D0265604

Prime Minister, Cabinet
and C   cutive

Edited by

R. A. W. Rhodes

and

Patrick Dunleavy

M
St. Martin's Press

First published in Great Britain 1995 by
MACMILLAN PRESS LTD
Houndmills, Basingstoke, Hampshire RG21 2XS
and London
Companies and representatives
throughout the world

A catalogue record for this book is available from the British Library.

ISBN 0–333–55896–0 hardcover
ISBN 0–333–55528–7 paperback

10	9	8	7	6	5	4	3	2	1
04	03	02	01	00	99	98	97	96	95

Printed in Malaysia

First published in the United States of America 1995 by
Scholarly and Reference Division,
ST. MARTIN'S PRESS, INC.,
175 Fifth Avenue,
New York, N.Y. 10010

ISBN 0–312–12616–6

Library of Congress Cataloging-in-Publication Data
Prime minister, cabinet and core executive / edited by R. A. W. Rhodes
and Patrick Dunleavy.
p.   cm.
Includes bibliographical references and index.
ISBN 0–312–12616–6
1. Prime ministers—Great Britain.   2. Cabinet system—Great
Britain.   I. Rhodes, R. A. W.   II. Dunleavy, Patrick.
JN405.P75 1995
354.4103' 13—dc20
                                                94–49141
                                                  CIP

Contents

List of Tables

List of Figures

Notes on the Contributors

Alan Beattie is Senior Lecturer in Government at the London School of Economics and Political Science.

June Burnham is a researcher in the Department of Government at the London School of Economics and Political Science.

Patrick Dunleavy is Professor of Government at the London School of Economics and Political Science and author of *Democracy, Bureaucracy and Public Choice* (1991).

Robert Elgie is Lecturer in Politics in the Department of European Studies at Loughborough University and author of *The Role of the Prime Minister in France, 1981–91* (1993).

Peter Fysh is a Lecturer in the Modern Languages Department at Nottingham Trent University.

Simon James is visiting fellow in Politics, University of Newcastle upon Tyne and author of *British Cabinet Government* (1992).

G.W. Jones is Professor of Government at the London School of Economics and Political Science and editor of *West European Prime Ministers* (1991).

Leo Keliher gained his docrorate at the London School of Economics and Political Science in 1987, and is now Director – General of Queensland Emergency Services.

Michael Lee is Emeritus Professor of Politics at the University of Bristol.

David Marsh is Professor of Government at the University of Strathclyde and author of *The New Politics of British Trade Unionism* (1992).

David Richards is a research student in the Department of Government, University of Strathclyde.

R.A.W. Rhodes is Professor of Politics at the University of Newcastle upon Tyne, author of *Beyond Westminster and Whitehall* (1988) and editor of *Public Administration*.

Anthony Seldon is Senior History Master at Tonbridge School, co-founder of the Institute of Contemporary British History and joint editor of *Ruling Performance* (1987).

Martin J. Smith is Lecturer in Politics at the University of Sheffield and author of *Pressure, Power and Policy* (1993).

Helen Thompson gained her doctorate at the London School of Economics and Political Science in 1994, and is now Assistant Lecturer in Politics, University of Cambridge and Fellow at Clare College, Cambridge.

Introducing the Core Executive

R.A.W. RHODES

Themes

For too long students have studied the textbook prime minister. When doing a subject for the first time, it is obviously necessary to discuss its 'conventional wisdom', so generations of students have rehearsed the arguments for and against prime ministerial power. However we must challenge the conventional wisdoms, try out new ideas and learn new ways of studying the subject. This collection of essays, some reprinted from the pages of *Public Administration*, many of them new, both supplements conventional textbook accounts and provides a new perspective on prime minister and cabinet.

The book has three objectives:

1. to introduce students to the academic literature (Part One),
2. to survey and interpret contemporary history from Wilson to Thatcher (Part Two), and
3. to provide original empirical studies of the core executive in action (Part Three).

However we have been more ambitious than this summary suggests. There are two extra themes to which we continually return:

4. to identify the strengths and weaknesses of different ways of collecting information on prime minister, cabinet and core executive, and
5. to discuss the different interpretations of prime minister, cabinet and core executive.

1

We encourage students to adopt a critical stance not only to an author's arguments but also to the ways in which the evidence was collected. We expand on all these themes below.

Summary

Part One surveys the literature. In Chapter 1, Rod Rhodes examines work on the prime minister and cabinet. He asks 'Where are we now?', concluding that the existing literature is theoretically weak, conservative in its methods and leaves too many questions unanswered. He argues for a focus on the *core executive* or 'all those organisations and procedures which coordinate central government policies, and act as final arbiters of conflict between different parts of the government machine'. He then turns his attention to the question, 'Where are we going?', identifying relevant theories, new methods and key topics for future research. He concludes that we must focus on the range of institutions which form the core executive; compare the strengths and weaknesses of the several available theoretical approaches; undertake more fieldwork of the core executive in action; and employ more, and more sophisticated, methods to take advantage of the information already in the public domain. In short, this chapter sets out in some detail the themes of the volume as a whole.

In Chapter 2, Martin Smith, David Marsh and David Richards review the literature on the role of central departments. Although departments are key actors in the policy process, the literature is institutional and static, ignoring political interactions both within departments and with other departments and governmental actors. They argue for a focus on the network of relationships, internal and external, in which departments are embedded. The remaining chapters set out to repair the defects identified in Chapters 1 and 2.

In Part Two we survey contemporary history from Wilson to Thatcher. In Chapter 3, Simon James provides a basic account of the way relations between prime minister and cabinet have changed since 1963. He dismisses the prime ministerial government argument, but identifies three important changes: growing international decision making, decision making by cabinet committee and the use of full cabinet as a sounding-board. This account contrasts sharply with, for example, Michael Foley's (1993, pp.264–8) thesis about the rise of the British presidency. In other words, Simon James provides an *interpretation* of changes since 1963 (see below).

Simon James's chapter provides essential background on key

characteristics of, and central actors in, British government, using an historical approach. The next two chapters not only introduce an important topic, Margaret Thatcher's rise and fall, but start our exploration of the way to study the core executive. In Chapter 4, George Jones provides an authoritative account of the fall of Margaret Thatcher. He employs the tools of the contemporary historian, drawing on newspaper accounts, memoirs, interviews and other primary sources when available. Because it is such a good example of the approach, it is worth asking, what are its limits?

Many existing ways of collecting information can be described, unkindly, as the 'Max Bygraves method', or 'I wanna tell you a story'. In other words, the book or article provides a chronological narrative of a person, an event, an era or an institution. There is nothing wrong with this approach. In the 'Guide for Further Reading', Rod Rhodes lists some excellent biographies of prime ministers which are essential sources for anybody studying the core executive. But all methods have their limits and in this case they revolve around the use of theory. Any story involves interpretation or a theory for making sense of the millions of 'facts' about a person or an era. For a social scientist that theory must be explicit. It should be clear why the author chose to study that topic in that particular way. We deliberately highlight the issue of interpretation by calling Part Two, 'Interpreting History'. We also provide concrete examples of the way social science theory can inform contemporary history.

First, by including a second account of the fall of Thatcher as Chapter 5, we are not being perverse because Martin Smith employs explicit theory to interpret the event. This power-dependence theory stresses the ways in which politicians depend on one another because each has resources the others need (Rhodes, 1981). Smith emphasises the ways in which Margaret Thatcher depended on others throughout her premiership. He introduces a theme we will return to in Part Three: the constraints on an ostensibly strong premier. We are not claiming that Smith provides a better or a definitive account of Thatcher's fall. All we want to do is to show that social science theory can make a distinctive, explanatory contribution and to provide an opportunity for the reader to assess that contribution. Second, in Chapters 6 and 7, we provide an example of a different debate, this time about methods. In Chapter 6, Anthony Seldon uses oral history to provide the best available account of the organisation of the Cabinet Office between 1979 and 1987 (for example, he is the main source for the relevant sections in Chapter 3). Despite the secrecy which surrounds the core executive, Anthony Seldon shows what a determined, skilled historian can achieve. His chapter also raises questions about the reliability of information gathered by interviewing elite actors.

In Chapter 7, Michael Lee discusses the pitfalls of relying on such interviews. Again, this debate is not about which author is right and which is wrong. It is about understanding the strengths and weaknesses of a particular way of getting information. Nobody would ignore information from interviews with key participants, but how much credence do you give that information? In the social sciences a common way of handling information of unknown reliability is 'triangulation'; that is, cross-checking information from interviews against information on the same subject from two other sources (not just two other interviewees). Thus the researcher would look for the relevant official documentation (for example, minutes of a meeting), newspaper accounts written at the time and the diaries or memoirs of participants.

Finally, in Chapter 8, Alan Beattie unpacks the notion of ministerial responsibility, showing that it has deep historical roots. He also shows it is a contested concept by identifying the Whig and Peelite interpretations. The Whig version which stresses the responsibility of ministers to Parliament is for many people the conventional view of ministerial responsibility. The Peelite version stresses the responsibility of ministers *for* policy, not *to* Parliament. This independent authority of ministers is an essential precondition of strong government. Beattie shows that the Whig version is incoherent. It mixes the brute fact that ministers (or the few) govern with representative values which stipulate decisions by the many. The Peelites like brute facts; they choose governmental power. So do governments, and constitutional reform aimed at strengthening ministerial accountability to Parliament has floundered and foundered over the last 50 years.

Thus, in the study of contemporary history, there are at least three broad areas of debate. Historians disagree about what happened, how to interpret what happened and how to get the information about what happened. When a student reads an account of Margaret Thatcher's fall, it seems so final. The printed page bestows authority on the story. In reality, history is contested; it involves debate and in this respect it is the same as any social science.

In Part Three we present new empirical accounts of the core executive in action and return to questions of theory and method. Chapters 9–11 all use the case method both to explore some theoretical propositions and to describe core executive behaviour. The case method is a common and controversial tool of social scientists. It is controversial because critics claim the findings cannot be generalised. To be blunt, this criticism is wrong, provided the case study is 'theory-laden'; that is, provided it systematically explores propositions explicitly derived from theory (see Eckstein, 1975; Yin, 1984).

Patrick Dunleavy's analysis of the Westland affair in Chapter 9 illustrates this argument. He applies four theories of the state to the crisis. The pluralist governmental politics model stresses the range of actors involved and the complexity of decision making. The instrumental Marxist model stresses the pre-eminent role of business and the elite decision-making process. The 'New Right' account focuses on policy entrepreneurs and the clash between a spending minister and guardians of the public purse. Finally the symbolic politics interpretation sees the crisis as a series of games involving leadership challenges, leaking secrets, executive–Parliament relations and mass media battles. The lessons of this analysis are not that any one interpretation is 'right' but that we should conduct comparative analyses of a series of decisions to test the several theoretical models. Or to make the same point in a different way, it is as difficult to interpret events as it is to collect the information about them.

There is an important substantive conclusion in Dunleavy's analysis of Westland: he demonstrates the limits to prime ministerial power. Although often described as domineering, and lauded to the skies for her strong leadership, Margaret Thatcher seemed powerless to stop a careening Michael Heseltine.

In a less controversial context, Leo Keliher also shows, in Chapter 10, that the ability of the core executive to direct specialised policy networks is severely limited by its lack of information and technical expertise. The Alvey project aimed to boost Britain's information technology industry. Although Thatcher had firm views on the policy and regularly intervened, her actions were either counterproductive or evaded at the implementation stage by the bureaucracy and organised interests.

Helen Thompson's account in Chapter 11 of Britain's entry into the European Exchange Rate Mechanism (ERM) concludes that decisions were dominated by personalised, non-institutionalised leadership interventions by Geoffrey Howe, Nigel Lawson and Margaret Thatcher. She criticises both policy network and institutionalist theories of policy making, pointing out that for many economic policies the core executive simply takes decisions and that institutional approaches do not encompass the strategies of the key actors.

Taken together, the three case studies produce a daunting list of constraints: international decision making, lack of information and expertise, recalcitrant policy networks of bureaucratic and organised interests, and powerful political rivals coupled with the need to maintain cabinet support, the lack of time and the risk, uncertainty and pressure of events. It is a wonder that anything is achieved and not at all surprising that many prime ministerial interventions are sporadic, counterproductive or ineffective.

In the final two chapters we show that statistical analysis is an essential tool for anyone seeking to understand core executive behaviour. Readers should not be intimidated by our use of statistics. It is important to show that understanding the ways in which British government works is not just a matter of examples and counterexamples. It can be the object of statistical analysis. We have excluded the technical details, although we provide references for the interested reader. We use simple descriptive statistics and we 'translate' the various tables in the text.

In Chapter 12, Patrick Dunleavy and George Jones analyse the prime minister's active participation in Parliament. They measure the change in this activity from 1868 to 1990. There has been a long-term decline in prime ministerial speeches, a stepped decline in debating interventions and a significant decrease in question answering. Statements from the prime minister increased after 1940 but declined in the 1980s. The authors conclude that the accountability of the prime minister to Parliament has declined.

In Chapter 13, Patrick Dunleavy provides an introduction to cabinet committees and then analyses the distribution of influence in John Major's cabinet committees. He identifies a clear 'first division', comprising the prime minister, foreign secretary, defence secretary and chancellor of the exchequer, and then shows that influence is segmented between domestic policy ministers. Above all, he demonstrates that simple statistics not only confirm our commonsense knowledge of the cabinet but also help us to analyse coalition behaviour among cabinet members.

Conclusion

This volume provides theoretical interpretations of core executive behaviour, demonstrates the value of employing a plurality of methods and fills important gaps in our knowledge. But it does not perform miracles. It cannot fill all the gaps in our current knowledge of the core executive. For example, we have not included any comparative material because that is the subject of a separate collection (Weller *et al.*, 1995). Also in April 1995, 15 projects, costing some £1.75 million and funded by the Economic and Social Research Council (ESRC) under its 'Whitehall Programme', will start. It will lead to a major improvement in our understanding of the way in which British government works (Rhodes, 1993). We cannot anticipate the findings of this programme. Also many changes are under way which could fundamentally alter, for example, the civil service and its relationship to ministers and the core executive (HMSO, 1994). So it is too early to provide a comprehensive account of the British executive at work. None the less, we do make a significant contribution to developing such an account both empirically and by suggesting ways of improving the study of the subject. Above all we stress that interpretation is every bit as important as fact finding. If we are to improve our understanding of British government, it will come about through the comparative testing of several theories and the use of a wider range of methods to collect and analyse information.

Acknowledgements

This collection had a long gestation. Its origins lie in papers presented by Pat Dunleavy and Rod Rhodes to the Annual Conference of the Political Studies Association at the University of Aberdeen in April 1987! Our collaboration first bore fruit, in a special issue of *Public Administration*, in spring 1990. Three articles survive from this issue of the journal in their original form (Chapters 6, 9, and 10). We would like to thank Basil Blackwell Publishers for permission to reprint these articles. We must also thank Martin Burch (University of Manchester) and William Wallace (St Antony's College, Oxford) for their help and forbearance. Chapter 1 was first published in the special issue but it has been so extensively revised that it is most accurately described as new.

Our interest in the core executive continued. As editor of *Public Administration*, Rod Rhodes actively sought new material. He also set up the ESRC's research programme on the changing nature of British central government, known as the 'Whitehall Programme'. This programme had its origins in a workshop held at the University of York on 13–14 April 1992. Two of the papers presented at this workshop are published here (Chapter 1 (part) and Chapter 2) and we would like to thank the ESRC for their financial support. Patrick Dunleavy, with several colleagues and doctoral students at the LSE, continued with his empirical work. All the material in this collection is a product of the collaboration between *Public Administration* and the LSE. Again we must thank Basil Blackwell Publishers for permission to reprint the articles by Martin Smith, David Marsh and David Richards (Chapter 2), Martin Smith (Chapter 5) and Michael Lee (Chapter 7). We also thank Cambridge University Press for permission to reprint the article by Patrick Dunleavy,

George Jones and others (Chapter 12). Chapters 3, 4, 8, 11 and 13 are published for the first time.

The editors would also like to thank several colleagues for their help. At different stages, Brendan O'Leary and Alan Beattie helped to edit the collection but, for various reasons, had to withdraw from the project. We are grateful for their efforts. We must also thank the Department of Politics, University of York and the LSE's Public Policy Group for their financial contribution towards the cost of preparing the manuscript.

Rod Rhodes would like to thank Mary Brooks for her usual secretarial help; and Charlotte Dargie for research assistance in checking the 'Guide to Further Reading'. Most important, Rachel Bayliss helped to compile the references, put the final manuscript together, read the proofs and prepared the index. Without her enthusiastic and above all speedy assistance, the book would have been delayed even longer. We are sure our publisher Steven Kennedy, finds the thought that we could have been even later almost inconceivable. We appreciated his patience. Debts and disclaimers of the individual authors are noted within chapters, as appropriate.

PART ONE

Surveying the Field

1

From Prime Ministerial Power to Core Executive*

R.A.W. RHODES

Introduction

Much work on the UK executive still focuses on long-running 'chestnuts of the constitution', especially the controversy about the relative power of the prime minister and the cabinet (Heclo and Wildavsky, 1974, pp.341–3). Mackintosh's (1962, 1968) study crowned the debate with an impressive summary of the historical evolution of cabinet government, but over the last 30 years little systematic fieldwork-based research into the prime minister or cabinet government has been published (the major exceptions are Hennessy, 1986; James, 1992; but see also Herman and Alt, 1978; Headey, 1974). Although this topic lives on as a standard controversy much raked over by students and newspaper columnists, in political science it has been an inactive field.

This chapter focuses on the British 'executive', especially the 'core executive'. This term is used in a broader sense than usual. Textbooks on British government typically refer to 'the executive' (for example, Norton, 1984; Kingdom, 1991) and limit discussion to the power of prime minister and cabinet. In fact, what constitutes the executive varies from policy area to policy area. Departments take important policy decisions with little or no reference to the cabinet and prime minister. Equally, central coordination, for example the Treasury's role in economic policy making, is not a function solely of the prime minister and cabinet.

---

* This chapter incorporates material from Dunleavy and Rhodes (1990) and Rhodes (1993) which is re-used with permission.

11

The term 'executive' is used here to refer to *the centres of political authority which take policy decisions.* In other words, the executive institutions are not limited to prime minister and cabinet but also include ministers in their departments. The term 'core executive' refers to *all those organisations and procedures which coordinate central government policies, and act as final arbiters of conflict between different parts of the government machine.* In brief, the 'core executive' is the heart of the machine, covering the complex web of institutions, networks and practices surrounding the prime minister, cabinet, cabinet committees and their official counterparts, less formalised ministerial 'clubs' or meetings, bilateral negotiations and interdepartmental committees. It also includes coordinating departments, chiefly the Cabinet Office, the Treasury, the Foreign Office, the law officers, and the security and intelligence services. The label 'cabinet government' was the overarching term for (some of) these institutions and practices but it is inadequate and confusing because it does not describe accurately the effective mechanisms for achieving coordination. At best it is contentious, and at worst seriously misleading, to assert the primacy of the cabinet among all organisations and mechanisms at the heart of the machine.

Unfortunately the term 'executive' has recently picked up new connotations with the creation of 'executive agencies'. To compound misunderstandings further, the government uses the term 'core' when referring to the policy-making parent department. To avoid confusion, I refer to agencies and departments. The qualifying adjectives are unnecessary. Indeed they are question begging. Thus the term 'executive agency' assumes, for example, that agencies have no role in policy formation. In fact the role of chief executives and their relationship to departments continues to evolve.

The term 'core executive' and the broad definition of the 'executive' are working hypotheses. I use them to raise the issues of coordination and fragmentation in central government. The term 'core executive' directs attention to the extent and efficacy of, and the various mechanisms for, coordination. The 'executive' focuses attention on the policy-making role of departments and their relationship to the core executive. Above all, my terminology provides a neutral description of the subject. It does not anticipate or prejudge the results of empirical research.

This chapter answers two questions: 'Where are we now?' and 'Where are we going?' Thus the next section reviews the *academic* literature on the prime minister and the cabinet, not ministerial diaries and memoirs, arguing that the debate about the relative power of these two institutions is stultifying. I set the scene by briefly sketching the conventional wisdom on prime minister and cabinet and identifying the defects of such a focus. This conventional wisdom both restricts the questions posed about the core executive and ignores the diversity of approaches. In the second section I identify and describe six variants of the prime ministerial government–cabinet debate, concluding that the literature is theoretically weak, is conservative in its methods and leaves many questions unanswered. The third section asks 'Where are we going?' and answers the question by arguing for a focus on the 'core executive'. I identify some promising theories, innovative methods and key research questions which need to be explored if the analysis of the core executive is to blow fresh air on a musty topic.

Where are We Now? The Conventional Wisdom Defined

What is the standard controversy surrounding studies of the British executive? Advocates of the prime ministerial power thesis argue that the prime minister is more powerful than the cabinet because he or she is leader of the party, has the power to appoint and dismiss ministers, chairs the cabinet and controls its agenda, has more opportunity to amass considerable personal popularity with the electorate through skilled use of the media, appears on an international stage as a world leader and because freedom from departmental responsibilities enables him or her to intervene over the full range of government policy. (See, for example, Benn, 1980; Crossman, 1963; Mackintosh, 1968; Madgwick, 1986.)

Advocates of the cabinet government thesis counter these claims by pointing to the constraints on the prime minister. Thus the party cannot be ignored, it has to be listened to; ministers have their own bases of support within the party and even the country at large; constitutional conventions require the government to act collectively; public visibility can be two-edged, with the prime minister being blamed when things go wrong; appearances on an international stage serve merely to highlight how little such jamborees achieve; and the prime minister lacks the expertise and advice necessary to intervene effectively in the complex world of departmental policy making. (See, for example, Jones, 1985b; Madgwick, 1986, 1991; Norton, 1988.)

The arrival of Margaret Thatcher gave an additional twist to these arguments. It is argued that she was a particularly dominant leader, providing an important precedent for her successors. This increase in prime ministerial power was supported by an enhanced role for, and increased numbers of, advisers at Number 10. Evidence of her dominance can be seen in her interventions in departmental policy (for example, local government finance, football hooliganism) and by, for example, the extensive use of prime ministerial powers of appointment of top civil servants. But, in this seemingly endless round of assertion and counterassertion, it is argued that Thatcher's domineering leadership style isolated her from both party and cabinet and the latter in particular was instrumental in bringing her down (Alderman and Carter, 1991; Jones, ch. 4 below; Norton, 1992). The size of the Number 10 unit cannot be compared, even remotely, with that of a ministerial department. The evidence for the political appointment of civil servants is scanty at best. Intervention brought its own problems. Her initiative on football hooliganism embarrassed Mrs Thatcher when her pet scheme had to be abandoned in the wake of the Hillsborough disaster. Local government finance in general, and the community charge in particular, contributed to her downfall, constituting perhaps, to continue with a footballing, rather than a fashionable cricketing, metaphor, the most spectacular own goal of the postwar period.

There are several problems with this textbook approach to the study of the British executive. King (1985a, pp.3–7) has cogently identified some of the defects, arguing that the literature is 'thin' and 'uniform'; 'Old arguments are . . . rehashed'; propositions are advanced 'without testing them against reality'; and 'the same materials are endlessly recycled'. In other words, neither side in the debate can marshal much by way of evidence to support their conflicting claims. Original field work is at a premium. To make matters even worse, important questions are almost totally neglected. Again King (1985a, pp.3–7) has pointed out that the 'variety and fluctuation' in prime ministerial involvement and the effects of a changing context are ignored. Indeed 'important aspects of the prime ministership are dealt with not at all or only in passing'.

Third, the debate adopts an institutional perspective betraying little or no interest in other theoretical perspectives. For example, Thatcher's leadership style has greatly preoccupied commentators, but this subset of the literature does not draw upon existing theoretical perspectives to interpret the phenomenon. There is nothing equivalent to Barber's (1972) systematic analysis of the personality of American presidents (although see Berrington, 1974; Foley, 1993; Iremonger, 1970). Nor has the literature on business leadership been explored, even though it provides a 'contingency theory of leadership' (Lawton and Rose, 1991, ch. 7; McCall, 1977) which explores the 'fit' between leadership style and the context within which a leader operates. The usefulness of comparing several different interpretations of the same event – known as the multitheoretic approach – was demonstrated as long ago as 1971 by Allison in his account of the Cuban missile crisis from three different viewpoints. Students of the British executive have yet to follow his example (for a brief exception, see Dunleavy, ch. 9 below). Finally, and paradoxically, by focusing attention on the prime minister versus cabinet debate, the conventional wisdom misrepresents the existing literature. There have been several attempts to move beyond its confines. A more sympathetic reading of the literature identifies several variants which suggest future avenues of exploration and support the argument that attention should be switched to the core executive.

Varieties of Institutionalism

There are six models which can be distinguished in the debate about prime ministerial power, many of which advance both an explanation (of how things work) and a prescription (of how things ought to work). The models are prime ministerial government, prime ministerial cliques, cabinet government, ministerial government, segmented decision making and bureaucratic coordination.

Prime Ministerial Government

This is conventionally seen as the exertion of authority solely by the premier, or monocratic government. The prime minister's personal predominance in decision making can be demonstrated in three possible ways: by a general ability to decide policy across all issue areas in which he or she takes an interest; by deciding key issues which subsequently determine most remaining areas of government policy; or by defining a governing ethos or 'atmosphere' which generates predictable and hard solutions to most policy problems. As a result, other ministers' freedom of manoeuvre is constrained, making them simple agents of the premier's will.

The first version of the argument has conventionally been criticised because of the mismatch between the time and workload pressures inherent in the prime minister's office and the complexity of policy making and administration in the modern extended state. The job (of any cabinet minister) 'is a conveyor belt to exhaustion and under-achievement all round, a predicament reflected in . . . the finished policy, which is all too often defective and immensely difficult to implement' (Hennessy, 1986, p.184). These limitations acquire added force given the demands on Downing Street. A hyperactive premier can considerably enlarge the scope of issues he or she addresses compared with a more relaxed or less hard-working incumbent. Yet international summitry, overseas visits and visitors, and similar events consume much of the prime minister's time, greatly restricting her or his scope of attention and capacity to follow up issues.

The other two versions of the case for monocratic authority are not open to such obvious objections. Prime ministerial control of key issues is plausible, and visible, during economic or international crises, such as the pre-devaluation period, 1964–7, or limited wars (see Seymour-Ure, 1984). However such events are relatively rare and prime ministerial control over the kinds of 'key issues' is less certain. The ideological authority version is more limited in its application, because some recent prime ministers (such as Wilson) have apparently had no such guiding principles. The version fits Margaret Thatcher's premiership well enough (Young, 1989).

Thatcher's period of office converted the monocratic version of prime ministerial power into an orthodoxy (Young and Sloman, 1986; Wapshott and Brock, 1983) which many academic authors have also supported (Burch, 1983; King, 1985b; Minogue and Biddiss, 1988):

> What we have established through the testimony of many intimate witnesses is the crucial importance of her personality to what her government does. Her politics proceeds from her character. Her style of leadership turns heavily on her being a woman. . . . This is her time dominated by her character. (Young and Sloman, 1986, p.142)

> [Thatcher] had no choice, given her aims and determination, but to lead in an unusually forthright, assertive manner. Partly this was a matter of her personality: she is a forthright and assertive person. But it was at least as much a matter of the objective situation in which she found herself. She was forced to behave like an outsider for the simple reason that she was one. (King, 1985b, p.116)

> [Thatcher] reaches out for decisions; she reaches out for people. She also reaches out for ideas . . . (King, 1985b, p.126)

She pushed out the frontiers of her authority from the moment she took office in 1979 (King 1985b, 137. See also Foley, 1993).

Yet if the Thatcher era apparently highlighted the strengths of the monocratic approach to prime ministerial power, it also rather graphically demonstrated its dangers and limitations. The resignations of Michael Heseltine over the Westland affair (Linklater and Leigh, 1986), Nigel Lawson over the role of Sir Alan Walters as the prime minister's economic adviser and Sir Geoffrey Howe over European Community policy all illustrate that a domineering style can impose heavy costs on a prime minister (see Barber, 1991; Jones, 1990). It also proved too easy for observers adopting the monocratic line of argument to collapse into hagiography, describing Thatcher as a leader who 'towered over all her contemporaries'; had an 'unwavering purpose'; evoked 'admiration and detestation for one identical reason: she is "big"'; and 'falls short of greatness, but radiates dominance'. In short, 'I do not believe that in our lifetime we shall ever look upon her like again' (Finer, 1987, p.140).

Prime Ministerial Cliques

An alternative interpretation (popular in other countries as well as the UK) argues that the premier's authority and influence are collective attributes of her or his inner group of advisers. No single individual can hope to impose leadership on the complex core executive of a large, modern nation state, let alone upon the wider executive. Political leadership cannot be narrowly conceived as personal initiatives or interventions in decision making. It is rather the product of a process of constructing, maintaining and providing political clout to a set of political and administrative influentials. An extended team or coalition can generate ideas and applications of the premier's basic values, monitor a broad scope of government policies, tell a broad range of actors and institutions about the premier's intentions and regularly and reliably follow up on policy implementation to prevent the premier's input to decisions being ignored or forgotten.

Historically in the UK, this approach has been associated with arguments about whether there is an 'inner cabinet' of influential ministers and cabinet committee chairs. The general academic consensus is that there is no coherent pattern, it is haphazard, and the debate has become tepid (James, 1992, p.194; Walker, 1970, pp.39–40).

A second version of the clique model posits an *éminence grise* exerting a disproportionate influence upon the premier's choice of policies and individuals. In earlier periods, people nominated for this role included Horace Wilson for Chamberlain or Lord Cherwell for Churchill. More recently media and academic observers have focused on close and trusted advisers such as William Armstrong, the head of the civil service at the time of the Heath government (Hennessy, 1986, p.80), members of the prime minister's personal staffs, such as Marcia Williams, Wilson's political secretary (Haines, 1977) and Thatcher's powerful press secretary, Bernard Ingham (Cockerell *et al.*, 1985). Since the mid-1970s a more corporate focus developed, with the premier's Downing Street advisers emerging as distinct 'players' in some policy decisions: for example, Sir Alan Walters' role in economic policy making. In addition, the prime minister has been closely linked to specific civil service units in the Cabinet Office, such as the Central Policy Review Staff (CPRS) in the late 1970s and the Efficiency Unit in the 1980s (see Lee, 1974; Blackstone and Plowden, 1988), in the Treasury, such as the Financial Management Initiative (FMI) Unit and later the *Next Steps* unit, and elsewhere, such as the intelligence services.

The episodic extension of Thatcher's advisers to cover most key policy areas, and the substantial upgrading of the personnel who serve as advisers on economic affairs and foreign policy, and in the Policy Unit, have sparked a controversy about the creation of a fully-fledged Prime Minister's Department (Berrill, 1985; Weller, '83; Jones, 1980, 1983). The increasing salience of news and media management in core executive operation in the 1970s and 1980s, and especially the centralisation of the government information services under Bernard Ingham, extended the scope of the prime ministerial clique to include a variety of presentational experts, news manipulators and 'spin doctors' (Cockerell *et al.*, 1985; Cockerell, 1988; Margach, 1978; May and Rowan, 1982, pp.101–57). Paradoxically for a premier credited with much personal influence by critics and admirers alike, Thatcher had an extended network of advisers, image consultants, speech writers and intellectuals, although their influence has tended to be episodic rather than continuous.

Critics of this trend argue that prime ministerial cliques undermine the official allocation of ministerial briefs and departmental advice giving, creating a parallel power network inside the executive. In effect there is a counterbureaucracy duplicating formal governmental structures. Other critics see the premier's clique as a way for a highly biased selection of external interests to gain privileged access to the centre of decisions. In the late 1970s under Callaghan, these external inputs mixed trade union and labour movement influentials with corporate business elites. In the 1980s, the networks plugged into the Thatcher government were confined to major finance and industrial capitalists, together with a few less conventional business entrepreneurs and assorted right-wing think-tanks or intellectuals.

The clique view expresses a long-running liberal fear that the top political executive is not accountable for its policy making. A re-

lated worry draws attention to the dangers of a premier constructing a tightly knit set of advisers insulated from outside networks or
experiences. They can develop a strong group consciousness and
awareness of their elite influence. Janis (1972) argues that groups
can become divorced from outside networks and experiences and
develop a 'groupthink' syndrome in which policies are developed
and pursued for lengthy periods in the face of mounting external
evidence of policy failures or fiascos, which the elite group simply
ignores or discounts. The community charge, or poll tax, may
perhaps be an example of such cut-off 'groupthink'.

Cabinet Government

Exponents of cabinet government were scarce in the 1980s. The
justification for collegial decision making, that it takes account of a
diversity of departmental interests, remains unchanged. Until
1990, the continuing importance of the cabinet was asserted in a
defensive fashion. Because of governmental growth and the complexity of decisions, the executive became a 'fragmented set of
overlapping decision arenas' in which the cabinet gives 'the system
a focus but which itself takes only a small proportion of decisions in
full session' (Mackie and Hogwood, 1985, pp.31–5). Similarly
Barnes (1989) acknowledges that in the 1980s the cabinet's actual
discussions focused on legislative timetabling, foreign affairs, public expenditure and pre-budget discussions, and the occasional
'fire-fighting' issues. None the less, he argues that cabinet has a key
residual role as court of appeal both for ministers radically out of
sympathy with a general line, and for a premier confronted by a
ministerial colleague who insists on ploughing her or his own
furrow. Because of the legal and constitutional pre-eminence of
ministers in policy making (see below), a prime minister faced with
a minister who refuses to toe the line agreed by a majority of
colleagues may be forced to take the issue to cabinet to be authori-
tatively resolved, as Thatcher did during the Westland affair (see
Chapter 9 below). Proponents of the cabinet government thesis
were more assertive after Thatcher's fall and many saw the lack of
cabinet support as a decisive factor (Alderman and Carter, 1991;
Jones, Chapter 4 below).

Ministerial Government

This term was coined by Jones (1975) to describe the British
executive. He argues against prime ministerial dominance, less
in terms of the vitality of cabinet as a collective decision-making

organ, and more in terms of the capacity of political and administrative departmentalism to limit the premier's influence. The key problem of cabinet

> has been how to organize itself to cope with the tremendous increase in the amount, complexity and inter-relatedness of its business. . . .
>
> The over-riding objective of the Prime Minister is . . . to hold together the Cabinet, which is potentially fragmented. (Jones, 1975, pp.41, 57)

Similarly Heclo and Wildavsky detect a key 'debility' where cabinet members are also 'chief executives of their own departmental empires, empires where their individual reputations are made and/or unmade. . . . Everyone knows they serve themselves by serving their departments' (Heclo and Wildavsky, 1974, pp.371, 369).

> The form and structure of a modern Cabinet and the diet it consumes almost oblige it to function like a group of individuals, and not as a unity. Indeed, for each minister, the test of his [*sic*] success in office lies in his ability to deliver his departmental goals. . . . No minister I know of has won political distinction by his performance in Cabinet or by his contribution to collective decision-making. To the country and the House of Commons he is simply the minister for such-and-such a department and the only member of the Cabinet who is not seen in this way is the Prime Minister. (Wass, 1984, p.25)

There are both legal–constitutional and political reasons for the continuing pre-eminence of individual ministers in making decisions within their departments:

> In constitutional theory, the minister continues to take precedence before the ministry. In law it is the minister who is usually responsible for the actions of the ministry. . . . A minister has unlimited liability for political mistakes made by his ministry. . . .
>
> A minister's position at the top of a hierarchy is an ambiguous eminence. The minister is answerable for everything that happens within the ministry (and often outside it), yet is remote from what is done by officials at the base. (Rose, 1987, pp.18, 232)

This general position is reinforced in many areas of government decision making by legal constraints on the ways in which ministers exercise parts of their responsibilities. In general, when ministers are exercising quasi-judicial functions, and in some cases where they are appointing people to head quasi-governmental agencies, overt interference by their colleagues (even by the premier) is illegitimate, and could be embarrassing if publicised. Usually neither cabinet nor the prime minister can seek to *decide* such issues, irrespective of the weight of a premier's known attitudes with the minister responsible. This reliance on 'Chinese walls', on government in compartments, works best in the case of such 'enclave' areas as the 'independent' Law Officers (Marshall, 1984, pp.111–17; Marshall and Moodie, 1967, pp.144–50). It is apparently ineffective in other areas, such as the supposedly separate ministerial controls over the five main security services: M15, GCHQ, SIS, Defence Intelligence Staffs and Special Branch (Richelson and Ball, 1985).

Politically the foundations for ministerial roles are also strong. Most ministers spare little thought for policy issues controlled by their colleagues, unless their own department has a stake in them. Attempts by one minister or department to acquire responsibilities or functions from another, or occasionally to assimilate a department whose rationale has dwindled, are the chief reason for outside interventions – and these efforts are rarely successful. The prime minister's role inside the government is unusual because he or she alone can regularly or legitimately take an interest in 'specific areas of micro-policy' on a wider front. But Callaghan's experience of trying to influence domestic policy making is typical: 'In each case it involved intervention in the normal Whitehall processes and often upset the respective departmental Ministers and officials who believe that Prime Ministers should not trespass on their policy cabbage patches' (Donoughue, 1987, p.7).

Ministerial responsibility plays an important role in defending policy turfs. Collective decision making has dwindled. The demands for governmental solidarity policed from Downing Street have expanded. The regular reshuffling of ministers, and the continued casualty rate even under one-party government in the 1980s (for data, see Alderman and Cross, 1985, 1986), generated strong reasons for ministers to reinforce political departmentalism to safeguard their positions. Some observers suggest that Margaret Thatcher's ministers sought to counteract her efforts to intervene in policy making across many issues by keeping business away from formal cabinet machinery or interdepartmental committees (Burch, 1989). Conflicts formerly pushed up to cabinet committees are now settled bilaterally between the ministers concerned, often via correspondence alone. The strengthened role of junior ministers in the 1980s may reflect these efforts to internalise more policy making within the department, or at least resolve issues with other departments without prime ministerial scrutiny (Theakston, 1987). The large majority in parliament strengthened the interest of Conservative backbench MPs in particular subject areas, usually amongst those MPs sitting on a select committee, and created parliamentary 'clienteles' to whom ministers need to pay attention.

There were other countervailing tendencies to Thatcher's apparent monolithic control during the 1980s. In the early years, strong Treasury control of public expenditures reinforced monocratic authority (Dunsire and Hood, 1989). But the economic boom of the mid-1980s led to a more relaxed attitude towards public expenditure and encouraged a departmental fight-back. There was a shift away from Treasury control of minutiae to global target setting and non-interference, as long as targets were met. The Financial Management Initiative's stress on decentralised cost control reflected a similar trend (Gray, Jenkins *et al.*, 1991). So too did the developing pattern of cash limits administration, and the replacement of rigid manpower controls by running costs controls and manpower targets (Thain and Wright, 1990b). Finally the *Next Steps* proposals for hiving off 75–90 per cent of civil service manpower into executive agencies (see below pp.34–5) could strike a further blow at Treasury controls (hence the opposition of its public expenditure control divisions to the proposals). In the 1990s one scenario sees stripped down policy-making departments taking on much of the current role of the Treasury's public spending divisions. The departments would be the 'sponsors' controlling the expenditures and targets of the numerous agencies and quasi-government organisations. These reforms imply the continuing diffusion of effective policy control to the sectoralised departments. Only the wholesale privatisation of departmental activities is likely to reduce radically the scope of ministerial responsibility and control (Jones, 1989, pp.254–8).

The Segmented Decision Model

This model suggests that some of the conflicting claims of the previous models can be simply resolved by agreeing that the premier and the cabinet operate in different policy areas, with ministers operating below the interdepartmental level at which cabinet machinery becomes involved. Prime ministerial control is strong in strategic defence, foreign affairs and major economic decisions, but genuine cabinet or ministerial decision making predominates over almost all other aspects of domestic policy.

> In public policy, a Prime Minister is doubtly constrained. Positive requirements to emphasise party management and the presentation of self limit the time that can be devoted to policy. The primary responsibilities of departmental ministers also constrain the involvement of Downing Street in policy making. *Where the Prime Minister is most involved, British government is now inevitably weak: this is true of the management of the economy as well as foreign affairs.* (Rose, 1980a, p.49; emphasis added)

This segmented pattern helps to explain why most commentators have detected increased prime ministerial influence in the modern period, while evidence of the prime minister's weak involvement in large areas of domestic policy continues to accumulate. For example, Donoughue describes Callaghan's decision to concentrate on some key domestic decisions in which he wanted to inject a new policy direction – including the sale of council housing, improving educational standards, the Finniston inquiry into the British engineering profession and the Annan Commission on the BBC. Yet by the end of his term it was 'difficult to claim much evidence of success' (Donoughue, 1987, p.124). Thatcher's longer tenure of office provides some similar instances of long-running but equally ineffective prime ministerial involvement. To the earlier examples of football hooliganism and local government finance can be added the Alvey programme (see Chapter 10 below), the campaign against litter and the common agricultural policy of the EC, amongst many others. The premier has great influence over strategic decisions which, in turn, influence many specific issues, but the resulting system cannot usefully be described as 'prime ministerial government', for four reasons. First, although the premier may play a key role in 'objectively important' issue areas, some of the most critical aspects of domestic policy making always remain open to cabinet or ministerial decision.

Second, the power-dependency relations between the premier and key ministers in foreign affairs, defence and economic policy making do not fit neatly into the mould suggested by enthusiasts for prime ministerial government. Premiers cannot directly or single-handedly determine basic policy directions in any of these areas, nor even easily influence the range of decision options considered. Prime ministers can select and reselect the personnel involved, and may be able to arbitrate particularly uncertain or difficult decisions. But appointing key figures to major positions creates power-dependency effects. A premier may not be able to impose her or his line on an appointee short of dismissal. The succession of public disagreements between Thatcher and Lawson over the direction of economic policy during 1987–9 dramatised the prime minister's inability to control a major department. Nor can premiers normally assume a dominant position in all three strategic areas simultaneously. They may not even be able to staff all the relevant cabinet committees with reliable supporters. While Thatcher successfully packed the economic committees in her first-term government, her control over foreign policy was weaker before 1982; for example, she had to accept the decisions leading up to the independence of Zimbabwe which brought Robert Mugabe to power (see Smith, Chapter 5, below).

Third, UK policy making is increasingly influenced by the European Union (EU), and numerous other international agreements (for example, policies to combat global 'warming', controlling dumping at sea, or regulating the security of air travel). This change has tended to erode the concept of a discrete category of 'foreign affairs' in which the prime minister, foreign secretary and Foreign Office play the predominant roles. The early postwar defence and treaty-based commitments (like NATO) buttressed the insulation of strategic policy from wide ministerial involvement. But trends since the 1970s have worked in the opposite direction by involving more and more ministers and departments in direct negotiations with overseas counterparts about sectorally specific policies (Wallace, 1986; Byrd, 1988). There has been a progressive transition to joint UK–EU control of some key policies previously controlled in Whitehall, such as monopolies and mergers policy, or the setting of clean water and environmental standards (Ward, 1990). Such policy areas have also become more important in wider EU relations because of the transition to a single European market in 1993. These changes have extensively constrained prime ministerial control over external relations policy. In short, although the segmented decision model does not answer this question, it does ask if government policy can be effectively shaped by any elements of the executive, either acting alone or in combination. The external constraints may leave little room for domestic choices.

The Bureaucratic Coordination Model

This model claims explicitly that the core executive has limited control over the rest of the government machine, and that cabinet, and even individual departmental ministers, play minimal roles. Most policy choices are effectively defined by the processing of issues within Whitehall. There are two versions of this thesis, one left-wing and the other associated with the 'fatalist' new right.

The left view is the simplest and best known, portraying the civil service as 'an elite arrogating to itself political power' (Sedgemore, 1980, pp.26–32 and ch. 4) which is an obstacle to the introduction of effective socialist reforms by Labour governments. (See also Benn, 1981, especially ch. 3; Castle, 1973; Crossman, 1975, pp.23–6, 342–3, 614–21; Kellner and Crowther Hunt, 1980, chs 4 and 5.) The key mechanisms for undermining more radical ministers have been the enormous growth in the effectiveness of interdepartmental committees, civil service manipulation of information flows to ministers and the ability to bid issues past 'troublesome' departmental ministers to the prime minister for 'safer' resolution. Sedgemore (1980) stresses 'the convergence of bureaucracy' (p.34): the shared interests between the civil service, the EC bureaucracy, the Confederation of British Industry (CBI) and the Trades Union Congress (TUC) in sustaining routinised bureaucratic control of issue processing. Deradicalised Labour premiers play a superficially important role in this account – but only as the final arbiter or tie-breaker in deadlocked inter-agency conflicts or as the stooges for unified bureaucratic interests. They are not genuine controllers of the policy machine or initiators of new policy directions.

The new right version of this viewpoint provides an analogous explanation of why the Heath government or even Thatcher's new right government have failed to make major cuts in public spending. Civil service obstruction of radical measures reflects a strong bureaucratic drive to maximise budgets and oversupply outputs. But the mechanisms of civil service power are much the same as in the left account, stressing bureaucratic monopoly of information, the ability to tone down, blunt or delay initiatives and efforts to marginalise political advisers and initiatives in a rapidly moving flow of short-term problems and issues. Bureaucratic conservatives can also successfully orchestrate vested interests to oppose ministerial proposals threatening to the status quo. Strong pressures are brought to bear upon departmental ministers to opt out of difficult reform tasks and instead 'go native' in their fiefdoms. The prime minister and other non-departmental ministers, together perhaps with the Treasury, are the only actors likely to keep up new right pressure for micro-policy changes. But they are vulnerable to pressures to reflate public spending as part of the political–business cycle, such as the consumer spending boom orchestrated in the run-up to the 1987 election.

Several contributors have sought to move beyond the prime minister versus cabinet debate in an effort to capture the complex

of relations at the heart of the machine. The ministerial government, segmented decision making and bureaucratic coordination
models all point to a view of the executive in which there are
multiple actors whose *relative power* shifts *over time* and *between policy
areas.* In other words, it is factually inaccurate to assert, by using the
phrases 'prime ministerial' or 'cabinet' government, that these
institutions invariably and inevitably either coordinate government
policy or resolve central conflicts. 'Who coordinates?' is an empirical question. It is quite possible that the prime minister and/or the
cabinet play this role, but the point must be documented, not
asserted. Unfortunately there is no coherent theoretical alternative
to the prime ministerial power versus cabinet government debate
to guide the search for evidence. Indeed there is not a great deal of
empirical research. Case studies are the dominant research
method and there are precious few of them. Any review of the
literature compels the conclusion that we know little about the
British executive.

As one way out of this theoretical and methodological impasse, I
propose that we adopt a differentiated model in which the relevant
executive varies over both time and policy area. There is no one
executive but multiple executives. The phrase 'core executive',
because it refers to a range of central institutions, captures this
essential variability. Which brings me to the question of how to
study this core executive.

Where Are We Going?

This section is structured around the defects of the existing literature, focusing on the theories, methods and research questions
which need to be explored if we are to repair the gaps in our
knowledge. And there are many such gaps.

Basic accounts of several executive institutions are lacking. The
examples include ministers of state, permanent secretaries, central
departments, think-tanks and audit agencies. This collective ignorance also encompasses constitutional change and extends to
the role of the several executive institutions in the policy process.
Rapid change in British government and politics further
compounds the problem.

The postwar period witnessed the growth of the welfare state,
the professionalisation of government, retrenchment under the
impact of economic recession and new right ideology, the widespread impact of the European Community, the fragmentation
of bureaucracy with the allied spread of new methods of service
delivery, the changing relationship with, and expectations of, citi-

zens (now known as consumers), the impact of new technology and the 'new public management' with its sharp divorce of policy and administration. We must assess the impact of these and other changes on the British executive before we can begin to explain their variable effects on, and results for, executive behaviour.

There is little theoretical literature on the executive. For example, the new public management or 'managerialism' leans heavily on the teachings and techniques of private-sector management. Their relevance to the public sector continues to be a matter of debate, but there is still no management or organisation theory developed explicitly for the context and purposes of the public sector (Rhodes, 1991). Both empirically and theoretically, therefore, there is much to be done.

Developing Theory

There is a lack of theory in the study of the executive. Recently two theoretical approaches have commanded considerable attention: the 'bureau-shaping' theory of departmental budgetary behaviour (see, for example, Dunleavy, 1989a, 1989b, 1991, 1992) and the policy network theory of policy formulation and implementation (see, for example, Marsh and Rhodes, 1992b; Rhodes, 1988).

The bureau-shaping model significantly modifies the classic rational choice view of bureaucrats. In the classic version, bureaucrats are rational, self-interested actors seeking to maximise their agencies' budget. In the bureau-shaping model, the bureaucrats remain rational and self-interested actors, but their behaviour varies both with the type of budget and the type of agency.

Dunleavy's (1991, ch. 4) bureau-shaping model of bureaucracy distinguishes between both types of budget and types of agency. He identifies four types of budget (see Figure 1.1): core (salary and running costs), bureau (core plus capital expenditure and transfer payments made direct to individuals and organisations), program (core and bureau budgets plus funding supervised by agency) and super-program (all foregoing plus supervision of funds raised by other agencies). He also distinguishes between delivery, regulatory, transfer, contracts and control agencies. He argues that budget maximisation by officials depends on their rank, type of budget and type of agency. Thus a rational middle-rank bureaucrat will seek to maximise the core budget because it will improve job security and enhance career prospects. On the other hand, the rational top-rank bureaucrat will maximise the bureau budget because it boosts bureau prestige. Moreover the incentive to

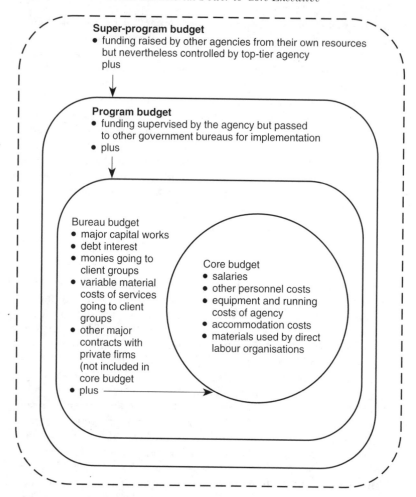

Figure 1.1   *Components of core, bureau, program and super-program budgets*
Source: Dunleavy (1991, p.182) (reproduced with permission).

maximise will be strongest where there is a close relationship between core, bureau and program budgets, as in the case of delivery
agencies. In other words, there is great variation between bureaucrats in the extent to which they have incentives to maximise their
budgets. In place of budget maximisation as an explanation of
official behaviour, Dunleavy introduces the notion of 'bureau-
shaping'. He argues:

> rational bureaucrats oriented primarily to work-related utilities
> pursue a *bureau-shaping* strategy designed to bring their bureau
> into a progressively closer approximation to 'staff' (rather than

'line') functions, a collegial atmosphere, and a central location. (Dunleavy, 1991, pp.202–3)

Thus national-level delivery agencies will become control, transfer or contract agencies and the central bureau will take on a small, central, elite character. In short, rational bureaucrats work in varied settings and have a choice of maximising strategies. They do not just maximise their budgets.

This model not only explains variations in budget-maximising behaviour but it can also be put to empirical use. Dunleavy (1989b, 1991, pp.188–91, 213–17) shows that his agency and budget typologies can be operationalised to describe the organisation structure of British central government. This empirical work will soon cover the USA and Australia. In addition, the typologies are being elaborated: for example, following Hood (1983), each agency type is said to have a distinct set of tools for interacting with the outside world (Dunleavy, 1992). Thus regulatory agencies rely on making rules (authority) whereas delivery agencies have their own staff to implement policy (administrative organisation).

Dunleavy would be the first to admit that the bureau-shaping model is at an early stage of development. However it already offers a way of comparing, for example, central agencies throughout the EU. More ambitiously, it ought to be possible, in principle, to describe and explain variations in budgetary behaviour between member states. Finally it can predict and explain administrative change: for example, Dunleavy (1989a, p.268) claims that the model explains why policy-level bureaucrats favour hiving off parts of their departments as separate agencies. In short, the bureau-shaping model has great potential and deserves exhaustive testing.

Recent work in Britain on policy networks has its roots in the Economic and Social Research Council's initiative on central–local government relations. The initiative was based on a power-dependence model of the relationship which argued that organisations are dependent upon each other for resources and have to exchange them to achieve their goals. These sets of interacting, interdependent organisations were described as 'policy networks' and five types of networks were identified (Rhodes, 1988, pp.48–77). They are listed and defined in Table 1.1. (For a more detailed history of the concept, see Marsh and Rhodes, 1992b, ch. 1; and for a critical discussion see ch. 11.)

Policy making by policy networks is a form of private government. The relevant central department, interest groups and other governmental bodies regularly and routinely decide on policy and only occasionally refer it to either Parliament or the cabinet. Policy networks are alliances of bureaucrat and professional across types and tiers of government, including the EU. In effect each policy network is the executive for its functional area of government. For example, Rhodes (1988, pp.237–55) argues that local and central government are interdependent. Although the centre enacts the law and provides a high proportion of local income, local government has the professional skills and organisational resources to implement the policy. They need each other if a policy is to work. Normally the Department of the Environment and the representative associations of local government formed a national intergovernmental network (see Table 1.1) to discuss local government finance and other matters of mutual concern. However, in the 1980s, the Conservative government adopted a unilateral style of policy making. The intergovernmental network became highly conflictual and local government resisted central interventions. A policy mess ensued in which neither level of government could achieve their objectives. In denying their interdependence, they frustrated each other's actions.

Such interdependence is characteristic of the relationships in the (multiple) executives of British government and of their relationships with the core executive (see Smith, Chapter 5 below), so a focus on policy networks provides the means for exploring the nature of the executive and its relationship to the core executive. Rather than comparing decision making by departments, future

TABLE 1.1   *Policy community and policy network: the Rhodes model*

Type of network	Characteristics of network
Policy community/territorial community	Stability, highly restricted membership, vertical interdependence, limited horizontal articulation
Professional network	Stability, highly restricted membership, vertical interdependence, limited horizontal articulation, serves interest of profession
Intergovernmental network	Limited membership, limited vertical interdependence, extensive horizontal articulation
Producer network	Fluctuating membership, limited vertical interdependence, serves interest of producer
Issue network	Unstable, large number of members, limited vertical interdependence

Source: Marsh and Rhodes (1992b, p. 14) (reproduced with permission).

research should compare the different types of networks, each with a central department at its heart, their relationships to the core executive and the ways in which they adjusted to the pressures of the 1980s. This approach could not only describe the changing patterns of internal and external relationships of a department but also analyse the impact of organisational change.

The advantage of both these bureau-shaping and policy networks approaches is that they offer new vantage points from which to view 'conventional' topics such as ministerial accountability. Instead of taking one of the chestnuts of the constitution – that is, the power of the prime minister, collective cabinet responsibility, ministerial accountability to parliament – as the unit of analysis, they use a classification either of agency and budget types or of policy networks.

Developing Methods

Traditional approaches to the study of the executive – for example, telling the story of a current event or describing institutional and legal arrangements – are no longer sufficient because they are atheoretical. There are other ways of studying the executive. Three methods have great potential.

First, Dunleavy *et al.* (1990) show how to use quantitative methods to document the frequency and type of appearance in the Commons by prime ministers since 1868 (see Dunleavy *et al.*, Chapter 12 below). The same techniques could be used to compare the relationships of ministers to Parliament. Moreover, I provide only one illustration of the usefulness of quantitative methods. They can be used in many other areas: for example, the changing ministerial composition of cabinet committees (see Dunleavy, Chapter 13 below) and prime ministerial popularity (Hudson, 1984).

Second, it is not necessary to use only a single case study. Robert Yin (1984, pp.48–9) argues that multiple case studies are analogous to experiments because they follow a replication logic: that is, each case predicts similar results or produces contrary results for predictable reasons. A multiple case research design is more robust and allows us to generalise with greater confidence. There are no multiple case studies of the British executive although several studies show that, without access to cabinet papers, illuminating individual cases can be written (Bruce-Gardyne and Lawson, 1976; Barnett, 1969; Linklater and Leigh, 1986).

Finally we need an archive of oral administrative history. More than 50 senior officials retired in the 1980s. Most will only speak off the record. Interviews with them, stored if necessary under the 30-year rule, would provide an invaluable research resource for future generations of researchers.

It is commonly alleged that access is the key problem limiting research in the field. However researchers with a proven record can surmount most problems. Also the times they are a-changing. There is a willingness to help and grounds for believing there will be greater access to civil servants and more information about the policy process (Butler, 1992).

Multiple sources of data are already available, including the following:

- *Hansard* (parliamentary debates and questions, select committee hearings);
- white papers, green papers and other official publications (including official statistics);
- media reports, including television documentaries as well as newspaper reports and investigations;
- memoirs, autobiographies and diaries;
- biographies;
- interviews with past and present ministers and officials;
- seminars under Chatham House rules;
- cabinet papers, available after 30 years (and William Waldegrave has offered to review access to official papers beyond the 30-year rule for historians on a case-by-case basis); and
- other secondary sources, whether written by participants, journalists or academics.

In sum, there is already much material in the public domain. (See James, 1992, for an illustration of the scope for syntheses based on published material.)

Undoubtedly all of these research methods and sources have some serious limits for studying the executive. The choice of methods has been too conservative in the past. Available sources have not been fully exploited. Secrecy and restricted access may be a problem, but there is still a great deal of work that can be done.

Key Questions

There is an urgent need to provide up-to-date accounts of the executive 'at work'. There are three key research themes of particular interest to the student of politics: the 'hollowing out of the state', the fragmenting governmental framework and ministerial and managerial roles and relationships.

Hollowing Out the State. I use the catchphrase 'hollowing out the state' (Rhodes, 1994, pp.138–9) to refer to:

(a)   privatisation and limiting the scope and forms of public intervention;

(b)   the loss of functions by central and local government departments to new service delivery systems (such as agencies);

(c)   the loss of functions by British government to European Union institutions; and

(d)   limiting the discretion of public servants through the new public management, with its emphasis on managerial accountability and clearer political control of the civil service through a sharper distinction between politics and administration.

This phrase is argumentative. I do not claim that it provides an accurate summary of the British executive in the 1990s. It is a plausible hypothesis which raises questions important to both academic and practitioner. Thus Sir Robin Butler (1993) identified four major changes in the British civil service in the 1980s and 1990s: the changing pattern of public ownership, the reform of public-sector management, the spread of competition and increased openness. Clearly there is substantial overlap between Butler's trends and 'hollowing out the state' (see also Osborne and Gaebler, 1992). Agencies and the impact of the European Union are particularly important topics.

The devolved management systems of the new public management and agencies raise questions about the extent of delegation and accountability, managerial and political. They range from ministerial accountability to Parliament through discretion in local pay bargaining to computerised management control systems. Potentially agencies and market testing provide a unique opportunity to explore change in the public sector and the Citizen's Charter is seen in Whitehall as the next significant step in the continuing reform of public management. There is one particularly challenging hypothesis: that the core executive is squeezed from the top (the EU) and the bottom (agencies). As a result, three questions are of prime importance. First, can departments develop a strategic management ability to steer their agencies? Second, to what extent is the ability of the core executive to coordinate central departments eroded in the hollow state? Finally, are current trends weakening the horizontal integration, or the village community, of the civil service? Is it being eroded by the vertical linkages between department and agency? In other words, there is a major research task simply to describe the ways in which the core executive is challenged by, and responds to, 'hollowing out'. (For a more detailed discussion, see Rhodes, 1994.)

The European Union has a widespread impact on the British executive. The emergence of transnational policy networks leads to a routinised, sectoral policy-making process. British interests will be 'represented' by the relevant functional agency in British government but it will be only one of several actors which could include local or regional authorities as well as more conventional interest groups. The policy process is complex and accountability scarcely exists. Yet again, there is no authoritative account of EU decision making, separate from the 'high politics' surrounding such events as Maastricht. There is a need to document the impact of the EU on the administrative procedures and decision making of the British executive. There is also a need to map British partici- pation in the labyrinth that is the committees and working groups of the Commission. Finally how has the EU affected the role of the executive in other member states? Luhmann (1982) argues that advanced industrial societies are 'centreless', meaning there are several centres of policy making. To what extent do West European democracies have fragmented executives? Has the EU contributed to this fragmentation? We need to compare the impact of the EU on the executives of the member states.

The Fragmenting Governmental Framework. I use this phrase to focus attention on the increasing institutional fragmentation of British government and its effects on the policy process. Basic information is not available. For example, what are the effects of creating an agency? What is the role of the department? How does separating policy (department) and administration (agency) affect strategic management? To what extent do the political demands of life in the department drive out strategic management? Do the relation- ships of an agency differ from those of a non-departmental public body? How do agencies affect Treasury control? In short we need an up-to-date account of the policy process. Also such an account would normally involve case studies of the core executive 'in ac- tion' and would provide, therefore, an opportunity to develop the replication approach to multiple cases.

I am specifically concerned here with function-specific policy making by policy networks. Studies of networks focus on the way sets of organisations work together. Applied to British government, this approach must work outwards from the departments to analyse their complex set of relationships. They would inevitably cover, therefore, links with the core executive and the conditions under which policy is referred to it. However a key foundation for such empirical work has been missing until recently. There is remarkably little substantive work on the character, resources, commitments or policy behaviour of British central departments. (For a review of the relevant literature, see Smith, Marsh and Richards, Chapter 2 below.) Whitehall's structure as a loose federation of departments is widely acknowledged, yet the nature of these component organisations has not been studied. The Treasury and a few other central departments have been the subject of developed political science studies (for example, see Heclo and Wildavsky, 1974; Thain and Wright, 1992; Wilks, 1987). The pioneering efforts of Hood and Dunsire (1981) to develop a quantitative 'bureaumetrics' approach to studying central state agencies have been supplemented by other studies (Rose, 1987; Dunleavy, 1989a, 1989b). The huge variation in department size, resource and implementation roles is now much better charted. A systematic disaggregated picture of departmental responses to cutbacks in staff and money has been drawn for the first time (Dunsire and Hood, 1989). The key requirement now is for organisational studies with a strong decisional (rather than institutional) focus in order to provide an empirical picture of a highly fragmented executive in which patterns of departmental, ministerial and core executive activity vary between different types of issue. Such studies will be most valuable if they are comparative. It is commonly argued that departments have distinguishing departmental philosophies: see, for example, Roy Jenkins (1971) on working in the Treasury and the Home Office. There has never been a systematic comparative study of the similarities and differences of departments.

Ministerial and Managerial Roles and Relationships. The traditional roles in the executive and the core executive – minister, senior officials, cabinet, prime minister – have changed and are changing. It is incredible that there has been no basic account of the roles and relationships of ministers and permanent secretaries for nearly 20 years. The most recent major study is Headey (1974)! How have their roles and relationships changed, and why? The volume of academic research on prime minister and cabinet is scarcely any greater. There is no authoritative account of the way in which the cabinet and its support system have changed. There are no histories of several key institutions within the core executive in the postwar period, such as the Cabinet Office (Mosley, 1969; Seldon, Chapter 6 below) and the Prime Minister's Office. We need to answer the basic question, 'Who does what, to whom, when, where and why?'

Basic information gathering, important though it may be, is not enough. We need to explain the changes and for that we need theories. Unfortunately existing institutional perspectives are at best atheoretical and at worst inadequate. It is in this area we are most in need of theoretical innovation. We also need to employ more sophisticated methodological techniques. There are several promising sources of theoretical and methodological innovation. Here I focus on the study of leadership.

Psychology and psychotherapy have provided the theoretical basis for several studies of the American presidency. With few exceptions, 'psychobiography' has not caught on in the UK (Foley, 1993, pp.151, 307 n.7, 308 n.12). The literature awaits assessment. Similarly the subfield of political psychology has not thrived in the UK. There is a vast literature on leadership, its traits and context (Hermann, 1986; Simonton, 1987). It focuses on either the great men of history or business leaders. The subject matter does not need to be so exclusive. Doig and Hargrove (1987), for example, analysed innovation by comparing the careers of administrative entrepreneurs in American government. Their main research tool was comparative biography, which has enormous potential for the study of administrative and political leadership in British government.

Simon James (Chapter 3 below) describes the changes in prime minister–cabinet relations under John Major. Why have relationships changed? Many commentators on British government stress the contrasting styles of Thatcher and Major. The various theories of leadership, however, direct attention to individual characteristics, the organisation and its context, leadership style, the task to be performed, expectations about the leaders' behaviour, and organisational and group objectives. In short, no one variable will explain the changing pattern of relationships and I know of no study which systematically evaluates the importance of these several variables for understanding British political leadership (although, for a partial exception to this generalisation, see Foley, 1993).

Conclusions

The state of the art in British core executive studies leaves plenty of room for improvement, but there are grounds for expecting some progress. Upon close inspection the institutionalist literature has proved to be diverse and to support a fragmented or differentiated interpretation of the British executive. Further progress requires a focus upon the range of institutions which constitute the core executive, a theoretical approach which compares the strengths and weaknesses of different approaches, more field work to provide case studies of the core executive in action, and greater methodological sophistication to make full use of the data which are already available. No one volume, let alone an edited collection, can hope to correct all these defects, but this book goes some way towards illustrating the way forward. It provides theoretical analysis, case studies of core executive decisions, quantitative analyses and institutional studies. Indeed I would argue for just such a variety of approaches and methods in the study of the core executive. Abstruse theorising and advanced quantitative analysis would be as debilitating as the unthinking adoption of the institutionalist approach has been over the past two decades. This volume heralds a new decade of eclectic theoretical and empirical research.

2

Central Government Departments and the Policy Process

MARTIN J. SMITH, DAVID MARSH AND DAVID RICHARDS

It is widely accepted that government departments are the key policy-making institutions in British politics. In addition to being the primary administrative units, departments are the focus for most of the policy process. However, in terms of research into central government, they have received relatively little attention. Much more work has been done on the prime minister and the so-called 'core executive' which, although the locus of 'heroic' policy making, does not play a decisive role in all, or even most of, the stages of the policy process.

Even when departments have been studied the analysis has been limited. Some attention has been paid to the organisational structures of departments and how they have changed. Nevertheless, with the notable exceptions of Heclo and Wildavsky's (1981) *The Private Government of Public Money* and Thain and Wright's (1992) recent study of the Treasury, there is little work on the politics of departments. Discussion of internal policy making has concentrated almost solely on minister–civil service relations, while analysis of relations between departments has been limited to department–Treasury interaction. There has been a significant body of work on the cabinet but it has been dominated by the discussion of prime ministerial power. In addition work on interest group–department relations has strongly emphasised the interest group perspective. Consequently analysis of departments has avoided some of the key relationships and so it has been both narrow and shallow. The present chapter will review the literature on departments, outline some of its limitations and highlight the importance

of departments in a comprehensive understanding of core executive relations.

Departments: What They Are and Why They Are Important

As Hogwood (1992a) has pointed out, it is contentious even to list
government departments. Hood and Dunsire (1981, p.40) believe
that 'the question is a deep legal (indeed philosophical) one and
there is certainly no single and all-encompassing definition of such
a thing'. This point is demonstrated by the plethora of definitions
of, and schemas for, classifying government departments. Many
authors include only the departments which are headed by cabinet
ministers (see Rose, 1987; for similar lists, see Madgwick, 1991,
p.20; Clarke, 1975, p.65; Hennessy, 1989).

Such lists, however, are partial. In contrast, a number of authors
have offered much more comprehensive definitions of government departments (Drewry and Butcher, 1988; Dunleavy, 1989a;
Hood *el al.*, 1978; Hood and Dunsire, 1981; Pitt and Smith, 1981;
Pollitt, 1984). Dunleavy (1989a, p.273), for instance, disaggregates
departments recognising that many have departmental agencies
attached. Consequently he identifies 44 'ministerial departments
(and elements of)' and lists a further 38 'non-ministerial departments, departmental agencies, and other semi-detached agencies
etc'. Hood *et al.* (1978), when beginning their research into the
management of government, soon found that there was 'no single
or self-evident definition of "a central government agency" in Britain'. They point out that different government lists offer varying
lists of agencies that are attached to departments and, perhaps
most ironically, the departments listed in the Treasury's ' "Memorandum on the Estimates" are by no means the same departments
which actually appear in the estimates' (Hood *et al.*, 1978). Consequently they distinguish between departments which are five-star,
that is the departments which appear on all five departmental lists
and the departments which are four-star appearing on four, and so
on. They finally accept a total of 69 departments.

For the sake of clarity we have chosen to use the list of 61
departments in the *Civil Service Year Book* definition. Of these, 19
are headed by cabinet ministers and a further two, the Law
Officer's Department and the Lord Advocate's Department, are
defined as Departments of State.

Having defined departments, we are still left with the question of
whether they are an important unit for research. The thrust of
much analysis of central government over the past two decades
is that the prime minister has become increasingly dominant in

relation to departments. The Crossman thesis (supported by Benn, 1981) which emerges from the diaries and his more academic writings (see Crossman, 1972) is that the department minister is highly dependent on the prime minister: 'each Minister fighting in the Cabinet for his Department can be sacked by the Prime Minister any day. We must be constantly aware that our tenure in office depends on his personal decision' (Crossman, 1972). The view generated during the Thatcher era was that, if a minister wanted to succeed, she or he needed the prime minister's support and that bilateralism was the key to policy development (Hennessy, 1986). This thesis, while often explicitly rejected, has frequently provided the implicit research agenda (see Riddell, 1990; Gamble, 1988). The most recent literature provides a heavy focus on the prime minister (see Barber, 1991; Madgwick, 1991; James, 1992), providing a good indication of how little attention has been paid to departments as a focus of research. There is too much emphasis on the prime minister; there always was, but this was exacerbated by the emphasis on Margaret Thatcher and her policy style (see King, 1985b; Minogue, 1988).

There are reasons to believe that even during the Thatcher government the central unit of policy making was the department. Except on particular issues of interest to the prime minister, or of central strategic policy, or a high level of controversy, the majority of policy making occurs within departments. This fact has been acknowledged in much of the public administration literature. Smith and Stanyer (1976, p.144) recognise that 'in British central administration the main organisational unit is the department or ministry . . .' Cross (1970, p.38) reinforces this view: 'The ministerial department is the nodal point of the British Administrative system . . . It is through the agency of government departments that policy is formulated and implemented.' This view is given further impetus by the study by Bruce-Gardyne and Lawson (1976, pp.80–117) of the abolition of resale price maintenance (RPM):

> The story of RPM abolition should be enough to dispose of the canard that the departmental minister under the modern British Cabinet system is – or at any rate needs to be – the Prime Minister's poodle. He can have a mind of his own, and he can assert a decisive influence of his own . . .

There are a number of limits on the power prime ministers can have over departmental ministers. The prime minister clearly does not have the time or knowledge to be involved in all areas of policy. He or she lacks the bureaucratic support that the minister has in a particular area. Moreover much department policy is routine and of little interest to the prime minister. Prime ministers cannot continually sack ministers and will lose support if they are constantly interfering in the work of departments. Cabinet ministers often have their own resources in terms of party and public support and so can be difficult to remove. In 1988, the prime minister could not prevent Nigel Lawson following an exchange rate policy which she directly opposed because he was seen as the architect of Britain's economic miracle and was strongly supported throughout the cabinet and the party (Lawson, 1992). To an extent, Margaret Thatcher's demise was a consequence of her sacking too many senior ministers (see Chapter 5 below).

Through their concept of the 'core executive', Dunleavy and Rhodes (1990) demonstrated that the notion of prime ministerial power is too simplistic to help in understanding the workings of central government (see also Chapter 1 above). Power within central government is based upon resource dependencies (Rhodes, 1981) rather than a zero-sum conception of power, so the relationship is not one in which the prime minister directs cabinet ministers; rather the prime minister needs departmental ministers in order to exercise power. This statement does not mean there is cabinet government. As we suggest below, the role of the cabinet in policy making is limited. Little, if any, policy originates in the cabinet. Its role is to arbitrate between conflicting ministries, to make strategic decisions and to approve major policy changes which might affect other departments (see Crossman, 1972; Headey, 1974; Mackintosh, 1977; Hennessy, 1986).

Thus departments are the key policy makers for the majority of policies within British central government. The central unit of analysis is not the prime minister, the cabinet, civil servants, ministers or interest groups (although these areas are obviously important in their own right) but the departments. Nevertheless departments for a number of practical and theoretical reasons have been subject to relatively little research. Theoretical, epistemological and practical problems resulted in researchers focusing more on the pressures on government than government itself. When they have investigated central government, they have either adopted an 'administrative/managerial approach' by examining organisation, or what might be called a 'constitutional approach' by focusing on the constitutionally important institutions of the prime minister and cabinet. Too much research on central government is artificially bound by the perennial question of prime ministerial versus cabinet government. An outline of some of the work done on departments will amply demonstrate this point.

Departmental Studies

A comprehensive study of government departments was conducted under the auspices of 'The New Whitehall Series'. These studies were written by permanent secretaries or ex-permanent secretaries and published mainly during the 1950s and 1960s. This series included about 20 volumes covering most of the main ministerial departments of the time (for a selection, see Bridges, 1964; Emmerson, 1956; Jenkins, 1959; Pile, 1979; Sharp, 1969; Winnifrith, 1962). The studies were largely institutional and descriptive. They provided an outline of the historical development of the respective departments, described their work and provided a comprehensive outline of their structure and agencies. They undoubtedly provide useful, if somewhat dated, sketches of the policy-making processes within departments. They also summarise the key policy changes. For example, the study by Pile on the Department of Education and Science (DES) examines the impact of demographic and social changes on the department and education policy. This study also provides a fairly legalistic account of the relationship between the DES and the Local Education Authorities (LEAs). Thus Pile (1979, p.24) suggests that the 'education service is operated as a partnership between the central authorities and the LEAs'. In doing so, he removes all the politics from this highly political relationship (see Rhodes, 1988, p.3). However not all the studies are completely depoliticised. Winnifrith's (1962) study of the Ministry of Agriculture Food and Fisheries demonstrates how agricultural policy was influenced by the economic conditions facing Britain after the war.

There have been a smaller number of academic studies of individual departments. For instance, there are a whole range of policy studies covering different areas (see, for example, Klein, 1989, on health; Grant, 1982, on industrial policy; Lowe and Goyder, 1983, on environmental policy) but rarely, if ever, do these books examine departments in detail.

Education is the subject of several studies (see Kogan, 1975; Jennings, 1977; Saran, 1973; Salter and Tapper, 1981). Interestingly Salter and Tapper criticise the other studies for focusing on a pressure group approach to educational policy. In this way, Kogan (1978), when examining educational change, does not deal with the Department of Education until the last chapter. Even then the focus of the analysis is on how the department responds to pressure groups and the outside environment. Salter and Tapper do emphasise the importance of the DES. They suggest that the discussion of educational policy takes place within a 'bureaucratic process which is far from passive in its policy preferences'. They use a combination of a Marxian and state-centred approach to suggest that:

> [the DES] is in a position to arrange not only the agenda of the negotiations but also to advise on the financial considerations involved in particular policy outcomes and the changes in the state apparatus required in order to implement certain policies. (p.92)

Salter and Tapper's work is certainly an advance on most investigations into the DES (and even other departments), but they say little about the internal relationships within the department and how, in particular, the process of agenda setting occurs. There have been other fairly descriptive departmental studies, for instance Clarke (1971) on the Ministry of Technology and Roll's (1966) article on the Department of Economic Affairs.

Pitt and Smith (1981) provide one of the few political analyses of a government department, the Post Office. They examine how the organisational structure affected the department and the ways in which its behaviour and policy was influenced by its relationship with the Treasury. They then demonstrate the impact that 'hiving off' had on the ability of the Post Office to make policy and so are concerned with the ways in which organisational structures affect policy outcomes. They conclude: 'The case of the Post Office shows that the achievement of organizational flexibility is neither straightforward nor painless. Constitutional reform does not necessarily produce change' (Pitt and Smith, 1981, p.131).

Despite the importance of departments, there have been relatively few detailed studies of the internal structures and processes of individual departments. Those that do exist are brief, descriptive and dated. The only department to be studied in any detail is the Treasury (Bridges, 1964; Brittan, 1964, 1971; Heclo and Wildavsky, 1974; Pliatsky, 1982, 1989; Roseveare, 1969; Thain and Wright, 1990a, 1990b, 1992; Young and Sloman, 1984). The key book is Heclo and Wildavsky's *The Private Government of Public Money* (1981). The Treasury, because of its role as the provider of finance, is the central department in Whitehall. All departments need money and so the Treasury has access to every department. The Treasury also has a central role in the supervision and development of all departmental spending plans. Consequently the Treasury frequently influences policy decisions. As Heclo and Wildavsky suggest, 'since nearly all policy involves some expenditure, the Treasury gets the opportunity to know about the principles and has some hand in the shaping of all departmental policies'. They emphasise how the Treasury maintains dominance through the use of the 'folkways' of Whitehall. However, while these folkways provide the Treasury with a central role, they also restrict its ability to cope with new problems. The focus of Heclo and Wildavsky is on the culture of Whitehall and how this defines and delimits the informal and formal relationships which exist within the Treasury and between the Treasury and other departments (pp.li, 1).

The limited number of actors and their spatial concentration means the 'cooperation of operating departments is essential' (p.7). Thus a relationship of trust and dependence has developed between the Treasury and the departments. Moreover, in order to maintain its dominance over specialist departments, the Treasury 'must claim a special expertise that belongs to no other department. That it indeed does so is an important part of the Treasury culture' (p.42).

Heclo and Wildavsky's account is also interesting because it focuses on one of the key aspects of the policy process – Treasury–department relations – about which they make a number of points. First, the relationship is often ambivalent. While departments admire the Treasury, they also 'fear it' (p.77). Second, they see civil servants as the cement of the relationship: 'Cooperation is facilitated by the fact that, despite departmental allegiances, all officials are part of a greater civil service society' (p.80). Third, disputes between the departments and the Treasury are settled by discussion in 'early, bilateral consultations between Departments and Treasury officials on a face-to-face basis'. Fourth, although the relationship is based on trust, departmental ministers are also involved in a game where they try to get as much from the Treasury as possible. Hence Kenneth Clarke admitted that he added substantially to his public expenditure submissions to the Treasury. Thain and Wright (1992a, p.8) point out that 'the strategies of departmental ministers representing a variety of different pressures will normally dictate additional public expenditure'. Fifth, cooperation between departments is rare but does occur when 'they find a common interest in assaulting Treasury rules that affect them all adversely' (p.96).

Heclo and Wildavsky (1981) also place a great deal of emphasis on the role of the principal finance officer. The PFO's position is interesting because she or he has to be Janus-faced: in a sense she or he represents the Treasury to the department and the department to the Treasury. There clearly is a substantial gap in our knowledge of PFOs and the work they do and how they develop Treasury–department relationships.

Heclo and Wildavsky provide a useful analysis of a department. They identify many of the key issues that need to be investigated:

how informal relationships work, how relationships develop between departments, how Whitehall excludes certain interests and the importance of culture in the policy process. They do not, however, say much about the internal organisation of the Treasury, although they do point out the inadequacies of organisational charts and the importance of informal relationships, structures and meetings (pp.7, 68, 71–3). The weakness of their approach is that it is almost an impressionistic, symbolic interactionist approach to government departments. The authors focus strongly on individuals and their 'presentation of self' after the inculcation of departmental values and so say little about structural constraints and organisational dynamics, and how they affect individual actions. They also more or less completely ignore the role of outside actors and thus present the Treasury as a hermetically sealed organisation. Perhaps their major omission within the context of the Treasury is to ignore the role of the City and the Bank of England (p. lxx). The Treasury is the nexus of financial and economic policy in Britain and consequently relations between the City and the Treasury are crucial to understanding the policy process (see Moran, 1984). It seems impossible to examine economic and financial policy making without looking at these external factors.

Thain and Wright (1992) to an extent update the analysis of Heclo and Wildavsky. They show that a great deal has changed. The Treasury's annual survey of expenditure is now the central element of control over public expenditure. Although much remains the same: 'the principles governing its preparation, the methodology employed and the conduct of negotiations between the Treasury and the departments have changed' (Thain and Wright, 1992, p.23). Thain and Wright emphasise that the whole process has been formalised. Nevertheless, they argue (ibid.):

> The medium of exchange in the bidding process has been little affected by the formalisation of the survey procedures. Most decisions about the allocation between programmes continue to be made as the result of mutually acceptable agreements negotiated between the Treasury and the spending departments; a few become the subject of bargaining conducted by Ministers face to face in bilaterals.

Thain and Wright provide a political account of the relationships within the Treasury and between the Treasury and other departments. They point out that within the expenditure process there are distinct sets of interests (Thain and Wright, 1992, p.193). More importantly,

There is a small, permanent, stable, cohesive and exclusive policy network focused on the [expenditure] survey process. Membership is precisely defined by the circulation list of the Survey Guidelines, some 200 officials (and their ministers) from about two dozen Whitehall spending departments. The inner core of key members is equally defined by the 'inner PESC' of PFOs and senior Treasury Officials. Relationships within the policy network are regulated by policy rules which determine the agenda of expenditure issues and how they are handled, and behavioural rules which govern the conduct of members towards each other when they transact expenditure business. (pp.194–5)

Thain and Wright are aware that internal relationships are highly political and are structured by the values, rules and roles of policy networks. Indeed they do an excellent job in updating Heclo and Wildavsky. In particular, their work tells us a great deal about the current relationship between the Treasury and departments and concerning the form and content of negotiations between them. They also indicate the approach which needs to be taken to other government departments.

Comparing Departments: Structure and Organisational Change

Whilst the studies of individual departments, with the exception of the Treasury, have been limited and few, there have been a number of studies which analyse a range of departments in order to compare their structure and organisational change. One of the earliest comprehensive studies is Chester and Willson, *The Organisation of British Central Government* (1957; 1968). They give a brief outline of the development of central government, the size of the civil service and the number of departments. More recently, Hennessy outlines the structure of the main departments and gives information on their budgets and management systems. He also provides a vignette of each of the departments. For example: 'The DTI is the Ethel Merman of the Whitehall scene – it has had more come-backs than can be counted' (Hennessy, 1988, p.432; this is a theme also pursued in Hogwood, 1984). Hennessy then goes on to point out the clashes that have occurred in departmental philosophy in the DTI. Yet, again, Hennessy's account is largely descriptive and anecdotal.

An attempt at a more systematic analysis of departments is made by Hood and Dunsire (1981). Their stated aim was 'emphatically not to discover the government's policy secrets merely to map its organisational structure ... in fairly simple terms' (Hood and Dunsire, 1981, p.38). They then devised 20 or so 'possible measures of administrative structures' which they grouped under five headings: (1) specialisation and differentiation; (2) expertness; (3) dispersion; (4) number of associated bodies; (5) measures of hierarchy. Subsequently they used this 'objective' information to assess each of the departments against these criteria. These measures created a multidimensional map of the way departments related to each other. They analysed departments on various criteria in order to establish 'the extent to which any other department appeared more than once among its three nearest neighbours in the various analyses' (p.153). It appears that the connections Hood and Dunsire established are based on quantitative similarities rather than any 'real world' political interactions.

Dunleavy (1989a, 1989b, 1991) has used the 'bureau-shaping, model to provide an 'architecture of the British central state'. The bureau-shaping model suggests that bureaucrats 'try to reshape their departments as small staff agencies, removed from lines of responsibilities and hence more insulated from adverse impacts in the event of overall spending reductions in their policy area' (1989a, p.252). This model demonstrates that 'many contemporary administrative systems are multi-organisational and less hierarchical in their operations than classical accounts assume' (1989a, p.252). Dunleavy then goes on to analyse different definitions of budgets and five main analytic types of agencies. He demonstrates that the extent to which budgets increase depends on the type of budget and the type of agency involved. So the bureau-shaping model would expect little budget maximising by control agencies and Dunleavy demonstrates that this is the case (see 1989b). Although Dunleavy offers explanation rather than description, by explaining the impact that certain organisational goals and structures have on outcomes, he is doing so at a fairly high level of aggregation. There is no examination of the internal processes of departments. Hence Radcliffe (1991, p.41) claims that Dunleavy's study is 'strongly non-political in that ministers themselves and the political environment in which departments operate are largely absent'.

One central area of departmental research has been the impact of organisational change. This work has ranged from studies of single departments (Hogwood, 1984) through comparisons of two departments (Radcliffe, 1991) to comparison throughout government (Pollitt, 1984). Clarke (1975) examines organisational change between 1914 and 1974. He concludes that changes occur as the result of 'underlying forces at work', such as increasing various cabinet places, improving coordination and increasing the size of departments: 'All these considerations suggest that changes have come about as a result of gradual realisation that it was practicable to reduce the number of major departments radically' (Clarke 1975, p.93). However Hogwood (1992b) demonstrates that since 1974 there has been some shift away from ever larger departments (for example, the splitting of the DHSS). He maintains (1992b, p.175):

> There has been some shift toward rationalisation and consolidation of functions. Government departments now much more closely correspond to the major public expenditure functions ... But an equally important feature has been the frequency of changes, though the pace of change has slowed down since the mid-1970s.

Pollitt (1984) traces the organisational changes that have occurred within government since 1964. He mainly describes the process of decision making that occurred and outlines the structural changes that resulted from policy decisions. In his view decisions to change structures 'usually emerge from private informal discussions between the Prime Minister and the head of the Civil Service' (1984, p.125) (Hogwood, 1992a, offers a different interpretation).

Radcliffe (1991) provides a detailed examination of the impact of organisational change on two government departments. His concern was with the way the 1970 white paper, 'The Reorganisation of Central Government', was implemented in relation to the creation of the Department of the Environment and the Department of Trade and Industry. He examines how a departmental ethos was established in the new departments and how various agencies were integrated. He concludes by suggesting that the impact of the secretary of state was important in determining the effectiveness of reorganisation (1991, p.192). He also demonstrates that those with executive or highly specialist functions were the most resistant to integration.

In some ways these studies of the impact of change on the machinery of government have been the most detailed and comprehensive analyses in the research on British departments. This focus has continued during the Thatcher era. Margaret Thatcher had a significant impact on government through privatisation, the Financial Management Initiative (FMI) and the Next Steps agencies (see Lee, 1980; Greenaway, 1985). Although Delafons (1982) demonstrates that concern with management and efficiency has been developing since the 1950s, the 1980s is the era of the 'new public management' (NPM) with its concern to reverse or slow government growth, privatisation and the development of automation (Hood, 1991). In Britain the NPM has taken a number of practical forms. First, the FMI was launched in 1982 with a number of aims:

> to provide managers in departments with clearly defined objectives; to promote clear specification of responsibilities for both resources and operations; to provide the necessary support (information, training and related management resource) for the execution of responsibilities.
> (Cmnd 8616, quoted in Gray, Jenkins *et al.*, 1991, p.47)

The goal was to provide each department with a management system which enabled the minister to obtain information on the department's operations and use of resources (Gray, Jenkins *et al.*, 1991; for systems in each department, see Hennessy, 1989). Second, this concern with financial management and the '3Es' of economy, efficiency and effectiveness led to the development within government of more performance indicators to assess an organisation's performance (see Carter, 1988, 1991; Carter *et al.*, 1992). Third, there were the Next Step agencies. The hiving-off of government agencies is not a new phenomenon (see Jordan, 1976), but it achieved a new impetus under the Thatcher government and had a significant impact on the organisation of departments.

Next Steps developed from the Ibbs Report (Jenkins *et al.*, 1988) which suggested that, in order to improve efficiency within government, 'agencies should be established to carry out the executive functions of government within a policy and resource framework set by a department'. In this way departments will be reduced in size with the slimmed down 'core' responsible for policy while the agencies assume executive functions and deliver services. Although the chief executive is responsible to the minister, he enjoys managerial independence within a preset budget and will be judged by results. As Hogwood points out (1993, p.3), although such agencies marked a radical change in the British context they bring Britain more in line with the Swedish and US models.

By January 1993, 76 Next Steps agencies had been established, with a further 26 under consideration ('Parliamentary Companion', no. 14, January 1993). A number of assessments of these new agencies have been published (see, for example, Davies and Willman, 1991; Efficiency Unit, 1991; Flynn *et al.*, 1990; Goldsworthy, 1991; Hogwood, 1993; Price Waterhouse, 1990; Radcliffe, 1991; RIPA, 1991; Treasury and Civil Service Committee, 1990).

The agencies vary enormously in size, ranging from 30 employees (the Wilton Park Conference Centre) to 65000 (the Social

Security Benefits Agency). In fact a number of agencies employ more people than some departments. The origins of agencies is varied; some were previously separate non-ministerial departments (for example, the Intervention Board), others separate units within departments (as with the Driver and Vehicle Licensing Agency), while a third group had no prior autonomy. There is also considerable variation in the way agencies are funded, with some receiving 100 per cent government funding while others raise all their revenue from fees or charges (see Hogwood, 1993).

More generally issues of departmental change are important for what they tell us about the way structure affects policy. Many of the researchers discussed above seem content to describe the structural change and problems with implementation rather than dealing with the questions of how these changes affect the internal politics of the departments and the policy process. The literature on policy networks demonstrates that departments often provide the core of a policy network (see Jordan, 1990; Marsh and Rhodes, 1992b; Smith, 1990). Frequently the departments provide a focus for a closed relationship which has substantial impact on policy outcomes through its ability to exclude particular groups and issues from the policy agenda (Rhodes, 1988; M. Smith, 1992). This raises the question of how departmental structures affect policy outcomes and how changes in the structure of departments affect particular policy networks.

Russell (1989) and McInnes (1990) demonstrate how the structure of the Department of Energy has constantly favoured certain interests and policy outcomes over others. McInnes (1990, p.18) maintains that 'The Department of Energy is structurally biased in favour of some interests. . . .' While energy conservation has its own division within the department, as has atomic energy and gas, these fuels also 'have powerful groups outside the department, furthering their interests; energy conservation does not. In these circumstances it is easy to see why energy conservation – the fifth fuel – remains relatively under-utilised, despite its great economic efficiency' (p.19). The point is confirmed by Russell (1989). Hence the way the Department of Energy is structured biases policy outcomes. Because energy conservation lacks external resources and a national organisation there is little pressure to make it a priority or to try to win resources from the Treasury for such a policy.

There has been relatively little detailed research into government departments and what does exist tends to be a highly descriptive and technocratic approach to organisational change. The focus of departmental research needs to be much more on the power of departments and how they are involved in the processes of policy making. What is important about departments is not the formal organisational structure but the types of relationships that departments have internally, with other departments, with the co-ordinating institutions and the outside world. There is a limited range of literature dealing with these issues.

Re-analysing Departments

Relations within Departments

Much of t-he research reviewed hitherto focuses on departments and defines the department as the unit of analysis. This sub-sequently ignores the relationships and politics within depart-ments. If departments are policy-making bodies, then much of the process of policy making goes on inside the departments. It is therefore important to analyse the internal relationships within departments. Departments are not unified organisations with sin-gle goals. Departments are divided into divisions responsible for major functions and headed by an under-secretary with two or three divisions grouped under a deputy secretary (Smith and Stanyer, 1976).

Thus the relationships between these sections are a central site of much of the political process. It is important to remember that 'Most activities occur without Ministerial scrutiny' (Kogan 1971, p.48) and therefore much internal politics occurs between civil servants rather than between civil servants and ministers. Gray and Jenkins (1985) stress that there is a tendency within departments 'to fragmentation which functional differentiation might promote' (p.92). So for many departments there are conflicts over which interest or function should be given primacy. For instance, in the Ministry of Agriculture, Fisheries and Food it seems that the el-ements of food, environment and consumer interests are often submerged under the interests of agriculture (Smith, 1990). Simi-larly Ponting (1986, pp.98–9) highlights how the rivalry between the services,

> mainly for money but also for power is bitter and continuous . . . Every year there are wrangles over the splitting up of the De-fence Budget, often reaching the ludicrous situation where one service would rather see money wasted than being spent on a rival.

The rivalries and conflicts have become greater with the establish-ment of 'super' departments where many different functions are

amalgamated into one ministry and where rivalries are often reinforced by the fact that a junior minister is placed in charge of a
particular section (Theakston, 1987).

Within departments there are often functional, political and
technical divisions. Rose believes that the unity that is frequently
imposed on departments is misleading: 'a ministry lacks a central
nervous system' (Rose, 1987, p.239). Thus much of the interaction
within departments is informal and based on negotiations.

Despite this potential for conflict, many discussions of departments have talked of the strength of the 'departmental view'.
Radcliffe argues that there is an accepted departmental view which
develops over time and is submitted to the cabinet through the
minister and may result in the failure of collective decision making
(Radcliffe, 1991, p.19). Bruce-Gardyne and Lawson (1976, p.109)
demonstrate that one of the reasons for the abolition of RPM was
that the Board of Trade kept the issue alive: 'pressing on successive
governments and successive Ministers, a specific departmental
policy grounded in a clear departmental philosophy'. Many commentators have suggested that Britain's industrial policy (or lack of
it) owes much to the dominance of laissez-faire beliefs within the
Treasury and the Board of Trade (Gamble, 1990; Grant and Wilks,
1983; Hall, 1986; Zsyman, 1983). Britain's economic decline has
been blamed on the Treasury's negative view of government spending and concern with specific economic indicators (Brittan, 1964;
Eatwell, 1981; Pollard, 1982).

Such is the importance of the departmental view that, in the
creation of the new 'super' ministries in the 1970s, the establishment of a departmental view was seen as being a high priority
(Radcliffe, 1991). These values are central to the department. They
can unite or divide a department, they limit the policy options and
access to the policy agenda, and they may divide departments
against each other. Yet, as Gray and Jenkins (1985, p.32) point out,
'we know little about how values and interests develop or about
how administrators are politicised in terms of interests which they
might seek to promote'.

An area of internal departmental politics which has been sub-
jected to much research is minister–civil servant relations. There
are a number of approaches to this question. The constitutional
view sees civil servants responding, at the very least, to the framework established by ministers (Butler, 1989; Wass, 1984; Wilson,
1976; Young and Sloman, 1982). The conspiracy view believes that
civil servants have a particular viewpoint, whether it is as a class or
elite, and they use their resources and informal networks to thwart
ministers who try to follow policies of which they disapprove

(Benn, 1981; Sedgmore, 1980). The elitist view sees civil servants as coming from a particular class and this creates a view of the world which is pursued by the elite's dominance of the system and the interrelationship with the political elite (Hennessy, 1989; Kellner and Crowther Hunt, 1980; Miliband, 1969). Finally the bureaucratic view sees civil servants as having access to particular bureaucratic resources which gives them advantages over their ministers (Gray and Jenkins, 1985).

It is clear that much of the time civil servants make policy and that they have the experience, knowledge and time that is not available to ministers (Kogan 1971, p.42). This often places a minister at a severe disadvantage in relation to his or her civil servants. The diaries of Benn, Castle and Crossman reveal that the minister–civil servant relationship is often difficult. Nevertheless Crossman (1972) points out that civil servants need ministers to represent the department in cabinet and to the Treasury and the public. Therefore it is too simplistic to see the relationship as one of conflict. Ministers can frequently choose the agenda of policy (Kogan, 1971; Headey, 1974) and civil servants see it as their role to support the development of these issues. As Theakston (1987, p.106) states:

> Life in Whitehall is not lived in a state of permanent conflict between ministers and civil servants. Analyses of policy-making which focus on adversarial confrontations between ministers and the civil service oversimplify and distort. Relations are complex and fluid, and the lines of division are more often than not to be found not between the political and bureaucratic elements in government but within them as alliances of ministers and officials compete with each other to advance particular goals or defend common interest. (See also Drewry and Butcher, 1988, p.82)

Relations between Departments

Ponting (1986, p.102) relates:

> Much of the work of Whitehall is institutionalised conflict between the competing interests of different departments. Each department will defend its own position and resist a line that, while it might be beneficial to the government as a whole or in the wider public interest, would work against the interest of the department.

This conflict can take a number of forms. It can be bilateral, whereby departments attempt to sort out a problem which concerns shared territory, or it can be multilateral and formal, where an issue involves several departments and can only be resolved in a cabinet committee. Frequently the conflicts occur over issues of expenditure or territory (see Madgwick, 1991). Crossman records how in his first meeting with his permanent secretary at the Ministry of Housing she told him that he had been responsible for selling the department down the river because of Wilson's decision that Fred Willey should be in charge of planning: 'As soon as she realised this, Dame Evelyn [Sharp] got down to a Whitehall battle to save her department' (Crossman, 1975, p.25).

Yet the Westland affair demonstrated that conflicts frequently concern policy. The Department of Trade and Industry fought an intense battle over whether the Westland helicopter company should be saved by a European consortium or the US company, Sikorsky. The intensity of the battle was such that it involved secret meetings of ministers and various interests, leaks to the press and the eventual resignation of two ministers (see Chapter 9 below and; Linklater and Leigh, 1986). Similar policy conflicts were revealed during the salmonella in eggs affair (Smith, 1991).

Nevertheless, despite the continued presence of interdepartmental conflict (see Street, 1988, on Aids policy; Parkinson and Duffy, 1984, on inner cities), most conflicts do not reach the level of Westland or salmonella. Gray and Jenkins (1985, p.40) assert: 'the organisational politics of Whitehall that encourage interdepartmental compromise reflect a mutual dependence on not publicising issues'. In the majority of cases if issues of conflict are not resolved informally they will be resolved either in cabinet committees or interdepartmental committees of officials. In the view of Smith and Stanyer (1976, p.168) the official committees:

> are now thought to have almost constitutional significance in British government and to reflect an aspect of our political culture. Certainly it is a phenomena which dominates any scene involving interaction between officials especially when representing different departments.

Of equal importance are cabinet committees. These are the main forum for resolving interdepartmental conflicts. As Crossman wrote, 'Harold Wilson is keeping to the rule that we should only discuss things in Cabinet which we can't resolve in a Cabinet committee' (Crossman, 1975, p.202).

The fact that so much of government is departmental and subject to conflict means that 'To resolve conflicts of interest, Cabinet

Ministers must participate in a continuous round of intra-Cabinet negotiations, involving bilateral discussions, Cabinet committees, lobbying the Prime Minister and formal Cabinet meetings' (Rose, 1987, p.82). Therefore an important aspect of government is coordination among these departments.

Coordinating Departments in the Centre

In this section we examine briefly how departments relate to the key coordinators, in particular the prime minister, the Treasury, the cabinet and the Cabinet Office. Ministers prefer not to take decisions to a higher authority because it reduces their autonomy. Nevertheless, on certain occasions, particularly where there are increases in expenditure, conflicts between departments or major changes in policy, the departmental minister has to obtain the approval of the Treasury or the cabinet. In addition, the prime minister often sees his or her role as one of coordinating government policy and so insists on knowing what is going on.

In constitutional theory the cabinet should be the central coordinating body. However Mackintosh (1977, p.629) concluded

> that the Cabinet is no longer the nineteenth-century body which took virtually all the decisions, where legislation was worked out, the Parliamentary programme devised and in which ministers could raise any issue. The change in party organisation, the volume of business and the subject-matter of politics have put great power in the hands of the Prime Minister.

Ministers are too overloaded and cabinet meetings are too short and ill-informed for the cabinet to be a significant decision-making body. 'The infrequency and short duration of cabinet meetings limits the amount of business that can sensibly be discussed' (Burch, 1988, p.41). Many items of legislation are not discussed in cabinet and so important issues are resolved elsewhere. Cabinet does provide some overall coordination by reviewing decisions and the main strategic issues, yet Castle (1980) gave the impression that cabinet was the arena for the continuation of the departmental battle, while Crossman suggested that, in cabinet, ministers were looking for allies rather than enemies. He still argued that this reduced the room for free discussion (1975, p.47). Consequently he felt that real discussion rarely occurred in cabinet (p.202). In fact Hennessy (1986) identifies a quantitative decline in the amount of business that is going through cabinet. This leads Burch (1988, pp.45–6) to conclude that the ability of the cabinet even to oversee effectively, let alone control the business of government, is bound to be limited. This suggests that coordination has shifted elsewhere. One obvious candidate, especially over the past 10 years or so, is the prime minister. According to Madgwick (1991, p.167):

> The rule of prime ministerial non-intervention rests on a fundamental perception of the role of the Prime Minister. He or she is concerned with strategy, the totality of the government's work, with popular and party political matters and only with 'micro-policy' in moments of crisis.

However the prime minister seems to have a continual role in the 'grand issues' of economic and foreign policy. The role of the prime minister in coordination depends in large part on the premier's strategy. Wilson, in particular phases, preferred to set the broad framework of policy and then appoint ministers that he trusted to develop detailed policy (Kogan, 1971; Wilson, 1974, 1979). Thatcher favoured bilateral arrangements with particular ministers, which allowed her to restructure particular policy areas. For instance, in 1988, she took charge of the NHS policy review (Klein, 1989). This raises an important question concerning the degree to which prime ministers intervene in departmental policy making and how much autonomy ministers have on a day-to-day level. Obviously it depends to some extent on the minister and the prime minister, but the policy freedom of a department is a crucial research area.

A formal institutional coordination role is provided by the Cabinet Office. 'The Cabinet Secretariat helps the Prime Minister draw up the agenda of the Cabinet, processes departmental submissions, keeps Cabinet minutes, records its conclusions, circulates them to departments and tries to ensure they are implemented' (Jones, 1975, p.50). Because the Cabinet Office coordinates departments, implements cabinet decisions and has a high level of authority (the permanent secretary in the Cabinet Office is the head of the home civil service) it does have an impact on policy (Madgwick, 1991). However, returning to the notion of departmental policy, there is obviously an important question concerning the extent to which the Cabinet Office can influence departments. Seldon (Chapter 6 below) suggests that during the 1980s the Cabinet Office was less of a power house and an initiator than it had been under John Hunt (1973–9). Although Lee (Chapter 7 below) thinks there have been some more significant developments in the Cabinet Office and asks whether recent developments have created a system at the 'centre of the machine' which is more than different aspects of the persona of the cabinet secretary.

Until 1983, the strategic function of the Cabinet Office was strengthened through the CPRS. Set up by Heath, 'The idea was to get research done and ideas worked out on broad aspects of policy free from any departmental commitment or bias' (Mackintosh, 1977, p.518). Hence the intention was to provide a basis for collective decision making as policy would be considered in strategic rather than departmental terms (Jones, 1975). It was linked to Programme, Analysis and Review (PAR) in an attempt to break down departmentalism (Gray and Jenkins, 1985; Drewry and Butcher, 1988). However the CPRS was not liked by the departments and had no authority over cabinet ministers (Radcliffe, 1991). It gradually became more adjusted to the 'community surrounding it' (Heclo and Wildavsky, 1981). Thatcher saw it as just another part of the civil service machine and so abolished it.

Perhaps the most effective coordinating department is the Treasury. As the Treasury has to be consulted on all spending plans and through the principal finance officer has contact with all departments, it is the one organisation in central government with access to each department and has the means to achieve departmental compliance. As Edward Boyle said, 'Much the biggest limitation on any Minister of Education is the need to get Treasury agreement' (Kogan, 1971, p.103). The importance of the Treasury is emphasised by Gray and Jenkins (1985, p.80):

> formal networks are typified by contacts between the Treasury and the spending departments, especially during the public expenditure survey. Here the formal battles that occur over the allocation of resources are actually played out against a background of the relevant section in the Treasury liaising with a particular department's finance division.

In addition the Treasury has been successful at sending Treasury officials into all departments. This central role means that the Treasury has had a significant impact over the general direction of policy. For Middlemas (1991, p.455), 'The Treasury emerged as a superior partner in negotiating how the postwar settlement would work in practice, because it managed to relate all aspects of the government to its concept of regime'. Middlemas also claims that economic crisis and the introduction of cash limits led to a strengthening of the Treasury's policy role in the 1970s and 1980s: However it is important to stress that the Treasury's coordinating role has often been restricted to the single criterion of public expenditure (Brittan, 1964) and often it has not been very successful in that aim (Madgwick, 1991).

Departments and the Outside World

A further important area of investigation is the relationship of departments to the external environment. One area where there has been substantial work is on the issue of departments and their relationships with interest groups. There is almost limitless information on interest groups and how they influence, or attempt to influence, policy, but most of this literature focuses on the groups rather than the departments, and departments are treated as aggregate organisations which interact with the groups (possible exceptions are Cunningham, 1992; Klein, 1989).

An area of increasing importance and which has also been underresearched is the relationship of departments with the EU and its impact on the policy process. Edwards (1992, p.65) points out that there has been 'a largely gradual process of adaptation within departments to the growing range of issues falling within the Community's competence and which therefore have to be negotiated in Brussels'. Benn and Barnett suggest that the policy process shifting to the EU can increase the autonomy of both ministers and civil servants (Barnett, 1982; Benn cited in Young and Sloman, 1982, pp.79–80).

Finally there is the question of relationships with the semi-external organisations, which were touched on earlier, such as quangos, the new regulatory bodies and the Next Steps agencies. Hogwood (1990) reveals that, despite its rhetoric, the Conservative government set up over 30 new bodies. There are a whole range of questions relating to these bodies concerning how they operate, their relationships with departments and how they might expand or contract in the future.

Conclusion

Keeton (1970, p.141) warns: 'During the last century and a half a major revolution has occurred in the structure of politics. . . . It is the progressive transfer of government function from Parliament, and in some measure, from the Courts of Law to government departments.' While there is certainly much academic discussion of departments, little of this has come to terms with the position of departments in the policy process. Departments are the key policy makers. Most policy is made within government departments, but there is very little research on the way in which departments make policy and how their structures and ideologies affect policy outcomes. But much of the literature is descriptive, merely outlining the formal organisational structure. The literature which goes beyond description tends to deal with administrative rather than political questions and some of the central questions have barely been tackled. This failure to deal with the important questions partly reflects the atheoretical approach of much of the literature (with a couple of notable exceptions: Gray and Jenkins, 1985; Pitt and Smith, 1981).

Consequently many of the extant studies fail to deal with basic political questions such as: where does power lie, how is the policy process organised and what types of networks exist within and between departments? Too much attention has been paid to entire departments as units of analysis and so there has been no disaggregation to allow an analysis of the internal workings of a department. There are only two studies which really tackle these issues systematically and both deal with the Treasury. Yet with Heclo and Wildavsky in particular there are problems which result from their emphasis on the role of individuals, cultural determinism and lack of consideration of the external environment.

In addition, there is a lack of theory to deal with the policy process within departments. Clearly, as Gray and Jenkins and Pitt and Smith demonstrate, there is room for the organisational and bureaucratic politics literature to be used in the study of British departments. Similarly, although the focus of the policy network literature has been on intergovernmental relations and interest group–government relations (see Marsh and Rhodes, 1992b), much could be done to adapt this literature to 'internal' networks. Certainly Pitt and Smith (1981, p.22) argue that it would be 'interesting to plot the networks of interactions among organisations of which government departments are the focal point'. More specifically Laumann and Knoke (1987) have made a quantitative analysis of these type of relationships in the United States.

Rhodes (1981) demonstrates the need to see power in terms of dependence rather than as a zero-sum game. Hence the need to develop a much more sophisticated analysis of the relationships between departments and in particular between the departments and the centre. Much of the popular analysis of the past decade sees Margaret Thatcher dominating government and 'hand-bagging' departments. The reality was that she was limited in the extent to which she could intervene in particular departments. She was also dependent on the support of cabinet ministers and on particular important issues, for example exchange rate policy and entering the ERM, she was forced to submit to their views.

Further theoretical issues are raised by the relationship between structure and agency within departments. Through their analysis of departmental views and organisational change, many of the studies of departments seem to be implicitly concerned with questions relating to the role of ideology and structure. However these questions have rarely been theorised. The level of freedom of individual ministers, the ways in which values are inculcated and the impact of structures on policy outcomes are central issues which need to be theorised and investigated. The theoretical literature on structuration and the social construction of institutions could be adapted to the analysis of departments (see Berger and Luckman, 1967; Giddens, 1986).

If we are to understand the dynamics of central government, it is necessary to provide some detailed investigations of departments and the context within which they operate. It is necessary to examine the nature of departmental views, how they are inculcated and how they affect policy. It is important to study the relationships within and between departments and the extent to which they are formal and informal. We also need to evaluate how the organisation of these relationships affects policy and to look at the problem of coordination. For all the gaps in our knowledge, however, it is clear that departments are the key policy-making institutions in Britain.

PART TWO

Interpreting History

3

Relations between Prime Minister and Cabinet: From Wilson to Thatcher*

SIMON JAMES

Whatever else may have been said about Margaret Thatcher, she made the study of cabinet government interesting again. In the 1960s and 1970s this field of scholarship, always bedevilled by the thirty-year rule, remained obscured by the sleepy commentaries of Ivor Jennings and the presidentialist simplifications of John Mackintosh. Thatcher shook this dusty subject back to life. Suddenly the character and health of cabinet government became a live issue: political commentators ruminated about it, backbenchers murmured about it, Heseltine and Howe resigned over it, and ultimately it became a factor in Thatcher's downfall.

In point of fact she worked less of a revolution in the cabinet machine than was – and still is – popularly believed. Commentators overstated the extent of the changes she made to the system, and underestimated the changes that her predecessors had wrought. They would have done well to remember Sir Ian Gilmour's perceptive observation in 1969 that those who believe in prime ministerial government overrate the Prime Minister's power today, and underrate his power in the past (Gilmour, 1969, p.206). The difference in Thatcher's approach was to a large extent one of style and openness: while Heath, Callaghan and, above all, Wilson manipu-

* This article draws on the contributions of guest speakers at the seminar on 'British Cabinet Government' held under Chatham House rules – that is, the discussion could be cited but not attributed – at the London School of Economics under the chairmanship of John Barnes. The author is grateful to Mr Barnes for allowing him access to the seminar.

lated the system subtly, she did so overtly. They were oblique, she was direct.

In the current system the dynamics of policy formulation *do* differ in important ways from those of the 1960s. Today cabinet discussions range more widely but decide much less, far more decisions are taken in committee and much interministerial business is transacted without going before any formal ministerial meeting. Yet the prime minister's influence and role – or rather his or her potential influence and the repertoire of roles open to him or her – are probably not much changed from 30 or even 60 years ago.

In trying to identify exactly how cabinet government under John Major differs from practice in the 1960s, it is important to disentangle structural, permanent developments in the system from transient features, such as the conjunction of particular ministerial personalities at a specific time, and the temporary changes made necessary by atypical crises, such as a run on sterling or the Falklands campaign. Unfortunately it is precisely this type of untypical event which tends to breach official secrecy and make headlines, popularising a distorted view of the system. The less dramatic events that constitute the bulk of cabinet work will pass unpublicised. Despite this drawback, this chapter will try to trace the changes in relations between prime minister and cabinet since the Wilson government of the 1960s. That epoch makes a suitable point of comparison, firstly, because it is the most recent period for which we have detailed accounts of policy making, in the shape of the Crossman, Castle, Benn and Gordon Walker diaries and, secondly, because the portrayals of the system in those diaries tend to be accepted as the state of the art as far as cabinet studies are concerned.

This chapter will look at developments across those three decades in seven areas: the changing role of the cabinet; the committee system; the impact of transnational policy making; relations between the prime minister and his or her colleagues, and their effect on policy-making; the prime minister as leader; inner cabinets; and the state of collective responsibility.

The Role of the Cabinet

The conventional wisdom of the 1980s, fostered by journalists and ex-ministers, was that the cabinet had become a greatly diminished force. Undoubtedly these days less business is going to cabinet, and fewer decisions are being taken there. But this must be seen in the broader context of a general pushing down of the level of decision making in the cabinet system. Although it has become a common-place of political science that ministers are overburdened with work – an observation amply confirmed by ministerial diaries – within the interdepartmental ministerial machinery there has been a conscious decision to push the level of decision making downwards. Questions of Procedure for Ministers (QPM) discourage ministers from bringing matters to cabinet or committee unless there is 'an unresolved argument between ministers' or unless they 'raise major issues of policy or . . . are of critical importance to the public' (Cabinet Office, 1992a, p.3; also see the box overleaf).

A great impetus to this 'pushing down' of business was given in the 1960s by Wilson, who made a number of piecemeal changes to the cabinet system which, codified in QPM and perpetuated by the Cabinet Office, added up to a major change in the operation of the system:

- The reduction of cabinet meetings to one a week, instead of the two common in the 1940s and 1950s, and avoidance of the practice, beloved of Churchill and Macmillan, of adjourning a difficult discussion from one meeting to another, or to a special meeting later in the same day.
- Flowing from the above, greater delegation to cabinet committees.
- The gradual formalisation of a substructure of four main standing committees – overseas and defence, home, economic and legislation.
- An expansion of the Cabinet Office staff, brigaded in functional units that shadowed these committees.
- The biasing of the system against appeals from committee to cabinet by allowing them only if the chairman of the committee gave his consent.
- The reinforcement of the Treasury's position by giving the chief secretary a seat in the cabinet and allowing the Treasury unlimited right of appeal from committee to cabinet if a policy requires expenditure from the reserve.

These changes came about simply because governments in the 1960s had become busier. The leisurely methods of Churchill and Macmillan were not adequate to cope with the growth of government activity and speed of events, which explains why Wilson's streamlining of the system was perpetuated by his successors. Indeed Wilson (1976) saw the changes as piecemeal, not realising they were such a far-reaching package of reforms.

The practical effect of the growth of committees was a marked change in the cabinet's role, as demonstrated in its agenda. Wilson and Callaghan perpetuated the tradition of opening with two

QUESTIONS OF PROCEDURE FOR MINISTERS

'QPM', as it is inevitably known in Whitehall, first appeared in 1945 when the cabinet secretary, Norman Brook, persuaded Prime Minister Attlee to circulate a note on general cabinet procedure to his colleagues. It remained a confidential document until John Major published it in 1992. Since its first appearance, QPM has expanded almost fourfold, from 37 paragraphs in 1945 to 134 paragraphs in 1992.

QPM is largely a practical document, a list of do's and don'ts. However the contents repeatedly stress the collegiate responsibility of ministers and the need for proper coordination of policy between departments. Although much comment on QPM has focused on the sections relating to cabinet business, only the opening 20 paragraphs deal with cabinet and committee procedures. These lay heavy stress on collective responsibility, and set out at length the practical arrangements for giving adequate notice of business to other ministers and clearing proposals with the Treasury and law officers. A second, brief, section deals with Parliament, concentrating almost exclusively on the practical arrangements for parliamentary statements.

The bulk of the document deals with the conduct of ministers in their departmental capacity. There are clear rules on the appointment of parliamentary private secretaries, special advisers and members of outside bodies; and on ministers' constituency interests to prevent clashes of interest. There is a reassuringly puritan code of conduct on foreign visits, the receipt of gifts and personal financial interests (for example, membership of Lloyd's). There are no less than 20 paragraphs on the public presentation of policy – a demonstration of the vital part this plays in government life. Repeatedly the document stresses the need to seek clearance from the prime minister or his or her office on appointments and major presentational issues, although the rigid rules constraining ministerial interviews and press writings appear to have been relaxed since the 1970s.

The formal standing of the document is debatable. It is promulgated by the prime minister, on the advice of the cabinet secretary, apparently without prior discussion with cabinet colleagues. It is the premier's document, and he can alter it at will. It is effectively binding on ministers. One cabinet secretary, Sir Burke Trend, described it as 'not a constitution, merely some tips for beginners – a book of etiquette'. But ministers who breach the prescribed procedures find themselves in serious difficulty. Certainly Wilson explicitly cited it when disciplining junior ministers who openly criticised government policy towards Chile, and when reproving the defence secretary for not clearing a speech on Northern Ireland with his colleagues.

Peter Hennessy, starting from the premise that in Britain precedent is the only constitution we have, has argued that QPM is the nearest thing we have to a written constitution for British cabinet government. It is also an oddity from the point of view of comparative studies. The many European and Commonwealth countries who operate forms of cabinet government usually have written constitutions, but these say little or nothing about the operation of the central executive. In Britain, QPM reverses the position.

QPM is usually updated with the appointment of each new prime minister. Copies can be obtained from the Private Secretary to the Secretary of the Cabinet, 70 Whitehall, London SW1A 2AS (Tel. 071-270 3000). A small charge – currently £5 – is made. Copies of the current list of cabinet committees can be obtained from the same source, free of charge.

standard items: the forthcoming week's parliamentary business and a report on overseas developments by the foreign secretary. The remainder of the agenda consisted almost entirely of issues referred up from committee for decision, occasionally because of their innate importance, but usually because a minister had been allowed to appeal to cabinet. There was no slot for 'any other business', nor for the discussion of broader issues of policy or strategy, and the version of QPM issued at the start of Callaghan's government prohibited ministers from raising matters orally except with the prime minister's prior permission (*New Statesman*, 14 February 1986). The cabinet was primarily a court of appeal and focused on casework.

As the 1980s progressed, Thatcher's cabinet moved to a different practice. Appeals to cabinet were firmly discouraged, to the point where they became relatively rare, and cabinet meetings became rather short. Professor Hennessy tells us that, by the mid-1980s, the number of papers put annually to cabinet for decision had fallen to 60 or 70, compared to an average of over 300 three decades earlier (Hennessy, 1986, pp.99–100). It became accepted practice that policy should be decided in committee. A marked example occurred at the height of the cabinet disagreement in February 1986 over whether to allow Ford's bid for Austin Rover. Revolt was simmering amongst Conservative backbenchers, but the cabinet that discussed the issue lasted only one hour, and the decision to prevent the sale was taken at a prolonged meeting of the Economic

Affairs Committee held in the cabinet room as soon as the cabinet dispersed (Fowler, 1991, pp.238–9).

To compensate for this the nature of cabinet meetings changed (see Chapter 6 below). Early on in her premiership, Margaret Thatcher reintroduced a standing item for EC business. There had been such a standing item in Heath's day, but Wilson had dispensed with it. By Thatcher's time the volume of EC business made this a regularisation of an existing necessity: the expansion of the EC's policy competence and progress towards the single market meant that EC business cropped up at most meetings anyway, and what was on the agenda of the Council of Ministers in the coming week was becoming as significant as next week's parliamentary business.

More significant was the addition in the mid-1980s of a standing item on home affairs, which was given a leading slot as second item, after parliamentary affairs. This departure was significant. Ministers were encouraged to tell their colleagues of significant developments in the near future and to explain issues within their responsibilities which were making headlines. There was a degree of formality to this: QPM requires ministers to give the secretary of the cabinet a week's advance notice of business to be discussed, although presumably urgent developments are not excluded (Cabinet Office, 1992a, p.6). The more significant decisions taken by committee were also reported. But, with a few significant exceptions such as the annual pre-budget cabinet, detailed discussions took place in committee (Wakeham, 1993).

How does this affect the cabinet's control over policy? On the plus side, it will allow the cabinet to range freely over the issues of the moment, rather than remaining fettered strictly to the issues listed on its formal agenda. It will be more involved in the moulding of current policy. On the debit side, its involvement is limited to influence rather than control. It will act as a sounding board at which a minister canvases political opinions. Ministers can encourage, or sound a warning, or indicate that such a proposal might be administratively sound but politically intolerable. This loss of control must be tempered by three considerations. Firstly, even in its heyday under Baldwin or Churchill, the cabinet as a whole only ever considered two or three issues at any meeting. Secondly, it was only ever consulted fairly late in the day, when the main lines of policy had been laid down, and any change it made was marginal or a dilution. Thirdly, policy control is still exercised in committees by groups of ministers.

In short, the cabinet has undergone a series of transformations in its role. From 1945 onwards it moved (although not at a steady rate) from being a *decisive* body, considering and deciding on specific issues put to it for consideration, to being *a court of appeal*: adjudicating on issues referred up to it from committees at the appeal of individual ministers, a transformation greatly encouraged by Wilson's procedural changes in the 1960s. In the early 1980s it seemed to go through a phase when, like the Privy Council, it was almost *residual*: an article by Martin Burch (1985) discussed whether cabinet had become no more than a decorative remnant of the former system, meeting briefly to register decisions taken at a lower level. However the introduction of standing items on EU and home affairs have changed it into a *discursive body*, meeting to discuss government business in a general way, but leaving decisions to be taken at other levels. It is much more like the cabinets of the nineteenth century: a gathering of political colleagues reviewing general developments rather than focusing on particular issues.

The Committee System

The evolution of the committee system has been entirely a product of the growth of the cabinet's workload. As the official guide to cabinet committees up to 1945 shows, until the Second World War committees were infrequent, *ad hoc* affairs, usually short-lived, with the exception of the Committee of Imperial Defence and a standing committee on legislation (Wilson, 1976). Of necessity, committees proliferated during the war, and since then a network of committees underpinning the cabinet has been a permanent feature of Whitehall life.

Since Macmillan created the defence and oversea policy committee in the 1960s, the main pillars of the structure have been four main committees: one on foreign and defence matters; one on economic affairs; one dealing with legislative issues; and one covering 'home affairs' – broadly, non-economic domestic subjects. But as John Major showed, when he published the structure, memberships and terms of reference of committees in 1992, there are many other standing committees and subcommittees (Cabinet Office, 1992b). Some of these have become extremely powerful in their own right: especially EDX, a committee appointed in 1992 under the chairmanship of the chancellor to take control of public spending discussions, (it existed in embryonic form as the 'Star Chamber' under Thatcher) and OPD(E), the subcommittee coordinating EU policy.

In addition to the standing committees and subcommittees, *ad hoc* committees are set up outside the standing structure which deal with particular issues. They are known by a number prefixed with the abbreviation MISC or GEN, that prefix changing from one government to another. These MISCs and GENs are generally smaller than standing committees and subcommittees. That is not entirely surprising: standing committees cover a range of policy and have to accommodate a wide range of members whose interests may only occasionally be affected by decisions: for instance, the ministerial committee on the environment (EDE) includes the foreign secretary and the national heritage secretary, neither of whom will always have a stake in the business being discussed. These seem to be set up at the rate of about 25 a year: certainly Margaret Thatcher had reached the 100 mark in her first five years in government (Lawson, 1992, p.58) while the unveiling of cabinet committees in 1992 revealed that, in his first 15 months, Major had reached 24.

Does the development of an extensive committee system strengthen or weaken the prime minister in relation to his colleagues? The instinctive reaction is to assume that it allows him to divide and rule, to pick and choose which committee will consider an issue, and to pack the committee to suit his purpose. Furthermore he chairs the main committees and chooses the chairs of other committees.

Certainly the prime minister's ability to decide whether a matter is dealt with by a large standing committee or by a smaller body offers scope for manipulation. This is particularly true of MISCs and GENs. Of their nature they are created and lapse suddenly and irregularly. The result was in the past, and presumably still is, that ministers do not know all the time which committees other ministers are serving on. For example, in the 1960s, Barbara Castle was obviously unaware that Tony Benn was serving on a committee on nuclear weapons – a subject that greatly interested her (Benn, 1988). And if ministers are not aware that a certain MISC or GEN exists, obviously they do not know to ask for the minutes.

Practice on the membership of committees is a complex question. Self-evidently, any minister with a direct departmental interest in a question has to be a member of a committee discussing it. The grey area is the appointment of additional members. Harold Wilson described the prime minister as having a 'positive duty . . . to ensure that the principal Cabinet committees, including *ad hoc* groups set up for a specific problem, are not packed with adherents of a particular departmental or political viewpoint. It is for him to ensure that a Cabinet committee is the Cabinet *in parvo*, a microcosm of the Cabinet itself' (Wilson, 1976, p.87). This would be achieved by appointing one or two members who were not departmentally involved to the committee. The drawback is that this takes up ministers' time: Shirley Williams has recorded that by the end of the Callaghan administration she was serving on some 20 committees, most of them covering issues outside her departmental remit (Williams, 1980, p.87).

In fact there is ample evidence that Wilson himself ignored that duty on occasion and slanted the memberships of committees to obtain particular outcomes: Barbara Castle described in detail how he rigged the membership of the committee that worked up her proposals for trade union reform, 'In Place of Strife' (Castle, 1984). But he could exercise this power only if not under scrutiny: the committee that prepared the way for the 1975 EC membership referendum was scrupulously balanced between pro-marketeers, anti-marketeers and agnostics (despite Castle's (1984, p.292) complaints).

The political balancing of committees seemed to fall into disuse under Margaret Thatcher, although to judge by her memoirs and those of her colleagues her government was as ideologically riven – first over economics, then over Europe – as Labour in the 1970s. Committee memberships appear to have been constructed on a purely functional basis: ministers were appointed only if the business impinged on their departmental responsibilities. This allowed for the reflection of all administrative interests in a discussion, but not always all the political interests. The only known exception was that Thatcher reserved a seat on her economic affairs committee for a dissident 'wet', first James Prior, later Peter Walker (Ridley, 1991, p.29).

The list of Cabinet committee memberships published in 1992 suggests that John Major, too, determines committee memberships on a purely functional basis, although Michael Howard appeared to be highlighting an exception after the 1993 cabinet reshuffle when he drew attention to the fact that, despite his move to the Home Office, he remained a member of the Economic Affairs Committee (Howard, 1993). The chairs of standing committees for the first time became transparent in 1992. One of the most striking features is that the prime minister chairs nine out of the 16 standing committees himself. Not all committees are equally important or meet equally frequently, but particularly significant is that Major chairs two key bodies: the committee on economic and domestic policy (EDP) and the committee on defence and overseas policy (OPD). It is also an interesting insight into a prime minister's preoccupations that four of the other seven committees he chairs are concerned with foreign affairs: the Gulf, nuclear defence, European security and Hong Kong, and two with matters allied to foreign policy: Northern Ireland, and intelligence and security. (The other committee he chairs is science and technology.)

The list also showed that the chairs of other committees are dominated by the leaders of the House of Commons and the House of Lords. Predominant is the leader of the Lords, Lord Wakeham, who chairs all other sensitive committees on the domestic front: the committees on home and social policy; industrial, commercial and consumer affairs; the environment; local government; and subcommittees on public-sector pay.

A further raft of committees is chaired by the leader of the Commons, Antony Newton, responsible for the committees on legislation, health, and civil service pay. Other subcommittees are chaired by ministers on a functional basis: the foreign secretary on European questions and eastern Europe, the home secretary on terrorism, and so on. But the majority of committees are chaired by either the prime minister or the leaders of the Commons and the Lords who, by the nature of their posts, have to work closely with the prime minister and so are likely to keep him informed about developments in the committees they chair, and to discuss with him how issues might be handled.

The prime minister, then, could influence, although not control, the work of committees if he wished. For all that, the existence of a committee system probably weakens rather than strengthens his hand. Firstly, this diffusion of decision making removes some subjects from his direct oversight. Self-evidently, he does not have the time to chair every meeting himself. Secondly, in the 1970s and, more markedly, the 1980s, there seems to have been a far greater willingness to do business by correspondence between ministers. This can be either by exchange of letters on a minor issue or, on more important issues, by a circular letter sent round the members of the appropriate committee. The committee meets only if another minister objects (see, for example, Pliatsky, 1984, pp.36–7; Burch, 1990). This must make it even more difficult for the prime minister to control developments. Thirdly, it is probably easier for a skilful prime minister to influence discussion at cabinet than in a committee. Since most committee members are selected on a functional basis, most of them are *parti pris* in a discussion. At cabinet, in contrast, most members will not have a stake in the matter at issue and will be open to persuasion in the course of discussion; and that discussion is guided by the prime minister and to some extent influenced by his views. Bernard Donoughue, senior policy adviser to Callaghan, identified in the cabinet a 'King's party': 'Most of them owed their positions in the cabinet to the personal favour of the prime minister . . . the prime minister expected them to follow his lead, and they recognised that in the end they would do so' (Donoughue, 1987, p.90).

If committees actually weaken prime ministers' grip on events, why have they allowed them to proliferate? The main factor is undoubtedly the pressure of business. This factor is structural, making this 'downwards shift' of policy making an inevitable and permanent feature of the system. It is worth noting two temporary factors, both products of a prolonged spell of government by one party, which have encouraged this trend to an unusual degree over the past 15 years. One is the political 'house-training' of ministers: after an unusually long spell in government, Conservative ministers have developed a close appreciation of the tolerances within the system and of their colleagues' likely reactions to a proposal. They can gauge in advance what their colleagues' likely reactions will be, and will not take matters to a full committee meeting, still less to cabinet, unless they are confident that they stand a good chance of effecting a change.

Secondly, there is a discernible difference between Conservative and Labour approaches to decision making, identifiable in the political culture of each party. Broadly speaking, Conservatives are happy to refer decision making to one person or a group of people because this allows speed and efficiency. Labour politicians in contrast tend to put a premium on collective control, which involves management of policy – or at least ratification of decisions – by a group, many of whom will not necessarily have executive responsibility for it. This difference in party culture shows clearly in party management and policy making: Labour's National Executive Committee and its network of subcommittees provide a more rigid conduit for processing decisions than the Conservatives' informal and personal methods. In this contrast the influence of local government is marked: amongst Wilson and Callaghan's ministers local government experience was common, much less so amongst Conservative ministers. Inevitably Labour ministers tended to look back to their municipal experience, in which decisions could lawfully be taken only by a committee and not by an individual councillor. The implication is that, if and when a Labour government returns, there may be a much greater propensity on the part of its members to appeal to cabinet against adverse decisions at committee, and possibly greater reluctance to settle matters by correspondence.

The Impact of Transnational Policy Making

A particular impact on relations between the prime minister and his or her colleagues, and a topical one in the light of debates over the 'hollowing out of the state', has been the impinging of international organisations onto the autonomy of British government.

In the 1960s and 1970s, the impact was most evident in the expansion of international summitry, with British prime ministers jetting off to meet their foreign counterparts and making agreements which their cabinets later had little option but to accept. Two *causes célèbres* were Macmillan's trip to Nassau, where he committed Britain to the Polaris nuclear submarine project, and Wilson's talks on board HMS *Tiger* with the prime minister of Rhodesia, which produced a possible formula for reconciliation. The axis built up between Callaghan, President Carter and Chancellor Schmidt had all the makings of a very powerful focus for influencing international policy – it seems in particular to have served to make West Germany reflate earlier than Schmidt wanted – but the advent of Margaret Thatcher cut the party short.

The cabinet is pretty well shut out of these events: the prime minister goes off and enjoys a fairly free hand. Admittedly Macmillan contacted his cabinet from Nassau to let them know what he was doing, but with the prime minister on the other side of the world they could not do much to restrain him, even though some of them disliked the Polaris deal. Wilson and Callaghan seem either to have ignored the cabinet, probably because they knew their colleagues were more inclined to argue than Macmillan's, or to have given their cabinets only bland and tedious reports.

Since the late 1970s, the growth area of international business has been the EC. One development that has greatly affected the prime minister–cabinet balance is the European Council. This twice-yearly meeting of heads of government and foreign ministers has a rather nebulous constitutional standing but, because its meetings occur towards the end of each country's six-month tenure of the EC presidency, it tends to be seen as some kind of cumulation, and so becomes the focus of the presidency's policy efforts. Its practical importance was shown not just by the Maastricht summit but by the series of European Council meetings that led to it, which removed obstacles over which the Council of Ministers had struggled. The Council of Ministers itself, in its various guises – Council of Agricultural Ministers, Council of Foreign Ministers, and so on – has also grown in power and has met increasingly often, as the EC has progressively expanded its policy competence into fields previously under the sole control of national governments.

The impact on British policy making is deep because the point of decision has been shifted upwards from the cabinet and its committees. The European Questions (EQ) committee spends its time, not taking definitive policy decisions, but agreeing negotiating positions that its representatives will adopt in Brussels. Up to a point the committee can agree the permissible margin for compromise, but in the end whoever is sent to the Council of Ministers must be given a mandate to agree to whatever majority opinion will bear – especially now that weighted majority voting has taken a hold on the Council's procedures.

From this follows a weakening of the cabinet and a strengthening of the prime minister. Firstly, the prime minister has tremendous scope for personal initiative. It is clear from Castle's and Benn's diaries that even in the 1970s the cabinet was having great trouble exercising restraint on Wilson and Callaghan's activities at EC summit meetings and in their regular bilateral meetings with other European leaders. Thatcher approached these meetings in the frame of mind that assumed that she could change her mind and commit her government in the same way as did President Mitterrand and Chancellor Kohl. Certainly the battle to reduce Britain's budget contribution was hers: she decided how long to hold out, and when to give in (Thatcher, 1993, pp.60–86).

Secondly, far more personal discretion has to be given to a minister attending the Council of Ministers: the EQ committee or cabinet may map out the margin for manoeuvre, but once the meeting in the Commission building in Brussels gets under way he or she may find – or may claim – that the negotiating position agreed in London is untenable. If he or she finds himself or herself in a minority and under pressure to compromise he or she may be invited to 'reflect by telephone' – a euphemism for ringing home for permission to give ground. Since cabinet and the EQ committee cannot be kept in permanent session to deal with this eventuality, he or she has to ring the prime minister. Self-evidently, this puts the prime minister in a position of greater power than his colleagues. True, he may sometimes have no option but to say, 'Well, do the best you can', but at least – unlike the rest of the cabinet – he has been consulted on the political tolerability of what is being proposed.

The balance may have been partially redressed in the cabinet's favour by the change in the nature of cabinet meetings. Margaret Thatcher's restoration of European affairs to a standing item in cabinet allows a more systematic discussion of EU business over the week past and for the week to come. And most ministers now have a keener appreciation of European affairs, because the EU now impinges on so many departments, and because ministers in a party that has been so long in power have become quite knowledgeable about the odd ways of the Union.

The Prime Minister, His or Her Ministerial Colleagues and Policy Making

Although the cabinet and its committees are the mechanism through which policy is coordinated and cleared with – or amended by – colleagues, every cabinet minister has, in addition to this mechanism, a direct relationship with the prime minister, and a sense of responsibility to him or her.

The prime minister needs to take an interest in any significant development and will expect to be informed of any forthcoming crisis and consulted on any new initiative. To the departmental minister, this relationship can be an asset: it gives him early warning of the prime minister's views on his work, and alerts him to any objection that the prime minister may raise to a policy initiative. The prime minister's approval is also a weapon that he can deploy against opposition from ministerial colleagues, especially the Treasury. The diaries of Castle and Crossman show how they exploited their link with Wilson to their departments' advantage: conversely Benn's diaries show how he was hindered by his poor relations with Wilson and Callaghan.

This relationship does not supplant the role of collective discussion by ministers, it supplements it. But it can be used by a prime minister to kill off an initiative he dislikes, or at least to issue so strong a warning that the minister may judge it imprudent to press the idea. Thatcher gained a reputation for acting as judge and jury on some policy initiatives in the middle years of her premiership: Sir Geoffrey Howe described her as 'the past mistress at marginalising cabinet committees and deciding issues in bilaterals' (*The Financial Times*, 23–24 October 1993; Hennessy, 1986, pp.98–103).

It is far more difficult for a prime minister to do the opposite and impose a policy of action on a minister who resists it. The dynamics of Whitehall are such that any policy initiative that is to last the course has to come from a departmental minister. His department possesses the expertise and knowledge of the facts, and it dominates the 'policy network' that will refine and manage the policy long after the prime minister has moved on to other subjects. Even if the premier launches himself into a policy field, it is very difficult for him to sustain the initiative without the lead department's expert help, let alone against its indifference or hostility. The prime minister lacks the time to harry an obstreperous colleague, and may be reluctant to risk the political and personal friction that this would cause.

Here again the foreign secretary and chancellor are in a class apart. With them the premier has close and continuous dealings on developing policies, while he sees other ministers less often and on specific issues (James, 1992, pp.140–41, 149–51). Partly this is due to the importance of the subject matter: diplomacy and the health of the economy dominate the prime minister's life in a way that other subjects do not; partly it is due to the nature of the subject: foreign affairs and economic policy tend to be continuous processes, while other policy areas are a succession of more or less discrete events.

In his authoritative article on prime ministerial power (Jones, 1987b, pp.36–66), Jones argued that one of the most potent restraints on a prime minister is that he is surrounded by colleagues who are his rivals and who consequently are keen to keep him in check. This theory may have been true when it was first propounded in the late 1960s, since at that time Wilson, fearing (with justification) a putsch by Jenkins or Callaghan, created some three or four further 'crown princes', as a means of dividing and ruling. But few prime ministers face that kind of rivalry. At any one time there are at best two or three other members of the cabinet who are potential claimants to Number 10. The remaining 20 or so are either in mid-career, or are nearing the end of their tenure, or are new to the cabinet, and in any of those cases they are unlikely to want to pick a fight with the prime minister.

The prime minister has comparatively limited discretion about who he appoints to his cabinet. There will always be a dozen or so people whose experience, abilities or political following assure them a cabinet place, and parliamentary parties are not so rich in talent that they can allow themselves the luxury of under-promoting able people. The prime minister's freedom of manoeuvre is much greater, however, in allocating portfolios between cabinet colleagues. Oddly this is less true of the exchequer and Foreign Office than of more junior cabinet offices, because two or three other key figures usually have a claim to those posts. For something like half to two-thirds of the inter-war period, these two offices have been held by powerful figures, who have often been rivals to the prime minister. This must affect the premier's ability to impress his views on the policy they are pursuing. One thinks, for example, of the trouble Eden had controlling Macmillan, or the uneasiness during Wilson's first government of his relations with Brown, Callaghan and Jenkins. Senior figures who fill these offices but who have no obvious claim on the premiership, like Lawson and Carrington, are exceptions to a rule.

Lesser cabinet offices can be filled with a greater measure of discretion. At any one time, between one-third and one-half of the posts in a cabinet are going to be politically sensitive, in the sense that they are crucial to the government's success, and the prime minister can make sure his preferred appointees fill those posts. Throughout her governments Margaret Thatcher, like Callaghan before her, kept the posts of secretary for trade and industry and chief secretary in the hands of those in sympathy with her policies. Those few ministers she felt constrained, early on, to appoint to sensitive appointments, notably Prior to employment, were moved as soon as political circumstance permitted. The upshot is that, oddly, the prime minister may devote much of his or her time to dealing on a daily basis on issues key to the government's success with a foreign secretary and chancellor he would not necessarily have chosen and may not particularly like, while on other issues he may deal less regularly with other ministers who may be more in tune with his thinking.

How does this affect policy? The prime minister's minimal role in policy making is as a coordinator, making sure that one minister's plans do not clash with another's, and acting as broker in resolving clashes of opinion. But he also has a considerable discretion to take a more active part either by taking sides in a conflict between departments, or by firmly pushing a certain policy line himself. More than anything else, what distinguishes one prime minister's style from another's is the balance between being a coordinator and being an activist.

In practice all prime ministers of recent times have developed fairly clear views on the main economic and foreign issues of the day; the difference between them has tended to be pointed up in domestic affairs. Heath and Thatcher – rather similar in this respect – tended to form very clear opinions on issues, although they were not averse to changing their minds and becoming converted to equally strong contrary opinions, as both did on Northern Ireland. Wilson, Callaghan and Major tended towards a less committed approach, often agnostic but holding strong opinions on certain subjects: Wilson's doomed commitment to trade union reform in the late 1960s, Callaghan's hostility to reform of official secrecy and Major's traditionalist views on education.

A significant factor in differentiating one premier's style from another is the extent to which they give a policy lead, and the style in which they go about it. The contrast between Wilson and Thatcher is instructive. He was a machine politician, at ease with the civil service, dextrously working through the network of cabinet committees and the established mechanism for interdepartmental cooperation. Thatcher, in contrast, had the instincts of an outsider, was sceptical of officialdom, supplemented the conventional machinery with informal meetings, and drew on advice from outsiders. Partly it was a matter of personal convictions: Wilson had clear views on a minority of issues, mostly economic and diplo-

matic, but in other areas was content to let colleagues provide a
lead. In contrast Thatcher, unusually for a prime minister, seemed
to bring strong views to most issues: not just central issues like the
economy and Europe, but 'lesser' areas of policy, like law and
order, and social security. She pressed her views firmly on her
colleagues: discussions were characterised by the responsible minister stating his case, followed by the prime minister giving her
view. This was the framework within which subjects were debated,
and ministers who disagreed with the prime minister were made to
fight their corner hard. The portrait should not descend to carica-
ture: on many issues Thatcher had no particular opinion or, if she
did, kept it to herself. But, more than most premiers, she made her
mind up early and put her views up front (see, for example, Hurd,
1993).

The Prime Minister's Leadership Role

The foregoing leads to the prime minister's broader role as leader
of the government. Evidently, more than most facets of central
government, this varies according to personality. On this subject,
Asquith bequeathed to the world his one memorable saying: 'The
office of prime minister is what its holder chooses and is able to
make of it' (Earl of Oxford and Asquith, 1928). Asquith himself, of
course, had exemplified his dictum by his own failure of leadership
at the low point of the First World War.

It is important to remember that the prime minister is *expected* to
lead, not only by the country at large but by backbenchers and by
ministerial colleagues. They want him to give a sense of purpose, to
inspire the party at the conference, to mince the opposition in
Parliament and to win the next election. As far as policy goes,
they want purpose, cohesion and no nasty parliamentary re-
bellions; when ministers disagree, they want the matter sorted out
swiftly and without public embarrassment. Two or three senior
members of cabinet might not be too upset if the prime minister
bungles it because they might gain promotion, possibly even the
succession, if he goes – although prime ministers are seldom, if
ever, overthrown in office: Mrs Thatcher was the first peacetime
prime minister to be overthrown for 70 years (see Chapters 4 and
5 below).

Leadership in government consists of possessing a cohesive set
of policies, communicating a sense of purpose and appearing to be
in command. These three elements are distinct, and it is possible
for a prime minister to show mastery of one but not of another.
Thus Wilson, in the early stages of his first government, did not

have a particularly clear set of policies: most obviously there were unresolved contradictions between the commitment to domestic economic expansion and his 'great power' aspirations to defend sterling and maintain defence commitments. However he kept party and public opinion satisfied because he gave the impression of dynamic purpose and seemed to be in command of events – until after the election of 1966. In contrast, the Callaghan government lost the 1979 election not for want of a clear set of policies but because it gave a disastrous impression of having lost control of events.

A prime minister's ability to imprint his leadership on his government depends greatly on external circumstances. Firstly, the public mood will set the parameters of his initiatives. For example, Attlee in 1945 and Thatcher in 1979 rode to power on the crest of a wave of public opinion that demanded radical change, even though neither of them was at the moment of their election a particularly inspirational character. Conversely, although Macmillan had considerable intellectual gifts and presentational skills, the strategic pretensions that he reveals in his memoirs – in world affairs and in domestic economic matters – got nowhere much because the tide was not with him; public opinion was not much stirred by the need for a National Economic Development Council or the chance to play Greece to the Americans' Rome.

The prime minister's room for manoeuvre also depends on the stage in the electoral cycle at which he or she takes charge. Thatcher had the inestimable advantage of starting in opposition. Her party had lost two successive elections and needed to redefine itself; she had the luxury of four years in which to imprint her ideas and personality on her party. In contrast, Major's scope for imprinting his outlook on his party was restricted because he took over in mid-term. The business of presenting and justifying government policies to the public had to be carried on: he did not have the same time or scope to redefine the party's orientation. Instead he took over the reins of a government bumping at high speed along a largely predetermined track. Curiously one indispensable facet of leadership skills is knowing when to retreat. Every government occasionally discovers that it has ventured onto thin ice, and fright sets in. At such moments, a prime minister needs a ruthless capacity to sacrifice the government's pride and limit the damage. In her earlier years, if one of her policies backfired, Thatcher showed a shrewd appreciation of when it was necessary to retreat. The government's decision to back away from a coal dispute in 1981 was a striking example of a government cutting its losses. A hallmark of Thatcher's later years in office was a growing inflexibility, notably on the community charge and on Europe. In marked contrast, one of the characteristics of the early months of Major's premiership was the pragmatism with which he lanced several boils which had been causing parliamentary and public irritation: child benefit was increased, cold weather payments to the elderly went up twice, and compensation was paid to haemophiliacs infected with the HIV virus – all small measures which his predecessor had fiercely resisted as matters of principle.

Yet although ministers want leadership, they do not want the prime minister to behave in a capricious or arbitrary way. They want the views of ministers to be valued, their management of departmental policy to be respected, and they expect a say – if not necessarily the final say – in major questions of policy and in the overall direction of the government.

Inner Cabinets

One other aspect of Major's government deserves mention: the emergence in the first year of his premiership of an inner group of ministers, occasionally referred to in the tabloids as the 'A team', meeting quite regularly with the prime minister to discuss policy. We are dependent for details of its work on press reports, according to which it met frequently in the run-up to the 1992 general election, and at moments of crisis in the subsequent year: at the time of sterling's withdrawal from the ERM, the coal mines closure crisis, and high points of the prolonged campaign to persuade parliament to ratify the Maastricht treaty. Its existence probably reflects in part Major's more collegiate style, and in part the fact that his most senior colleagues had exceptionally long experience of office.

This subject passes in and out of fashion as a subject of academic debate. The term 'inner cabinet' suggests a group of senior ministers meeting collectively and regularly to discuss the main lines of government policy and giving shape and coherence to overall policy. It can basically take two forms: a formal committee, like other cabinet committees, meeting to an agenda, its decisions having the same standing as decisions of the cabinet itself, or a looser group without the same formal standing, but meeting fairly regularly and having a reasonably consistent membership.

In terms of this distinction, there has been only one formal inner cabinet since the Second World War: the parliamentary committee set up by Wilson in 1968, which he remodelled as the management committee in 1969. It was set up in response to criticism of a lack of central leadership within the government; Crossman in particular urged upon Wilson that an inner cabinet was essential (an implicit requirement being that Crossman should himself be a member). The activities of this body are documented in the Castle and Crossman diaries, but it is difficult to discern any systematic purpose to its work. It discussed the issues of the day – the management of bills in parliament, pay settlements, the finance bill, race relations, education – but all in a desultory way, with little in the way of clear decisions. Often its agenda was dictated by that day's newspaper headlines.

One suspects that Wilson was indulging in his typical vices of gimmickry and window dressing, especially since more often than not business required over half the cabinet to attend. The inner cabinet occasionally met before full cabinet, to which its discussions were repeated: ministers who belonged to the inner cabinet were irked by this repetition, and those who did not resented their exclusion. A farcical note was added by the expulsion of Callaghan in May 1969 for his dissent over 'In Place Of Strife' and his readmittance several months later. Probably this body served Wilson's purpose simply by existing: it absorbed the energies of his more restless senior ministers and spread the blame for any lack of leadership. The experiment was not recreated when Wilson returned to office in 1974.

Informal inner cabinets are more common, but by their nature more difficult to identify. In the most detailed study of these groups, Phillips (1977) identifies a group which operated throughout Attlee's government, always with a core of Bevin, Morrison and Cripps, but with a varying fringe cast. In other cases the membership is harder to identify: Eden seems to have had a small group consisting of Macmillan, Salisbury and Butler, but for obvious reasons it was cut short. Macmillan (1972, pp.22–3) records consulting an inner cabinet of sorts after the 1959 election, but it soon lapsed.

The truth seems to be that inner cabinets are only one of a variety of sources of advice on which prime ministers draw. Most premiers, for example, have a particular relationship with the one or two senior colleagues who chair key cabinet committees: Macmillan with 'Rab' Butler, Wilson with Houghton, Thatcher with Whitelaw. Some meet regularly with a group of quite junior colleagues whose views chime in with their own: Churchill seems to have had this kind of relationship with Brendan Bracken, Lord Beaverbrook and Lord Cherwell. Thatcher in the early years of her premiership used to eat and chat with a disparate group of (then) junior figures including John Nott, John Biffen, Nigel Lawson and Norman Tebbit: 'we met, informally, outside cabinet committees, and we, I think, gave moral support to Mrs Thatcher that the policies we believed in were right. To some extent those who didn't agree with us in the cabinet were rather put on one side. . . . we met sometimes at No. 10, sometimes over a meal, occasionally over breakfast' (Knott, in Whitehead, 1985, p.367).

Sometimes prime ministers prefer just one adviser: Callaghan's key confidant seems to have been the indispensable Michael Foot, and Thatcher in mid-premiership seems to have relied first on Parkinson, then Tebbit. At other times prime ministers go it alone: that was true of the last years of both Macmillan and Thatcher, and Heath, after losing MacLeod and Maudling early on, had no senior colleagues to turn to.

In short, although in his informal inner cabinet Major appeared to have reintroduced a fairly rare beast in cabinet life, there was nothing about it to suggest that it would become a permanent feature of the landscape, and everything in the past to suggest that it was a transient phenomenon.

Collective Responsibility

What of collective responsibility in all this? Over the past 30 years, with fluctuations, the cabinet has managed to observe the old rule that all ministers defend every policy as if it is their own. The duty of collective responsibility is adamantly enshrined in Questions of Procedure for Ministers: 'Decisions reached by the cabinet or min-isterial committees are binding on all members of the government' (Cabinet Office, 1992a, p.17). But although ministers' obligation to toe the line on policy remains theoretically as rigid as ever, many of the structural changes over the past 30 years have lessened individual ministers' say in making the policy that they are bound to: only one cabinet a week, far more issues dealt with in small committees and far more 'mandated discretion' given to ministers attending the EU Council of Ministers.

For all that, as Crossman (1963) pointed out 30 years ago in his controversial introduction to Bagehot, this obligation to observe collective responsibility is strictly enforced by prime ministers even though the collective element of government has declined. Prime ministers are not slow to crack the whip when ministers step out of line. Wilson did this ostentatiously in his last government: in 1974, he publicly demanded and obtained from three ministers promises that they would toe the government line on Chile when attending the party's National Executive Committee, and the following year he sacked Eric Heffer for speaking against membership of the EC.

At the same time, the prime minister has absolute power to decide when collective responsibility shall be relaxed (Wilson relaxed it during the 1975 EC referendum campaign), when to enforce it rigorously and when to turn a deaf ear to a coded message of dissent, as Thatcher, with surprising forbearance, did towards dissidents like Sir Ian Gilmour in the early 1980s. This discretion has extended to prime ministers unofficially giving themselves a dispensation, such as Wilson's blatant leaking to the press and Thatcher's ill-concealed disdain for her own government's policy on the ERM.

Unavoidably this variation has given rise to discontent, which breaks out in four ways. Most dramatic, there are occasional explosions, the most memorable of which is the Westland affair. Then there are running campaigns of dissent, which in the long term are probably more disabling to a government: the running battles between Wilson and the opponents of 'In Place of Strife', and the barely-coded economic dissent of the 'wets' in the earlier years of the Thatcher governments. Deliberately undramatic, but quite effective, is the tactic of mutinous silence. The best example was Lawson's taciturn failure to endorse publicly the community charge, except for a few grudging words extracted from him in the Commons at question time. And finally, discontented ministers leak to the press.

The extent to which prime ministers manage to hold their colleagues in line depends very much on the atmosphere they manage to create in cabinet: what matters is not only that ministers should be involved, but that they should *feel* that they have been involved. Heath seems genuinely to have cared about his cabinet's views – it is often forgotten that he ran the most united cabinet of the last three decades – but his austere personality gave colleagues the impression that he often went his own way. Conversely Callaghan's colleagues were reassured by his relaxed, avuncular manner and remembered the solicitude for their views that he had shown at the time of the International Monetary Fund (IMF) crisis. But in fact his personal grip on key policy issues was easily as firm as Thatcher's; in the later years of his brief time in Number 10 he ran economic policy from a secret body called 'the seminar', and at international summits he acted as he chose, pursuing plans for international economic development and exploring the acquisition of Trident missiles.

The most marked change of styles since the 1960s has been that between Thatcher and Major. Her antipathy towards her cabinet, as a group and on occasion as individuals, became a rich mine of anecdotes. She was impatient with large meetings, which she felt wasted time, but perversely her style of discussion was itself very time-consuming; in Whitelaw's words, 'Her unquenchable appetite for argument is rather trying . . . It can be very wearing' (1989).

That, as much as helicopters, lay behind Heseltine's resignation. This head-on approach seems also to have heightened the likelihood of her being overruled by her cabinet, which happened to her with a frequency unknown to her more cautious predecessors. On at least three issues – public spending cuts in 1981, a radical review of public expenditure in 1982 and membership of the ERM – she was overruled on issues so crucial to the government's policies that they could easily have broken her administration (and indirectly, the ERM conflict did precisely that).

Once Thatcher threw in her hand, all three contenders for the succession committed themselves to a return to what they described as the true traditions of cabinet government (*The Times*, 26 and 27 November 1990). Not only did this appear to suit Major's temperament, but it also recognised the presence around him of a group of experienced colleagues (Hurd, Heseltine, Clarke) who had held office since 1979. A piece of negative evidence suggesting that the collegiate sense is much stronger in the Major government is the absence of semi-public rows between ministers which periodically erupted under Thatcher. Indeed Major has made a public virtue of the revival of collegiality: the collective agreement of cabinet was invoked by the prime minister and senior colleagues to protect chancellor Lamont when he came under criticism after sterling's withdrawal from the ERM, and again to justify the reintroduction of the Maastricht Bill to the Commons in the autumn of 1992 (Major in *The Times*, 18 and 19 September 1992; Fowler in *The Times*, 5 October 1992).

For all this, it is notable that the underlying machinery of the Cabinet did not change. Major's cabinet meetings may be more discursive than Thatcher's, but not more frequent. The focus for decision making remains at committee level.

Conclusion

We return therefore to the starting point. There have been extensive changes in the past three decades, but the substance is different from the public appearance. Even at the zenith of Thatcher's standing in her cabinet, we were a long way from prime ministerial government.

Instead three long-term structural changes have occurred, half unnoticed by the public. The first is the development of international decision making, under which the decisions of cabinet and committees have become less definitive and subject to being amended or overruled at international level. The second is the pushing down of decisions to committees, a logical consequence of long-term trends in ministerial workloads, which future governments may alter marginally but not substantially. Thirdly, the reversion to a more discursive type of cabinet meeting, more a sounding board than a court of appeal, is likely to endure: if ministers are to tolerate being bound to support decisions in home policy taken at committees they do not attend, they will want at least some handle on policy as it evolves.

Of these changes, the growth of the international dimension clearly gives the prime minister greater control over policy. For the rest, the relationship between prime minister and cabinet remains substantially as it has been for the better part of two centuries: a variable balance of forces dependent on the political clout and abilities of individuals, all of them manoeuvring within the confines of an essentially collegiate system.

4

The Downfall of Margaret Thatcher*

G.W. JONES

Introduction

This chapter examines the resignation of Margaret Thatcher as prime minister to uncover what it shows about the power of the British prime minister and of the cabinet. It is not a chronological narrative but an analytical explanation, unravelling the threads of a story. The plot is rather like a detective novel by Agatha Christie. Was Thatcher's resignation 'the grandest political suicide in modern British history' (Young, 1991), or was it murder and, if so, 'who dunnit?' For those who like to know the ending early on, so they can appreciate the twists leading to the dénouement, it was not suicide: she was murdered. Three daggers were plunged into her, two injuring her seriously and one fatally. The first was wielded by the British people, expressing their views in the European elections, by-elections and opinion polls; the second blow was struck by the Conservative party in the House of Commons, withdrawing its support at a critical moment; but the mortal wound came from the cabinet, which rejected her.

Hubris and Nemesis

The downfall of Thatcher in November 1990 may seem sudden. Eighteen months earlier, in May 1989, she had celebrated 10 years

---

* An early version of this chapter appeared as G.W. Jones, 'Mais qui a tué Maggie?', *Pouvoirs*, 58, 1991. I must thank June Burnham and Brendan O'Leary for comments on a draft of this chapter, and R.K. Alderman and Neil Carter for showing me the typescript of their article (Alderman and Carter, 1991) before publication. Their judgement, 'The Cabinet was the crucial body' (p.139) is mine too.

as prime minister. She was thought to be going 'on and on and on' to her fourth successive general election victory. She had achieved a remarkable political predominance: the longest-serving prime minister this century and second only to Lord Liverpool (1812–27) for continuous service as prime minister in modern British history; party leader since 1975; the winner of three general elections, in 1979, 1983 and 1987; and enjoying a majority of almost 100 in the House of Commons. She was the real leader of her government, assertive and interventionist. She seemed to dominate her ministers, who were often depicted as terrorised or 'handbagged' into subservience. The 'Iron Lady' was said to have diminished the cabinet, preferring to operate through smaller groups of ministers; and if any opposed her she sacked them. By November 1990 she was the sole member of her 1979 cabinet still in government: she was the great survivor. Unlike any other prime minister, she had given her name to an 'ism'. She was the first female British prime minister. On the world stage she was the longest-serving elected leader of a major power, jetting from summit to summit to promote the national interest. She had won a war, in the Falklands, and claimed she was responsible for the worldwide triumph of privatisation and decline of communism. Yet within 18 months she was toppled from her pedestal.

Thatcher's ejection from the premiership was the most dramatic since Neville Chamberlain's in 1940: the first example since then of a prime minister in good health and eager to continue being elected while her own party still enjoyed a majority in the Commons. (A good account is Young, 1991, pp.542–91.) It showed that three key constraints on a prime minister, the voters, the party in Parliament and the cabinet, could not be ignored or flouted with impunity.

The Voters Turn

Thatcher's ascendancy over the British electorate should not be exaggerated. First, her party obtained its largest vote, 43.9 per cent, in the general election which installed her in office in 1979; and her governments were returned to power with fewer votes in 1983 and 1987 (42.4 per cent and 42.3 per cent, respectively). More voted against her party than for it, but the distortions of the British disproportional electoral system magnified her party's electoral plurality into an overall majority of seats in the House of Commons. Second, for much of her period in office, from 1980 to the mid-1980s, the Labour party alienated voters by adopting extreme-left stances and pursuing internal sectarian disputes. Third, as a result of Labour's move to the left, a significant centre movement, the alliance between the Liberal and Social Democratic parties, arose in British politics. It obtained around a quarter of the vote, and allowed the Conservatives to 'divide and rule' by splitting the anti-government forces. Fourth, there were specific circumstances in each of the three general elections fought by Thatcher which made her party successful. In 1979, the incompetence of the Labour government during the winter of discontent of 1978–9 in managing the economy and mastering the trade unions meant that more voted against the Labour government rather than positively for the Conservative party. In 1983, the Conservatives benefited from victory in the Falklands and an upturn in the economy, boosted by oil sales, which improved the balance of trade, and government revenues. In 1987, a booming economy, although temporary and manipulated by the government, seemed to persuade voters to put more trust in the government's record than in the opposition's warnings and promises.

So Thatcher was not as secure as she apparently looked in May 1989 (Crewe, 1990). Indeed at the same time as celebrations of her decade in office were taking place in Downing Street black clouds loomed. Her popularity and that of the government began to fall, and this was soon reflected in electoral defeats. In a by-election in May 1989, one day after the anniversary of her 1979 victory, her party lost to Labour the Welsh seat of the Vale of Glamorgan, with Labour's share of the vote rising by 14.2 per cent and the Conservatives falling by 10.5 per cent on the 1987 general election. In the elections for the European Parliament on 15 June 1989, Thatcher took her party to its first election defeat under her leadership when Labour gained 13 seats from the Conservatives: Labour's share of the vote rose 3.7 per cent and the Conservatives fell 6.7 per cent on 1985.

The monthly poll of opinion polls in *The Guardian* had the Conservatives always in the lead from June 1987 until May 1989, when Labour and Conservatives received equal levels of support. In the following month Labour was eight percentage points ahead of the Conservatives. Until the end of 1989, Labour polled around 47 per cent and the Conservatives about 37 per cent. At the start of 1990, Labour's lead increased, from 12 per cent in January, to 16 per cent in February and to a record 24 per cent in March, but it fell thereafter: in September it was down to 9 per cent, though in October it rose again to 11 per cent. The standing of the Conservative party was worse in the autumn of 1990 than it had been at the same time in 1989. Gallup's personal rating of Thatcher's performance as prime minister at only 23 per cent satisfied in April 1990 was the lowest for any British prime minister since polling began in the late 1930s, and had not significantly improved by the start of November 1990, when her rating was 25 per cent, with 71 per cent registering dissatisfaction.

In March 1990, the Conservatives lost the Mid-Staffordshire by-election with a 21.4 per cent swing to Labour from the 1987 election, its best by-election performance in 50 years. In the May 1990 local council elections the Conservatives lost around 200 seats. There was little to cheer them in by-elections later in 1990. In October they lost the 'safe' seat of Eastbourne on a 21 per cent swing which turned a Conservative majority of 17 000 into a Liberal Democrat majority of 4500; November saw further swings against them in Bootle and Bradford North, of 11.2 per cent and 15.8 per cent respectively, and in Bradford they were knocked into third place. Thatcher's leadership was an electoral liability for her party.

Why the People Turned

Why had the slump in public support occurred? The Labour party was more electable than in the early 1980s. Neil Kinnock had adopted a firmer style of leadership. He had tamed the extreme left and conducted a major review of party policy, moderating policies that had previously alienated voters. Labour displayed more unity generally and its front bench presented an effective and competent team in the House of Commons. The Alliance disintegrated with an internecine split between the Liberal and Social Democratic parties, polling nearer 10 per cent rather than its previous 25 per cent, which made Labour seem the only alternative government.

But the main reasons for decline in the government's fortunes were failures in policies closely associated with Thatcher, especially management of the economy and the poll tax (Sanders, 1991, p.258). The results of British general elections are mainly determined by the state of the economy. The key voters whose swing is critical tend to judge a party by its record in government, above all by how far it affects the living standards of themselves and their families, and how optimistic or depressed they are in their expectations about the future of the economy.

A sense of an economic miracle reaching its peak in 1988–9 was transformed gradually into one of economic malaise. The chancellor of the exchequer, Nigel Lawson, had relaxed controls over money supply, cut rates of income tax, reduced interest rates and kept the pound high, in line with the German mark, but when balance of trade and payments figures turned to Britain's disadvantage and inflation re-emerged, interest rates were raised to record levels to dampen demand and counter inflation. These high interest rates triggered a major recession. Yet only in the summer of 1990 did the government seem to recognise that the country was in the grip of a recession. Labour was able to castigate the government for mismanagement of the economy.

After 10 years in office the Conservative government could no longer blame Labour governments of the 1970s for current economic ills, especially after claiming in 1986 and 1987 that its policies were responsible for a British economic miracle, with bank base rates in June 1988 falling to 8.5 per cent. In August 1988, these began to creep upwards, reaching 13.5 per cent in February 1989 and 15.5 per cent in December. In October 1990, bank rate was eased slightly, to 15 per cent, to appease the Conservative party conference. The high base rate caused high mortgage interest rates, which hit hard those who had been encouraged to buy their houses when rates were low, for instance in June 1988, when the basic rate was 9.76 per cent. In August the rate rose to 11.5 per cent and by March 1989 to 13.46 per cent. It continued to rise, reaching its height in April 1990, when it stood at 15.40 per cent. It had fallen a little by November 1990, to 14.65 per cent (Central Statistical Office, 1987–91). Inflation rose to nearly 10 per cent in 1990. There were record deficits in the balances of trade and payments. 'The balance of payments deficit during 1989 (at £20.3 bn) was the largest ever recorded, representing over 3% of GDP' (Sanders, 1991, p.236). Unemployment increased. This economic deterioration, bearing hard on voters through loss of jobs and rising prices, with many people unable to repay house mortgages and a large number of bankruptcies, was the root cause of the erosion of public support for the government from the spring of 1989.

However the poll tax (or 'community charge', as the government called it) was the reason for the sharp decline in the government's and Thatcher's popularity. As local councils set the rate of the poll tax in March and April and people became aware of the size of bills they would have to pay, so there was a dramatic fall in Conservative support. There were far more losers than gainers from the tax, and the losers protested more loudly than the gainers expressed their gratitude. Marches and demonstrations occurred throughout the country and Trafalgar Square witnessed the worst riot since 1886. Poll tax bills were higher than had been predicted by the government and most of the blame was laid on the government and in particular on Thatcher, who had pushed the poll tax through her cabinet against the wishes of many reluctant or sceptical ministers. It was seen as Thatcher's tax (see Crick and van Klaveren, 1991).

At the Mid-Staffs by-election in March 1989, the poll tax was identified as the single most important issue driving voters from the Conservatives. Many Conservative backenchers, even those who had voted for the tax, became alarmed and urged changes to cushion their constituents from its impact. During the summer of 1990, anxieties over the poll tax receded as the government increased central grants to local authorities to soften its effects, and Labour's lead in the opinion polls slipped. Economic indicators – inflation, interest and house mortgage rates – however did not significantly improve; and the main source of anxiety of voters again became the economy. The worrying problem for the Conservatives was that those hit by the deepening recession and poll tax were not only traditional Labour voters in the inner cities, the North, Scotland and Wales, but increasingly citizens in the South, South East and Midlands, and especially the skilled working class, the C2s, who had been attracted to vote Conservative earlier in the 1980s.

Another sore weakening the government was its image as the enemy of the public sector and public spending. Thatcher and her government were seen as champions of low taxation and privatisation, while Labour promoted itself as the party in favour of public expenditure to maintain and improve standards of education, health care, housing and public transport, especially capital expenditure on infrastructure. Labour's complaints of private affluence amidst public squalor seemed to win the electorate's support.

Thatcher embodied the government. Her direct style, the crusading spirit of her conviction politics and her adversarial approach won great loyalty from her devotees but so polarised opinions that those opposed to her were intensely antagonistic. In many people's eyes she was the government, and when its policies were so clearly failing she bore the brunt of the blame.

The Conservative Party in Parliament: Increasing Unease

These developments in the country unsettled Conservative MPs. Career politicians feared loss of their seats at the next general election: they would miss their chance of appointment to government or, if already ministers, the perquisites of office and hope of further promotion. As the general election came nearer their alarm intensified. There were increasing rumblings in the media from backbenchers wanting Thatcher to step down. Her very longevity in office became a disadvantage: on the Conservative backbenches were many she had disappointed by not appointing them to office and others she had dismissed. A total of 95 had been in the House of Commons since 1979 and earlier and had not been appointed to office, while another 78 were no longer holding ministerial office (*The Times*, 12 April 1990). More and more felt it was time for a change.

In autumn 1989, Thatcher's leadership of the party was challenged for the first time in 14 years (Norton, 1990). A backbencher, Sir Anthony Meyer, stood against her, and 60 of the 374 Conservative MPs failed to vote for her. Meyer made his challenge as a stalking horse to provoke a more serious rival, Michael Heseltine, into standing. Since his resignation from the cabinet as secretary of state for defence in January 1986 during the Westland crisis, Heseltine had campaigned ceaselessly to promote his chances as the successor to Thatcher. He put forward alternative policies, involving a more pro-European orientation, more government intervention in the economy and higher public expenditure to help industry and the inner cities. He courted fellow MPs, speaking on their behalf in their constituencies. Although he never expressed a direct challenge to Thatcher as party leader, and said he could not foresee any circumstances in which he would stand against her, he was seen as her chief internal opponent (Ingham, 1991, p.389), and one likely to seek her position if the party wanted a change of leader. In 1989, Heseltine did not believe the time was ripe.

However the leadership ballot of 1989 revealed the prime minister's vulnerability. She was on probation. If she failed to restore the electoral fortunes of her party by the time of the opening of the next sitting of Parliament in November 1990, she was likely to face a more formidable challenger, most likely Heseltine. A general election had to occur no later than early July 1992, so November 1990 was the last practical occasion to oust the prime minister and put a new one in place with sufficient time to make a mark on the party and country to win the next general election. The downfall of Thatcher is explained by her failure to improve the electoral chances of her party in the 12 months after the leadership contest of November 1989.

Thatcher failed to pass the ultimate test of a party leader: to bring the party electoral success. She looked like a loser in the autumn of 1989 and more so in the autumn of 1990.

The Cabinet: Asserting Itself

Just as parties in the Commons are affected by changing moods of public opinion, so the cabinet comes to reflect the changing moods of the governing party in the Commons. The prime minister, by losing support in her party in the Commons, became vulnerable to a loss of confidence by her cabinet. Increasingly in 1989 and 1990 she seemed to be losing control of the cabinet, as she had in the previous Parliament in late 1985 and early 1986 over the Westland affair. In July 1989, she undertook a major reshuffle of her cabinet, demoting Sir Geoffrey Howe from secretary of state for foreign affairs to lord president of the council and leader of the House of Commons, and in October her chancellor of the exchequer, Nigel Lawson, resigned when she refused to sack her economic adviser, Sir Alan Walters.

The main issue behind these cabinet disputes was the government's attitude to the European Community, a topic of little interest to most voters but of great importance for elites. The EC split the Conservative party. One section wanted closer integration, for economic and political union; another group, some of whom wished the UK had never joined, viewed the EC simply as a free-trade area, which they wanted to expand to encompass all European nations; and yet another faction wanted Britain's national interests vigorously asserted against those of other member states which they saw more as rivals than partners. Thatcher was supported by the second and third factions.

The European issue had long festered within the Conservative party. It had been at the root of the Westland crisis in 1985–6, when Heseltine resigned, when prevented from rescuing an ailing helicopter company with a European consortium rather than an American buy-out. The issue of European monetary integration became salient again in the summer of 1989. The government's stated policy was that Britain would join the Exchange Rate Mechanism (ERM) of the European Monetary System (EMS) when the time was ripe. While Thatcher was adamantly opposed to it, and never believed the time was ripe, the chancellor, Lawson, and the foreign secretary, Howe, wanted Britain to join and forged an alliance to press her to make a firm commitment to do so. Before the Madrid European summit meeting in June 1989, Lawson and Howe pushed Thatcher to accept more relaxed conditions for Britain joining the ERM of the EMS than she apparently had wanted. In revenge for this 'Madrid ambush' she demoted Howe in the July reshuffle. He made his resentment public and insisted on being given the honorific but empty title of deputy prime minister and the official residence of the chancellor. In this imbroglio Thatcher alienated the home secretary, Douglas Hurd, by at one point offering his portfolio to Howe. She did not sack Howe, although they were clearly at odds over a major matter of policy.

She had shown a similar inability to sack the recalcitrant Heseltine. She never felt strong enough to dismiss ministers who had significant followings in the party. Howe was well-liked, an amiable and non-abrasive figure, of whom Denis Healey had said that to be attacked by him was 'like being savaged by a dead sheep' (Healey, 1989, p.444).

Nor did she sack Lawson, or move him, despite appearing to be opposed to some of his policies. She recalled from the USA her former economic adviser, Sir Alan Walters, in May 1989. He was opposed to Britain's entry into the ERM and to further European integration. She had public rows with the chancellor over his policy of tying the pound sterling to the German mark as a substitute for Britain's entry into the ERM. In October 1989, Lawson's patience at last snapped and he confronted Thatcher with a choice: either she sacked Walters or he would go. She refused to be dictated to by a minister and Lawson resigned. Walters himself then resigned. The main beneficiary of these moves was John Major, whom the prime minister appointed to his first full ministerial post in place of Howe at the Foreign Office in July and then to Lawson's place at the Treasury in October.

The prime minister seemed to be losing control over the cabinet: she was failing to carry out the essential prime ministerial task of keeping the cabinet together (Jones, 1987b, pp.8–12; 1990, pp.2–8). Ministers seemed to be pursuing their individual policies and were not being reined in by the prime minister to follow either her own views or those of the cabinet. In the aftermath of this episode Sir Anthony Meyer launched his challenge against Thatcher in November.

There were three further signs of the prime minister's problems with managing cabinet. In December 1989, Norman Fowler resigned as secretary of state for employment, ostensibly to spend more time with his family, and in May 1990, Peter Walker felt the same need and resigned as secretary of state for Wales after serving in Thatcher's cabinets since 1979. In July 1990, Nicholas Ridley was forced to resign as secretary of state for trade and industry following an outcry over his intemperately hostile remarks about other member states of the European Community, especially Germany, which many thought reflected the prime minister's own views.

One reason for Thatcher's increasing difficulties in managing the cabinet was that it contained no one with the stabilising impact of Lord Whitelaw, who had resigned after a stroke in late 1987. Nigel Lawson detected a change of mood at 10 Downing Street following his departure. His absence led to a 'bunker mentality', pervaded by a deep-seated and destructive paranoia (*Independent*,

12 July 1981). Whitelaw's soothing ways no longer helped oil relationships between the prime minister and other ministers (Whitelaw, 1989).

The prime minister was able to survive disturbances in the cabinet between the summer of 1989 and autumn 1990 because her opponents never mounted a concerted attack against her. They acted like those ministers in 1981 who had protested against the government's monetarist economic policies but failed to stand up to the prime minister and acted 'wet' (Gilmour, 1992). They did not unite behind a coherent alternative. She endured because they were so pusillanimous; and the electoral prospects for the government seemed to improve during the summer of 1990.

The worst effects of the poll tax for the current year seemed to have worn off and extra money was made available to reduce its impact in the following year; Iraq's invasion of Kuwait in August and the ensuing Gulf crisis promised to elevate the stature of the prime minister and return support to the government, as had happened during the Falklands war; and in October the European issue and, some hoped, Britain's economic ills seemed to be nearing solution when the chancellor of the exchequer announced that at last Britain was joining the ERM. This announcement was made at the Conservative party annual conference when the government presented itself as a united 'right team' under the prime minister. The government, following past precedents as a general election approached, seemed to be ready to relax its tight controls over public expenditure. Pundits started to think that the government still had sufficient time to pick up enough support to win the next election, but it would need to get the economy right and reduce mortgage rates.

However the prime minister's position in cabinet was not as strong as it appeared. She could not easily move Major and Hurd again so soon after appointing them chancellor and foreign secretary if she disagreed with them; so they were in very strong position and probably pushed her into accepting British entry into the ERM, which until then she had opposed. Her cabinet was becoming more of a constraint on her, reflecting the growing disillusion about her leadership among her party's MPs.

The Final Blow

So what caused the downfall of the prime minister, who seemed to be recovering from the battering by the voters, her party and cabinet? The story of the final days' events has been told in Anderson, 1991, pp.98–194; Baker, 1993, pp.364–421; Clark, 1993, pp.341–69; Ellis, 1991, pp.6–47; Fowler, 1991, pp.347–56; Ingham, 1991, pp.379–98; Parkinson, 1992, pp.20–39; Pearce, 1991, pp.137–60; Ridley, 1991, pp.219–252; Shepherd, 1991, pp.1–52; Thatcher, 1993, pp.829–62; and Watkins, 1991, pp.1–28).

With the resignation of Sir Geoffrey Howe from the government on 1 November the worm turned: 'The fuse was lit' (Ridley, 1991, p.223). The issue was still Europe. At a Rome European Council meeting on 27 and 28 October, Thatcher had been in a minority of one against the other 11 members over the timetable for European monetary union. Once again she had vigorously assserted her reluctance to embrace monetary integration; at the concluding press conference in Rome she described the other European leaders as living in 'cloud cuckoo land' (Ridley, 1991, p.231). Later, in a prepared statement to the House of Commons about the Rome meeting, she first expressed a more moderate line agreed with her ministers to allay the adverse impression created by her attitude in Rome, yet in impromptu answers to parliamentary questions she again expressed her determined opposition to monetary union and repeated emotionally, 'No. No. No' (*HC Debs*, 30 October 1990, cols 869–90). This outburst reflected her fundamental disagreement with views she had had to accept to keep her cabinet together, and raised again the issue of her domineering and abrasive style. At Madrid and Rome she had listened to her ministers and done what she personally did not believe in, but back in the Commons her real attitude bubbled out. She seemed to be treating her colleagues with scant respect and undermining them. Howe could take no more: it reminded him of the way she had resisted his and Lawson's earlier efforts before the Madrid summit in 1989.

Howe's resignation not only highlighted divisions in the Conservative party over Europe but also raised the question of a possible challenge to Thatcher in the leadership elections at the start of the coming parliamentary session. Some thought it was Howe's own bid, testing the water to see if anyone would nominate him. However the more likely challenger was Michael Heseltine, who had been courting Conservative backbenchers and publicising his claims since his own resignation from the cabinet in 1986. Some even suspected Howe had concerted his resignation with Heseltine, but no evidence sustains that allegation. Heseltine did not mount an overt challenge at first, pleading again that he could not envisage 'foreseeable circumstances' in which he would stand against her. But the unforeseen took place on 13 November when Howe made his resignation speech in the Commons. The dead sheep turned into a rottweiler and delivered 'the death blow' (Ridley, 1991, p.346).

It was the most dramatic resignation speech in years and brutally savaged the prime minister. It had two themes: there had been a long-standing split in the cabinet over Europe; and Thatcher's leadership undermined ministers. Howe had proclaimed in his earlier letter of resignation that 'Cabinet government is all about trying to persuade one another from within', but he told the House of Commons he found his attempts to pretend there was a common policy 'risked being subverted by some casual comment or impulsive answer'. Of Thatcher's approach to government he said: 'It is rather like sending your opening batsmen to the crease only for them to find, the moment the first balls are bowled, that their bats have been broken before the game by the team captain' (*HC Debs*, 13 November 1990, cols 464–5).

This 'unforeseeable' circumstance gave Heseltine his chance. He was urged by supporters to stand and by enemies to 'put up or shut up'. It seemed as if the Thatcher camp was urging him to stand in order to smash him with a massive defeat. He said he would stand. His campaign emphasised his pro-European credentials and his willingness to resort to state intervention for economic and social purposes. He projected himself as being more likely to lead the party to a victory in the next general election than Thatcher. This judgement was confirmed in a flurry of opinion polls and was spotlighted by the startling by-election defeat for the Conservatives in Eastbourne. Here a solid Conservative seat, held at the 1987 election with a majority of 17 000 by Thatcher's former parliamentary private secretary, Ian Gow, who had been murdered by the IRA, was converted by a 21 per cent swing into a Liberal Democrat majority of 4500. Another telling blow delivered by Heseltine was the promise of a fundamental review of the poll tax. His candidature looked particularly attractive to Conservative back-benchers fearing loss of their seats.

The electoral process for choosing a Conservative party leader had been established in 1965 when the party was in opposition. It was never intended to be used to unseat a prime minister (Alderman and Smith, 1990). Each year at the start of the parliamentary session nominations for leader could be made, within 28 days of the Queen's Speech announcing the government's legislative programme. It was to consist of three ballots. This system was devised to ensure the eventual winner had the widest possible support in the party and had not gained only a bare majority or plurality. In the first ballot the winner needed a majority of all Conservative MPs, plus 15 per cent more than the runner-up. A week later, at the second ballot, into which new candidates could come forward, the winner needed 50 per cent of the vote plus one vote. If that were not achieved then a third ballot, two days later, was to be held between the three top candidates in the second ballot and the system of voting would be by single transferable vote, the second preference votes of the bottom candidate being redistributed among the other two.

Thatcher made four tactical errors in the run-up to the first ballot. First, she fixed the closing date for nominations as 15 November, only eight days after the Queen's Speech, ostensibly to end the speculation (Thatcher, 1993, p.836) but more probably to deny Heseltine time in which to campaign: but he had been campaigning for years and she was in need of more time in which to solicit support.

Second, she relied on a lacklustre and complacent campaign team, containing no current cabinet ministers: a bunch of 'has-beens' who were no match for the more bustling group supporting Heseltine (Thatcher, 1993, pp.840–41, 843, 850; Clark, 1993, pp.354–5). Nicholas Ridley criticised them for setting out 'merely to canvass, rather than to persuade' (Ridley, 1991, pp.241–2). Their confidence was based on their defeat of Meyer in the previous year.

Third, she gave few interviews to the media in the opening days of the campaign, but then as if in last-minute desperation gave some press interviews in which she attacked Heseltine for personal ambition and for advocating Labour party policies of intervention and corporatism. She urged a referendum on the European single currency, which raised once again the image of her speaking without taking account of her cabinet colleagues. (*The Independent*, 19 November 1990, *Sunday Telegraph* and *The Sunday Times*, 18 November 1990, *Financial Times*, *Daily Telegraph* and *The Times*, 19 November 1990, carry the interviews.)

Thatcher's final error, which was to cost her dearly, was to attend the Conference on Security and Cooperation in Europe in Paris in the crucial final few days before the ballot. Her decision to go to Paris was based on the view that she should emphasise her position as a prime minister of eleven and a half years standing, and surround herself with the aura of a leader on the international stage who had helped bring victory to the West in the Cold War (Thatcher, 1993, p.836). The drawback was that she was not on hand personally to coax and woo the few MPs she needed to win over for victory in the first round. Thatcher was reported as saying 'if she had been in London at the time of the ballot, instead of attending a summit in Paris, she would have won the leadership on the first ballot' (*The Guardian*, 29 May 1991).

There were 372 Conservative MPs. On Tuesday 20 November Thatcher obtained 204 (55 per cent) and Heseltine 152 votes (41 per cent); 16 ballot papers (4 per cent) were spoiled. Thatcher was four short of victory. She had only just missed it: if two who had voted for Heseltine or four abstainers had voted for her she would have won. But for her absence in Paris she might have won over those critical few. She could not have missed the Paris meeting without provoking the accusation that she was panicking through weakness, but she could have arranged a later ballot.

Within minutes of hearing the result she stated that she would go into the second round. She selected a more high-powered campaign manager, the secretary of state for energy, John Wakeham. She seemed determined to stay leader. Even as she left Downing Street on the next afternoon to make a statement about the Paris summit, she said: 'I fight on. I fight to win' (*Financial Times*, 22 November 1990). Yet within 24 hours she had given up. Who was responsible for this change of mind? Who Dunnit?

One argument is that she was already fatally wounded, damaged beyond repair, by the blow from the parliamentary party (Barber, 1991, p.23). Although 55 per cent of the parliamentary Conservative party voted for her, it was not enough under the rules to give her victory. Her decision to carry on alarmed some MPs who had voted for her. They feared that by going on she would plunge the party into bitter internal warfare. She might win narrowly and limp on wounded, lacking authority and unable to stop a Labour victory in the general election, or else she would be defeated and the party would find itself led by Heseltine, thus jeopardising the Thatcherite achievements of the last decade. Some had grave reservations about Heseltine, and thought him likely to split the party with his pro-European and allegedly collectivist policies. Some MPs had voted for Thatcher in the first ballot out of loyalty but felt they had to change to another candidate to defeat Heseltine in the second. They wanted her to resign and allow a cabinet minister to stand against Heseltine.

From the moment of the announcement of the results of the first ballot there were all sorts of meetings, cabals and plots. The chief whip was given the task of sounding out backbenchers, and by lunchtime on the Wednesday he and other leading figures of the party in Parliament and in the country, the 'men in the grey suits', reported their findings to Thatcher. Two trawls of Conservative peers by Lords Colnbrook and Denham revealed two to one support for her. The president of the National Union of Conservative Associations found that about 70 per cent of Conservative associations, or at least their chairmen, in England and Wales wanted her to stay, while Kenneth Baker reported (Baker, 1993, p.401) that 'messages sent to Central Office had been 90% in her favour'. Heseltine's assiduous wooing of local parties had apparently been a failure. The majority of Conservative members of the

European Parliament wanted her to go. The message from the Commons was less conclusive. The executive of the backbench committee, the 1922 Committee, was divided but reported that backbenchers wanted a wider choice. The chief whip himself felt that Thatcher could not win, but the other whips, by 11 to two, felt she could. Although there was some slippage from the Thatcher camp, there was still strong support for her, but the result would be painfully close (*Daily Telegraph*, 20 November 1990; *Financial Times*, 22 November 1990; *The Independent*, 23 November 1990). She needed to obtain 50 per cent plus one vote or face a third ballot. Thatcher was not deflected by these reports. That afternoon she made her 'I-fight-to-win' statement. So neither the parliamentary party nor the party in the country delivered the fatal blow.

The cabinet killed her: not because it formally met as a cabinet to deliver a collective verdict but because its members, and only its members, expressed the views which finally persuaded her to resign. She decided not to concentrate her efforts on winning over backbenchers directly but to mobilise cabinet ministers. She put herself at their mercy (Thatcher, 1993, pp.850–51). The opinions of cabinet ministers were first canvassed over the telephone by the leader of the House of Commons, John MacGregor (*The Times*, 23 November 1990). He is said to have reported that of the 17 cabinet members (excluding Thatcher, Hurd and Major, who proposed and seconded her, and the two peers) 12 felt she should resign and five felt she should stay on. To verify that assessment Wakeham and Thatcher's parliamentary private secretary, Peter Morrison, suggested she speak to cabinet members individually. The decision not to have the cabinet meet to discuss the issue was intended to avoid a row and subsequent damaging resignations (Baker, 1993, p.403).

On Wednesday from about 6 pm to 8 pm Thatcher interviewed ministers individually in her room at the House of Commons. She saw 15 cabinet members that evening (Anderson, 1991, p.142; Thatcher, 1993, pp.850–55). As a result of what they said she decided to resign, despite last-minute appeals for her to stay in the running from some right-wing backbenchers and three junior ministers from the 'No Turning Back Group', who visited Number 10 that evening. She announced her decision first to the cabinet the next day, at an unusually early meeting, at 9 am.

What did her cabinet colleagues tell her in answer to her question: 'Do you think I should go on?' It was reported, but later denied, that some had threatened to resign if she stayed on. She later said no one threatened to resign. At least two (Parkinson and Baker) are said to have begged her to remain; two (Brooke and Waddington) wanted her to stay on but felt she would lose. But the overwhelming majority declared they believed she could not win or, if she won, she would lead a divided and demoralised party (see also Thatcher, 1993). They said support for her was collapsing, because backbench MPs feared they would lose their seats if she remained leader; they felt they were blighted by her and would switch to a more likely general election winner. Most of her cabinet colleagues asked her to step down to let another cabinet member enter the second ballot with a better chance of beating Heseltine. After meeting Norman Tebbit and some junior ministers who urged her to fight on, Thatcher returned to 10 Downing Street, talked it over with her husband and, sleeping on it overnight, decided she would resign; she told the full cabinet the next morning.

Nesta Wyn Ellis wrote, 'Apart from Denis Thatcher's husbandly concern for her feelings and dignity, only one factor prevented [her] from a fight to the finish with Heseltine. It was the evidence, brought to her by a number of colleagues, that her vote was slipping and too many MPs were changing sides' (Ellis, 1991, p.31). Thatcher admitted later that she considered briefly staying on as prime minister even if she had lost. She might retain the premiership without being party leader (see Brazier, 1988, pp.17–22 on this constitutional issue): 'I could have said "It is only the leadership of the party. It is not for prime minister, therefore I will continue as prime minister because I was elected as prime minister and I have never been defeated by the people and I have never been defeated by parliament as a whole".' She quickly dismissed this idea because 'she would probably have split the party' (*The Times*, 29 May 1991; also *The Guardian*, 29 May 1991).

The way was now open for Hurd and Major to enter the contest. In the second ballot Major had 185 (49.7 per cent), Heseltine 131 (35.2 per cent) and Hurd 56 (15.1 per cent). Although Major was two short of the winning number, there was no third ballot, as technically required by the rules, because both Hurd and Heseltine withdrew, pledging loyalty to Major. So Major was elected Conservative leader, and the next day was asked by the Queen, who had just received Thatcher's resignation, to be prime minister. The irony is that Thatcher had received more votes than Major, 204 as against his 185, and more had voted against him, 187, than had voted against her, 168. As Thatcher said, on opening the cabinet on 22 November, 'It's a funny old world' (*The Independent*, 23 November 1990).

She had caved in to cabinet pressure. She felt she had lost the support of her cabinet. 'Her own Cabinet had deserted her in her hour of need' (Baker, 1993, p.407). To govern she needed authority emanating from the cabinet: it was not there. Her confidence was shattered, because her ministers would not mount a credible campaign on her behalf (Thatcher, 1993, pp.850, 855–6; Baker, 1993, pp.407–8). They felt she could not win in the second ballot or, if she did just win, she would lack authority. Whether their judgement was right we will never know. About 40 backbenchers were said to have voted for her at the first ballot out of loyalty and intended to switch on the second. However she might have picked up some previous supporters of Heseltine and waverers. In the event she never put it to the test. Having taken the advice of her cabinet she resigned. Her backbenchers had not killed her: the mortal blow came from the cabinet.

Conclusion: Who Murdered Thatcher?

Margaret Thatcher did not commit suicide. Until the final Wednesday evening she was determined to fight on. She may have neglected her best interests. She chose a feeble initial campaign team and brought forward the date of the ballot, denying herself time to win over waverers. She courted the backbenchers in the Commons too late and ineffectually. Her parliamentary private secretary, Peter Morrison, 'found it hard to reach those parts of the party where her influence needed to be reinforced' and the whips' office was criticised for not vigorously supporting the leader (Anderson, 1991, p.102). Thatcher immersed herself in the Paris summit and appeared in the House of Commons Tea Room only on the final Wednesday afternoon: the first time in 18 months, which seemed like a sign of panic. Indeed she might never have had to face a contest had her office not goaded Heseltine to 'put up or shut up'. On the crucial night in the Commons she agreed to see cabinet ministers individually and allowed them to range wider in their opinions than simply saying whether they would support her in the second ballot. More generally she had persisted in unpopular policies and become remote from her backbenchers, usually performing in the Commons only at the twice-weekly Question Time, and neglecting to make regular speeches, statements and interventions in debates (Dunleavy *et al.*, 1990; and Chapter 12 below). Negligence or misadventure may be possible verdicts, but she did not deliberately seek her own downfall in an act of suicide.

She was murdered: assaulted by blows from three sources. First, the British people expressed their hostility towards her, her government and its policies, and proclaimed they were more likely to vote Conservative under another leader in a series of public opinion polls from June 1989 to November 1990, in the European elections of June 1989, in the local government elections of May 1990 and in repeated by-elections right up to November 1990. This public disaffection came from the government's policy failures, overwhelmingly in economic management which produced high inflation and high interest and mortgage rates, and in the poll tax. She was personally identified with these policies. She seemed to be leading her party to electoral disaster against a revitalised Labour party.

The second blow was struck by her party in the House of Commons (see Baldwin, 1991, pp.5–8; Gamble, 1991, p.88; Benyon, 1991, p.107; Shell, 1991, p.272; Young, 1991, p.590). To be prime minister and remain in office the Conservative leader needs the support of the party in the Commons. It has the power of life or death over a prime minister and government. When it seemed she was leading the party to electoral defeat at the next election, thus failing in the main task of a party leader, the party increasingly turned against her, sending her a warning in November 1989, when Sir Anthony Meyer stood against her, which was intensified in November 1990 in the first ballot. She was brought down in November 1990 for not improving her performance in the year after the Meyer challenge to make victory at the general election likely. But the party in the Commons never actually killed her. She attained 55 per cent of their vote, four short of the winning number. It was within her grasp to remain leader had she fought back and stood at the second ballot. But even when told she might have the numbers on her side. Thatcher's view was that 'if her cabinet was against her, numbers no longer mattered' (*The Economist*, 1991, p.24).

The cabinet struck the third and final blow: 'The rats got at her' (*The Independent*, 23 November 1990). Her decision to resign was taken only after listening to the views of cabinet colleagues (see Anderson, 1991, p.143; Shepherd, 1991, p.51; Ingham, 1991, p.396; Parkinson, 1992, p.37; Watkins, 1991). Although the cabinet never met as a collective body to discuss her leadership, the meetings with individual cabinet ministers constituted the equivalent of a cabinet, acting as if they were a cabinet and, although not all members thought she should resign, the weight of opinion was sufficient to convince her she had lost the support she needed to continue. She no longer commanded the confidence of those whose backing was essential, her cabinet colleagues.

Thatcher's past dominance over them came about because they had been 'wet' in the face of her assertiveness. Now they turned against her and pulled her down, reflecting a mixture of personal and party ambitions. They wanted to win the next election and to preserve what as a cabinet they had achieved. They feared that the outside challenger, Heseltine, might win and shift policy too far from the cabinet's line and split the party, so an insider from the cabinet was needed to run against him. The eventual winner was the one who looked most likely to win the next election, maintain party unity and preserve the 'Thatcherite' inheritance. Heseltine might have been an election winner, but would have split the party and led in a different direction. Hurd did not look as much an election winner as Major, nor as likely to preserve the Thatcher approach. Major seemed to score highly on all three counts, although eventually Major's style and some of his policies were different from Thatcher's, provoking mutterings of dissent in the spring and early summer of 1991 from Thatcher's most dedicated former supporters.

Thatcher's demise came about because of a combination of interacting factors: Heseltine's campaign for the leadership from the moment of his resignation from the cabinet in 1986 to the ballot of 1990; government policy failures, especially as regards economic management and the poll tax; the deepening recession and unpopularity of the prime minister and government; and backbench MPs' anxieties over the prospect of losing their seats and the prime minister's neglect of her supporters in the Commons. All these factors were significant, indeed necessary, in undermining her position but they were not sufficient to destroy her. The final straw was the cabinet.

Thatcher felt cabinet ministers had concocted a line to put to her: treachery with a smile by those she had appointed. Kenneth Baker (1993, pp.398–9) believed this 'common purpose' was planned at a meeting of some ministers at the home of the deputy chief whip, Tristan Garel-Jones (Parkinson, 1992, p.37). Despite much gossip of plots by cabinet ministers to remove her, even as early as 1988, there is no hard evidence that any such scheme was hatched. Ellis surveyed the rumours (1991, pp.17–30) and noted a distinction between 'discussion of strategies on a "what if?" basis, and the deliberate pursuit of a campaign to destroy the Prime Minister. Among Westminster insiders, strategies for the succession were being discussed, as they will always be discussed after a certain length of office-holding' (ibid., p.28). However Ingham (1991, p.379) records: 'I am singularly unimpressed with conspiracy theory. I do not believe there was a plot within her party to bring her down . . . I do not believe there was a premeditated and organized coup in November 1990.' Anderson (1991, p.99) takes a similar view: 'The conspiracy theory has only one problem: an entire lack of evidence.' Pearce (1991, pp.137, 140–44) agreed, describing her fall as 'the culmination of a period of spectacularly poor judgments by her, quarrels with foreigners, heel-diggings at the EC, and a breakdown of normal give and take with senior colleagues . . . The wonder with a leader so poised on the hair trigger of her emotions is not that she went but that she took so long.'

A theory about a one-man conspiracy developed over the role of John Wakeham. Ostensibly her campaign manager, he was depicted by Watkins (1991, p.12) as not so much her 'cheerleader' as her 'undertaker'. It is suggested he advised the prime minister to consult cabinet members individually so she could more easily be told she should go. He may initially have supported her but quickly saw she had lost the support of backbenchers. He knew she would not trust any message from the chief whip that she stand down, since Timothy Renton was known to be part of the Howe camp, and so he thought up the consultation with cabinet members as a means to reinforce any whips' message that backbenchers were turning from her. If the cabinet had met as a collective group, arguing with each other, she might have decided that no one would do any better than she was doing and have carried on. So Wakeham was presented as the man who brought her down. He later denied any such motive, as indeed did two other ministers, Kenneth Clarke and John Gummer, who were alleged to have met Wakeham to plot her downfall (*Sunday Express*, 17 November 1991; *Daily Telegraph*, 18 November 1991). Indeed ministers facing the prime minister alone may have been more vulnerable to her influence than if linked together with like-minded colleagues. Shepherd (1991, p.22) gives a more plausible explanation: Wakeham 'wanted to provide her with independent verification of whatever she was told by Renton.' (See also Fowler, 1991, p.353.)

Professor Norton argues 'not that there was a conspiracy but that disparate events, over which no one had control, combined to produce an outcome that surprised a great many, including the participants' (Norton, 1991, p.5). Richard Maher, scriptwriter of the ITV production, 'Thatcher: the Final Days', said: 'It's more the story of a set of mistakes made through being overconfident and out of touch. One way of describing it would be as a Tragedy of Errors. Alternatively, it can be seen as a tragedy of hubris, of not being able to see the world as it really is' (*The Sunday Times*, 8 September 1991). Even her advisers were blamed: 'For all the talk of conspiracies. Thatcher ultimately fell because her courtiers were too obsequious, too blind to her political mortality, to warn her of the gathering storm' (*Financial Times*, 7 September 1991). *The Economist*'s survey of the evidence about plots concluded there was no conspiracy (*The Economist*, 9 March 1991, p.24).

James (1992, p.96) argues: 'Mrs Thatcher's overthrow came about because she was unwise enough to quarrel with senior colleagues and treat them poorly, at the same time as a powerful centre of opposition coalesced on the backbenches around Michael Heseltine and opinion polls showed her to be an electoral liability.' Even then, he notes, she was safe until Howe resigned over European policy and made his resignation speech.

The cabinet acted only at the end: the final link in the chain. Popular discontent caused by failures of policy provoked backbench disaffection which ultimately stimulated the cabinet to strike. Thatcher had become out of touch with the British people, her party in the Commons and finally the cabinet. They all played a part in bringing her down, but in the end the *coup de grâce* was given, not by the parliamentary party or by the British people, but by the cabinet (*The Independent*, 23 November 1990). Margaret Thatcher was only as strong as her cabinet ministers let her be.

5

Interpreting the Rise and Fall of Margaret Thatcher: Power Dependence and the Core Executive

MARTIN J. SMITH*

The limitations and difficulties of the traditional debate about prime ministerial versus cabinet power are discussed in Chapter 1. Here I set out an explanatory model of prime ministerial power which recognises that the power of the prime minister is variable and therefore power within the core executive depends on context; that prime ministerial power depends on institutional resources as well as individual attributes; that any definition of power must be relational; and that power is dependent on interaction rather than command. There is mutual dependence within the core executive. It should also be apparent that each of these factors interact, so the relationships which develop depend on their context and are therefore difficult to generalise. Of course, a number of these points are recognised to some degree in the traditional debate, but they need to be developed into a more systematic account of core executive power with less emphasis placed on the volition or personality of individual leaders.

The work by Dunleavy and Rhodes (1990; see also Greenaway, 1991) suggests a way out of the impasse on prime ministerial

* I would like to thank Neil Carter, Fiona Devine, Andrew Gamble, Rod Rhodes and the participants of the University of Sheffield Department of Politics postgraduate seminar for comments on earlier drafts of this chapter. I would also like to thank Suzanne Presland for gathering the material on Margaret Thatcher's resignation and the University of Sheffield research fund for providing funding.

power. They widen the focus of analysis by looking at the core executive which includes the prime minister, key departments, senior civil servants, cabinet and cabinet committees rather than just the cabinet or the prime minister. They also suggest that analysis of government decision making has to be disaggregated by looking at particular decisions in specific areas rather than the prime minister or cabinet in general. Subsequently they propose that the prime minister tends to be dominant in specific areas such as strategic economic decisions whilst ministers are dominant over the majority of domestic issues. They note the increasing complexity and segmentation of government and the strong bureaucratic foundations for departmentalism. Importantly they note an increasing shift towards departmentalism as a way of keeping political issues from Margaret Thatcher and this may have created 'a range of subtle countervailing tendencies to Thatcher's apparent monolithic control during the 1980s' (Rhodes, Chapter 1 above, pp.21–2; Dunleavy and Rhodes, 1990, p.13).

The other key element of Dunleavy and Rhodes' analysis (Chapter 1 above, pp.23–4) is the emphasis on power dependency. Ministers have resources and therefore the exercise of prime ministerial power depends on the support of ministers. This suggests that power, rather than being a zero sum game, is actually the result of dependencies. Rhodes (1981, p.98) derived the power dependence framework in relation to local government and suggested that:

(a) Any organisation is *dependent* upon other organisations for *resources.*

(b) In order to achieve their *goals,* the organisations have to exchange resources.

(c) Although decision making within the organisation is constrained by other organisations, the *dominant coalition* retains some discretion. The *appreciative system* of the dominant coalition influences which relationships are seen as a problem and which resources will be sought.

(d) The dominant coalition employs *strategies* within known *rules of the game* to regulate the *process of exchange.*

(e) Variation in the degree of *discretion* is a product of the goals and the relative power potential of interacting organisations. This relative power potential is a product of the resources of each organisation, of the rules of the game and of the process of exchange between organisations.

This notion of power is useful for examining prime minister–cabinet relations. Both prime minister and cabinet have resources. The prime minister has patronage, the authority to intervene in key policy areas and the ability to direct resources. Ministers have the responsibility, knowledge and administrative capabilities to develop policies in their own particular areas. Ministers, particularly if they are senior, will have their own political authority. To an extent resources derive from each other. The prime minister's authority derives from the cabinet, the ministers' position is determined by the prime minister. To achieve goals they exchange resources; they need each other. There are frequently coalitions between the prime minister and senior ministers, particularly, the chancellor, and this coalition can set the framework for the overall determination of policy and so to an extent 'regulate the process of exchange'. Finally it is clear that the relative power of actors is highly variable.

As a consequence the power of the prime minister and the cabinet is not fixed but varies according to the resources available, the rules of the game, administrative ability, political support, political strategies, relationships within the core executive and external circumstances. After winning an election, the prime minister has the clear support of voters and MPs and so has greater freedom to use resources than at times of poor polls and economic problems. However the prime minister's power will also vary according to the issue in question. In certain issue areas the prime minister might have the authority to intervene but if it is a policy area in the remit of a minister with high authority and popular support the influence of the prime minister might be less. For example, after the 1987 election Margaret Thatcher had limited ability to intervene in economic policy because Nigel Lawson was seen as a very successful chancellor by Conservative MPs. Wherever the prime minister intervenes he or she must weigh up the costs of intervention and a minister must assess the cost of resistance.

As Dowding points out, in order to understand power we need to evaluate the capacities of actors, which depend on the resources they have available: 'But looking at these resources is not enough to measure their capacities, for those resources will only allow actors to bring about outcomes under certain conditions' (Dowding, 1991, p.5). Prime ministerial resources are institutional and strategic, such as patronage, formal control of the cabinet and the ability to make policy bilaterally with a minister. Unlike other models of prime ministerial power, the personal strategy which a premier develops can be seen not as a result of prime ministerial personality but as deriving from strategic choices facing them (Clegg, 1989). It will change according to external support and the particular policy area, the circumstances and the resources of ministers. The choice the prime minister makes can greatly affect his or her ability to influence outcomes and they can choose a range of strategies or modes of behaviour in different circumstances. She or he can be dominant, collective, interventionist or a coordinator (see Figure 5.1). In a particular policy area at a certain time the prime minister might be collective – as Margaret Thatcher was over the Falklands. At others he or she might be interventionist – as Thatcher was over health policy in 1989. How the prime minister, and indeed ministers, choose to use their resources can have a great impact on power.

A minister with limited resources may have a disproportionate influence on policy if he or she has an effective strategy for using the resources. Thus ministers can most simply present the prime minister with threats or offers which will change his or her incentive structure (Dowding, 1991). For example, ministers can threaten to resign at a critical point, as Howe and Lawson did in 1989 (see pp.119–21 below). Alternatively ministers can provide offers of support in return for particular action by the prime minister. Ministers can also develop coalitions in order to influence cabinet committees or to try and force a particular action by the prime minister (see Chapter 13 below). For example, Thatcher eventually agreed to ERM membership when she realised that she had very little support in the cabinet for not joining (see Chapter 11). Other tactics can be used to defeat the prime minister, such as leaking. Patrick Jenkin was able to stop cuts in social security

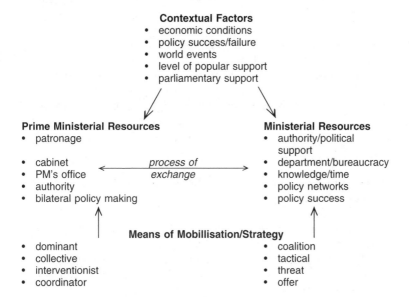

Figure 5.1   *A model of prime ministerial power*

spending by reading out in Cabinet manifesto commitments to maintain the level of benefits, (Young, 1989, p.212).

Although the prime minister has superior resources, he or she is still dependent on other actors for cooperation, support and legitimacy, and this dependence changes according to the overall context. For example, after John Major won the 1992 general election against the odds, one might have expected his authority to be high, so that he would have substantial freedom in his use of prime ministerial resources. However a poor economic situation, combined with the mishandling of other policies and falling support in the polls, undermined his electoral success. Consequently he was forced to make a number of concessions to backbenchers on coal mine closures and on the Maastricht treaty.

The power dependence model improves on the traditional approaches to the prime minister, for a number of reasons. First, it develops a notion of power which recognises that power does not belong to the prime minister, nor is it an attribute of an institution. Instead ministers and the prime minister have resources. Power is their capacity to use these resources but the use of resources is dependent on the particular circumstances of any situation. Second, power is relational and not a zero sum. Thus this model does not see power as directly causal. Within central government the prime minister cannot force a minister to act in a certain way. Ministers and prime ministers are dependent on each other and therefore they might both gain or lose from a situation. Third, power is not reduced to personality. The use of resources does not just depend on the 'style' the prime minister *chooses* to adopt. Fourth, by examining the context within which decisions are made the model is able to explain why the power of actors within central government varies. It can explain why an apparently well-resourced prime minister can fail. Fifth, the model ends the dichotomy between cabinet and prime minister, highlighting the complex interrelationships that exist within the core executive, and so provides a more realistic account of the central government policy process.

Prime Ministerial Power and the Resignation of Margaret Thatcher

Existing journalistic and academic explanations of Thatcher's resignation tend to be highly individualistic and short-term narratives, which fail to place the resignation within the context of prime ministerial power (see, for example, Alderman and Carter, 1991; Anderson, 1991; Norton, 1992; Geelhoed, 1991; Ranelagh, 1991; Watkins, 1991; Young, 1991). Some pay attention to policy failures

– in particular the poll tax, but also the economy and Europe (Norton, 1993; *The Times*, 12 March 1991; Watkins, 1991; Wilson, 1992). Others focus on Thatcher's loss of support on the backbenches owing to a failure of political management and declining electoral support (Ellis, 1991; Norton, 1992; Young, 1991). The most short-term accounts focus on a 'cock-up' and poor tactics both by Thatcher's campaign team and by the prime minister in the way they handled the run-up to the re-election campaign, how they handled the campaign and actions after the first ballot (Alderman and Carter, 1991; *The Economist*, 9 March 1991). Thatcher supporters suggest a conspiracy, particularly from within the Treasury (see *The Times*, 5 December, 1990; *The Economist*, 9 March 1991; Riddell, 1991). Others blame Thatcher's personality (Prentice, *The Times*, 15 July 1991). Finally a number focus on her relations with cabinet colleagues and in particular the impact of Geoffrey Howe's resignation speech (James, 1992; *The Economist*, 9 March 1991; Lawson, 1992; Watkins, 1991).

Undoubtedly many of these factors did play a role in Thatcher's downfall, and the most thorough accounts stress that there were multiple causes of the resignation (see Alderman and Carter, 1991; Jones, Chapter 4 above; Norton, 1993; Watkins, 1991). Nevertheless, because of their failure to deal with issues of power, these treatments have mainly provided a narrative rather than an explanation. And even when explanations are provided they focus on the events immediately surrounding the resignation, such as tactical errors (Norton, 1993, p.54; Alderman and Carter, 1991, p.125) and particular policy failures. But they fail to examine whether these were a *cause* of the downfall or factors that *enabled* Thatcher to be removed from office. They also place a great deal of emphasis on Thatcher's style (Norton, 1993; Watkins, 1991).

By contrast I argue that, while the factors outlined above did contribute to Thatcher's demise, one of the key explanatory variables was the undermining of her relations of dependence with cabinet colleagues. The breakdown of this relationship occurred over a long period and started at least as early as the Westland affair. To understand this process we must look at the resources she had, the strategy she used to employ those resources, and how both the resources and strategy were affected by the changing context.

Dependency and Dominance in the Thatcher Cabinet

During Thatcher's period in office, her relationship with the cabinet changed greatly. Initially she was relatively dependent on senior ministers, a situation from which she struggled hard to escape between 1979 and 1985. She wanted a great deal of control over particular aspects of policy. Nevertheless she continually ran up against the changing limits of her domination and was reluctantly forced to recognise her dependence on members of the cabinet.

Thatcher's dominance was at its height after electoral victories (particularly after 1983 and 1987), after policy successes (such as the Falklands and during the economic revival of 1987/8) and when she built alliances within cabinet and cabinet committees that allowed her to dominate potential opponents. Although Thatcher did not have a majority of supporters in her first cabinet, she managed to ensure that she controlled economic policy by containing policy making within a small group of ministers (Young, 1989, p.148; Harris, 1990). As late as November 1979, despite its importance and radicalism, there was no discussion of economic policy at all in cabinet (Pym, 1984; Young, 1989, p.157). Thatcher was able to use her control of government machinery both to prevent full cabinet discussion of economic policy and to establish an economic cabinet committee in which her supporters had a majority.

This method of creating *ad hoc* committees in order to circumvent a cabinet in which she was not in a majority became common throughout the Thatcher period of office (Hennessy, 1986; Ridley, 1991; Wapshott and Brock, 1983). According to Lawson (1992, p.128):

> she sought to fragment any dissident voices. What had started off as a justified attempt to make effective decisions in small and informal groups degenerated into increasingly complex attempts to divide and rule. More and more, decisions were taken in very small groups in which she had hand-picked the balance of membership to ensure the outcome that she had sought.

In addition to sealing off certain areas of policy, Thatcher imposed her dominance despite opposition within the cabinet in the 1979–85 period because the 'wets' were divided. They lacked a strategy or alternative; they were loath to provide coordinated, overt opposition; they had little parliamentary support; and they did not have an alternative leader (Butt, *The Times*, 20 September 1981). In addition, Thatcher improved her position through selective sackings and a 'divide-and-rule' strategy. By 1981, she had either removed or isolated most of her cabinet critics and so greatly strengthened her own position (Burch, 1983; Young, 1989).

Thatcher was then in a strong enough position to enable Howe to present the 1981 budget which involved taking £3500 million out of the public sector borrowing requirement (PSBR) despite the strong opposition of a number of 'wets'. 'The cohesion of viewpoints between Treasury ministers, the Prime Minister and their advisers constituted a formidable force driving policy forward' (Burch, 1983, p.411). She had supporters in economic positions, a coherent policy and a lack of a coordinated opposition and thus was able to direct economic policy.

One of Thatcher's greatest periods of freedom in relation to the use of resources came after the Falklands war which 'elevated Mrs Thatcher to a new level of public esteem, hitherto untouched' (Young, 1989, p.280) and allowed her to put 'her personal stamp on an extraordinarily wide range of policy decisions' (King, 1985b). Then the 1983 electoral victory allowed her to remove the remaining critics from the cabinet. Again, after the 1987 election, a slightly less clear-cut victory than 1983, the prime minister was in a position of relative freedom. Although she now had some critics from the right, such as Tebbit and Biffen, they had no real support and were outside the cabinet (Young, 1989, p.520). Consequently the prime minister could push through the poll tax, despite some significant opposition (Lawson, 1992; Watkins, 1991).

Throughout this period, despite having a cabinet seemingly opposed to many of the policies she supported, Thatcher managed to control key areas of policy. However she was still partly dependent on the cabinet. Her strength was based on her 'dry coalition' on key cabinet committees and her relationship with Howe. Together they were in a position to dictate 'the appreciative system' and to determine the rules of the game concerning how cabinet operated and the direction of policy. Thatcher's position was clearly strong because of the context of political success and the fact that she seemed to provide the only viable option for Britain's economic problems, but she was also strong because she exchanged resources with Howe. On several occasions her senior colleagues did limit her actions.

The selection of Thatcher's first cabinet highlights her awareness of the need to maintain support from key figures within the party. She had worked with Heathites in opposition and kept a number in the cabinet. Moreover, in achieving her economic goals, Thatcher was highly dependent on her chancellor and the Treasury team. It was Geoffrey Howe who devised the Medium Term Financial Strategy (MTFS) and was prepared to implement it despite hostility from many quarters. Without the chancellor's support it would have been unlikely that the cabinet would have accepted the economic strategy.

Even with this support there were some significant defeats. In 1980, Patrick Jenkin cleverly prevented the loss of £600 million from the social security budget and Pym reduced the proposed cut in defence spending (Wapshott and Brock, 1983; Young, 1989, p.212). In 1981, the cabinet showed the limits of its tolerance when faced with a demand for more cuts in public spending, even after the highly deflationary 1981 budget. Young (1989, p.218) writes:

> After a swingeing budget, and against a background of civil breakdown – even as the cabinet met, the Toxteth district of Liverpool was recovering from another night of highly publicised violence between police and unemployed youths – [Howe] presented a paper which solemnly announced a preliminary demand that next year's projected spending should be cut by £5000 million.

The response was a rebellion in the cabinet which spread beyond the 'wets' to Thatcher loyalists such as John Biffen and John Nott (Young, 1989) and the paper was withdrawn. Thatcher's attempt to implement an even more stringent budget at a time of recession and rising unemployment failed. The government's support in the polls was low and Thatcher had not ensured that she had an alliance within the cabinet to support the policy. Despite her apparent dominance, she still needed assent from a majority of cabinet members, and lack of support limited her room for manoeuvre. Thatcher was convinced that the economic policy was right but she 'knew that there were too many in the Cabinet who did not share that view' (Thatcher, 1993, p.149).

In the early period of her premiership, Thatcher was aware of her dependencies on cabinet, the parliamentary party and, in particular, the Treasury, and so was forced to back down on a number of issues (Kavanagh, 1987). William Whitelaw played the role of ensuring that the prime minister retained the support of key cabinet members. As Hugo Young (1989, p.235) aptly points out: 'Power and its management were Whitelaw's forte: acquiring it, maximising it, deploying it, ensuring as far as possible its retention.' Later, as she became more secure in her position, the prime minister paid less concern to her dependencies. Yet changing circumstances and the position of colleagues in a way made these relationships more important. It was the undermining of mutual dependence at times of crisis that eventually resulted in her demise.

The Undermining of Dependencies

After 1985, Thatcher increasingly ignored her dependence on other colleagues despite the fact that circumstances and policy failures actually made these relationships more important. Partly she chose the wrong strategies. According to James (1992, p.98), 'She told ministers what she thought they ought to be doing. If they disagreed, she berated them. If they persisted, they argued it out in Cabinet or committee. If a minister argued too often, he was sacked.' Important decisions were made without any reference to cabinet (Walker, 1991). Thatcher's office often conducted whispering campaigns against ministers who had fallen out of favour. And the prime minister frequently undermined collective responsibility by distancing herself from decisions of colleagues (Young, 1989; Ellis, 1991; Lawson, 1992). As a *Times* leader (27 October 1989) observed:

> Her manner of governing has been a means of infusing the administration with energy, and of carrying through vast and in many respects admirable reforms. It did not however involve winning the trust of colleagues, carrying them with her, proving to them that, since she had appointed them, they could count on her support. Her method, whether conscious or not, has always been to manipulate subordinates and stab them in the back when they have outlived their usefulness.

This had the effect of frustrating ministers within cabinet and it left many disgruntled ex-ministers on the backbenches. Anderson (1991, p.10) calculates: 'During Mrs Thatcher's last year as Premier, the disgruntled ex-ministers and frustrated non-ministers numbered at least half the Parliamentary Party.' In addition, the prime minister had a habit of annoying ministers by interfering in the departmental policy process and imposing policies – from a half-informed position – on departments. The result was that she was directly identified with policy failures as well as successes (Young, 1989). This strategy of dominance had a worse effect when combined with poor management. Thatcher paid insufficient attention to her supporters outside cabinet (Norton, 1992). She relied on the whips for filling junior posts and this meant that many of her supporters did not get posts in government (Baker, 1993).

Through her strategy, Thatcher not only undermined the support of potential enemies but also that of close friends. Lawson (1992, p.696) points out that the prime minister frequently made policy statements which departmental ministers, often her supporters, later had to deny. However she went even further and actually developed rifts with some of her closest allies, such as Norman Tebbit and John Biffen (Watkins, 1991). Lawson (1992, p.937) reports that, after July 1989, Thatcher behaved little better towards her colleagues: 'The press briefings by Ingham became ever more presidential and Margaret's trust in – and dependence upon – her kitchen cabinet ever more pronounced.' In July 1990, Thatcher became even more isolated when she lost almost her last close ally in the cabinet, Nicholas Ridley, who was forced to resign after making some uncomplimentary remarks about Germany. Increasingly surrounded by her own advisers, she became cut off from the cabinet and the backbenches, and no longer ensured that she cultivated the support of MPs as she had in the past. As early as March 1990, it was reported that 'up to a quarter of Tory MPs want her to quit before the next general election' (*The Times*, 12 March 1990) and that she was even losing support on the centre right (*The Times*, 26 March 1990). Rather than being dependent on the cabinet, she was dependent on her advisers.

The Westland affair was in retrospect a turning point, a dispute over whether the Westland helicopter company should be bailed out by a European consortium or by the US company, Sikorsky (for a full account, see Chapter 9 below, and Linklater and Leigh, 1986). 'The dispute created a major row involving the Cabinet, a Cabinet committee, several departments of government, individual ministers, the government law officers and officials in No. 10' (Barber, 1991, p.92). The affair resulted in the resignation of two ministers and for a time Thatcher thought that she might not survive the crisis. It demonstrated graphically that, despite her electoral position and the Falklands war, Thatcher was vulnerable and fallible. It also indicated that there were problems of management in government (Jenkins, *The Sunday Times*, 2 February 1986). Thatcher allowed Heseltine to disregard the conventions of cabinet government; she become involved in an apparently minor issue; and she herself repeatedly broke the conventions of cabinet government. 'After Westland, following the bombing of Libya, the prime minister's weight in the cabinet balance of power was held by her colleagues to have been reduced, and her dominant style to have been tempered' (Young, 1989, pp.495–6).

Thatcher's authority was decreased so that she could no longer realistically pursue a strategy of dominance. Lawson (1992, p.375) reveals how he revived Geoffery Howe's target of a 25 pence in the pound tax rate despite Thatcher's dislike of targets because 'weakened by the Westland affair', the prime minister, 'was in no condition to oppose it'. In Heseltine, the Westland affair placed on the backbenches a figure of sufficient seniority and authority to provide a significant leadership contender at a later date. After Westland the government appeared to lack direction and it backed down on issues such as the abolition of state earnings-related pensions (SERPS) and the selling of Land Rover (Young, 1989). More importantly:

The longer-term effects of the Westland affair, however, were wholly adverse. The lesson that Margaret took from it was that her colleagues were troublesome and her courtiers loyal. From then on she began to distance herself from colleagues who had been closest to her – certainly those who had minds of their own – and to retreat to the Number 10 bunker, where the leading figures were Charles Powell and Bernard Ingham. (Lawson, 1992, p.680)

Thatcher's handling of the issue indicated her lack of awareness of her dependence on cabinet. Her response was to undermine these links even further and thus begin the path to destruction.

The Westland affair was also indicative of the issues surrounding Britain's relationship with Europe, which ultimately played a key role in Thatcher's resignation (Harris, 1990). Thatcher had a different view of the EC from many of her senior colleagues. But rather than build alliances or compromises she tended to override or undermine opposition. The central issue was Britain's membership of the Exchange Rate Mechanism (ERM) and the impact that this had on her relationships with two senior figures in her cabinet, Nigel Lawson and Geoffrey Howe. (For a full account, see Chapter 11 below.)

Most of the cabinet believed that Britain should join the ERM, while Thatcher became if anything increasingly opposed. The gulf opened up sharply at meetings in the autumn of 1985 and continued for five years, largely unclosed. Although Thatcher eventually made a commitment to join the ERM in 1989, 'she showed no sign of ever honouring it' (Anderson, 1991, p.53). Instead she used her position and authority to veto ERM membership. In doing so it could be argued that she was in a powerful position, but in ignoring the demands of senior colleagues she weakened herself because she ignored her dependence. Unlike the early period in office, however, neither side in the dispute backed down.

As chancellor of the exchequer Lawson had significant resources. He was in charge of the Treasury, which gave him substantial influence on economic policy. He was seen as the architect of Britain's economic revival and subsequently had tremendous authority in the Tory party (Watkins, 1991, p.96). And he had no ambition to be prime minister (*The Times*, 27 October 1989) and so could take political risks. Lawson's stock rose further in 1988, when he introduced a radical, tax-cutting budget. Despite Thatcher's isolation she was dependent on her chancellor. She could not sack him: he was (in her words) 'unassailable'. Thatcher admitted to Baker that she could not have sacked Lawson because 'I might well have had to go as well' (Thatcher, quoted in Baker, 1993, p.315).

Lawson used this position to override Thatcher's veto (Anderson, 1991, p.54). Keegan (1989, p.210) quotes one insider:

> By 1987 he thought he knew how to run the British economy and how to control inflation. He was hailed as the architect of electoral victory, the best chancellor the world had seen. It affected his judgement and it almost seemed possible that he could overrule the Prime Minister.

For example, Lawson and the Treasury worked on a scheme for a return to a general international system of managed currency without reference to Downing Street and which he advocated at the annual meeting of the IMF (Keegan, 1989). And from February 1987, the chancellor established an unpublicised stable rate of exchange for sterling with an unofficial ceiling of D-Mark 3.00. Eventually, according to Keegan (1989, p.222), 'the Prime Minister finally rumbled his exchange rate policy'. In March 1988, Thatcher insisted that sterling be allowed to find its own level and relations between Thatcher and Lawson became increasingly difficult (Young, 1991; Lawson, 1992).

A year later, in combination with the foreign secretary, Howe, Lawson returned to the fray. Before the Madrid summit of June 1989, Howe and Lawson effectively threatened to resign unless Thatcher made a specific commitment to join the ERM, which in the end she seemed to do publicly (see Chapter 11). She was in a weak position. It would have been very difficult for her to survive the resignations of her two most senior cabinet ministers. She was further weakened by the party's poor showing in the European elections and by the fact that there was almost a coordinated campaign by the economic elite for Britain to join ERM.

Understandably the Madrid démarche did not improve relations between Lawson and Thatcher. The normal mutual dependence which seem to exist between the prime minister and the chancellor disappeared (Ridley, 1991, p.211; Thatcher, 1993, p.714). Thatcher effectively forced his resignation a few months later, further undermining the sources of her authority. Britain was facing severe economic problems and Lawson's resignation undermined economic and political confidence. 'She no longer enjoys the confidence of a substantial and growing element within [the Conservative Party] and may be hard put to regain it' (*The Independent*, 27 October 1989). The balance of power, it seems, had changed within the cabinet as a result of the government's poor position in the polls and the divisions with the chancellor (*The Independent*, 27 October 1989). Kenneth Baker warned Thatcher that she was in danger. And 'the back-benchers let it be known that they had told Margaret to get her act together . . .' (Baker, 1993, p.316). With this loss of power, Hurd (the new foreign secretary) and Major (the new chancellor) were able to force Thatcher into joining the ERM. 'After all, having lost so many Ministers, the leader could hardly afford to lose them as well' (1991, p.570).

Thatcher's treatment of Sir Geoffrey Howe also demonstrated indifference to dependency relations. She apparently treated Howe with rudeness and disdain for many years. After Madrid, the relationship deteriorated further and Thatcher exacted revenge by sacking him as foreign secretary without any consultation and making him just leader of the House of Commons (after offering Howe the Home Office without consulting the then home secretary, Douglas Hurd) (*The Times*, 26 July 1989; *The Independent*, 27 October 1989). This move made Howe very resentful and relations worsened, particularly over Thatcher's view of the EC. After the Rome Summit in October 1990, she agreed her Commons statement with Hurd and Major. However, when asked questions, she deviated from government policy and attacked developments in the European Community. For Howe this was the final straw and he resigned, taking care to direct his resignation speech so as to damage the position of the prime minister.

> It is the symbolism of Sir Geoffrey's resignation that makes it significant. The fact that Mrs Thatcher could not keep someone as inoffensive and as accommodating as the deputy prime minister in her cabinet only fuels public discontent with her highhanded ways. When things are going well Mrs Thatcher can get away with dragooning the Cabinet into whatever causes she chooses. When things are going badly . . . her imperious style only increases her unpopularity. (*The Sunday Times*, 4 November 1990)

The speech directly opened the way for Michael Heseltine to stand against Thatcher for the leadership.

The other important factor in Thatcher's undermining of her own position was the poll tax, which directly affected many backbenchers who feared the loss of their seats. In a 1985 memorandum, Lawson (1992, p.574) concluded that 'The proposal for a poll tax would be completely unworkable and politically catastrophic.' He was supported in his opposition by a number of senior ministers (Young, 1991). However Thatcher continued to push through the policy despite cabinet and party opposition and hence, when the problems of the policy became apparent, she was blamed and her standing with Tory MPs was significantly weakened by it.

The events immediately surrounding Thatcher's resignation are discussed elsewhere (see Chapter 4 above). The point of this chapter is to show that Thatcher's downfall was not a result of Michael Heseltine, her campaign or even loss of backbench support. She undermined her own position by not realising that the exercise of her power depended on maintaining the support of colleagues, rather than destroying it. She made the wrong strategic decisions in relation to her use of resources. Geoffrey Howe (1993) argued:

> We could have avoided the clashes over ERM entry in 1989 which ruptured irretrievably the once-solid troika which Nigel Lawson and I had formed with Mrs Thatcher. One cannot help feeling that her own reputation might be the greater today – indeed she might even still be in power – if she had not tested that relationship to destruction in pursuit of an ideological obsession.

The backbenchers' votes might well have ultimately led to Thatcher's demise, but she would have been much more likely to survive if she had retained the support of the cabinet. Thatcher was prepared to go on to the second ballot until she became increasingly aware that cabinet support was slipping away. At least 10 cabinet ministers thought that she could not win. Kenneth Clarke and Malcolm Rifkind were prepared to resign if she stayed on and a group of cabinet ministers 'really did want a change of leader' (Baker, 1993, p.404). Thatcher recognised that her area of greatest weakness during the election campaign 'was among Cabinet Ministers' (Thatcher, 1993, p.847). She saw that she could have gone out and mobilised backbenchers but that first it was necessary to have the full support of the cabinet:

> a prime minister who knows that his or her Cabinet has withheld its support is fatally weakened. I knew – and I am sure they knew – that I would not willingly remain an hour in 10 Downing street without real authority to govern. (Thatcher, 1993, p.851)

Once convinced that she no longer had the support of the cabinet, Thatcher decided not to stand in the second ballot (p.853).

In 1981, the government was introducing unpopular policies, support in the opinion polls was low and the economy was in recession but Thatcher was strong because she maintained the support of the cabinet. Later things changed. A *Times* leader prophetically pointed out in October 1988: 'She could not indefinitely go on treating Cabinet ministers in the way she had done for a decade without at some point suffering politically disastrous consequences' (*The Times*, 27 October 1988). Thatcher was less dependent when her authority was high and policies successful, but with the disaster of the poll tax, economic problems and low popular support she needed the support of ministers. This list of factors provides the context of Thatcher's demise but not the cause. In this context the combination of Howe's speech, a ready challenger for Tory leader, a mishandled leadership campaign and backbench unease had an impact. However, it was Westland, the ERM and the resignations of Howe and Lawson which significantly weakened Thatcher. By 1990, she needed the support of her cabinet colleagues, but had undermined the relationship of dependency.

Conclusion

Earlier accounts of Thatcher's dismissal have not satisfactorily explained why such an apparently dominant prime minister was forced from office. They concentrate on personality rather than circumstances and relationships; they only examine the events immediately surrounding the resignation; they search for a simple linear causal explanation and thus they do not really examine the context within which Thatcher resigned. A few accounts do emphasise the importance of the cabinet in Thatcher's fall, but they do so in the sense of seeing the cabinet as constitutionally important. It was not the loss of cabinet support that was crucial for Thatcher, but the way she failed to recognise her dependence on the cabinet or to understand the patterns of dependence within the cabinet.

This chapter shows that the power of the prime minister varies greatly. Although prime ministers have a wide range of resources, in order to use their resources they are dependent on others. Thatcher fell because she increasingly failed to recognise her weaknesses and so chose the wrong strategy for employing resources. While Thatcher was 'aware of her strengths, she showed no insight into her weaknesses' (*The Guardian*, 23 October 1993). Undoubtedly there were occasions when Thatcher had great freedom to use her resources, but by 1990, when she was politically unpopular, policies were failing and there was unrest in the Conservative party, her dependence on the cabinet was greater than ever.

Thatcher's fall highlights the weaknesses of traditional approaches to prime ministerial power. British government is not cabinet government or prime ministerial government. Cabinets and prime ministers act within the context of mutual dependence based on the exchange of resources with each other and with other actors and institutions within the core executive. A prime minister can only be dominant with the support or acquiescence of cabinet and attempts at dominance without this support undermine the relationships of dependence. The power of the prime minister varies greatly according to the issues, the external circumstances and the resources of other actors within the core executive.

6

The Cabinet Office and Coordination, 1979–87

ANTHONY SELDON*

Introduction

This chapter examines the role and work of the Cabinet Office (CO) during the first two terms of the Conservative government, from 1979 to 1987. As the study ends at the general election in June 1987, the past tense will be used throughout, although inevitably many of the procedures and bodies described below continue. The title of the chapter speaks of the 'Cabinet Office', but most of it will focus on the work of just one part of that Office, namely the cabinet secretariat. In addition, the CO contained (in 1979) the Central Policy Review Staff (CPRS), the Central Statistical Office (CSO) and a small historical section.

The chapter sets out to describe how the Cabinet secretariat operated during 1979–87. No full study expressly on this subject has appeared in print before, yet the CO lies at the heart of British government. The chapter examines the principal organisational changes to the CO in the period; the function of the six secretariats within the cabinet secretariat; appointment and service of the CO staff; the office's role in coordinating and planning government business; the role that full cabinet and cabinet committees played during the period, and the support offered them by the CO; the work of CO officials with regard to agenda preparation, briefing chairmen and minutes; and, finally, it focuses on the role of the official at the apex of the office, the cabinet secretary.

*The author is grateful for the comments of Peter Hennessy, Professor G.W. Jones and Professor J.M. Lee on an earlier draft of this chapter.

Many difficulties were encountered in writing the chapter. Their existence no doubt explains the dearth of literature on this important subject. However imperfect the finished product and tentative the conclusions, the author felt it better to publish, and to put an account of the CO's operation, which he believes to be substantially accurate, on the record. The first and most obvious difficulty concerned secrecy. Researching any branch of the contemporary civil service brings one up against official secrecy, especially when tackling as sensitive a subject as the CO. Extracting information was complicated further by the lack of published information about the operation of the system. No organisational chart is published, and only four standing cabinet committees have been officially identified. The fullest and most accurate account to date of the operation of the system appears in Hennessy's *Cabinet* (1986) whose principal findings have been corroborated as substantially accurate by a number of independent officials who worked in or near the CO. But Hennessy had, of necessity, to rely upon the scarcely satisfactory resort of covert information gathering, hushed telephone calls and so on to build his picture of, as he describes it, 'the engine room of Whitehall'.[1]

Second, one necessarily had to rely on interviews, with all their imperfections, as a source (Seldon and Pappworth, 1983). One could not cross-check the accuracy of what was said owing to the lack of written material. Evidence varied greatly, depending on whether one was interviewing a minister or an official, serving or retired, senior or junior, and the period of involvement with the CO. Often those interviewed only saw the system in operation for part of the time and/or only saw parts of the system. Only one senior official (Robert Armstrong) and a handful of senior ministers (Margaret Thatcher, Lord Hailsham, William Whitelaw and Geoffrey Howe) saw the system in operation throughout the eight-year period. Readers of this chapter cannot see where the author is referring to particular interviews, because, being confidential, they cannot be included in references. Not even the number or identity of interviewees can be mentioned. The author endeavoured to interview witnesses who saw the system from a variety of different perspectives, but he is well aware of the possibilities of having been overinfluenced by interviewees expressing one particular viewpoint. The facts and opinions in this chapter must, inevitably, be substantially conditioned by the principal source. Interviews can be the kiss of death to objectivity. Ministers were, for the most part, poor interviewees. During the course of the research for this chapter, the author frequently had reason to wonder whether some former ministers had served in the same administration, so at variance were their accounts of the way that coordination took place at the heart of Whitehall.

A third complicating factor was that one was trying to describe a moving target. Although there were many procedural conventions, there was no one way of conducting business, and different pressures, crises, the imminence of elections and the need for secrecy, caused work to be handled in different ways at different times. The working of the system, moreover, was partly a function of the dominant personalities of the day: for the period under review there were three principal individuals concerned: Thatcher, Whitelaw and Armstrong. The presence of just one prime minister, the key actor in the process throughout the period under study might, *ceteris paribus*, have inclined it towards a degree of stability. But Thatcher conducted business within reason as she liked, as did other key actors in the story. One cannot, therefore, exaggerate the extent that formidable descriptive difficulties result from this essentially covert, flexible and fluid system.

Finally comes a problem of perspective. On one level, the cabinet secretariat was a relatively discrete unit, susceptible to isolated description; on another, it was the centre of a highly complex web of interlocking policy networks. Its operation only becomes full explicable when understood in conjunction with a wide variety of different institutions, of which the Treasury, Foreign and Commonwealth Office, Number 10 Private Office and overseas governments and agencies, especially in the European Community and Washington, are just some of the more important. To focus solely on the work of the CO, as this chapter does, thus gives inevitably a partial account of the centre of British government.

Changes, 1979–87

There were two main changes to the cabinet secretary's and the CO's role between 1979 and 1987, both of which produced increased work and responsibilities for senior CO officials.

Abolition of the Civil Service Department

After the abolition of the CSD and the attendant changes in November 1981, the CSD's functions were divided between the Treasury and the CO. This move affected the CO more than the subsequent demise of the CPRS, discussed below. The Treasury took over the pay and numbers functions of the CSD; the CO took over recruitment, training and personnel functions. The cabinet secretary in his capacity as (initially joint, subsequently sole) Head of the Home Civil Service took over responsibility for senior appointments. When he became cabinet secretary in 1979, Armstrong essentially did the job that Burke Trend (1962–73) and John Hunt (1973–9) had done before him; after the CSD was wound up, his responsibilities increased considerably. With the exception of Edward Bridges in 1945–6, who was at the same time head of the Home Civil Service, permanent secretary of the Treasury and cabinet secretary, no cabinet secretary had possessed so much responsibility before (although Norman Brook had a comparable task to Armstrong's, from 1956 to 1962 when, following Edward Bridges' retirement, Brook took over his job as Head of the Home Civil Service). Following the 1981 rearrangements, Armstrong had to change his *modus operandi*, for example, by increasing the scope of the deputy secretaries.

Before 1981, the cabinet secretary himself dealt with, signed and sent forward the briefs and approved the minutes for all cabinet committees in which the prime minister was in the chair. After the 1981 changes, Armstrong continued this practice for cabinet, but instituted a system where deputy secretaries, responsible for overseeing particular policy areas, briefed the prime minister direct and approved the minutes for those committees the prime minister chaired, except in those cases where Armstrong himself wanted to retain his former role. Armstrong himself saw this change not just as an essential relief to his own workload but as a sensible devolution of responsibility in its own right, since it served to enhance the role, job satisfaction and status of the deputy secretaries. This change served to justify the selection of officials of the highest calibre to fill the posts concerned and to make the appointments even more attractive to high-flying deputy secretaries from other departments.

From November 1981 to April 1983, following the premature retirement of Ian Bancroft as Head of the Home Civil Service, Armstrong and Douglas Wass (the permanent secretary at the Treasury) were appointed joint heads. By mutual agreement, Armstrong looked after the top civil service appointments, the most obvious manifestation of the Head of the Home Civil Service's authority. Armstrong consulted Wass on selections, as he did Peter Middleton, Wass's successor as permanent secretary at the Treasury, and it was Armstrong who, from 1981, chaired the Senior Appointments Selection Committee (SASC). When Wass retired in April 1983 at the age of 60, Thatcher decided to abandon the joint headship, leaving Armstrong sole Head of the Home Civil Service, a change which in effect did little more than make the nomenclature correspond with the reality that had existed from 1981 to 1983. Both of Armstrong's predecessors as cabinet secretary, Burke Trend and John Hunt, it may be noted, were delighted when the jobs of cabinet secretary and Head of the Home Civil Service were once again combined.

The demise of the CSD stemmed from Thatcher's and Derek Rayner's feeling that the office had lost its way since being set up after the Fulton report (in 1968). They felt that it had fulfilled a valuable function in early post-Fulton days, but its approach had since become increasingly theoretical and out of touch with the realities of the task of running large departments. The choices were few. It could have been put back into the Treasury, from whence it came. But neither Geoffrey Howe, the then chancellor of the exchequer, nor Wass, his permanent secretary, wanted it all back, nor did Armstrong wish to see it all go there. Handing over all the CSD's work to the CO was never considered a serious option, so the division of responsibilities described above came into being.

The prime minister retained her efficiency adviser, Rayner, and unit (organisationally working to Number 10 but physically situated in the Cabinet Office) and some efficiency and manpower work remained in the Management and Personnel Office (MPO). The Financial Management Initiative (FMI) was run as a joint Treasury–MPO operation. The principal impact on the cabinet secretary after 1981 was taking on the work of senior appointments to the civil service, and advising the prime minister on other public appointments, and on honours for the 'PM's list'.

At the time of the change in 1981, Armstrong had been keen to abolish the title 'Head of the Home Civil Service': he thought it would be sufficient for the cabinet secretary to take over the appointments task without the addition of the title. But he was persuaded of the case for not abolishing it and that there was a real role for someone to fill as head of the Home Civil Service. This role existed in part in relation to discipline matters concerning permanent and deputy secretaries, although no case arose in his time, in part because the Head of the Home Civil Service could provide a natural 'open door' through which other permanent secretaries could call in to discuss problems. His role as Head of the Home Civil Service was enhanced by the guidance he gave in February 1985 on the duties and responsibilities of civil servants. In its second refined version, published shortly before Armstrong's retirement, this in effect gave officials the right of appeal to the Head of the Home Civil Service on issues of conscience. These statements were remarkable for being the first by the Head of a Home Civil Service on the duties and responsibilities of staff since the headship of Edward Bridges (1945–56).

Subsequent changes came in the autumn of 1987, when the MPO was abolished. The office of the minister for the civil service remained in the CO, but some of the personnel work undertaken hitherto by the MPO went back into the Treasury. (2)

Abolition of the CPRS in July 1983

The demise of the CPRS, first established by Edward Heath in 1971 with Lord Rothschild at its head, has been much written about and need, therefore, be treated only briefly here (see Blackstone and Plowden, 1988). It is believed that its disbandment was a move which Armstrong did not particularly welcome, but that he accepted that there was not much to be said for retaining a body for which ministers no longer felt a need. It has been alleged that Armstrong argued for the retention of the CPRS (ibid., p.180). Overall it was a far less significant change to the work of the CO than the end of the CSD. When the CPRS was wound up, its scientific adviser, Robin Nicholson, was left behind in the CO, and a new science and technology secretariat was set up. Science and technology from about 1984 was the major area of expansion of the Cabinet Office's staff. The prime minister had for some time been wanting to give a clearer central focus to government policies and activities in relation to science and technology, and used the House of Lords Select Committee reports on the subject (under Lord Sherfield) and the subsequent government white papers on science, to provide the rallying cries (HMSO 1988). Subsequently the secretariat became even more active, especially under John Fairclough, since 1986 the head of the secretariat. Fairclough's quick impact owed much to his own personality and background: he was fundamentally a doer who came to Whitehall having been an executive in IBM (during 1983–6 he had been chairman of IBM's UK laboratories). Both Nicholson and Fairclough also benefited from a favourable climate in Whitehall, with Margaret Thatcher, reflecting no doubt her educational background, actively supporting their work. The secretariat helped raise the profile of scientific awareness at the centre of government in its effort to get to grips with major science issues and the distribution of resources.

The other main impact of the demise of the CPRS fell principally on the economic secretariat. Although the CO lacked the resources to undertake the investigation and research work of the CPRS, nevertheless after 1983 ministers looked to the CO (as head of a task force of officials from Whitehall departments) to take the lead in the production of *ad hoc* studies and analysis akin to those that hitherto had been produced by the CPRS. The economic secretariat bore the brunt of this new demand by dint of the fact that most of the studies commissioned fell within the economic sphere.

Secretariats

The work of the cabinet secretariat in 1979 was divided into four main secretariats: economic, home, overseas and defence, and European. Science and technology was added, as seen above, in 1983. There was also the intelligence assessment staff (IAS) which was inevitably more secretive and operated rather differently from the secretariats. Its work concerned a specific area and was only tangentially related to new policy and ongoing administration. Economic, home, and overseas and defence corresponded to the principal standing committees of cabinet. The economic secretariat was responsible for economic, industrial and energy policy. The home secretariat oversaw social policy, education, law and order and environment matters, and coordinated the government's legislative programme. The overseas and defence secretariat oversaw developments in the foreign and defence policy areas.

When the head of the intelligence assessment staff was Sir Antony Duff, he combined the tasks of chairman of the Joint Intelligence Committee (JIC) and assistance to cabinet secretary as coordinator of the security and intelligence services, MI5, MI6 and GCHQ, ensuring that their work was coordinated and information was supplied to those who required it. When he was succeeded as intelligence coordinator by Colin Figures, the two tasks were split; Figures retained the job of coordinator, and the task of chairman of the JIC passed to a deputy secretary (Clarke, 1988).

Each secretariat initially had a deputy secretary in charge (for example, the economic secretariat was headed successively by Peter le Cheminant, Peter Gregson, Brian Unwin and Richard Wilson). After a time, Armstrong decided to put the home secretariat in the hands of an under-secretary, who reported to him and (on certain matters) to the deputy secretary in charge of the economic secretariat. The change was a recognition of the fact that there was so much overlap between economic and 'home' areas (for example, local government finance) that it was a sensible rationalisation to combine the work of both secretariats.

The two 'proactive' secretariats were European, and science and technology. The other three secretariats were essentially 'reactive': they responded to outside pressures and did not as a rule initiate activities themselves. This distinction between 'reactive' and 'proactive' was itself a reflection of the structure of the policy networks in which the secretariats operated. The economic, home, and overseas and defence secretariats were working in areas with long-established and deep policy links within, and beyond, Whitehall. But the two 'proactive' secretariats, European (ES) and science and technology, did not operate to the same degree within a system of domestic policy linkages with the secretariats providing the focus. ES, created to provide a focus outside the Foreign and Commonwealth Office (FCO) to coordinate EC matters, was 'proactive' because of its relative independence (and, perhaps, comparative newness). Science and technology was 'proactive' because there was (and still is) only a loose policy community within the field of scientific research and its industrial application. (The author acknowledges his debt to Professor J.M. Lee for drawing his attention to this thesis.)

The European secretariat was a rather different body in other ways from the other main secretariats (Stack, 1983). On a trivial level, it was the only one whose existence was generally admitted: announcements of new heads were given to the press, and former heads' entries in *Who's Who* specify their task as 'head of the European secretariat'. The deputy secretary in charge always came from a home department with a strong European interest (for example, the Ministry of Agriculture, Fisheries and Food, the Department of Trade and Industry and the Treasury), as did the under-secretary below him. Of the two assistant secretaries, one always came from the FCO, the other from a home department. In view of the crucial importance of the FCO to the ES's work, it might appear odd that the FCO only had one of its own officials in at the third level. But the department of origin was not felt to be significant: what mattered was that the head of the secretariat carried weight with the FCO, and indeed with others in Whitehall, EC institutions and European governments. The unusually long length of service for deputies (over four years for Franklin and Williamson) also helped add to the standing of the secretariat's head. Hancock would himself have stayed longer had he not been promoted in 1983 to permanent secretary of the DES. The deputy secretary at the head of ES attended and briefed the prime minister personally for every European Council, and attended virtually every meeting of the Council of Ministers and cabinet when it discussed EC affairs.

The impulse for the ES's greater proactivity lay in its being expressly charged with responsibility for coordinating the government's policies and activities in relation to the EC across the board; hence it possessed greater authority for taking the initiative itself, rather than awaiting Whitehall departments to proffer instructions. The EC budget issue dominated the ES's work throughout the years 1979–84 and still played an important role thereafter.

After the Fontainebleau European Council in 1984, which saw a major settlement for Britain, the work of the ES began to develop rapidly on other issues, such as accession of Spain and Portugal, amendment of the Treaty of Rome (resulting in the Single European Act), the completion of the internal market and new areas of Community action such as environment and research. In the constant barrage of EC business, requiring frequent decision and cognisance of EC obligations, the ES was called on to evaluate the impact of various strategies on different departments, and of various departmental policies on overall government strategy in relation to Europe. Given that the government was not going to achieve its ends with EC members every time, the ES itself was often called on to advise and make judgements as to when to compromise and when to hold out. As a result the ES, often possessing an overview held by no other single Whitehall department, would itself be in a position to recommend strategies and policy decisions. The ES's work was thus different in kind, not just degree, from the work of other secretariats.

Cabinet Office Appointments and Staffing

Armstrong took pains to secure the very best deputy secretaries available in Whitehall, as Hunt had done before him. He leant heavily on them, and they were very much his own appointments. The meaning he might have attached to the words 'very best' had less to do with creative qualities than with impartiality, the ability to work very hard, to be able to command and hold the respect of officials in departments with which they were to be associated, and to have the ability to brief clearly and to summarise arguments impartially in a way that assisted and impressed committee chairs. Selections of under-secretaries would be discussed much more with others, principally with the heads of secretariats and with permanent secretaries in the departments from which they came. Assistant secretary and principal appointments were made even more at the suggestion of others. Efforts were made to achieve a balance of secondments from a range of Whitehall departments.

All officials in the cabinet secretariat (except the cabinet secretary) were on loan from other departments. Deputy secretaries (with the exception of those in charge of the European secretariat) stayed in the CO on average three years, under-secretaries and below for two years. The loan system and relatively brief duration was seen as a way of giving a wide number of promising officials experience at the centre. It also ensured a steady supply of appointees with fresh experience of the workings, personalities and problems of the departments from whence they came, which helped keep the CO fully in touch with, and in the confidence of, the rest of Whitehall. One of the features of the CO's organisational culture was the rapidity with which officials developed a personal loyalty to the CO after joining from their departments, for which they had often worked for a large number of years. No CO official during this period ever had to be called to order for promoting the interests of his or her department of origin, and departments in their turn very rarely complained about partisanship by officials once they were in the CO. Any temptation to promote the cause of an official's department of origin was more than countered by cultural and personal factors inclining him towards impartiality.

Armstrong never had a formal deputy, as Trend (1962–73) had done. Instead, on those occasions when a semi-formal 'deputy' was required, for example to sit on the right of the prime minister when Armstrong could not attend cabinet, he nominated his longest-serving deputy secretary. No single official, therefore, came at all close to rivalling him. Ministers were hard-pressed to name any CO official, other than Armstrong, who had made a particular impression upon them.

Ensuring that the CO was staffed to maintain the flow of work in peak periods (commonly June–July, and November–December) was a constant problem. Slack periods, conversely, as occurred principally in August and September, sapped morale. Armstrong encouraged flexibility, especially cross-overs between secretariats in either the seasonal peak or crisis periods: for example, during the Falklands war, in 1982, staff joined Overseas and Defence (OD) from another secretariat, and two non-CO staff were temporarily drafted in (from FCO and MOD). During the miners' strike, in 1984–5, the other main *ad hoc* crisis of the period, staff came over from other secretariats to join the economic secretariat, which shouldered the bulk of the extra work.

Cabinet Office Coordination and Planning

John Hunt (1973–9) held a regular meeting for senior cabinet secretariat staff each Friday. Armstrong had a regular meeting, usually each Thursday, to discuss cabinet and cabinet committee business for the following three weeks, and in great detail for the coming week. On the basis of this discussion, Armstrong would go to the prime minister and tell her what meetings to expect in the coming weeks, and what issues were likely to be coming up.

Armstrong inherited a system of trying to plan business six months ahead, the longest period it was deemed valuable to think ahead. His staff rang around departments to ascertain what topics would be coming up which would require discussion and coordination at the centre, so that there would be some semblance of logic and planning. The objective of the long-term look was to shape business ahead to avoid log-jams.

At these meetings Armstrong and the deputy secretaries would, in cases of doubt, and where the prime minister or other ministers had not made their own views known, decide which committee would take particular matters. Opportunities for discretion in practice were not large. In most cases it was considered a foregone conclusion to which committee business would go: subjects that fell in between committees were rare. Thatcher seldom challenged Armstrong's recommendations for the conduct of business: neither had Wilson or Callaghan queried Hunt's proposals, which were placed in the premier's weekend box following his own Friday meetings.

Cabinet Meetings

Opinions vary on whether full cabinet became less significant during the period. It is not relevant or necessary for this chapter to discuss in detail Thatcher's conduct of cabinet meetings (see Burch, 1988; James, Chapter 3 above; Jones, 1987b; Hennessy, 1986, pp.94–122). By increasing reliance on decision taking in formal committees and in informal meetings, Thatcher held cabinet meetings to one a week, although, as Jones (1987) has argued, a decline in frequency of cabinet meetings does not necessarily mean a downgrading of its importance. Thatcher's two immediate predecessors, Harold Wilson (1974–6) and Jim Callaghan (1976–9) summoned cabinet, on average, a little over once a week during the Whitehall year, with increased numbers during crises such as the IMF loan discussion (1976) or the 'winter of discontent' (1978–9) (Donoughue, 1988). The sea-change, from the pattern of having two full cabinets a week, as occurred for most of Trend's period as cabinet secretary, to only one cabinet, came in the early 1970s. The new demands of joining Europe, increased summitry responses and reactions, and recurring economic and industrial crises all put increasing strain on the centre. When Trend left the CO in the autumn of 1973, full cabinet was still the critical decision-making forum. By the time Hunt left in 1979, the principal standing committees had virtually replaced it as the principal axes through which decisions were made. Ministers confirmed that full cabinet under Thatcher was rarely a decision-taking body, but was instead a discussion forum. 'It is almost a confession of failure if a matter has to go to full cabinet for discussion – under Margaret Thatcher it seldom happens', said one cabinet minister. Another minister recalled few major decisions being taken in full cabinet in 1986, her last full year covered by this study: Westland, public expenditure and review bodies on pay being three prime examples.

Thatcher's preference was for taking decisions outside full cabinet in subordinate bodies over which she felt, rightly or wrongly, she had more control. She came to office in 1979 feeling, in part as the result of her experience as secretary of state at the DES (1970–74), that decisions taken by committee tended to be decided on the lowest common multiples rather than on more vigorous criteria. She also considered, again on the basis of her experience during the Heath government, that there was a danger that ministers could be distracted from departmental duties if required to sit on too many committees.

What function did full cabinet serve under Thatcher? Cabinet met at Number 10 on Thursdays, usually at 11 am. The premier sought to push through business as quickly as possible. Business was of two kinds: with and without papers. Meetings opened with the two standing items for which papers were not circulated. Parliamentary affairs for the following week came first. Before the cabinet, Thatcher chaired a half-hour (or so) meeting with the business managers of both Houses (that is, the leaders and chief whips) and the chief press secretary, Bernard Ingham, so she could be well briefed for the cabinet. At cabinet the item would be opened by the leader of the House giving a report on the forthcoming business of the House of Commons: the chief whip in the Commons would attend throughout cabinet meetings. If there were no particularly disturbing matters, Thatcher would try to keep discussion of this item to less than 10 minutes. She sometimes sought advice on how to handle PM's questions that afternoon in the House. The whole item could broaden out into a general discussion of policy, but she was generally reluctant to allow this to occur. The leader of the House might change the content of his announcement of the next week's business in the House following the discussion. Towards the end of the period under review, home affairs was added as a discrete item on the agenda after parliamentary affairs (hitherto discussions on home matters had often been slotted into discussions of parliamentary affairs). The new item provided a more formal opportunity for ministers in charge of domestic departments to raise current issues and problems.

Next came foreign affairs. Thatcher would ask the foreign secretary to make a report (approximately 10–20 minutes) which provided an overview of world developments of relevance to the

UK since the last meeting. Lord Carrington's (1979–82) reports were felt to be very entertaining, Geoffrey Howe's (1983 onwards) to be duller but thorough. When the foreign secretary finished, ministers would ask questions. It was the principal time in the week when cabinet ministers not directly concerned with foreign affairs would have the opportunity to discuss them. EC affairs arising were taken next: whoever had attended Community Council meetings, or had matters to raise, would be invited by Thatcher to speak.

The EC discussions brought to a close the first part of the meeting. What purpose did these talks serve? The discussion of parliamentary business allowed attenders to be briefed on what was coming up, to contribute and receive counsel on how to handle difficult business. The foreign affairs discussion served less obvious purposes, other than informing ministers: the full cabinet was not the forum where foreign policy decisions were taken. Several ex-ministers found difficulty in describing the purpose of the report and subsequent discussion. One should not, however, overlook the importance of these discussions of home and foreign affairs in giving practical meaning to the doctrine of collective responsibility. Attenders were provided with the opportunity to listen to and offer comments on the pressing issue of the day. Contrary to the statements of some, Thatcher positively invited contributions.

The second part of the meeting was devoted to *ad hoc* subjects on which papers were usually circulated in advance (normally not less than 48 hours beforehand). If there were financial implications of matters raised, the figures had to be agreed beforehand with the Treasury. The Treasury also possessed the right to demand a matter be raised in full cabinet, although in practice this occurred rarely. Typically one to four items would be on the agenda. Certain types of issues would be brought to cabinet's attention. Key economic and public spending questions would be discussed and decisions taken. In July of each year, the cabinet determined the overall level of public expenditure for the following three financial years. The decision, taken at one meeting only, was usually fairly straightforward, because most spending ministers reserved for a later stage their efforts to obtain their slice of whatever figures were chosen. Public expenditure discussions then took place in bilateral meetings between the chief secretary and spending ministers, the 'Star Chamber' (MISC 62) and/or the premier cleared up outstanding difficulties by October, and the result would be reported to cabinet. Cabinet would only rarely be brought in to help decide figures, as it did over the housing budget in 1984, when no agreement was forthcoming elsewhere. Thatcher generally disliked having detailed public expenditure decisions taken in full cabinet.

Crises, as over the future of Rhodesia, and issues of great political sensitivity, such as the civil service pay dispute in 1981, would be discussed in full cabinet. Committee chairs might seek ratification of decisions taken in their committees, but such ratifications were the exception, occurring when the decisions taken at subordinate level were considered of particular importance, the matter was highly sensitive, or it had been very controversial, with strong dissenting viewpoints. Under normal circumstances, cabinet ministers would hear about committee decisions via the minutes: their private offices would bring to their attention those decisions with a departmental or personal relevance. The bulk of this second part of cabinet was taken up by discussion of matters which could not be resolved in cabinet committee. Occasionally such matters could be quite trivial, as in Thatcher's first term when a longish discussion took place in cabinet on the siting of a law court at Reading, a matter over which she was in dispute with her law officers. A number of factors acted against too many of these decisions coming up from committees: committee chairs saw it as an admission of failure if they could not obtain decision within their committees. Thatcher herself made if plain that she wanted decisions taken lower down by the ministers in committee and that the group of 20 plus people in full cabinet made it not an appropriate forum for routine decision taking: ministers, moreover, would only be willing to bring a matter to full cabinet if they were fairly confident of winning, as defeat would be humiliating.

The Rationale of Cabinet Committees

If full cabinet had only a limited role in coordinating decisions in central government, attention must focus on subordinate bodies. Early in Thatcher's first administration the numbers of committees fell, especially the matching official committees, but by the end of her first term they were returning to former levels, as they had done earlier under Churchill, when he, too, on coming to power in 1951, had tried to reduce their number.

Cabinet committees were in several forms: the principal distinctions concern composition, whether they are peopled by ministers, officials or (very rarely in this period) a combination of the two; and whether they are standing or *ad hoc* (not to be confused with bilateral or multilateral *ad hoc* meetings with the prime minister and colleagues).

The four principal cabinet committees, the only standing committees whose existence was officially admitted, were Home and Social Affairs (H), Economic Affairs (EA), Overseas and Defence (OD) and Legislation (L). The first three were especially important. Meetings of H were considered by ministers to be more informal than EA, largely because the affable Whitelaw was in the chair, and he was considered to possess more of an open mind, and to be freer in his encouragement of discussion than Thatcher, who chaired EA and OD. Whitelaw's command also was in part due to the widely held belief among ministers that he knew Thatcher's mind and was very fully in her confidence. OD was chaired by Thatcher or, in her absence, by the foreign secretary. All primary and some secondary legislation would go to L, and it was the only one of the four to have officials on it in the form of parliamentary counsel. Queen's Speech and Legislation (QL) was chaired by Whitelaw and was responsible for advising cabinet on the substance and drafting of the Queen's speeches on the prorogation and opening of Parliament, and for recommending which bills could go into the next year's programme. A smaller committee than L, on QL sat the leaders and whips of both Houses. Ministers were especially keen to sit on EA or its principal subcommittees: if they did not, then they feared they might be considered to be not in the mainstream of political life. At times during this period, EA, which met at Number 10, became so large and unwieldy that the principal focus of action shifted to its subcommittees, for example on privatisation, as EA grew too large to take effective decisions itself.

Together, these four standing committees provided the critical nexus through which the major decisions of government were taken. Meetings were often highly rigid. Ministers in the know appreciated that, in trying to win the key arguments, timing, the support of the appropriate chair, the position of items on the agenda and prior lobbying of attenders were critical. Clever ministers cultivated the important relationships, which could include the chief CO civil servant responsible for the committee. Debate in the committees was often on legal matters: 'legal questions predominated', said one cabinet minister.

Thatcher possessed the surest of grasps over whom she appointed as chairs and selected to sit on which committees she considered key to her own priorities (the four standing committees, the principal subcommittees, and *ad hocs*). For committees she considered of secondary importance, she sought advice on chairs and membership from principal colleagues, especially Whitelaw. She leant heavily on Armstrong when it came to deciding which matters were to be decided in which committee, and which she would determine at any rate in the first instance, by discussion outside the formal committee structure.

Three of the four standing committees, H, EA, and OD, all made increasing use of subcommittees after 1979. The subcommittees varied considerably in authority, some being especially influential, such as E (PSP), the public sector policy subcommittee of EA (chaired by Nigel Lawson), or OD (SA), the South Atlantic sub-committee of OD, the so-called 'war cabinet' during the Falklands war, chaired by Thatcher. Cabinet ministers belonged to, on average, five committees and subcommittees and spent approximately six to eight hours a week sitting on them.

The *ad hoc* committees, the MISCs (GENs under Callaghan and MISCs under Wilson before him), had reached a total of about 200 by June 1987 since the beginning of Thatcher's premiership. Only about 10–15 MISCs, however, were active at any one time. The precise number is difficult to give because defunct MISCs were not formally terminated. As one CO official put it, 'old MISCs didn't die: they just faded away'. The rationale which explained why some tasks were given to subcommittees of standing committees and others to *ad hoc* committees was as follows: if a matter was considered essentially 'one-off' and transient, it was given to an *ad hoc* committee. The MISC committee which appeared the most glaring exception to this framework is the so-called 'Star Chamber' which might more logically have been, one might have supposed, a sub-committee of EA. However this apparent paradox is explained by the fact that the 'Star Chamber' was revived each year as a new MISC, and with an essentially different membership (only Whitelaw and the chief secretary of the day were fixed attenders. Other members consisted of non-departmental ministers and spending ministers whose figures had already been settled for the year). One witness suggested that its *ad hoc* status allowed Thatcher to exert greater influence over its activities and its chairman, Whitelaw, but this belief has little substance.

When there was a particularly sensitive issue, or one which gave rise to a good deal of controversy, Margaret Thatcher liked to have a multilateral (non-cabinet committee) meeting with small groups of ministers (sometimes accompanied by senior officials) to allow her to clarify her mind. It also allowed her to prepare a caucus ahead of full cabinet or cabinet committees. Another reason why she often favoured discussing business in non-cabinet committee meetings undoubtedly was a fear of leaking. She felt that cabinet committee minutes had a very wide circulation throughout White-hall, and although it was possible to restrict the circulation of minutes or parts of minutes of some committees, nevertheless she felt that meetings outside the cabinet committee system would be more secure.

A cabinet committee differed from any other Whitehall meeting in the following ways: it had a CO reference number; it was serviced by the cabinet secretariat; and the minutes were prepared in a certain form, for circulation by the CO. A multi- or bilateral meeting with the prime minister would usually have an official from the

CO in attendance, but Number 10 would take and circulate minutes in the form of a private secretary letter to the offices of the ministers present at the meeting. Another difference was that collective responsibility was not so formally engaged by meetings other than official cabinet committees. The niceties of the British constitution come into play here. It is now fairly well established that cabinet committees, whose membership is chosen, at least in theory, to be representative of the government as a whole, take decisions with the same binding force of collective responsibility on members of the entire government as decisions of full cabinet. The position is much less clear as to whether in practice the premier could take a decision with perhaps just one minister present and expect it to be generally accepted as binding on the entire government. Thatcher realised, like any incumbent at Number 10, that, the more ministers involved in decisions, the greater her clout in persuading sceptics of the legitimacy of the decision.

The vast bulk of decisions that required interdepartmental coordination, it should be noted, were never taken up by the CO. Matters were resolved on the telephone between officials, by letter, or by interdepartmental committees, often of just officials. One insider hazarded a guess that only 5 per cent of Whitehall interdepartmental coordination took place at the behest of the CO (with European Community matters the figure was far higher, as described above). In general the CO tended to become involved at a fairly high level. The CO certainly liked, though, to send an observer to the more important interdepartmental committees, so it could be kept informed of developments and have the information about what was going on in Whitehall which it regarded as all important.

Matters which were brought to cabinet committees or full cabinet were brought at the request of either the prime minister, individual ministers or the CO. The reasons for matters being brought into the centre were threefold: they were matters in which several departments were critically involved; they were of great intrinsic difficulty, even where only one department, or one department and the Treasury, was involved; or they were considered matters of great political sensitivity.

Opportunities for Official Influence: Agenda Preparation, Briefing, Minutes

If CO officials possessed scope for exercising their own views and asserting their own priorities, it would come in their roles as preparers of agenda, briefing chairmen, and drawing up minutes and circulating conclusions.

In particular, CO officials in secretariats (other than the European and science and technology) almost invariably found the agenda was drawn from two principal sources: either a ministerial committee wanting some matter to be looked at or a departmental minister asked for some topic to be discussed. The fact that agenda appeared in the three other secretariats to almost 'decide themselves' reflected the well-established policy network world in which they operated, as described above. Officials also built up the agenda by reading all the main correspondence and by seeing the papers of all relevant committees. Officials appeared to have executed this work in a way that was accepted as fair in Whitehall. The author was unable to find evidence of complaints by ministers between 1979 and 1987 about committee agenda being rigged by CO officials. Officials were responsible for circulating papers in advance of meetings: the aim was to do so at least 48 hours before meetings; there were complaints when the secretariats did not receive papers from ministers in time to circulate them that far in advance. Officials were also responsible for ensuring that the ministers who had an interest in matters being discussed attended the appropriate meetings: ministers strongly resented not being informed of meetings of interest to them and their departments.

Another main task was for officials to brief chairmen, usually in writing, before meetings. This function provided perhaps the greatest potential for influence. Briefs consisted of three aspects: technical advice on how to handle meetings, what papers to take in what order; where the line-up on positions and views was, and who was likely to support or oppose: finally, how the meeting might be concluded, what the chance was of getting a decision, what that decision might be, what action should be put in hand to give effect to the decisions, and what matters might be better to have decisions deferred. The concern of officials in this work appears to have been less to promote their own personally favoured courses than to ensure that the chairman had the information needed to handle the business most effectively. Officials had to rely very heavily on material submitted to the committee in identifying the options. Rarely did they have the opportunity to become 'experts' themselves.

On most items before cabinet, the cabinet secretary and at least one member (usually the deputy secretary) of the secretariat most directly responsible (for example the overseas and defence when a military matter was under discussion) would make a full record of the discussion in notebooks. From their notes, the officials would compile a draft minute to send to Armstrong's office later on the day of the meeting, 5 pm being the target time. (Some matters, as discussed above, would be minuted by Armstrong himself, if he felt it necessary that he do so.) Armstrong then collated and edited the drafts sent in by the secretariats, and produced a final copy of the cabinet's minutes. He would amend the drafts from his own notes which he made during the meetings, regardless of whether or not he was responsible for producing the first draft. His final record was never cleared with the prime minister or with the individual ministers concerned, contrary to the views of some. When completed, the minutes were sent off for reproduction and circulation. In the first instance, the minutes would be circulated to ministers in duplicated form, an unwritten CO rule being that full cabinet minutes should be circulated to all concerned in the first internal delivery of the next day following the meeting. After a period, minutes would be available in printed form on green paper. The cabinet secretary's own notes recorded during meetings, called the cabinet secretary's notebook, were counted as part of the public record, and will be preserved in the PRO (Public Record Office), where they could prove invaluable to historians as an almost verbatim guide to what was said in cabinet. However cabinet secretaries' notebooks are not being released under the 30-year rule, and historians will have to await the decision of the lord chancellor in the 1990s to hear whether the policy of exclusion will be continued. In contrast to the cabinet secretaries, the notebooks of the secretariats, containing notes made by them during meetings from which their draft minutes had been prepared, are all destroyed. All those concerned for historical accuracy may legitimately wonder why.

Minutes of committees would be prepared in a similar way to those of full cabinet, with the secretariat most directly responsible drawing them up. The standard technique was for a senior and a junior member of the secretariat to attend the committee and subsequently to produce independent drafts from their own notes. These drafts would then be exchanged, and differences checked with accounts in the notebooks. The senior official would then approve a single correct account for circulation around Whitehall the following day, although there was less need for committee minutes to be in the first delivery.

The minutes always concluded with a remit for action, preceded by the arguments. Some chairs would spell out exactly what they wanted to go in the minutes in their summing up: at other times it was left to the secretariat to sum up. But this did not give officials much scope for independent thought. It was a point of some pride among the officials concerned that the minutes were accepted by attenders as a fair and accurate record of what passed in cabinet.

When chairs or other ministers (very rarely) challenged the minutes, the officials' notebook would be brought out to verify the record given. Neither the chairs nor committee members would have taken kindly to any attempt by a secretariat official to put his own gloss on proceedings. Indeed the CO's acceptability in Whitehall was dependent upon the minutes being regarded as fair and unpartisan.

Cabinet Secretary's Power

Armstrong, as cabinet secretary, has been described as the most powerful civil servant of his day. No single postwar official, apart from Edward Bridges in 1945–6, and Norman Brook after Bridges' retirement in 1956, had as many responsibilities (for the fullest and most illuminating portrait of Armstrong, see Hennessy, 1987a).

In what did this power consist? The main manifestation of Armstrong's 'power' lay in his recommendations for appointment of top officials in Whitehall, when he had the ability to make or break careers. Although Margaret Thatcher exercised more personal say over top appointments than her predecessors, as the report of the RIPA Working Group (1987) into top appointments concluded, this still left Armstrong considerable freedom. The importance of her influence over appointments can be exaggerated; to cite one example, it is incorrect to say that the appointment of Clive Whitmore to succeed Frank Cooper as PUS (permanent under-secretary) at MOD was at her own instigation (Whitmore had previously been very close to her as her principal private secretary since 1980). In the great majority of cases, the premier had neither the will nor the inclination to interfere with Armstrong's recommendations. Armstrong chaired SASC, on which sat senior permanent secretaries, but it only *advised* Armstrong on senior appointments. Thatcher did not receive advice from SASC but only from Armstrong, who was independent-minded on the subject.

This role of the Head of the Home Civil Service aside (the other tasks of the Head of the Home Civil Service's office were relatively insignificant) it would be more correct to ascribe Armstrong's authority in his capacity as cabinet secretary as 'influence'. Even this influence can be exaggerated. The potential would have been all the greater with a new, unenergetic or indecisive premier. Thatcher was none of these, and had learnt much of the job in her first few months when Hunt was still cabinet secretary. Armstrong's influence pales into insignificance when contrasted with Brook's under Churchill, especially in Churchill's last two years at Number

10 (April 1953–April 1955) when he was often ailing, and sub-sequently under Eden (1955–7), and Brook's potential for influ-ence, as historians are only beginning to uncover, was immense (see Gilbert, 1988).

Armstrong nevertheless had considerable potential for influ-ence: talking each day to the prime minister, sitting by her side in cabinet and committees, counselling her and other senior minis-ters as to policy options and on the timing and form in which decisions should be taken. Armstrong was also able to call on his considerable knowledge of the way the machine operated, gleaned from a career of working close to senior ministers, and especially as principal private secretary to the prime minister (1970–75). The task of cabinet secretary did not just revolve around cabinet and committees. For instance, economic summits involved Armstrong in total for some 21 days a year, and preparation for them was very much a task relating to him in his capacity as prime minister's personal representative (or 'Sherpa') rather than as head of the Cabinet Office, using the FCO and Treasury for support in the four preliminary meetings and at the annual summit itself.

Commonwealth summits, in contrast, occurred biannually, and were less demanding of his time. After the creation of the Com-monwealth secretariat in 1965, the cabinet secretary retained re-sponsibility for coordinating the preparation of briefing for the British delegation to the heads of governments meeting, which he always attended as the premier's principal official adviser. Trend, the cabinet secretary at the time of the 1965 change, made his Commonwealth responsibilities very much a priority, in large part because of personal sentiment (a feeling reflected in his sub-sequent chairmanship of the Royal Commonwealth Society). Hunt and Armstrong gave the Commonwealth less time, partly a reflec-tion of increased workload. Armstrong himself abandoned the practice of the cabinet secretary attending meetings for Common-wealth senior officials, held in the off-years (1980, 1982, 1984 and 1986) in between heads of governments' meetings. The reasons were twofold: *ad hoc* domestic issues arose to make his attendance difficult, and attenders from other Commonwealth countries tended to be the official heads of their foreign or external minis-tries. In his place, the PUS at the FCO attended.

The risk of tension between the FCO and CO which these and other tasks might have produced was reduced considerably by the mutual determination of Armstrong and the PUSs at the FCO to make the system work harmoniously. Armstrong made it a positive priority to work closely and amicably with the three PUSs at the FCO during his period, Michael Palliser, Anthony Acland and Patrick Wright. Such personal efforts do indeed appear to have defused whatever personal tensions may have existed between the two bodies, at least at the highest level.

Another task of the cabinet secretary, and one which again brought him into frequent contact with representatives of the FCO, was that of principal official adviser to the prime minister on matters of security and intelligence. This was a task to which Armstrong brought a particular personal interest and experience by virtue of his contact with these matters in previous appointments – as principal private secretary to the premier (1970–75) and permanent secretary at the Home Office (1975–9). A high degree of involvement was foisted on him by his tenure coinciding with the Blunt, Hollis and *Spycatcher* affairs. The Blunt issue hit him just 10 days into his period in office, when Andrew Boyle published his *Climate of Treason* speculating on the identity of the 'fourth man'.

What factors, then, motivated Armstrong in the advice he offered? On one level, he was clearly influenced by the fact that he was a man, of upper-middle-class, cultured background, wedded to certain ideas on the proper ordering of society. But in this he had much in common with most of his fellow permanent secretaries. It is fairly clear that he was passionately concerned to do his job efficiently, to ensure that the prime minister and other ministers had all the information relevant to the taking of decisions. He saw it as of primary importance to ensure the orderly conduct of government and to see that ministers were fully informed of all the implications of carrying out certain policies. He wanted to ensure that ministers would never round on him and say, 'Why didn't you tell us?'

Hunt was a more forceful character than Armstrong. In the five months he served with Thatcher, he acted as a tutor to her while she learnt. Armstrong was always more in the faithful servant mould, who provided a rescue kit for Thatcher when occasion demanded. His personal mark was seen in relatively few episodes: for instance, in the negotiations for the Anglo-Irish Accord which led to the Hillsborough Agreement of 1985 (for which he led the negotiating team), in the GCHQ deunionisation affair, in the issue of guidance about duties and responsibilities of civil servants, over the conduct of Westland (during which he was determined to protect the civil service) and in the *Spycatcher* episode. In assessing the influence of the cabinet secretary, it is necessary to bear in mind the very real restraint of the need for him to take heed of and respect the views of permanent secretaries, especially the most senior ones. One can be overimpressed by the 'geography of power'. In Armstrong's case, proximity did not necessarily mean power. One can also be overinfluenced by visibility. With his public appearances before the House of Commons Select Committee investigating Westland and during *Spycatcher*, Armstrong became a better known civil servant than perhaps any other since the war. But he was by no means the most powerful civil servant during 1979–87. Middleton, to name but one, had far more influence on the evolution of policy during the period.

Conclusion

The CO between 1979 and 1987 is likely to be judged by historians as one which underwent some internal structural change, but in many other ways it will be seen as an unexceptional period during which the machine operated along lines already established. The Cabinet Office was indeed less of a power house and an initiator of action than it had been under John Hunt (1973–9). Armstrong himself, by dint of the length of his service, his intimate association with the most remarkable postwar premier, his combined responsibilities and his personality, is likely to be judged as exceptional. Robert Wade-Gery, deputy secretary and head of the OD secretariat from 1979 to 1982, stands out for his role during the Falklands dispute, and for helping produce plans used later to break the miners' strike (Hennessy, 1986, pp.32–3). Only two others, Franklin and Williamson, both of ES, appear to have had much personal influence on the outcome of decisions.

With these exceptions, the remaining officials who worked in the office appear to have left little personal mark on the substance of decisions. For them, backing personal hobby horses was anathema. Imbued with a high sense of duty, an outlook positively enhanced by Armstrong, they saw themselves as the servants of the whole Cabinet. It might appear implausible to those who believe in the ubiquity of civil service power, but, for the great majority of CO officials in 1979–87, the rewards were knowing that they had done their work expeditiously, invited the right people to committee meetings, briefed the chairman correctly, ensured that papers were circulated in good time, that decisions were taken in the light of the fullest possible information available at the time, and that clear instructions following meetings were sent to the relevant people in Whitehall. One ex-cabinet minister said: 'I never thought [CO] officials had any influence at all. I was constantly surprised that such clever men were content to preoccupy themselves on such pedestrian tasks.' A retired senior permanent secretary opined in similar vein, 'throughout my years in the civil service, I always thought the importance of the Cabinet Office was greatly exaggerated'.

Editors' Notes

1. In May 1992, John Major published a full list of his standing ministe-
    rial committees and sub-committees, along with their membership.
    His list did *not* include either temporary committees (GEN) or the
    committees and their membership under previous prime ministers.
    Anthony Seldon's chapter remains, therefore, a key source on the
    period 1979–87 and his methods are central to describing the heart of
    the machine. For an account of cabinet committees post-1992, see
    Dunleavy, Chapter 13 below.
2. John Major created the Office of Public Service and Science (OPSS) as
    part of the Cabinet Office in May 1992. OPSS brought together the
    Office of the Minister for the Civil Service with the Office of Science
    and Technology formed by amalgamating the Science and Technol-
    ogy Secretariat in the Cabinet Office and the Science Branch of the
    Department of Education and Science, now the Department for Edu-
    cation. As well as the Efficiency Unit, it includes units on Executive
    Agencies, Citizen's Charter and Market Testing.

7

The Ethos of the Cabinet Office: A Comment on the Testimony of Officials

MICHAEL LEE

Anthony Seldon's description of the Cabinet Office in Chapter 6 conveys very accurately the formulations of those he has interviewed. But his methods fall short of providing a full explanation of the Cabinet Office's position in British government. As he points out, interviewers are at the mercy of informants who unselfconsciously project an official self-image. They need to find ways of decoding the information they are given. By taking a longer time scale than the first eight years of Margaret Thatcher's premiership it should be possible to find a way of interpreting the material collected.

The Cabinet Office, at what was called in 1945 'the centre of the machine', is now an institution with its own customs and practices. Its structure has been shaped in response to the difficulties of relating domestic and foreign policies and to the exigencies of dealing with different 'policy communities' in these domains. A satisfactory explanation of its position would have to follow the changing character of executive authority and the displacement of Parliament from the mainstream of policy formulation. The Treasury has always been the central department *par excellence*, and the evolution of its power and procedures owes a great deal to the supply of revenue to the Crown through Parliament. There is now a considerable literature about the Treasury's position. The Treasury has been 'demystified' because descriptions of its methods of work do not endanger any myths about government responsibility and autonomy. Descriptions of the Cabinet Office retain a certain tone of deference and mystique precisely because the forces which are shaping its procedures are less tangible. Does Seldon's treatment of the subject bring us close to seeing the place of the institution in our system of government?

The character of the evidence Seldon has collected provides a clue to a deeper understanding. All senior officials wish to be remembered for their procedural efficiency and to deny suggestions that they exercise personal influence. The principal actors at the 'centre of the machine' appear to hold roughly the same views about their roles and functions. All are eager to demonstrate the importance of negative statements: the Cabinet Office is not a locus for civil service power; individual civil servants do not exercise personal influence or assert their own policy priorities. Few officials leave a personal mark on the formulation of policy when they are working within the central nexus of relationships between ministers and civil servants. All actors wish to emphasise the fluidity of cabinet business. There are no fixed rules; there is no one way of conducting affairs or of coordinating policies. The whole apparatus is personalised and secret. Few individuals are able to acquire an overall view of the interlocking parts. What matters are hard work, good briefing material and skilful chairing, not personal glory.

This ethos of the secretariat proper has been built up over a long period of time. The Cabinet Office as an institution should be examined in the context of its history before 1979. There are three features which mark out its present structure in Seldon's description. First, the secretariat proper proceeds as a set of deputy secretary organisations, each handling a separate policy field. A high proportion of Seldon's information comes from accounts of each deputy secretary's responsibilities. Second, this functional specialisation aids the delegation of responsibility and the division of labour. Seldon explains how briefing and minute taking are broken up into specialist tasks. Third, the meetings of full cabinet have become a discussion forum. The majority of important decisions are taken below that level. The important matters come to *ad hoc* meetings with the prime minister in the chair, or to standing committees.

The ethos so accurately described has its own vocabulary, which Seldon's treatment reflects. First, he picks up the terminology of his informants in describing a set of deputy secretary responsibilities as either 'proactive' or 'reactive'. Second, he quotes his informants saying that in cabinet committees 'legal questions predominate'. And third, he repeats the quite remarkable statement that the agenda largely decides itself. This evidence of official thinking aids the preparation of an understanding of the structure. With a little probing underneath the official folklore the proper history of the institution might be found. What will it look like?

First, the establishment of deputy secretary sections in the office arose directly from the need to make strategic decisions in both overseas and domestic affairs, sometimes separately and sometimes in conjunction. Perhaps the beginnings of the reallocation of duties lie in the Central War Planning Staff, the unit run from 1955 to 1957 partly as an exercise in preparations for nuclear war. The sectionalisation of the Cabinet Office followed its acquisition from the chiefs of staff of the Joint Intelligence Committee in 1957, and was a response to official opinion in favour of pushing some subjects down from cabinet and bringing other subjects up. The creation of the defence and overseas committee and a separate secretariat in 1963 was tied to the construction of a new 'federal' ministry of defence. The setting up of a secretariat for economic affairs followed the creation of the Department of Economic Affairs as an alternative to the Treasury. The evolution of the new deputy secretary commands during the 1960s and early 1970s was accompanied by a debate about the value of large departments which could settle matters below cabinet level and about the need for a greater 'central capability' in analysis of options at the centre. The creation of the Civil Service Department in 1968 provided an opportunity to give the Cabinet Office its own vote in the supply estimates. It sprang forth as an institution in its own right, not under the general wing of the Treasury.

The consequences of these developments were apparent in the selection and posting of officials to serve in the Cabinet Office on secondment from their departments. Deputy secretaries could look for suitable candidates familiar with specific areas of policy. Each section of the secretariat concentrated on its own field of policy; there was much less cross-posting within the office. Indeed it became possible to provide a team of different specialists to take the minutes of different parts of the same meeting. There were teething troubles. Contemporaries talked of the 'Christmas tree function' of the office which provided a home for any specialist group or private office that could be hung on its many branches. But during this period the methods of work began automatically to follow the contacts of the policy worlds and the policy communities with which each section of the secretariat had to deal. Deputy secretaries talked about 'being more into policy' and of 'knowing what the line-up is'.

An important aspect of the changing character of the office was the availability of senior Cabinet Office officials to act as the chairmen of interdepartmental committees. Before the late 1960s the Treasury normally provided the 'central' chairs. Table 7.1 shows that the expansion of the office took place largely during the 1970s. Setting aside 40 from the armed services, 400 of the rank of principal and above were posted to the Cabinet Office during the

15 years, 1965–79. During the previous 20 years the corresponding figure was 167. A major component in this expansion was simply the decision in 1968 to develop a central assessments staff in the handling of intelligence, and the commitment in 1971 to create a Central Policy Review Staff. Each of these bodies recruited staff from outside the civil service.

But the most significant expansion to affect the ethos of the office was the assignment of officials to both the deputy secretary sections and the private offices or special task forces. Senior officials came, not simply to run the procedures of interdepartmental negotiation at cabinet level, but also to be knowledgeable about particular policy communities. Another factor of some importance in this expansion was the sheer necessity of finding staff to handle secure communications.

Both Conservative and Labour governments used the device of recruiting private office staffs at the centre for ministers without portfolio or ministers with few departmental duties who were asked to undertake inquiries or negotiations. For example, Geoffrey Rippon as Chancellor of the Duchy of Lancaster in 1971 took charge of Britain's negotiations to enter the European Common Market; Edward Short as Lord President in 1974 was made responsible for a Constitution Unit dealing with legislation for the devolution of authority to Scotland and Wales. The EEC private office led to the creation of a new deputy secretary section of the office after negotiations were successfully completed. The European secretariat acquired the largest number of recruits after 1971.

By 1976, there were just over 900 members of staff in all grades. By the late 1970s the number of officials serving in the secretariat proper seems to have settled at a figure between 650 and 700. This meant that there were 70 or so senior officials on secondment from departments, and that the office was in future conceived as a collection of five or six deputy secretary 'brigades' with seven to 10 under-secretaries and up to 20 assistant secretaries. It is a pity that Anthony Seldon does not give the statistics for the 1980s. If one sets on one side the staff of the minister for the civil service, it looks as if 650–700 remains the magnitude of the secretariat. The Supply Estimates for 1988 (HMSO 1987, p.19) refer to 694. The office now merits an establishments and finance officer of senior rank.

The fashionable vocabulary which labels secretariats either 'proactive' or 'reactive' reflects the now established convention that each deputy secretary brigade can develop its own style of communication according to the business on its agenda or according to its own development of subjects for discussion. The four main secretariats and the four standing committees of cabinet which are publicly acknowledged to exist are the expression of the institutionalisation developed in the period before Margaret Thatcher's administration. During the 1970s the home secretariat was called 'home and social affairs' (HSA). As Anthony Seldon shows, the fifth secretariat, on science and technology, was partly the product of the abolition of the Central Policy Review Staff in 1983. The history of developing special units at the centre or special private offices during the 1960s and 1970s shows that the institution was being built on the cultivation of opportunities to be 'proactive'.

Second, the delegation of responsibility and the division of labour was an extension of the expectation that different policies required different channels of communication. A significant development of the 1960s and 1970s was that each secretariat loosened the conventions governing the propriety of who should speak to whom and who should copy papers to whom. Communications with departments or Number 10 were not all channelled through the private office of the secretary of the cabinet. If Cabinet Office officials were seen around Whitehall to be part of a team in a particular field of policy, then telephone calls and letters could be appropriately addressed without following formal channels. Just as Sir Norman Brook's tenure of the office of cabinet secretary was marked by the 'consolidation' of practice in the form of 'notes of guidance', so Sir John Hunt's incumbency produced sets of instructions that took account of changing conventions. Brook codified the practice of the Second World War; Hunt gave expression to the impact of international affairs on domestic policies. A proper history of the institution ought to contain evidence of the changes made in instructions to staff, and of the extent to which these rules were bent. It would be valuable to know how far there have been significant revisions of handbooks, manuals of procedure and desk-training programmes. A good antidote to the testimony of officials is hard evidence that the new ethos has been expressed in day-to-day instructions.

The habit of speaking about 'the predominance of legal questions' reflects the extent to which each secretariat has become engaged in the process of finding time in the legislative programme for those points within its remit which need translation into law. The European secretariat has obviously a special place in the handling of legislation required under the European treaties. But the other parts of the office are increasingly engaged in finding methods of administrative action which avoid recourse to legislation. The functional specialisations open up more opportunities to monitor what departments are doing. The basic convention that the cabinet has no formal powers, but invites a minister to take action on its behalf, may be acquiring a new meaning.

TABLE 7.1 Postings to cabinet office from departments, five-yearly intervals: principals and above, officers in the armed forces noted separately (in brackets)

From	Posted to Econ. section before 1953	Secretariat proper				JIC after 1957	Total
		Defence section	Civil section	Private offices	Other assignments		
1. 1945–9							
Service depts		1 (8)					1 (8)
Overseas depts		4	4	1	2		11
Treasury	4		3				7
Other depts	3	3	11 (1)	2	3		22 (1)
Outside CS	10		3				13
	17	8 (8)	21 (1)	3	5		54 (9)
2. 1950–54							
Service depts		1 (10)					1 (10)
Overseas depts	1	3	2	1			7
Treasury		3	1				4
Other depts	5	3	14	2	1		25
Outside CS	1						1
	7	10 (10)	17	3	1		38 (10)
3. 1955–9							
Service depts		4		1		1 (10)	6 (10)
Overseas depts		2	1	1	3	1	8
Treasury		3	2	1	1		7
Other depts		5	8	1	1		15
Outside CS					1		1
		14	11	4	6	2 (10)	37 (10)
4. 1960–64							
Service depts		4 (2)	2	2	2 (2)	3 (8)	9 (12)
Overseas depts		5	2			4	13
Treasury			2				2
Other depts		1	10	2	2		15
Outside CS							15

TABLE 7.1 Continued

From	Def.	HSA	Econ.	Europe after 1971	Secretariat proper		CPRS after 1971	JIC and assessments after 1968	Total
					Private offices	Other assignments			
5. 1965–9									
MOD	4				4	4 (1)		6 (6)	18 (7)
FCO	5					5		12	22
Tr'y/CSD			5		2				7
Other depts	1	7	12		8	5		1	34
	10	7	17		14	14 (1)		19 (6)	81 (7)
6. 1970–74									
MOD	6 (3)		2	1	4	4	2	11 (18)	30 (21)
FCO	5			4	3	2	3	9	26
Tr'y/CSD	1	1	3	4	3	1	4	5	22
Other depts	2	8	6	15	8	19	6	5	69
Outside						4	14		18
	14 (3)	9	11	24	18	30	29	30 (18)	165 (21)
7. 1975–9									
MOD	7 (3)		1	1		2	2	9 (9)	22 (12)
FCO	5			8		1	3	16	33
Tr'y/CSD		3	2	2	4	1	7	5	24
Other depts	1	13	10	14	2	15	5		60
Outside							14	1	15
	13 (3)	16	13	25	6	19	31	31 (9)	154 (12)

Note: Figures for Treasury and Treasury/CSD after 1968 include also Customs & Excise, Inland Revenue, and Bank of England. Information officers and scientific officers have *not* been included.

The Cabinet Office plays a fairly direct part in the government's management of parliamentary business. Prime ministers used to act as leaders of the House of Commons and to conduct the leadership functions through their own private offices. Since 1961, the leader of the House has normally been a holder of one of the non-departmental portfolios attached to the centre. An under-secretary in the Cabinet Office has spent a large proportion of his time preparing briefs for whichever minister was leader.

Third, the limitation of formal business at full cabinet level is a continuation of the recognition that the prime minister's office is now dominated by foreign policy issues and by the special demands made by the international community on the head of government. Many of the proposals to create a prime minister's department during the 1970s sprang from a general awareness that the pres-sures on the head of government had multiplied, particularly through the increasing recourse to 'summit meetings'. Since the meeting of world leaders at Rambouillet in 1973 there has been a notable increase in Cabinet Office briefings of prime ministers on international affairs. This work far surpasses the arrangements made by the cabinet secretary before 1965 for the meetings of prime ministers in the Commonwealth. Sir Kenneth Berrill, the retiring director of the Central Policy Review Staff, told a university audience in 1980 that there was a case for 'more strength at the centre' because there were ineluctable forces at work moulding and expanding the role of the prime minister in all the major parliamentary democracies of the Western world. The prime min-ister's need for a system of secure communication to other govern-ments or British representatives around the world places the Cabinet Office in a special position. Decisions can be taken rapidly and in appropriate ways by *ad hoc* meetings and briefings. It is not surprising that cabinet is considered a forum for discussion. It is more suitable as a vehicle for airing general points at issue than as a body for collective decision making.

The idea that the agenda 'sets itself', to which Anthony Seldon refers, is a typical by-product of this environment. The agenda 'sets itself' in the sense that each specialist secretariat acts as the centre of a network of policy discussions across departments and between outside groups. Events in the world outside may well change the terms of the discussion.

There is still quite a long way to go before the Cabinet Office as an institution can be widely understood in a manner comparable with the literature on the Treasury. Anthony Seldon's emphasis on the question of Sir Robert Armstrong's personal influence diverts attention from the more difficult question: have recent develop-ments created a system at the 'centre of the machine' which is more than different aspects of the persona of the cabinet secretary? The 'proactive' elements and the delegation to deputy secretaries suggest that an institution is taking shape that goes beyond the traditional tensions between a cabinet secretary's service to all ministers collectively and his role as chief of staff to the prime minister.

The fact that ministers and officials are now prepared to be interviewed about the *arcana imperii* is itself evidence of change. It seems less important to insist on the fiction that some operations cannot be mentioned in the public domain. Anthony Seldon refers to the Joint Intelligence Committee and to the coordination of the security services. He has capitalised on the widespread disclosure of the names of cabinet committees, the use of subcommittees and of MISCs (*ad hoc* committees) as well as the 'multilateral meeting'. The setting of his chapter is the accepted belief, given widespread publicity by his colleague, Peter Hennessy, that Thatcher has reduced the significance of full meetings of cabinet, convened fewer meetings and kept a stricter surveillance over the use of cabinet committees.

The debate has moved beyond the issue which was voiced in the 1970s of whether to recognise the evolution of the Cabinet Office into a 'prime minister's department'. Seldon shows how Thatcher ran Number 10 and the Cabinet Office in tandem without any need for redesignation. Nothing has happened to transform a basic proposition of British government: a strong prime minister does not need a prime minister's department, while a weak prime minister who may need one lacks the power to create it.

The tasks performed at the centre by the secretariat proper may still seem fairly mechanical in nature. Sir Ivor Jennings, in *Cabinet Government* (1936), described them as the circulation of memoranda and other documents, the compilations of agendas, the summons to meetings, minute taking and archive preservation. Seldon quotes the surprise expressed that 'such clever men were content to preoccupy themselves with such pedestrian tasks'. Yet the institution of the Cabinet Office is clearly more than these routines. The latter should be considered in the context of the processes of consultation. Placing Seldon's account of 1979–87 in the context of pre-1979 developments brings home the importance of looking beneath the formulations that are common currency among the principal witnesses. Their particular interest in what is written or said in public should be but the beginning of developing a wider understanding. The task of putting interview material with documentary evidence may not yet be a practical possibility. But there may now be sufficient indications of how the Cabinet Office ethos has been formed for an adequate history to be prepared. The important questions to ask are just emerging.

8

Ministerial Responsibility and the Theory of the British State

ALAN BEATTIE

Britain lacks both a 'written constitution' and a codified system of public law, two features which are usually held to be essential for any coherent conception of 'the state' (Dyson, 1980, ch. 7). Despite this alleged handicap, the British do have a conception of the state. They invented one through the dominant concept of ministerial responsibility, which shaped the whole way in which government expanded between the 1870s and the 1920s. Long-lived attitudes towards the 'ministerial' state and ministerial responsibility which developed at this time continue to determine the arguments of those who defend the constitutional *status quo* in the 1990s, and of those calling for radical reforms in the system of government.

To understand the role played by ministerial responsibility, I first briefly review the way that modern British government developed in its formative period (1870–1930), which seemed to give priority to unifying and coordinating institutions (such as the cabinet) over forces for fragmentation (such as departmentalism in Whitehall). The second section shows that the subsequent development of an extended state began to undermine the idea of a unified state under ministerial control. Achieving unity and accountability through ministerial control survived as a normative aspiration through to the present day in two forms.

The more prominent version is the 'Whig' theory discussed in the third section, which stresses the need for political control to be paramount and for government to be held responsible for state actions. The 'Whig' view has encountered increasing problems in explaining and justifying British constitutional arrangements in the modern era. A less well-studied but equally influential 'Peelite' theory discussed in the fourth section takes a different stance: ministerial responsibility is justified primarily as a means of *limiting* democratic controls so as to ensure that the business of government can be efficiently carried forward. The conclusions briefly point to the relevance of the Peelite strand for the current controversy about constitutional reform.

The Rise of the Ministerial State

During its critical period of modernisation in the late nineteenth century, the coherence of British central government was seen to rest on a series of institutions and practices which were canonised in the Haldane report of 1918 (Haldane, 1918; Greenleaf, 1983, ch. 4; Thane, 1990). The logic and history of the perception was simple: Parliament was sovereign; the Commons now dominated Parliament; therefore the Commons should, through the responsibility of ministers, monopolise political control (Craig, 1990, pp.12–29). British government was a unity, founded on a ministerial/parliamentary monopoly of policy making.

Greatly reinforced by the impact of the First World War, these developments strengthened the 'coordinating' or 'horizontal' aspects of British government (Chester and Willson, 1968, ch. 1). Many previously independent agencies (such as boards) were incorporated into Whitehall departments, thus extending the scope of ministerial power (Willson, 1955). Civil service reforms replaced patronage recruitment with competitive examination, and organised recruitment into horizontal grades rather than vertical departments (Parris, 1969, chs 3–5). Treasury control entailed standardisation across departments and the establishment of an ultimate arbiter in the increasingly important area of public expenditure (Beer, 1956). Collective cabinet (as opposed to individual/departmental) identity and responsibility was promoted through the cabinet secretariat and an enhanced prime ministerial role (Mackintosh, 1962, pt V). The emergence of a national, programmatic, two-party system provided security of parliamentary tenure for governments in between elections, and transformed general elections from the choice of local constituency representatives into the choice of a national ministerial team. At the same time, party programmes welded disparate policies into a coherent whole (Lowell, 1920, ch. 24). The line between the public arena and the private (market or voluntary) arena was assumed to be clear. Governing was a matter of general rules rather than the promotion of particular ends (Attiyah, 1979, pp.388–97). And the machinery of government could be exhaustively defined by reference to the activities of ministers and civil servants. Organised interests, if noticed at all, were part of civil society rather than of government. The police, the judiciary and the armed forces were rendered 'apolitical' (and thus not part of 'the state') through the substitution of the rule of law and self-controlling professional ethics for ministerial responsibility (Vile, 1967, pp.339–40).

The desire to preserve the values of a state based on ministerial responsibility conditioned reactions to suggested institutional reforms. For example, the belief that 'administration' could be clearly and usefully distinguished from 'politics' had important implications. Civil servants must be insulated from all 'political' pressures except those of ministers: the Commons must have no direct supervision of bureaucratic activities (Finer, 1937). Civil service reform was seen as a matter of 'efficiency'. Whether this meant increased technical expertise, better managerial skills or 'value for money' mattered less than the fact that these changes had no 'political' implications. Policies were (or should be) determined by ministers; the bureaucratic role was one of efficient implementation (Sisson, 1976, pp.255–9). Moreover the preservation of executive unity ruled out segmental or discriminatory departmental reform. Any changes must be applicable to the whole of the public service in a standardised fashion, and none must undermine Treasury control (Hennessy, 1990, pp.689–729).

Executive unity also required vigilant efforts to avoid any 'official' or public ventilation of disagreements between ministers, lest departmentalism and internal inconsistencies in public policy be encouraged. This stance in turn implied that a collective ministerial monopoly of initiative and control was the only way in which parliamentary control of governmental power could be made effective and rational (Marshall and Moodie, 1967, pp.100–104). Ministers and public policy must be judged as a team and as a whole. Changing the system would risk transferring control from Parliament to the courts, undermining the two-party system and turning public policy making into an irrational battle between sectional interests (Lowell, 1920, ch. 23). The aim was to ensure that 'government' appeared to the individual subject as a unitary and consistent set of practices, rather than as a plurality of specialised individual tasks (Cranston, 1985, pp.269–72). As long as 'the government' was ultimately controlled by ministers, the location of responsibility was clear and parliamentary control thus assured (McKenzie, 1964, pp.635–49).

The preservation of a particular kind of party system was crucial to the ministerial state (Beattie, 1970). Programmatic parties provided the coherent basis for governmental policies and ministerial collegiality. Without them, public policy (like party 'platforms' in the USA) would become a pluralistic chaos of inconsistent proposals. For the system to be dominated by only *two* cohesive parties (whether or not they were ideologically based) was necessary for maintaining the clear location of responsibility, providing reasonable ministerial security of tenure, sustaining cabinet unity, permitting longer-term policy planning and allowing the aggregation of parliamentary and public opinion into genuinely national majorities (Bassett, 1964, pp.17–18).

The Growth of the Extended State

Of course this portrait of the ministerial state and its rationales is highly simplified. And even in its more refined forms such an 'ideal type' account was never the only strand in British constitutional thinking. However this strong justification helps to explain why academic studies and political developments in the period since 1945 have caused so many problems and controversies. Modern trends have revealed British government as pluralistic in its workings and deeply ambiguous about the functional and constitutional boundaries between political institutions. Postwar developments have presented doctrinal and practical problems because they differ so sharply from the normative and empirical assumptions of the theory of the ministerial state.

However the central problems of the ministerial state were present from its beginnings. The conception of the British state as a unified hierarchy governed by the principle of ministerial control emerged concurrently with the rise of 'collectivism' in party politics and public life, an approach which is inherently difficult to reconcile with any unitary, procedure-based view of the constitution and of the British state. Collectivism involves the expansion of public power into areas previously governed by market or voluntary arrangements. It entails the employment of public power to regulate or promote specific social and economic objectives, which in turn requires the exercise of executive discretion (Greenleaf, 1983, ch. 1). The institutional consequences are a commonplace of modern political analysis and they include the expansion of bureaucracy; the redistribution of power away from legislatures and ministers towards bureaucrats, electorates and organised interests; and the incorporation of interest and groups other than ministers and civil servants into the implementation of public policy ('corporatism'). The modern literature of British politics is largely the story of how these general trends have reverberated in the specific areas of the cabinet, the civil service, individual ministerial responsibility, the public/private divide, and the party system (Greenleaf, 1987, chs 3–4, 7).

The conventional view of the cabinet until the 1930s was that it was the body which had inherited the executive role of the monarch. The cabinet's collegiate character and its ultimate supremacy within the executive were unquestioned, reflecting the triumph of representative government and the ministerial state (Jennings, 1936, pp.338–40). There was little need to analyse how the cabinet actually worked. However John Mackintosh's seminal work represented a switch of attention away from the presumption of egalitarian ministerial collegiality and supremacy towards recognising the variety of institutions which shared or usurped the cabinet's monopoly of policy making and power (Mackintosh, 1962). He argued that the cabinet's central role was diluted by the independent role of cabinet committees and the bureaucratic institutions of the cabinet secretariat and interdepartmental committees. Within the cabinet, inegalitarian hierarchies were discerned in the existence of inner cabinets and the unique role of the prime minister. The hypnotic power of 'the media' drove ministers to use 'the Lobby' and 'off-the-record' briefings to evade the requirements of cabinet confidentiality (Rush, 1984; Dunleavy and Rhodes, 1990; Harris, 1990, ch. 8; and Rhodes, Chapter 1 above).

The defence of executive unity and coherence against the evidence of pluralism and internal cabinet diversity took one of two forms. One response was to accept that prime ministerial domination had indeed replaced collegiate cabinet government, but to argue that this development had established a 'presidential' system which had become a new source of executive unity, however baleful in its effects (Crossman, 1963, pp.51–7). A second argument was that the prime ministerial role was special only because it involved overall management and coordination rather than the exercise of policy power over individual departments. The delegation of aspects of cabinet business to its committees or to external bodies was also an efficient way of preserving collegiality, by preventing the cabinet from being overwhelmed by a mass of relatively unimportant detail (Jones, 1985a, 1990).

From the standpoint of the theory of the ministerial state, these defences involved either implausibilities or concessions. The first response fails to explain how one individual (the prime minister) could exercise so much control within the extended state. Crossman, for example, found no difficulty in arguing both that the sheer size and power of the bureaucracy in any one government department made it impossible to exercise individual ministerial control *and* that the prime minister exercised dictatorial power over all departments (Crossman, 1968, pp.47–9). A more persuasive version of the argument – that prime ministerial domination is 'segmental' or selective rather than comprehensive – (Rhodes, Chapter 1 above, pp.22–4) leaves open the questions of whether such prime ministerial intervention is arbitrary and of how (if at all) the areas not selected for prime ministerial control are in fact supervised and coordinated. The second response (claiming that collegial control still operates) concedes that cabinet delegation (or abdication) of scrutiny and control over large areas of executive action does create a 'responsibility gap', of the kind familiar to students of the relations between departmental ministers and their civil servants. 'Realism' dictates that we recognise that there are limits to the scope of collective control, while the normative power of the doctrine of ultimate cabinet responsibility prohibits changes (such as external legal controls) designed to 'fill the gap'. The problem is particularly acute in the collective responsibility or cabinet sphere because the doctrine that cabinet proceedings are confidential itself conceals the information necessary to assess the real scope of cabinet control.

Postwar studies of the civil service also questioned the assumption that it is subordinated to collective and individual ministerial control. Insofar as the extended scope of government enhanced bureaucratic power, ministerial control was undermined. 'The paradox of civil service reform' (Carpenter, 1952) was that the replacement of patronage by merit as a criterion of civil service recruitment in the period after 1870 reduced the scope for effective political control. The role of the Treasury could plausibly be represented, not as the embodiment of the 'horizontal'–coordinating function essential in a coherent state, but as the mere imposition of one departmental view upon others (Heclo and Wildavsky, 1981, ch. 3). Moreover the standardising ethos represented by the classic form of Treasury control was undermined by alternative methods of bureaucratic recruitment. Increased prime ministerial interest in senior appointments, recruitment from outside orthodox Civil Service Commission channels, and a new emphasis on interchange between the worlds of civil service and business, all combined to inject further subversive evidence of significant departmentalism, eroding the 'unitarian' view of the civil service (Hennessy, 1990, pp.373–6).

The recognition of departmental autonomies revealed further problems. First, it highlighted the tension or contradiction involved in the requirement of *both* collective/cabinet supremacy and individual ministerial primacy inside their departments, which implies that the bureaucracy faces a dilemma of divided loyalties. They are expected to be loyal both to the decisions of their individual departmental minister and to the potentially conflicting decisions of the cabinet (Greaves, 1947, ch. 6).

Second, to the extent that departments are free from 'horizontal'–collective control, this might enhance the power of civil servants rather than ministers. After the Crichel Down episode in 1954, ministers formulated new, 'more realistic', versions of the doctrine of individual ministerial responsibility. These emphasised the limitations on what ministers could be expected to know about the actions of their civil servants, and therefore reduced the extent to which ministers should be held culpable for their actions (Marshall and Moodie, 1967, pp.71–2). A 'responsibility gap' was thus created. Individual ministerial responsibility was now 'realistically' circumscribed in scope. But the 'unrealistic' version – that ministers are responsible in every sense for everything (Morrison, 1954. p.323) – was still available to exclude proposals to introduce external controls on civil servants whose actions fell outside the ambit of ministerial culpability (Robinson, 1987, pp.62–8).

Third, the new emphasis on departmental autonomies revealed conflicts within, as well as between, departments. 'The departmental interest' might be seen differently by various bureaucratic elements, reinforcing the impression of a diminished public service ethos and identity. To the controversial and threatened status of Treasury control was added the complex internal politics of individual departments (Gray and Jenkins, 1985, pp.73–80).

The concern with departmental autonomies also revealed particularly clearly the consequences of extended government action and 'collectivist' approaches for any rigid conception of the public/private divide. The perceived unity of British central government rested (and rests) upon the idea of ministerial responsibility: the role of ministers and (subordinate) civil servants is crucial. Even if the realities of departmental autonomy force a switch of emphasis from collective to individual ministerial responsibility, the logic survives. What these governmental actors do must easily be distinguishable in functional terms. An identifiable boundary between the 'public' (governmental) and 'private' (market and voluntary) spheres, and a traceable connection between ministerial decision and eventual public policy outcomes, is required.

But the phenomenon of corporatism undermines the plausibility of these assumptions. Under corporatism, policy and implementation are shared or bargained between public officials (ministers and civil servants) and actors whose status might seem to be 'private' – or at least unofficial – such as business leaders and trade unionists. Moreover theorists of corporatism often emphasise, not the formal/legal status of decision makers, but their real effects. Thus the decisions of (say) the City of London and multinational corporations may have greater 'public' ramifications than those of (say) the minister for sport. From the governmental point of view, corporatist relationships are necessarily department-specific or agency-specific: their workings depend upon the policy area involved and on the characteristics of the specific groups which are incorporated. Thus corporatism obscures the distinction between public and private roles, fragments policy making into a universe of discrete areas and makes it impossible clearly to calculate the precise causal contribution of ministers to policy outcomes (Birkinshaw *et al.*, 1990, pp.29–38; Lewis, 1990).

The extent of corporatism in Britain is disputed (Williamson, 1989, ch. 3), but it is only one example of the way in which extended state activity has made it difficult to calculate who influences outcomes. Civil servants necessarily participate in policy making in a way which cannot be captured by simple models of ultimate subordination to ministers. And the implementation of ministerial projects relies, not merely upon the cooperation of civil servants, but also upon a universe of other bodies and influences, including quasi-governmental agencies, public corporations, local authorities, organised interests, the European Community, the international economy, parliamentary and party responses, and the cooperation of ministerial colleagues. There are thus many relevant 'public' actors, ambiguities about what is to count as public power, and a pluralistic and shifting constellation of influences and constraints. The central importance (and even the identification) of the specific ministerial role becomes problematic (Rose, 1987, ch. 8).

Turning to the British party system, the idea of two cohesive and ideologically distinct competitors underwrites the idea that British central government is a coherent entity. Parties were assumed to be important because public policy should be the product of ideologically consistent party pressures (Rose, 1974, chs. 15–16) and/or because party discipline is the necessary basis of ministerial power and cabinet unity (Jennings, 1963, pp.328–31). However the mythological and historical coherence for government formerly provided by the party system is now dissolving. The contribution of party ideology to the formation of public policy is disputed (Rose, 1980b; Gamble and Walkland, 1984) and parliamentary cohesion is now more difficult to maintain (Norton, 1981, pp.200–230; Shaw, 1988). The relaxation of party rigidity underlies and is reinforced by the enhanced status of Commons select committees since 1979, raising the possibility of cross-party pressures (Drewry, 1989, ch. 21). Outside parliament, the emergence of multiparty voting (and hence of an 'unreliable' electorate) has undermined the authority and dominance of the two major parties, making 'hung parliaments' more likely and increasing the pressure for electoral reform (Bogdanor, 1981). There are signs that one consequence of the decline of traditional two-party politics has been an increased role for lobbyists, a move towards the pluralistic and fragmented policy making so feared by proponents of the ministerial state (Beer, 1982, ch. 1; Miller, 1990).

These developments have been not only widely recognised, but also widely welcomed: the two-party system has lost much of its former legitimacy (Beattie, 1975). Insofar as party ideology remains important, it is now more often seen as a baleful source of long-term conflict, policy failure and destabilisation than as a source of high principles or effective government (Finer, 1980, pp.203–24). Party cohesion is increasingly seen as the enemy of rational public debate and effective parliamentary control of the executive. Advocacy of electoral reform, multi-party parliaments, coalition governments and generally increased public participation in policy making all reflect the extent to which current views of representative government recognise the ministerial state as the problem rather than the solution.

The 'Whig' View of Ministerial Responsibility

So far in this chapter I have set out but not labelled the predominant doctrines about ministerial responsibility and the ministerial state. However there is no single view on these matters, no consensus which is shared by all protagonists. Instead the predominant view is only one of two well-worked-out and quite complex accounts of the way British government at the centre works, one of which I explore in this section, and the other in the next.

Choosing a descriptive label for the conventional wisdom about ministerial responsibility is difficult. Describing it as the 'Whig' view is justified because the doctrine originated with the high point of Whig influence in British politics, the 1832 Reform Act. Before then parliamentary sovereignty, conferring unrivalled and unlimited legal power on the 'trio' of King, Lords and Commons, had been established for over a century. But from the 1830s onwards, 'Parliament' was increasingly defined as the Commons alone, and the 'Whig' view of the state, enshrined in Bagehot's classic *The English Constitution* (1867), relegated the monarch to a merely symbolic role: 'the executive' now meant ministers alone.

Ministerial actions should reflect the wishes of the Commons in this account. If it was impossible or undesirable for the Commons to take policy initiatives itself (with ministers merely carrying out its orders) then the various mechanisms of ministerial responsibility would ensure that any discretionary decision making by ministers would be clearly limited and ultimately exercised in accordance with the will of the House. Ministers had no basis for their authority except the Commons. In the Whig doctrine, ministers should be given a monopoly of governing power because this arrangement was the only means by which public power could be made responsive, representative and participatory. Any public power not exercised by elected politicians, or not under their ultimate control, would be unresponsive, unrepresentative and therefore irresponsible (Vile, 1967, pp.220–23).

The Whig view was controversial in the nineteenth century because there were those who argued another rationale for ministerial responsibility, the 'Peelite' doctrine that government needed to be *insulated* from representative influences if it was to be effective, a view I discuss at length in the next section. Then, as now, there were also voices critical of ministerial responsibility because it cut across the concept of 'the rule of law,' a position set out in Dicey's influential *Law of the Constitution* (Dicey, 1915, pt II). Here the point of defining, scrutinising and controlling public power was not to further responsiveness, representativeness and participation. Rather the aim was to establish *predictability* in the exercise of power and to limit the scope of political decisions. Only if government was subject to clear, legal rules would men be free to pursue their private interests within a stable social context (Oakeshott, 1962). The rule of law view of responsibility did not provide a basis for 'the ministerial state', for its concern was not with whether public power was exercised by ministers, nor with whether there were opportunities for participation in public policy making. What mattered was that any source of public power should be subject to the *legal* test of rule of law criteria, employed by the courts. Indeed ministerial power, and responsiveness and participation in general, could lead to precisely those unpredictable, vague and constantly changing definitions of governmental scope which were incompatible with the certainties of the rule of law (Hayek, 1963, chs 7 and 16).

As the 'Whig' idea of ministerial responsibility has evolved, those most committed to it, and to the ministerial monopoly of public power, have been predictably hostile to the rule of law doctrine (Harlow and Rawlings, 1984, pp.1–21). They may concede that some public institutions, such as the judiciary, the police and the armed forces, should be excluded from the ambit of full and direct ministerial control. But even here the 'Whig' view relies on the unlimited scope of parliamentary sovereignty to ensure that these special, autonomous institutions play a subordinate, 'non-political' role: the 'big' questions should remain in the hands of a representative, responsive, participatory politics (Griffith, 1979). Nor is it surprising that the rule of law doctrine has been rejected as either a description or a justification of the modern British state. It is incompatible with the kind of expanded role for discretionary public power which has been a central aspect of British government since the late nineteenth century (Raz, 1983, pp.226–9).

Nonetheless, partly in response to 'rule of law' criticisms, the 'Whig' doctrine of ministerial responsibility was expanded to answer four key questions. In what sense are ministers responsible? For what are they responsible? To whom are they responsible? What constitutional values are served by the doctrine? (See Marshall and Moodie, 1967, ch. 4.) The first question – the definition of responsibility – has three main answers in the 'Whig' view. Ministers may be deemed responsible because, first, they possess *authorial power*, the responsibility that arises from an author's causal ability to produce (or avoid) specific consequences. Thus ministers are responsible for a policy outcome if they took (or were free not to take) the decision which resulted in the relevant outcome. Second, they are *accountable*. Ministers are obliged to give reasons, justifications and information about decisions. Third, they may be *culpable* or appropriately assigned blame: ministers are culpable for certain actions in the sense that they may be dismissed, criticised and sued. The fourth possible meaning of acting responsibly is that ministers behave correctly, acting with rectitude. Since the *rationale* of the 'Whig' doctrine is to force ministers to make policy responsive to public opinion, it follows that making ministers act with rectitude is either irrelevant or potentially dangerous.

The empirical validity of the distinctions between authorial power, accountability and culpability has been challenged. A wholly sceptical view of the empirical applicability of the 'Whig' version of ministerial responsibility would argue that, since ministers lack authorial power, and since accountability and culpability are either difficult or impossible to assign and to enforce, the 'Whig' doctrine should simply be jettisoned as irrelevant (Ridley, 1988).

However doctrines of ministerial responsibility have a normative as well as an empirical content: they specify what ought to be the case – as well as or instead of what is the case. So we need to examine the claims of the 'Whig' version of responsibility as a normative doctrine – including the idea that, insofar as actual political developments have diverged from the constitutional aims of 'Whig' doctrine, the real political world should be reformed to conform with 'Whig' moral aspirations. However, if a set of moral/

constitutional principles is either ambiguous or internally inconsistent, then it cannot serve as a useful guide to practical reform.
The 'Whig' doctrine of ministerial responsibility exhibits these
ambiguities and internal inconsistencies.

The concept of *authorial power* masks the fact that ministers play
two potentially incompatible roles simultaneously, as heads of individual departments and as members of the (cabinet-determined)
collective team, and that this is a 'zero-sum' relationship. The
question, 'who is the author of what?' is further blurred by the
absence of any convincing doctrine about the boundaries between
individual and collective ministerial rights: for example, the distinction between 'administration' and 'policy' will not work. One
aspect of the problem of authorial demarcation has important
implications for the concepts of *accountability* and *culpability*.
Cabinet confidentiality requires that the process leading up to
collective decisions is kept secret: ministers have an obligation
to explain and defend only the final, published, collective decisions (Marshall, 1984, pp.55–60). But the confidentiality rule in
itself denies Parliament (and everyone else) the information
necessary to identify the relative contributions of individual ministerial actors. Conversely it is inevitable (as in the Westland affair)
that any effective enquiry into controversial aspects of individual
departmental decision making will trespass onto the 'forbidden'
area of cabinet discussions (Hennessy, 1989). Without information, neither individual nor collective ministerial accountability
and culpability can rationally be distinguished or enforced. Hence
the possibility of invoking collective responsibility to shield individual ministers from the consequences of their errors (and vice
versa) does not arise simply from ministerial survival strategies
(Finer, 1989). It is based on the incoherence of the 'Whig'
doctrine itself.

Even without these internal problems, the concept of *authorial
power* potentially clashes with other aspects of 'Whig' doctrine.
Accountability and *culpability*, we have seen, require information
about the way power is being exercised. As the institutions
devoted to acquiring information (such as select committees, the
Ombudsman and so on) become more effective, two important
risks are run. First, there is no obvious way of preventing such
inquisition from developing into participation in decision making,
thus undermining the ministerial monopoly of authorial power
(Regan, 1986, pp.429–34). It is at this point that the potential
incompatibility between the 'Whig' aim of ministerial responsiveness to representative opinion on the one hand, and the location
of authorial power in ministers on the other, is most starkly
revealed:

a minister could not fairly be expected to defend policies in Parliament and 'carry the can' for errors of judgement and the like if he had not himself been responsible for formulating and implementing those policies . . . constitutional doctrine tends to minimise popular participation and produce an oligarchic, élitist, and authoritarian style of government. (Oliver, 1989, pp.116–19)

Second, it is inevitable that effective scrutiny of subordinates such as civil servants or the heads of devolved Next Steps agencies will reveal the existence of a universe of actions not directly known to or controllable *a priori* by the minister. At 'worst', recognition of the degree of discretion in the hands of subordinates will lead to efforts to enforce accountability and culpability directly upon them. Such a development simultaneously further undermines ministerial power, presents subordinates with the dilemma of divided loyalties (to the minister and to the inquisitor) and erodes the rationales of culpability mechanisms: parliament has no (formal) sanctions against civil servants (Robinson, 1987, pp.62–8).

It is sometimes wrongly assumed that the question of how decision-making rights (who should do what) should be allocated between ministers and others would be rendered irrelevant if full information about the decision-making process was available and if the process was opened up to wider public participation (Hanson, 1961, pp.215–18; Harden and Lewis, 1986, p.292). Sole reliance upon the notions of representation, responsiveness and participation is a weakness of the 'Whig' view of responsibility: but (however desirable in themselves) information and responsiveness are insufficient. The problem of allocation is parasitic upon the fundamental issue of how the purposes of any given public body are to be defined. In some cases (such as the nationalised industries until the 1980s, and *Next Steps* agencies currently) such questions are highly controversial. They will remain, whatever information and participation arrangements prevail; and so, therefore, will the question of allocation (Baldwin, 1988). Such allocation problems appear in all pluralistic political systems, and no constitutional rules, however unambiguous, are proof against evasion. But the normative grip of the doctrine of ministerial responsibility in Britain presents special difficulties. Neither 'privatisation' nor 'hiving off' need of themselves change public expectations. If ministers continue to be blamed by Parliament and the electorate for what happens in these areas, then the result is either an irrational system of culpability allocation or a standing invitation to ministers to 'interfere' in subordinate agencies' affairs in arbitrary ways.

The set of bodies *to whom* ministers may be deemed responsible extends far beyond Parliament and the courts. In the absence of any agreed doctrine ranking the competing rights of these bodies, jurisdictional disputes are inevitable. There is no consensus on the respective rights of select committees versus the floor of the Commons, or of electors versus Parliament. 'Off the record' briefings to the Lobby and the media in general may impinge on the 'Question Time' rights of the Commons, and the respective roles of judges and politicians in reviewing and controlling executive action are hotly disputed. It is not even clear that the Commons still possesses the ultimate sanction of removing ministers:

> If the constitution depends on usage and precedent, then it is now *unconstitutional* for MPs to frustrate the wishes of the electorate by voting so as to defeat their own party in Parliament. (Crick, 1968, p.17; emphasis in the original)

The 'Whig' doctrine of ministerial responsibility is thus neither clear nor consistent in its answers to questions about who is responsible to whom, in what sense, and for what. It is not merely that political practice fails to conform to the doctrine: the deeper problem is that the doctrine is to a significant degree *logically* inoperable. There are two competing ways of responding to these empirical and analytical problems.

A primary response of those committed to the 'Whig' view is to urge the restoration of full ministerial authorial power. The aim here is to make real the 'Whig' ambition of locating power in the hands of responsive politicians rather than in those of non-elected bureaucrats and judges (Jones, 1987b, pp.87–91). However the restoration of ministerial omnipotence faces considerable problems. To be practical it seems to require a radical departure from 'collectivist' politics. Clarifying (by reducing) the scope of ministerial authorial power requires the transfer of tasks out of the public sector and into the market or voluntary sectors – 'privatisation'. Even leaving aside the question of how far privatisation commands general agreement, a formal relinquishing of public powers does not guarantee the absence of *de facto* ministerial influence (through financial and other controls). In addition privatisation still requires a regulatory framework through which responsibility allocation and control problems will reappear (Veljanovski, 1987, ch. 7). And while a reassertion of ministerial control might solve the *accountability* problem (ministers would *answer questions* on everything), ambiguities and inconsistencies would remain in the concepts of culpability, in ideas about to whom ministerial responsibility is owed, and in the collective and individual versions of authorial power itself.

The 'Peelite' View of Ministerial Responsibility

The other main justification of a ministerial state is as long-lived as the Whig doctrine, and just as hard to label. It favours executive control to enhance stability (and not representation) and might be termed 'the Tory view', since its exponents are clustered more heavily in the Conservative party. But this approach also has exponents in other parties, among some Liberals in the nineteenth century and in Labour's ranks subsequently. It has also been described as 'the Whitehall view' because of its prevalence in the upper levels of the bureaucracy. Both its cross-party appeal and its resonance amongst senior civil servants make clear that the approach is not (simply) a party political one. Hence I have adopted the deliberately anachronistic 'Peelite' label, thereby also achieving a neat symmetry with the 'Whig' approach, and emphasising the Peelite view's similar historical origins in the early nineteenth-century debates.

The Peelite view regarded the decline of the monarch and the rise of popular claims as a serious threat rather than as a welcome opportunity for representative politics. The problem, as perceived for example by Sir Robert Peel and the Duke of Wellington in the 1830s and 1840s, was how to preserve social order in the face of popular pressures from below and in the absence of the power and status of monarchy. They did not share Whig confidence that the Commons would constitute a barrier against popular control. Indeed, even if it did, the Commons itself was both a dangerous source of pluralistic pressure and an unstable foundation for ministerial tenure. The Peelite aim was the preservation of executive power; and ministerial responsibility in that context enjoined that the executive, *rather than* Parliament and people, were responsible for public policy. The stress was on responsibility *for* rather than responsibility *to*. For the Whigs in the early nineteenth century, ministerial power was an insurance against the revival of monarchy; for Peelites it was a pragmatic means of preserving executive ascendancy (Hawkins, 1989, pp.652–4).

The preservation of order required that the executive possess a basis of authority partly independent of Parliament and the people. That independence might be based on the fact that ministers (and not the Commons) had inherited the powers of the royal prerogative, thus enabling them to employ common law as well as statutory authorisation (Amery, 1947, p.15). It might be based on the party system, provided that party was seen as a means of securing ministerial tenure rather than as a channel for the expression of 'representative' demands. It might even be based on 'appeals to the people', over the heads of the Commons, provided that the people could be persuaded to recognise the importance of preserving order. The persuasive process could employ the notion of rectitude – the duty of ministers to do the right thing rather than the popular thing – coupled with the representation of Conservative governments as the embodiment of national character, traditions and religion (Marsh, 1978, chs 4 and 5).

A necessary condition of 'doing the right thing' is that ministers are free to do so, and such freedom in turn required that ministers were not constrained by Whig mechanisms for enforcing responsiveness. From the Peelite point of view, both the rule of law doctrine advocated by Dicey and the participatory implications of Whig constitutionalism dangerously circumscribed the freedom of ministerial action, and such freedom was a condition of the preservation of governmental power (Clarke, 1947, p.47). Peelism is thus best described as a doctrine of 'strong', rather than either 'representative' or 'responsible' government.

Peelites are 'white marxists': government for them involves the suppression or management of social conflicts, and these functions require an unblushing recognition of the role of governmental coercion in the maintenance of social stability (Minogue, 1963, p.151). The instruments of government ('the state') include the police, judiciary and armed forces. These institutions are not regarded as neutral, 'non-political' bodies (reluctantly) rendered immune to representative pressures, as they are in the Whig view. Instead, for Peelites, insulation from political control is a possible condition of these institutions' effectiveness, but also something which can be overridden in the higher interests of social stability (Ewing and Gearty, 1990, ch. 7). The conflict between Whig and Peelite views on the role of coercion in politics has been historically played out in imperial and (most lastingly) Irish affairs (Curtis, 1963).

From both Whig and rule of law viewpoints, Peelite views imply arbitrary government: the concept of rectitude, the emphasis on order, and the suspicion of responsive/representative government appear as recipes for autocracy. But Peelite views are usually formulated in such a way as to suggest two qualifications to the necessity for 'strong government'. The first is that the role of 'representative' institutions such as Parliament and the electorate is diminished, not abolished. Although such institutions operate as 'long-stops' – as long-term constraints rather than immediate initiating bodies – they are sufficient to create a defensible balance between the requirements of order and the dangers of autocracy (Amery, 1947, ch. 1). The second constraint takes the form of an appeal to community. The dangers entailed in the exercise of public power have to be assessed (the argument goes) in the light of the character of those exercising such power (a question of trust) and on the assumption that Britain as a polity has a communal identity such that actions are constrained as much by traditions (mutual expectations) as by laws and other formal mechanisms of control (Scruton, 1980, pp.32–3). Autocracy is prevented not by bills of rights or by the doctrinal invocations of Whig theories. It is kept at bay by self-restraint (rectitude) on the part of those who exercise public power and by the force of the 'moral economy' subscribed to by those who are subject to that power (Attiyah and Summers, 1987, pp.32–4).

Peelite views served as a midwife to the rise of the ministerial state, not for the positive reason that 'ministers' were coterminous with 'the state' (as in the Whig approach), but for the negative reason that emphasising a central ministerial role was the most effective way of combating the pluralistic and destabilising claims of representative politics. But Whig and Peelite views could combine (from conflicting premises) to rationalise and justify the ministerial state. Both views involved the elevation of the ministerial role and entailed centralisation, the inclusion of hitherto autonomous institutions within the ambit of ministerial control, and approval of the unlimited scope which the doctrine of parliamentary sovereignty conferred on the Commons and on ministers.

Most currently discussed proposals for reforming Britain's constitution or political system are addressed almost solely to the problems and values of the Whig version of ministerial responsibility. They thus ignore the normative claims and practical influence of the Peelite view. The attraction of ministerial responsibility for many British political leaders is that it offers them maximum flexibility. They can avoid culpability by nominating areas over which they have temporarily or vaguely relinquished authorial responsibility; but they are free to intervene in these areas, when necessary, by invoking their ultimate sovereignty. Such flexibility turns the doctrine of ministerial responsibility into a weapon of 'strong government', to be employed against the participatory claims of Parliament and the electorate (Tant, 1990, pp.478–81).

To Peelites, the uncertainties arising from the above problems of responsibility allocation and definition are of minor interest, since the point of ministerial responsibility is to give the executive (including, but not solely, ministers) sufficient power to act with rectitude and effectively to preserve order. Who is responsible for what is a matter of (privately exercised) executive convenience. The coherence of the British state is seen to lie, not in any formal doctrine standardising the structure and duties of all public authorities, but in the executive, defined as that part of the constitution devoted to the maintenance of order and stability rather than to the reflection of the popular will (Amery, 1947, ch. 1; Sisson, 1959, p.151). The resulting variety and vagueness of public powers may offend proponents of both representative government and the rule of law, but may equally reflect a pragmatic recognition of the complexity and differentiation of the tasks of government (Marshall, 1980, p.31). The precise division of power within executive institutions is seen to matter less than its distribution between governmental and representative ('popular') elements. Ministers and civil servants, for example, have common purposes, encapsulated in the notion of Crown service. Thus, from the ministerial point of view, it is Parliament and the electorate (rather than the civil service) who are the adversaries.

In the Peelite view, Parliament and the electorate exercise only long-run, post mortem checks rather than short-run participatory rights (Maude and Szeremey, 1982). Such checks determine who governs, rather than initiating policy programmes indicating 'the will of the people'. Parliament and the electorate have sufficient information and power to discharge *these* limited functions; anything more (such as a Freedom of Information Act, electoral reform, or a bill of rights) would be inimical to strong and stable government (Butt, 1967, ch. 3). Moreover the doctrine of parliamentary sovereignty and the absence of clear and legally defined demarcations of power make the system a 'flexible' one in an additional sense. An opposition outraged by the way in which an incumbent government has used its 'strength' are themselves free to use the system for their own purposes when they win power. For example, nothing that Attlee's or Thatcher's governments did irreversibly changed 'the constitution': its Peelite structure and ethos remained intact and available for use by successors (Beattie, 1989, pp.140–43).

Peelite doctrine is influential beyond the confines of the 'Tory' party. It was a Labour prime minister who minuted that 'the underlying principle [is] that the method adopted by Ministers for discussion among themselves of questions of policy is essentially a domestic matter, and is no concern of Parliament or the public' (quoted in Hennessy, 1987b, p.52). It was a Labour prime minister, again, who judged that the rule of public cabinet unanimity did not apply 'in cases where I announce that it does not' (quoted in Marshall, 1984, p.57). An even more revealing episode is the manner in which Harold Wilson became prime minister in February

1974. Following an election in which no party won an overall
Commons majority, and after which the incumbent prime minister
(Edward Heath) failed to win sufficient Liberal support to stay in
office, a new prime minister had to be appointed. If Whig representative principles had applied, the formation of the new
government would have taken into account the distribution of
opinion in the Commons and/or the electorate: the Liberals had
won 19 per cent of the vote and a (pivotal) 14 seats, and the minor
parties together had won 25 per cent of the vote and 37 seats
(Bogdanor, 1983, pp.110–17). After his resignation, Heath was not
in contention for the premiership but Wilson was the leader of the
second largest party. So public and parliamentary opinion could
have been taken into account by (*inter alia*) commissioning Wilson
to discover whether he could command sufficient minor party
support to form a majority government, and leaving open the
circumstances in which another election might be called should
such negotiations fail to produce a government. What in fact happened was that Heath's resignation was followed by the Labour
leader's *immediate appointment* as prime minister. As the new incumbent in 10 Downing Street, Wilson was assured of full rights to call
an election should the Liberals (who had not been consulted)
refuse to support his government. The fear of an interruption in
the smooth, immediate, transfer of power between the two major
parties – of 'caretaker governments' and of protracted bargaining
which might involve the Commons as a whole (and even the electorate) – was decisive. To assume that the virtues of strong and
stable government are the only relevant considerations is to
conform to Peelite doctrine (Steed, 1983).

The Peelite view is seldom (at least in modern times) propounded with the articulation and openness of its Whig rival. It is
usually found informing governmental practices or, to the shame
of academics, in the perceptive fictional activities of Sir Humphrey
Appleby (Lynn and Jay, 1984) rather than academic treatises. Its
importance, and its role as an obstacle to reforms, does not stem
from any unique empirical view about how the system works – on
this there is a large measure of agreement between Whigs and
Peelites (Rees, 1977). It lies in the Peelite rejection of the constitutional *values* embedded in the Whig view. The survival of Peelism is
a striking refutation of the widespread view that, nowadays, everybody believes that the principles of democracy and the rule of law
are the only possible framework of political debate (Harden and
Lewis, 1986, ch. 9). Peelite opponents of political reform have
been neither ignorant nor uniquely self-interested. They are committed to the value of strong rather than representative (*or*, in its
usual version, responsible) government.

Conclusions

The ministerial state which emerged by the 1920s was underwritten by both Whig and Peelite constitutional doctrines. The rise of the extended, collectivist state revealed (rather than created) logical and descriptive shortcomings in the doctrine of ministerial responsibility. But these limitations were more damaging to the 'standard', Whig, doctrine of responsibility than to the Peelite alternative. 'Collectivist' purposes and the expansion of the state forced Whigs to choose between the fundamental value of representative government and the elevation of the ministerial role, and they have increasingly chosen the former (McAuslan and McEldowney, 1985). Since responsiveness was not the Peelites' basic constitutional value, their conception of the ministerial role was always more pragmatic: 'Whate'r is best administer'd is best.' Lack of ministerial responsiveness to popular opinion was therefore not a conclusive objection to ministerial monopolies of power. And if the preservation of executive strength in the face of representative pressures turned out to involve a dilution of the ministerial role (in favour of, say, civil servants or the market), that was doctrinally acceptable (Gamble, 1988, pp.145–54; Beer, 1965, ch. X).

The agenda for British constitutional reform since the 1970s has been set by Whigs disillusioned with the doctrine of ministerial responsibility but retaining their attachment to the values of representative government. Whig doctrine assumed that making the ministerial role central would minimise the role of non-elective institutions such as the monarch, the bureaucracy and organised interests. It assumed that the influence of the Commons would be maximised because ministers were members of that body, and depended for their existence on its support. These assumptions are now almost universally agreed to be implausible: if correspondence between public policy and public opinion is what is desired, then ministerial power is an obstacle rather than a means to its achievement. Ministers do not in fact generally exercise the degree of authorial power required by the Whig view. And even when they do it is not necessarily exercised in accordance with parliamentary and/or public opinion: ministerial control does not entail representative government (Prosser, 1986, p.220). Clear thinking about these issues would be much enhanced if the distinction between 'representative' and 'responsible' government were drawn more sharply than is usually the case. Ministerial responsibility means authorial power, or freedom to exercise rectitude, or an attempt (inspired by rule of law considerations) to define the boundaries of public power; and all of these imply that ministers govern and the remainder do not. Conversely representation nowadays involves political participation as a means of establishing the supremacy of the democratic will; and that which is decided by all cannot be the authorial or culpable responsibility of the few (Pennock, 1952). The standard formulation of Whig doctrine is simply incoherent:

> The notion of 'responsible government' implies *both* acceptance of responsibility for things done *and* 'responsiveness' to influence, persuasion and pressure for modifications of policy. (Turpin, 1989, p.56, emphases added)

Hence the choice, for Whigs, between ministerial responsibility and representative values. Peelites may or may not be ultimately vanquished, but they remain doctrinally unruffled: they chose governmental power from the beginning.

PART THREE

Empirical Studies

9

Reinterpreting the Westland Affair: Theories of the State and Core Executive Decision Making

PATRICK DUNLEAVY

In a seminal study published two decades ago, Graeme Allison developed three alternative interpretations of the Cuban missile crisis and in the process shed a great deal of light upon the operations of the American core executive in foreign policy areas (Allison, 1969, 1971). Yet the contrasting models he compared were all variants of a single theory of the state, pluralism. They differed from each other chiefly in using divergent methodologies and conceptions of the foreign policy process. More substantive differences about who controls the state apparatus and which social interests it serves were excluded from Allison's consideration. Most of Allison's critics additionally failed to distinguish between their disagreements with his historical narratives and dissent from the analytic models he discussed (Freedman, 1976; Cornford, 1974; Nossal, 1979; Krasner, 1972). Allison's later work ran together his 'governmental politics' and 'organisational process' models into a unified 'bureaucratic politics' account (Allison and Halperin, 1972; Halperin, 1974; Allison and Szanton, 1976). This complex model incorporates so many possible influences that it is indistinguishable from any applied pluralist account of decision making. As a result Allison's method of comparing alternative interpretations of a single historical episode has rarely been followed up (but see O'Leary, 1987a).

This chapter directly imitates Allison's method, but compares a set of applied models drawn from fundamentally divergent accounts of the way liberal democratic government operates. These 'theories of the state' play a central role in modern political science, bridging the gap between normatively based political thought and the eclectic forms of contemporary empirical analysis (Dunleavy, 1987b; Almond, 1988; Nordlinger, 1988; Lowi, 1988; Fabbrini, 1988). They analyse the interrelationship between governmental institutions broadly defined and civil society, in a way informed by particular moral values and conceptions of human nature, using distinctive methods and offering a consistent and integrated account of diverse political processes (Dunleavy and O'Leary, 1987; Alford and Friedland, 1985; Cox *et al.*, 1985; Self, 1985). Within every main theory of the state (pluralist, Marxist, the new right, and elite theory), a wide range of applied interpretations of core executive behaviour are possible. From each of these I have selected one view for analysis here – the governmental politics model; an instrumentalist Marxist account; a new right account in terms of 'policy entrepreneurs'; and the symbolic politics model.

The episode to which they are applied is the Westland affair of 1985–6, an acute political crisis which briefly threatened Margaret Thatcher's position as premier (Hennessy, 1987a; Madgwick, 1986). Westland is also an appropriate case study because it is one of the best documented recent UK policy crises involving the core executive. The first part of the chapter outlines a basic chronology of the Westland affair. The next four sections start by briefly setting out a theoretical position, which is then applied to the Westland affair. A brief conclusion examines the implications of the approach adopted here for future core executive research.

An Outline of the Westland Affair

The development of the Westland affair can be considered in five main stages.

Stage 1: Issue Recognition

Problems about Westland Helicopters Ltd. first reached ministers' agenda in a major way in mid-June 1985, several years after the small West Country firm began to run into difficulties. A takeover bid for Westland, 90 per cent of whose business consisted of building helicopters for the British armed forces, had been made by an entrepreneur, Alan Bristow. In the course of bid negotiations it became apparent that the firm's plight was much more acute than any outsiders had guessed, and Bristow's proposed takeover was publicly withdrawn. Westland had in fact become technically insolvent because of a venture into the civilian helicopter market, which proved disastrous when their W30 machine crashed in service in late 1983 and market demand subsequently collapsed. The company was left exposed because of a £90 million investment in production capacity and stocks for the unsaleable helicopters.

A ministerial meeting on 18 June chaired by the prime minister, Margaret Thatcher, was held to discuss the government's reactions to these events. Ministers refused to provide Westland with a short-term extra subsidy of around £100 million to bale the company out. Instead the Bank of England prevailed upon a specialist 'company doctor', Sir John Cuckney, to take over the chairmanship of Westland and safeguard the sizeable overdrafts extended to the company by two major clearing banks, National Westminster (£23 million) and Barclays (£17 million). Cuckney approached a number of possible sources about a capital injection, including British Aerospace (BAe), an Italian firm, Agusta, and the US helicopter giant, Sikorsky. Of these options only the Sikorsky deal developed or was actively pursued by Cuckney up to mid-September. Westland's dominant customer, the Ministry of Defence (MoD), was uncooperative. The Secretary of State, Michael Heseltine, initially suggested that Westland could go into receivership for all he cared, since B.Ae and the engineering firm GEC would probably then pick up the pieces.

However Westland's 'sponsoring department' within Whitehall, the Trade and Industry Department (DTI), broadly backed Sikorsky's long-term plan. The American proposals involved them injecting £30 million in cash and providing work for Westland; the banks converting their £40 million overdrafts into an equity stake; and public subsidies of various kinds amounting to nearly £200 million over several years. The attraction for Sikorsky (and its parent company, the huge multinational United Technologies) was that, if Westland built their successful 'Black Hawk' design, they might hope to break into, first, the British and, later, the European helicopter markets. The situation of apparent government unconcern about Westland's future changed radically at the end of September when Heseltine met the Sikorsky director in charge of negotiations and became alarmed that, if their association with Westland went ahead, his ministry would come under strong pressure to purchase large numbers of the American firm's helicopters. Heseltine came off the fence and began actively looking for an alternative 'European' solution to Westland's problems.

Stage 2: Emergence of Interdepartmental Conflict

Divisions between ministers became explicit at two meetings
in early October 1985 between Leon Brittan (who had just taken
over at Trade and Industry) and Heseltine. Both initially sought
to minimise the implications of Westland's crisis for their departmental budgets, which the DTI saw as best pursued by accepting
the Sikorsky plan. But at the second wider ministerial meeting
Heseltine secured his colleagues' acceptance for his plan to explore whether an alternative rescue package from European
corporations could be encouraged. Almost simultaneously the
French firm Aerospatiale and the German company MBB began
talks with Westland about intervening, and appointed a UK merchant bank to prepare a plan. Sikorsky countered by involving Fiat
as a 'European' co-partner (against Italian government policy) in
their capital reconstruction. Cuckney and the Westland board were
dismissive of any Franco-German alternative to Sikorsky–Fiat.

Yet, at the very end of November 1985, Heseltine rapidly put
together a meeting in his ministry of the National Armaments
Directors (NADs) of France, Germany and Italy, together with
representatives of Aerospatiale, MBB and Agusta. Concerned
about the threat of American penetration of the European helicopter market, the four defence ministries and the firms effectively
drew a ring-fence around the market, agreeing to standardise their
military purchasing on three helicopters to be built collaboratively
by the four companies. All these agreements depended upon a
European solution to Westland's problems being found. If the
Sikorsky rescue went ahead, Westland faced being squeezed out of
European markets, and even out of UK defence contracts if the
government were to accept the NADs agreement as binding.

Stage 3: Intense Political and Economic Conflict

The NADs agreement sparked an immediate row, with Westland
and Brittan immediately requesting that it should be withdrawn. At
two *ad hoc* ministerial meetings on 5 and 6 December, Heseltine
argued successfully for the agreement to be discussed at full
cabinet committee. By this time BAe and GEC had signed up as
members of the Euro-consortium, following urgings by Heseltine
and the Defence Ministry. At the Economic Affairs (EA) cabinet
committee on 9 December, Cuckney and his merchant banker
attended to explain Westland's position in person to ministers.
Heseltine asked for the NADs agreement to stand until the Euro-
consortium submitted its reconstruction plan to Westland at the

end of that week, at which point another cabinet committee meeting would discuss the issue. Apparently agreed by Thatcher, the follow-up meeting was subsequently scrubbed by Number 10 the next day. When the consortium plan did reach Westland it was unceremoniously rejected by Cuckney and the board, and Brittan announced that because of Westland's decision the government was not bound by the NADs agreement, which therefore lapsed.

Next week (mid-December 1985) Thatcher considered but abandoned an ultimatum to Heseltine publicly to toe the government's collective line that Westland's capital reconstruction should be made by the company's shareholders alone. Heseltine formally agreed to abide by this position at cabinet but reserved the right to answer 'queries' about the Euro-consortium's improved offer to Westland, which by 20 December was almost the same in its financial terms as the Sikorsky–Fiat plan. In practice, Heseltine campaigned actively for a European solution in Parliament and the media, his actions soon precipitating countervailing interventions by Brittan. By Christmas the dominant tactics of both the Thatcher–Brittan and Heseltine camps involved using the press to carry messages hostile to the opposing reconstruction plans, and so to influence Westland shareholders who were being circularised by their board about approving the Sikorsky–Fiat scheme.

In the New Year, Cuckney sought assurances from Thatcher that Westland would not be discriminated against by MoD or other European governments if the Sikorsky–Fiat plan went ahead. He received qualified support in a letter from the prime minister, considerably modified following pressure from the government's law officers whom Heseltine had prompted. Heseltine then got the Euro-consortium to send him questions which he could reply to, arguing that an Americanised Westland would have little future in European collaborative projects. In response, Thatcher and Brittan asked the government's chief law officer, Mayhew, to give a written view that Heseltine's letter was misleading in key particulars. (Mayhew was actually solicitor-general, the number two law officer, but at this stage he was deputising for his superior, the attorney-general, Havers, who was away ill.) Constitutionally, although the law officers are ministers, they are supposed to offer non-political professional advice, so that Mayhew's judgement was both influential and supposed to be kept highly confidential.

Mayhew despatched his reply to Thatcher on 6 January 1986. Selective extracts from his letter which spoke of 'material inaccuracies' in Heseltine's statement were immediately leaked to the Press Association by senior officials at the DTI and 10 Downing Street, following a prearranged plan, and with Brittan's express consent and Thatcher's implied approval. The leak provoked an immediate political storm hostile to Heseltine. In the next two days Brittan also leaned heavily on both GEC and BAe to reduce or withdraw their involvement in the Euro-consortium plan. In an impromptu meeting with BAe's managing director he apparently threatened to withhold DTI launch aid for the company's share of a civilian airline project (the European airbus) if it did not change tack. And at Cabinet on 9 January Thatcher demanded, without warning, that no minister should make any further statement or response on Westland without clearing it through the Cabinet Office first. Provoked beyond endurance, Heseltine stormed out of the meeting and immediately resigned.

Stage 4: Political Reverberations

Heseltine at once issued a full statement of his grounds for resig- nation and launched a very active media campaign against the Sikorsky–Fiat reconstruction and in favour of the European/ British consortium. In a Commons debate on 13 January, he raised a question about Brittan's attempt to lean on B.Ae. Brittan evaded a response to repeated questions by using hair-splitting language, and later that evening was forced to return to the Commons to apologise for misleading the House. Meanwhile the law officers demanded and secured from the prime minister an internal inquiry by the cabinet secretary into the leaking of Mayhew's letter – although not without some delay and a reported threat by the attorney-general, Havers (now back at work) to resign if the breach of confidentiality was not investigated. From 15 to 21 January the government's position seemed to be stabilising, as they easily survived a vote in the Commons and Brittan began to counterattack vigorously against Heseltine's media campaign.

However, on 22 January, Labour MPs named the DTI's press officer as the source of the Mayhew letter leak, at the same time as the cabinet secretary reported the results of his inquiry to Thatcher. On 23 January, in a weak Commons performance, Thatcher admitted that the leak was ministerially authorised by Brittan, but claimed that she had not been told about it (even though she later admitted being involved in the decision to ask Mayhew for a written judgement on Heseltine's statement). Despite her chief press officer at 10 Downing Street having been consulted in detail about how Mayhew's letter should be pub- licised, she also claimed that she had known nothing about how the leak took place until briefed by Armstrong the day before her speech. That evening a crowded meeting of the Conservative backbenchers' 1922 Committee indicated a surge of feeling that Brittan should resign, which he reluctantly did the following morning.

Over the following weekend Conservative MPs and journalists decided that this sacrificial victim was enough. They rallied round Thatcher to limit the severe political damage which the affair had caused. In a Commons debate on 27 January, the Labour leader, Neil Kinnock, made a general and 'political' opening speech, harassed by Tory interruptions, which denounced the prime minister but did not probe her role in the leaking of the Mayhew letter in any detail. Thatcher replied by reaffirming her ignorance of the leak, regretting the manner in which it had been carried out, and insisting that the whole affair would not deflect the government from its key policies. In the debate Heseltine agreed that the prime minister's speech should 'end the politics of the matter'. Thereafter, although controversy continued to surround inquests by two Commons select committees into the affair, the political crisis for the government and the Conservative party quickly receded.

Stage 5: Economic Reverberations

Heseltine's decision to resign removed the Euro-consortium's key promoter from the government's ranks and confirmed ministers' stance of leaving the Westland board to see through shareholders' acceptance of the Sikorsky–Fiat solution free from 'political' interference. As a result the press battle which had dominated the previous period gave way to two waves of share buying in Westland stocks, with 60 per cent of the company's shares being traded in the month from 9 January to 11 February in 5000 separate transactions, and often at prices well above those formally prevailing on the Stock Exchange. This phase was inaugurated on 9 January by Alan Bristow, the entrepreneur who had made but then withdrawn the 1985 takeover bid for Westland, who favoured the Euro-consortium plan. Next day, the multinational firm, Hanson Trust, which has close links to Conservative party leaders, began building up what eventually became a 15 per cent stake in Westland, by buying out an investment firm previously supporting the consortium plan. Hanson's packet of shares was cast for the Sikorsky–Fiat option. At this time British Aerospace and GEC also decided to downgrade their public role in presenting the consortium's case, reasoning that both their standing with government and their sales to the USA might be jeopardised by too close an association with an anti-Sikorsky position. A week's interregnum followed, during which the original Sikorsky–Fiat plan for a special capital reconstruction was put to the vote at a Westland shareholders' meeting on 17 January and failed to secure the 75 per cent majority needed.

Sikorsky–Fiat and the Euro-consortium then submitted revised capital reconstruction plans to be approved by a simple majority at a Westland shareholders' meeting on 12 February. Sikorsky began some buying of Westland shares, and its modest efforts in this respect were backed up in the next 10 days by mysterious interventions by individuals and companies with no apparent reason for getting involved. The new purchasers all bought just under 5 per cent of Westland shares (to preserve their anonymity) and at high prices, and their stakes were then used to back the Sikorsky plan. These purchasers included the Australian transport firm, TNT, owned by Rupert Murdoch, and nominee companies acting for firms and individuals in disparate locations such as Geneva, Montevideo and Panama. By the 12 February meeting, six nominee shareholders controlled over 20 per cent of Westland shares, and their votes helped to secure a Sikorsky–Fiat victory, with 68 per cent of the shares backing their reconstruction plan, to the Euro-consortium's 32 per cent.

The Governmental Politics Model

How can theories of the state illuminate the Westland affair? The governmental politics account views core executive decision making as a highly complex 'game', repeated over successive 'rounds' of multiple issues by a large group of different actors, each with their own distinct sets of interests (Allison, 1971, pp.144–80). Policy outputs result from the ways in which dozens of individuals play out their institutional and personal roles in the overall process, their skill in deploying arguments and resources, and their ability to make bargains and alliances with other players. There is no authoritative source of strategic direction; nowhere in the policy system are the varied objectives of diverse actors effectively integrated or prioritised.

> Most 'issues' . . . emerge piecemeal over time, one lump in one context, a second in another. Hundreds of issues compete for players' attention every day. Each player is forced to fix upon his issues for that day, deal with them on their own terms, and rush on to the next. Thus the character of emerging issues and the pace at which the game is played converge to yield government 'decisions' and 'actions' as collages. (Allison, 1971, p.145)

The policy process normally takes the form of a power struggle between basically instrumental actors. Individuals are motivated partly by diverse personal ambitions and commitments, and partly by role interests given by their agency positions ('where you stand depends on where you sit'). Most actors' behaviour is socialised, expressing not simple individual preferences but a complex of organisational, peer group and individual influences. In addition goal displacement processes characteristically convert instrumental bases for action into strongly developed convictions (ideologies) that advancing agency or personal interests will itself serve the national interest. Instrumental behaviour is also disguised and constrained by routing inputs to the decision process through specified 'action channels', which are relatively long-standing arrangements governing the procedures to be used for tackling an individual 'round' of an issue. Each action channel can normally only be operated by some players and at some particular points in the decision process. The set-up of action channels and the rules of the game confer advantages and disadvantages on participants, particularly since different actors see the same issues in different lights, only some of which may be capable of being explicitly considered in the decision process.

Despite the importance of action channels in structuring behaviour, the model stresses the openness and indeterminacy of much core executive decision making, especially under crisis conditions. The personalities of key actors, their judgement and individual standpoints, and the skill and timing of their decisional manoeuvres can all make a major difference in shaping policy outcomes. The conviction that many decisions could easily have been otherwise had different personnel been involved, or had a different sequencing of events occurred, of course accords closely with the ways in which most political practitioners themselves come to understand core executive operations.

This model offers a distinctive perspective on the Westland affair in three key respects. It draws a narrow boundary around the overtly 'political' realm. It stresses the diverse motivations of multiple political actors significantly involved in the affair. And it offers a sceptical/realist interpretation of people's behaviour, interpreting it as the responses of hasty actors reacting to immediate political stimuli.

Narrow Boundary

A pluralist view focuses in a restricted way on the most 'governmental' aspects of the Westland affair, arguing that only these events are relevant for analysing core executive behaviour. A major issue arose only after the signing of the NADs agreement provoked open interdepartmental conflict in early December 1985, which Heseltine took pains to make public. Initially the defence minister's campaign went no further than to breach the usual practices of ministerial solidarity, but by the end of the month Heseltine's activities were clearly beginning to call into question the more fundamental and constitutional conventions of 'collective responsibility'. His stance reflected a complex of personal ideological commitments, public interest judgements and ministerial power plays, which *The Economist* summarised as:

> a fight for a European approach to defence procurement, for more governmental involvemental in industry, for the rights of ministers to run their own departments with less back-seat driving from Downing Street, and, most of all, for the right of ministers to bring departmental policy issues to full cabinet. (4 January 1986, p.18)

The initial spiralling out of the issue into a major governmental crisis is explained by Brittan's willingness to play tough using a similarly unconventional rule book to Heseltine's tactics. Later Thatcher's uncharacteristic indecisiveness in bringing Heseltine back into line, combined with her apparent endorsement of a 'dirty tricks' campaign against him, fuelled the issue.

The governmental politics model would of course accept that there is empirical evidence of extensive networking between the business world and ministers over Westland, but would deny that political or governmental actors adopted the stances they did because of financial or economic pressures or linkages acting upon them. For a considerable period after the issue became public, ministers at both Defence and DTI were diffident about intervening, and concerned chiefly with limiting the consequences of a possible Westland failure for their broader budgets. As late as the end of September 1985, Heseltine minuted that no option except liquidation should be considered, while in mid-October 1985 the DTI formally encouraged the Westland board to seek a European rescue package. Thereafter what shaped ministerial protagonists' behaviour was almost completely the pattern of moves and countermoves within the central executive itself. Corporate linkages were at various points useful tactical resources which Heseltine, Brittan and Thatcher exploited to the full, but they did not shape their motivations in significant ways. The government's eventual position of letting Westland's shareholders decide between the two capital reconstruction proposals accurately reflected the sense of disengagement which characterised most cabinet members' views throughout the crisis.

Multiple Key Actors

A wide range of personnel and institutions were influential in determining the course and eventual outcome of the Westland affair. The rival groupings of Heseltine, MoD and the Euro-consortium, on the one hand, and Thatcher, Brittan–DTI and Westland–Sikorsky, on the other, were clearly the major protagonists in the issue, as the brief narrative of the affair given above demonstrates. But throughout its course their behaviour was extensively shaped by the interventions of non-aligned third forces. Within the core executive itself, Heseltine's independent campaign was so protracted and difficult for Thatcher to control precisely because it attracted a degree of conditional support from other ministers. At the meeting on 17 October 1985, Heseltine's criticisms of Sikorsky and his offer to put together a European rescue package attracted support from Norman Tebbit, the Conservative party chairman, and produced an instruction to the DTI to push Westland to develop a European alternative package. The meeting's endorsement provided Heseltine with the crucial space he needed to put together the NADs agreement by the end of November.

The forum initially chosen by Thatcher to scotch the NADs agreement was an *ad hoc* ministerial meeting (known as 'the club'), which included, besides Thatcher, Brittan and Heseltine, six less aligned or uninvolved ministers from major departments (Whitelaw, Howe, Tebbit, Lawson, McGregor and Biffen). Again Heseltine survived two meetings, on 5 and 6 December, because Tebbit and the foreign secretary, Geoffrey Howe, backed his demand that the NADs agreement should at least be discussed at the EA committee before being jettisoned. At the full committee three days later, almost the same cast of actors plus three extra ministers were not prepared to squash Heseltine's argument that the full Euro-consortium case should at least be put to the Westland board before the NADs agreement was scrapped. Their tolerance of Heseltine's position forced Thatcher to end discussions inconclusively and apparently to concede another EA committee meeting at the end of the week. Following Heseltine's resignation, the importance of non-aligned actors inside the core executive continued with the law officers adopting a markedly independent stance, and impelling the cabinet secretary in turn to go through the motions of impartially policing the behaviour of the prime minister's aides and one of her most loyal ministerial lieutenants. The cabinet as a whole also exerted some independent influence by pressuring Thatcher on 23 January into making the 'fullest possible' disclosure to the Commons about the results of the Mayhew letter leak inquiry.

Heseltine's resignation and the accompanying disclosures also involved non-aligned actors outside the core executive itself, especially in Parliament and the Conservative parliamentary party. The House of Commons demonstrated its independence on 13 January by forcing Brittan back to the Chamber late at night to apologise for his misleading responses that afternoon. The full-scale debate initiated by Labour two days later was also a testing occasion for Thatcher and Brittan, both of whom made ministerial statements and were visibly relieved to encounter little criticism or loss of support from backbench Conservatives. On 22 January the Commons became the focus of ministerial anxieties again when Labour backbenchers publicised the DTI press officer's role in leaking Mayhew's letter to the press, and the attorney-general's tactics in forcing an inquiry on Thatcher. From a pluralist perspective these events demonstrate Parliament's considerable influence as a control on core executive actions. They also directly triggered Thatcher's statement the following day. Conservative backbench reaction then made the sacrifice of Brittan's career virtually inevitable as a demonstration of parliamentary independence from the executive – a cathartic 'balancing of the books' for Heseltine – which thereafter allowed Tory MPs to swallow their doubts and anxieties and resume their customary loyalty to the prime minister. And even when the affair was resolved, two Commons select committee investigations enforced considerably more than normal disclosures by ministers and senior civil servants.

This record of involvement by non-aligned actors and institutions needs to be set in the more general context of a protracted media battle, in which both the Heseltine and Brittan–Thatcher camps claimed an almost equal number of coups and successes in getting their message across. Ministers, businessmen and other actors alike regarded mass media coverage as the barometer of which way the Westland battle was flowing. To some degree this special salience reflected the potential importance of the press in swaying the votes or stock market behaviour of the remaining Westland shareholders agnostic about the Sikorsky–Fiat and Euro-consortium capital reconstructions. But the generally critical stance of even rock-solid Conservative newspapers on the affair conforms to pluralist expectations of media independence.

Unplanned Actions

Exponents of the governmental politics approach would deny that the central actors in the Westland drama planned their moves much of the time. Allison's stress on the piecemeal emergence of issues in a climate of rushed decision making and imperfect information, and with many different matters competing for actors' attention, closely fits the Westland affair. Heseltine clearly knew what he was doing in promoting the NADs agreement, but his lame, delaying reactions thereafter to Brittan's and Westland's opposition revealed that he had scarcely thought through how to follow up the scheme once it was signed. Similarly Brittan's and Thatcher's key moves at later stages of the affair were often simply mistakes. When Brittan leaned heavily on the British Aerospace managing director to withdraw from the Euro-consortium he seems not to have anticipated the angry public reaction from the company which his intervention would cause. (Parenthetically and ironically it was exactly the same kind of behaviour which had earlier blotted Brittan's ministerial copybook as home secretary in 1985. Following a Thatcher statement to the US press deploring the 'oxygen of publicity' afforded to terrorists, Brittan crudely pressurised the BBC board of governors not to transmit an innocuous documentary about Northern Ireland which included interviews with Sinn Fein councillors. His action provoked a 24-hour strike by broadcasting journalists in protest at government censorship.) Similarly his disingenuous performance in the Commons on 13 January 1986 in refusing to admit the existence of a letter of protest from B.Ae was a spontaneous reaction to the immediate pressures of a Commons debate, as was the decision by Thatcher, sitting next to him in the Chamber, not to intervene to correct the misleading impression being created.

More surprisingly, neither Thatcher nor Brittan apparently anticipated any public outcry over the selective publication of details of the Mayhew letter when they set about securing the solicitor-general's written comments on Heseltine's pro-consortium pronouncement of 3 January. The implications of such a public breach of the government's previous hard line on prosecuting earlier unofficial leakers (such as Sarah Tisdall and Clive Ponting) never seem to have occurred to them. Brittan's lack of anticipation extended to giving direct ministerial sanction for the leak on the morning of 6 January, whereas Thatcher at least had some kind of 'cut-out', even though the leak was still directly authorised by her chief press officer at Number 10, Bernard Ingham.

The chain of unforeseen consequences continues with the 'leak inquiry' which Thatcher reluctantly conceded to the attorney-general to forestall resignations by the law officers. Her publicly avowed scrupulousness in not asking Ingham, Brittan or any other participant anything whatsoever about the leak of Mayhew's letter at any time between its publication and 22 January, when Armstrong communicated to her the results of his leak inquiry, might be interpreted in three ways. Perhaps her ability to stifle any curiosity about the incident reflected an extraordinarily prescient concern to preserve 'deniability' about her personal role in the whole incident. Alternatively it might reflect a complete failure to appreciate the public controversy which the leak occasioned, and the extent to which it raised a serious question about the continuation of her premiership – in a way which virtually no other behaviour in her term of office had so far done. The sudden switch of mood inside Number 10, from elation around about 20–21 January 1986, when Heseltine's post-resignation campaign seemed to be running into the sand, to sudden alarm on the day of Armstrong's report, seems to bear out this interpretation. Lastly, it might simply be explained as the pressure of other business competing for attention and leaving no time whatsoever for investigating what had gone wrong on this occasion.

By contrast to these events, Heseltine's impromptu resignation from the cabinet on 9 January was only partly unanticipated. The defence minister had no prior warning of Thatcher's *démarche* about clearing all statements on Westland with the Cabinet Office, and seems to have made up his mind on the spot. But the prime minister herself had carefully prepared the occasion. A previous letter to Heseltine requiring him to conform to ministerial solidarity conventions was drawn up by Thatcher, Cabinet Secretary Armstrong, Deputy Prime Minister Whitelaw and Chief Whip Wakeham in the course of a two and a half hour meeting on 18 December 1985. But it was promptly scrapped when Ingham arrived late at the meeting and advised against an ultimatum for fear that it would push Heseltine into resignation. The 9 January demand was more carefully phrased as an instruction to all cabinet ministers and was devised at a Chequers meeting the previous Sunday, attended by almost the same group as the 18 December meeting. Thatcher prepared for the contingency of a resignation by deciding on George Younger as possible replacement. So when Heseltine stormed out of cabinet, the name of his successor was made public within half an hour. If the rest of the cabinet was stunned, the prime minister quite obviously was not. Probably only the extent to which Heseltine's post-resignation statement tracked back and forth over the Westland saga, and raised quasi-constitutional criticisms of her style of premiership, was unexpected.

Marxist Interpretation

Orthodox Marxist accounts never offer any distinctive account of the core executive. Instead they assert that the detailed institutional arrangements within the state apparatus are purely superstructural. This stance has been strengthened by the tradition's well-known difficulties in analysing political leadership factors. Some central tenets of Marxism have been taken to imply that individual actors (such as political leaders) cannot shape social outcomes:

> The basic premise which informs historical materialism is not in doubt: it is that men and women, organised in classes, are the collective actors of history, but that the play itself is very largely shaped by forces which are not greatly affected by any single will or by the will of small groups of people.... Individuals, singly and in [non-class] groups, can certainly make a difference to the ways in which class struggles work themselves out: but that difference, in classical Marxism, is not very great and certainly should not be taken as decisive. (Miliband, 1983, p.134)

However there is a wide gulf between this theoretical attitude and Western Marxists' applied political descriptions, which vest considerable explanatory significance in major political leaders. Personalised labels such as 'Thatcherism' or 'Reaganism' are supposedly just convenient shorthand. Yet in practice leadership styles and leadership/regime succession seem to be ascribed 'heroic' significance in contemporary Marxist accounts. For instance, the deradicalisation of Labour policy making in the late 1970s or the electoral advance of US new right conservatism in the 1980s have been explained in these terms (Hall and Jacques, 1983; Piven and Cloward, 1982, pp.125–49). This tension between theoretical views and practical analysis is sometimes fudged by supposing that there are two 'layers' of historical evolution. One is a base-level groundswell of social development governed by the evolution of class struggles, while the other consists of superstructural variations around the trend of social development (Miliband, 1983). Leadership influences are important in causing these 'wobbles', some of which may obscure the realisation of an underlying pattern of class struggle for decades.

Most applied Marxist accounts relevant to core executive studies have followed an 'instrumentalist' position, fleshing out Lenin's claim that parliamentary government is 'tied by a thousand threads' to capitalist social interests and acts on their behalf. Political leaders and central government policy making are fitted into an overall characterisation of state activity as maintaining a capitalist social order, a limited or distorted form of liberal democracy and high levels of social inequality. The central role of political elites is 'the containment and reduction of popular pressure' (Miliband, 1982, p.1). The attempt to document this position and to offer empirical support for it in practice brings Marxist accounts into close approximation with 'power elite' studies, in the tradition inaugurated by C. Wright Mills (1956). Rather than undertake decisional research to produce a developed analysis of core executive operations, authors in both approaches have tended to retreat into detailing the narrow social background of political leaders and administrative elites (Greenberg, 1979; Miliband, 1969; Crewe, 1974).

An alternative Marxist position has been sketched by analyses of 'authoritarian statism' in Western democracies (Poulantzas, 1978). The idea here is that formal representative institutions have increasingly been bypassed by shadowy 'parallel power networks cross-cutting the formal organization of the state and exercising a decisive share in its activities' (Jessop, 1982, p.170). In Britain both Marxist and some liberal studies point to the creation of machinery with repressive functions in areas such as surveillance and news media manipulation by the intelligence services (May and Rowan, 1982); the piecemeal emergence of a coordinated national police force deployed for combating urban riots, major strikes and terrorism (Hennessy, 1985; Jeffery and Hennessy, 1983; Fine and Millar, 1985; Bunyan, 1976); and the highly insulated inner policy system controlling decisions about nuclear weapons, major defence systems and intelligence services (McLean, 1986; Hennessy, 1986, pp.23–63; Freedman, 1980; Richelson and Ball, 1985). The theory of authoritarian statism links these fragmented pieces of evidence about 'parallel power networks' with claims that a politically dominant party bloc has been created under the control of the core executive, in whose hands the administrative apparatus and political management of the populace are effectively unified: 'Real power is rapidly becoming concentrated and centralized at the summits of the governmental and administrative system, and, indeed, is increasingly focused in the office of president/prime minister at the apex of the various administrative structures with the resultant appearance of a personalistic, presidential/prime ministerial system' (Jessop, 1982, p.171). Again this theme finds echoes in left-wing analyses of the demise of cabinet government under Thatcher, and previously the primacy of the civil service departments under Labour governments of the 1970s, which left a political role only for a single chief executive as tie-breaker in intractable or unbargainable inter-agency disputes (Benn, 1980; Sedgemore, 1980, pp.49–87, 105–47).

Applied to the Westland affair, a Marxist position focuses on two main features: the construction of tightly integrated networks of core executive actors and agencies with business corporations and personnel; and the explanation of why the business/political networks in this case were internally divided, conflicting with each other rather than expressing a unified ruling class interest.

Power Networks

The Marxist account portrays the Westland affair as a power struggle between two closely integrated groupings of politicians/departments and corporations/capitalists (Figure 9.1). On the Westland side, the linkages between Cuckney, Brittan and Thatcher were numerous and close. Cuckney's background began in MI5 and his government contacts continued throughout his business career. For example, shortly before taking over at Westland, he finished a 10-year stint as head of an MoD front company running overseas arms sales. Once appointed at Westland following Bank of England intervention, Cuckney's first step was to shift the company's merchant bank to Lazards, chaired by John Nott, a former defence minister in Thatcher's government and someone with multiple Tory party contacts. Cuckney also brought into the Westland board Lord Fanshawe, a former MP and Tory loyalist ennobled by Thatcher. Also hired as a Westland publicity consultant was Gordon Reece, Thatcher's personal campaign adviser, who received a knighthood in the 1986 New Year's honours list and spent the preceding Christmas break at Chequers as the Thatchers' house guest. In addition to these overt contacts, Cuckney apparently received briefings about confidential government papers and discussion informally from a source inside Number 10. Cuckney had direct contact with Brittan and Downing Street at numerous points throughout the whole affair, even extending to speaking at a meeting of the prestigious EA cabinet committee (along with Marcus Aquis of Lazards).

On the corporate side of the Westland/Sikorsky grouping, Cuckney was also the central linking figure. As the Bank of England's selected 'company doctor', his key brief was to safeguard the interests of the National Westminster and Barclays banks. The banks' insistence kept Westland and Sikorsky wedded to a plan to issue 'preference shares' to Natwest and Barclays, long after the emergence of the Euro-consortium meant that obtaining the

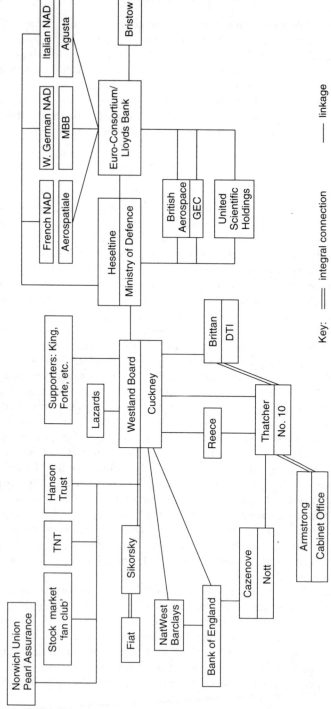

Figure 9.1 *Networks of business/governmental linkages in the Westland affair*

necessary 75 per cent majority at a special shareholders' meeting was impractical. Sikorsky/Westland's acceptance of preference shares kept the banks in line even when they were heavily lobbied by James Prior (chairman of GEC) and other business contacts of Michael Heseltine at the minister's insistence over the weekend of 4–5 January 1986. When the preference shares plan failed at the first Westland shareholders' meeting, the banks almost withdrew support from the revised Sikorsky/Westland reconstruction. But this occasion was the only one when their support wobbled: otherwise they endorsed all Cuckney's decisions. Cuckney's links to Sikorsky were built up over months of negotiations, and at a personal level became very strong on both sides.

How did corporations and capitalists apparently remote from any concern with Westland come to be involved on behalf of Sikorsky? Clearly Sikorsky themselves brought in Fiat, whose role in funding half the outside capital injection but leaving all the voting powers to Sikorsky seems odd. Fiat had to defy their own government's policy line in favour of the European solution to take their stake. After the Sikorsky reconstruction succeeded, Fiat fairly speedily sold their shares to the UK firm, GKN, suggesting that Fiat actually had no long-term interest in helicopters or Westland. Cuckney was involved directly in some of the 'fan club' activities on the stock exchange following Heseltine's resignation, such as the interventions of Hanson Trust in share buying and a meeting at Claridges Hotel between Faure (Sikorsky's president), Cuckney and Sir Gordon White (chairman of Hanson Industries) which tried to persuade Bristow to sell his pro-European shares. But the links which bound the other anonymous buyers of Westland shares to the Sikorsky/Westland axis can only be surmised. It seems clear that political considerations influenced both Hanson Trust and TNT, companies not exactly renowned for purchasing severely overpriced shares in almost bankrupt companies.

On the other side of the affair, Heseltine was unquestionably the key figure in the political/corporate linkages (Figure 9.1). He used his contacts in Europe to make many of the administrative and commercial contacts necessary to produce a single plan from Aerospatiale, MBB and Agusta, backed by official support from the French, West German and Italian governments, culminating in the NADs agreement. Heseltine's personal linkages to the consortium continued after he left office, but his ministerial role seems to have been more important in organising the British backing for the European solution. British Aerospace and GEC initially professed an extreme lack of interest in Westland. However both joined the consortium at a latish stage after heavy lobbying from MoD. Both firms then radically downgraded their public rule in promoting the consortium case following Brittan's pressure on them and the replacement of Heseltine as secretary of state for defence by George Younger, a Thatcher loyalist. The only other major UK corporation to support the consortium bid as a shareholder was United Scientific Holdings, a major defence contractor whose managing director, Peter Levene, was made head of the defence ministry's procurement executive by Heseltine in 1984.

A Marxist account describes the whole character of the Westland affair as a closely integrated, interpenetrating and overlapping battle between effectively unified business/political coalitions. Deals and direct contacts between politicians and corporate interests were the repeated currency of the affair, as in Brittan's controversial 'warning off' of British Aerospace or Heseltine's secret offer to Cuckney on 23 December 1985 in which (presumably) concessions on MoD contracts were to be traded for the Westland board reappraising its opposition to the consortium plan. At the margin some of these dealings might have shaded into potential corruption, as in Bristow's allegation that he was told a knighthood could be available as part of a *quid pro quo* for selling out his shareholding to Sikorsky/Westland. But such factors are small details in a broader picture of a closed policy process dominated by linkages between capitalists and Conservative politicians.

Explaining Elite Divisions

A more difficult problem for a Marxist account is to explain why the bifurcated networks shown in Figure 9.1 conflicted with each other so sharply and disruptively. Traditional Marxist views stress that the role of the state (and hence of the core executive) is to integrate government with the needs of capital, a view also developed in 'power elite' studies. Yet in the Westland case, although business/government linkages are obvious, the elite as a whole appears as internally divided. Far from unifying otherwise centrifugal elite groupings, the core executive was a key locus for divisions to open up and magnify. Marxists could argue that in a residually competitive capitalist system intra-elite divisions occasionally arise, especially where foreign capital becomes involved in previously closed defence procurements. These conflicts of interest will be reflected inside government because of 'the play within the state apparatus needed to ensure the coordination of a divided dominant class' (Cockburn, 1977, p.50).

A more sophisticated Marxist account pictures the Westland affair as a struggle between distinct 'fractions' of capital. Historically in Britain the Conservative party has been able to arbitrate politically between large, multinational and finance capital interests, on the one hand, and medium and small domestic industrial capital, on the other. But in the Westland affair the normal closed and private intra-party channels for balancing conflicting capital interests broke down, so that government had to become overtly involved in resolving the issue. The interests of external monopoly industrial capital (United Technologies, tactically backed by Fiat) allied with finance capital (NatWest, Barclays, the Bank of England and Cuckney) found consistent political support from Thatcher, Brittan and the DTI in wanting to open up defence contracting to 'free' competition. By contrast, British Aerospace and the three European helicopter/aircraft firms involved in the consortium closely fit the pattern of medium-sized industrial companies, whose main insulation against international competition was political protection by their national governments. Classifying GEC in these terms is more difficult.

The pattern of political/departmental alignments with business which occurred over Westland was not unique. In a range of previous and subsequent decisions involving conflicts between monopoly capital and medium capital, the prime minister and her closest aides and ministerial allies consistently sided with monopoly capital interests, against resistance from other ministers defending British medium capital. In 1986, Thatcher and the DTI both backed a plan for British Leyland to be sold to the US multinational General Motors, which was thwarted by ministerial and backbench Conservative opposition. Within six months of the Westland affair, Thatcher and her Number 10 staff were intimately involved in securing the cancellation of the MoD's £1000 million contract for the British Nimrod early warning system developed by GEC, and its replacement by an American competitor manufactured by Boeing. In 1988–9, the Nimrod line-up of interests recurred in a dispute over the choice of a main battle tank between a US model marketed by the giant General Dynamics corporation and a British rival manufactured by the medium-sized Vickers company. In this perspective, the Westland affair can be seen as simply one instance of a wider struggle for hegemony in British public policy between differing fractions of capital and their associated ideological wings of the Conservative government.

The Policy Entrepreneur Model

New right authors have transferred the economic concept of entrepreneurship to political settings. Economic entrepreneurs found new firms, promote organisational improvements in existing firms, or develop new products, with a view to making profits. Political entrepreneurs supply leadership to collective interest organis- ations (such as interest groups or political parties), with the aim of maximising their personal power, social status, public fame or other perquisites of high political office (Frohlick *et al.*, 1971). They are pure utility-maximisers, seeking benefits and avoiding costs. When entrepreneurs subsidise fledgling organisations, they do so, not from ideological convictions or political principles, but to secure a long-term personal return. This approach has been applied most to explain organisational entrepreneurship by party leaders, interest group campaigners or managers of competing local governments. In these contexts the pay-offs for political entrepreneurs clearly increase with organisational size or effective- ness (such as party support, group influence or community growth).

Within government, policy entrepreneurs are chiefly elected politicians who scan the horizons of their institutionally defined office, picking up and promoting ideas, problems and solutions which will have favourable consequences for their careers. Middle- ranking politicians badly want to be re-elected or promoted and to secure favourable publicity to these ends. Hence they are keen to associate themselves with new ideas or initiatives which attract attention. But they place little stress on following through or criti- cally assessing these initiatives. This orientation can create 'politi- cal hyperactivism' which inflates public expenditures (Minogue, 1978). Middle-rank politicians constantly on the look-out for op- portunities to extend their reputations use public funds to launch initiatives, heedless of their long-term costs or cumulative drain on state revenues.

Central political leaders (such as presidents, premiers or those in charge of finance ministries) are unlikely to share the simple expenditure-boosting orientation of politicians in charge of spend- ing agencies. Core executive actors are not so directly pressured by special interests as middle-ranking politicians in any given issue area. Instead they have to balance conflicting imperatives, to court popularity by conceding special interest demands in many differ- ent issue areas, or to pursue electoral success by stabilising or reducing the overall burden of taxation on citizens and enter- prises. Much will depend upon the balance of support and opposi- tion on particular issues, with even central political leaders bowing to majority opinion on cases where support is strongly mobilised and opposition is diffuse (Wilson, 1973, ch. 16). Leaders can also leave alone 'no-win' situations where opposition outstrips diffuse support, and entrust diffusely supported and opposed issues to the bureaucracy. But the behaviour of central political leaders becomes more indeterminate where both support and opposition to an issue are concentrated (as in the Westland affair). Unless the issue is of very strategic importance (such that a premier or president perceives an opportunity to enhance their reputation or ensure their place in the history books), the likelihood is that the preferences of central political leaders will diverge systematically from those of middle-ranking politicians more deeply involved in the issue. Finally, in a new right administration such as Thatcher's government, core executive resistance to spending proposals should clearly be greater.

In the policy entrepreneur account, administrative elites behave in a simple fashion, championing causes which facilitate budget maximisation by their own agencies, which boosts their welfare (Niskanen, 1971). Departments unite in defence of resources which safeguard their collective interests from political interference, such as official secrecy, or the 'professional' self-regulation of the civil service in the UK. But to a limited degree departments also compete with each other for scarce resources, especially for finance where overall budget levels are fixed, and for the support of central political leaders when a premier or president can greatly determine the pecking order or gradients of influence between agencies. In these situations a spending department might on occasion gain more by opposing a budget-boosting proposal but raising its 'credit' with central leaders than it loses by passing up the opportunity to secure a new increment of finance.

The policy entrepreneur account presents an uncluttered picture of the conflicts in the Westland affair. Heseltine is portrayed as a conventional hyperactivist politician willing to spend public money like water in pursuit of personal advantage. The MoD was similarly concerned to expand its patronage over contractors and its links with Europe. By contrast, Thatcher and her group had the unenviable task of drawing a line to limit governmental involvement. Brittan and the DTI might have had some stake in a budget-boosting solution for Westland, but much less than MoD; and they judged that they stood to gain more political credit from supporting the Thatcher line.

Explaining Heseltine's Behaviour

On this model a policy crisis arose chiefly because Heseltine had 'gone native' at the Defence Ministry, internalising the armed services' goals uncritically, and responding more to sectional interest group pressures than to overall public interest considerations. His campaign clearly used policy initiatives to promote his standing with Tory MPs and wider public opinion. Heseltine's basic position was indicated as soon as Westland's troubles surfaced in early June 1985. At the first ministerial meeting to consider options he suggested that the company be given a £40 million temporary subsidy, split half-and-half between his ministry and the Treasury. This help was to come on top of a subsidy of £65 million which the Overseas Development Administration (ODA) had earlier agreed to give Westland to finance the sales of a consignment of its W30 helicopters to India. In fact the Indian government soon concluded that, even with this much 'support', the W30 design was unsuitable for them. They modified this stance only after a good deal of high-profile lobbying by Thatcher and (probably more effective) a secret additional payment to them of £10 million directly by Westland – a sweetener designed only to trigger the ODA assistance which the firm needed so desperately. In addition the DTI had given Westland 'launch aid' of some £40 million, nominally in the form of a repayable loan to help design and produce the W30, three years earlier. This sum would clearly have to be written off under Heseltine's scheme. The purpose of the temporary subsidy proposal was to allow Bristow's withdrawn bid for Westland to be reactivated – at a total cost to the taxpayer of some £145 million.

When the first Heseltine attempt to inflate the public budget was defeated by Treasury resistance, the pressure for an undercover injection of public money continued. The original Sikorsky rescue package for Westland entailed the government's purchasing the company's whole stock of unsaleable W30s, thereby raising the previous ODA subsidy of £65 million to £120 million and unlinking it from an Indian sale (which was then very much in doubt). In addition, the DTI launch aid for the W30 would be written off, and the Department of Employment would chip in around £25 million to ,fund necessary redundancies at Westland's plants. Heseltine raised no objections to these provisions, but professed himself alarmed at the spectre of the MoD being pressurised into purchasing Sikorsky's Black Hawk helicopters, for which the UK armed forces had no procurement needs. The realism of this alarm needs to be assessed against the record of the MoD under Heseltine's successor, Younger, which had no subsequent difficulty in resisting pressure from Westland to purchase Black Hawk.

The development of Heseltine's campaign for a Euro-consortium rescue demonstrated a thinly disguised preference for further direct governmental intervention. Rather than doling out overt subsidies, Heseltine's solution proposed to prop up Westland by insulating it (and the rest of the European helicopter industry) from international – that is US – competition. The strategy of cartelising all military helicopter contracts across four European firms, plus the commitment to three standardised designs for the full range of British, German, French and Italian defence uses, made the NADs agreement the defence equivalent of an almost risk-free venture for the firms involved. It was little wonder that, with this level of distortion of markets in prospect, British Aerospace and GEC were prepared to sink their previously expressed lack of commercial interest in Westland and get involved in adding some corporate muscle to Heseltine's otherwise unimpressive consortium. Over and above the public but unquantified sums involved in the NADs solution, Heseltine clearly used the scheduling of contractually committed MoD payments to try and pressurise the Westland board into 'playing ball' with the Euro-consortium, as well as dangling before the company's eyes a follow-on order for six Sea King helicopters. Heseltine almost certainly offered Cuckney additional inducements in the form of MoD contracts or assistance during the course of a long and still secret telephone conversation with him on 23 December 1985, provided that the Westland board would accept the Euro-consortium rescue package.

On the policy entrepreneur model the Euro-consortium was from the outset and throughout its brief existence a creation of Heseltine's fertile imagination and activist ministerial style: its construction and momentum owed almost everything to his patronage. The consortium's failure to attract support from more than 4.4 per cent of uncommitted Westland shareholders – compared with the 19 per cent who backed Sikorsky's solution – amply expresses the balance of commercial advantages involved, once Heseltine himself no longer held office at MoD.

Explaining Central Leaders' Position

Thatcher and Brittan/DTI did not accept the original Sikorsky rescue plan, rapidly making clear to Westland that the government's commitments were limited to retrieving the Indian government sale, plus possibly writing off the DTI's launch aid (on the grounds that the money was already lost). They stuck to this position, with the launch aid wiped on 11 December 1985 and the Indian sale agreed two weeks later. They justified the resulting £105 million drain on the public purse as less than would be entailed by any alternative course of action (especially liquidation for Westland). In addition they argued that the Sikorsky deal was a 'private-sector' solution because the Americans were putting up £30 million and the banks and institutional shareholders some £45 million, creating strong 'market' incentives for the rescue package to work, and hence minimising the likelihood of further calls on government. The Thatcher/Brittan line of leaving the issue to Westland shareholders to decide was originally quite genuinely designed to let market considerations override ministerial fetishes or enthusiasms. It implied no new governmental aid for Westland, even though it could hardly help but continue some already committed market distortions.

The Symbolic Politics Approach

The symbolic politics approach offers a sceptical elite theory interpretation of the core executive in which political leadership plays a key role in determining mass perceptions of governmental or regime behaviour: 'Governmental leaders have tremendous potential capacity for evoking strong emotional responses in large populations. . . . [They] become a symbol of some or all the aspects of the state: its capacity for benefiting and hurting, for threatening and reassuring' (Edelman, 1964, p.74). Yet the very salience of relationships between political leaders and the mass of citizens, and the importance of symbolic politics in leaders' toolkits for manipulating public opinion, cast doubt upon the dominant framework for presenting and analysing core executive behaviour (Elder and Cobb, 1983, pp.18–27). 'We are taught to believe that there is "someone" in charge of government and that there must be a reason for every governmental act' (Anton, 1967, p.38). Query these basic premises, however, and very different interpretations of core executive activity open up (O'Leary, 1987b).

Citizens want to believe in leadership myths. Western electorates suffer from deep-rooted psychic anxieties that their countries' highly complex political and administrative systems are not really controllable by anyone. These concerns manifest themselves in strong waves of public support for those leaders who can project an image of competence and authority, and in rapidly increasing resentment of apparently ineffective presidents or premiers:

> The public official who dramatises his [*sic*] own competence is eagerly accepted on his own terms. The illusion is created that planning of consequences and of the future is possible in far greater degree than it demonstrably is. Because it is apparently impossible for men to admit the key role of accident, of ignorance, and of unplanned processes in their affairs, the leader serves a vital process by personalising and reifying the pro-

cesses. . . . Incumbents of high public office become objects
of acclaim for the satisfied, scapegoats for the unsatisfied, and
symbols of aspirations or of whatever is opposed. To them are
constantly ascribed careful weighing of alternatives and soul-
searching decisions. That the premisses for decisions are largely
supplied and screened by others and the decision itself [is]
frequently predetermined by subordinates' decisions is not
publicized. Decision making at the highest levels is not so
much literal policy making as dramaturgy. (Edelman, 1964,
pp.77–8)

Strong pressures elsewhere in the political system help to sustain
this picture of incumbent leaders controlling the machinery
of government. The mass media need a highly personalised representation which simplifies the narrative difficulties of describing
complex public choices. Individual leaders can also be held accountable for results in a way that impersonal policy processes
cannot, a key illusion which political opponents have every interest
in maintaining. So neither the media nor the opposition parties
have any incentive to disillusion voters about the real scope for
core executive activity to shape or control policy outputs.

The symbolic leadership model has not been much applied,
since some key propositions are hard to operationalise. For
example, leaders are said to be able to 'dramatise their competence' in either an active style (like Thatcher) or a passive style
(like Reagan) (Edelman, 1964, p.80). But then there is no objective indicator of 'competence'. Leaders who project competence
are simply those who are perceived as doing so by the mass public,
so they are almost definitionally more successful than those who do
not. However these problems mainly concern the impacts of symbolic leadership, rather than the ways in which political leaders
create and sustain leadership images – these 'production' activities
can be studied directly.

The symbolic politics model would interpret the Westland affair
in a distinctive way by stressing that, in most aspects of the crisis,
things were less than they seem. The objective stakes and activities
involved in the struggle over the capital reconstruction of a small
helicopter company were never intrinsically important to the development of government policy. Instead what mattered were the
political appearances or symbols which came to be associated with
an otherwise mundane issue. Four different but interlocking
'games' can be distinguished – over leadership succession, leaking
of government 'secrets', government–legislature relations and
mass media battles.

Leadership Succession

Perhaps the most obvious level at which symbolic politics pervaded the Westland affair was the way in which Heseltine's refusal to accept normal ministerial solidarity conventions came to be viewed as either a leadership challenge to Thatcher directly or at the very least as a bid to become heir apparent. The defence secretary was always at pains to present publicly his campaign for a Euro-British solution to Westland's difficulties as grounded on defence procurement considerations. But, at the very beginning of October 1985, Heseltine rated the problems of Westland very low on his agenda of concerns, so much so that he could still envisage liquidation of the company with equanimity. Yet within two and a half months the affair had become a potential resigning issue for him. What had changed in the interim? Heseltine had clearly invested considerable effort and some of his prestige in a European rescue effort by assembling the NADs agreement. (In doing so he capitalised on his contacts and reputation with other European defence ministries, carefully built up in the campaign for a European fighter aircraft deal concluded earlier in 1985.) Clearly, too, the unfolding tussle between Heseltine on the one hand and Brittan and Thatcher on the other created a sequence of incidents with their own dynamic and momentum, where Heseltine could make plausible links between his Westland position and broader issues about the constitutional rights of cabinet ministers.

However neither of these effects is commensurable with the extent and speed with which both Thatcher and Heseltine forced the issue during December 1985 and the first week of the new year. As the Westland crisis began to emerge from the relatively private circles of Whitehall committees, company boardrooms and small items on the papers' financial pages, it metamorphosed in a radical fashion. Given normal British government conventions on minimising public disagreements between ministers, Heseltine's open campaign against the prime minister's line was almost bound to end up being coded by others as a leadership challenge of some kind. Thatcher's own indecisiveness in November and December 1985, her failure to bring Heseltine quickly to heel, undoubtedly added to the magnification of the issues involved in Westland. An important part of the techniques Thatcher had always employed to dramatise her own leadership competence was the assertion of her unwillingness to bargain, trade or compromise with dissenters inside her government. Stated forcefully in a famous 1978 interview, it was backed up with well-publicised purges of independent-minded ministers in September 1981 and after the 1983 general election. By December 1985, Thatcher was partly a prisoner of her carefully cultivated reputation for ruthlessness.

The chronology of events demonstrates how telescoped was the period of transition for the Westland affair from minor policy squabble to leadership challenge. On 12 December 1985, Heseltine used a cabinet meeting formally to record his dissent about the cancelling of the second EA committee meeting the previous week, thereby bringing all his ministerial colleagues rather dramatically up-to-date on the Westland saga. He followed up this move with a weekend of heavy leaking to the press designed to counter the public announcement by Brittan that the NADs agreement would lapse. And on 18 December the defence minister testified to the Commons' Select Committee on Defence, evoking a favourable reaction from most members, including a majority of Conservatives present. That same afternoon Thatcher tore up the first *démarche* to Heseltine demanding he adhere to a collective governmental line on Westland, for fear that its despatch would precipitate his immediate resignation. Over Christmas 1985, Heseltine was already contemplating the possible need to resign. The following weekend he refused to accept direct appeals or instructions from 10 Downing Street not to be interviewed on a radio current affairs programme, so long as a taped interview given earlier by Brittan was going out. These steps meant that, without an escape route being provided by Thatcher, any further forcing of the issue by Number 10 would commit Heseltine to join a string of ambitious and strong-willed ministers – such as Lord Randolph Churchill, Aneurin Bevan and Selwyn Lloyd – who picked on apparently small-scale pretexts and forced them through to resignation as part of a wider challenge for the political or ideological leadership of their parties.

Leaking of Government 'Secrets'

A great deal of the specifically political crisis associated with the Westland affair was bound up with the whole issue of disclosing government papers to the media and the Armstrong leak inquiry. No face-value interpretation of departments', ministers' or the premier's behaviour in this area makes any sort of sense. Trying to analyse actions in terms of constitutional or quasi-constitutional conventions quickly runs aground on stark inconsistencies in the standards applied to different actors' behaviour. Only a 'reading' of events in terms of their varying symbolic presentation allows us to construct a coherent account of why the crisis unfolded as it did.

Before the Westland affair the Thatcher government was zealous in representing unauthorised leaks of information by civil servants not just as breaches of confidence and employment contracts, but also as deeply damaging for the freedom with which ministers and their advisers could debate issues in making decisions, and in several cases potentially a threat to national security. The same stance continued after Westland, for example, with the expensive and ineffectual attempts to restrict or ban international sales of the *Spycatcher* book. These attitudes always sat very oddly with the increasingly well-known system by which ministers and their press officers give 'authorised' briefings to journalists in an effort to slant media coverage their way on contested issues (Cockerell *et al.*, 1985). The Westland affair saw a record number and scale of such briefings: 'The Official Secrets Act had been in ribbons. At one point, irate ministers were reading whole chunks of cabinet papers directly to journalists' (*The Economist*, 4 January 1986, p.18).

Most constitutional observers have tended to conclude:

> Whatever the distorting effects of the monopoly of some kinds of information by the government and the existence of techniques for exploiting this monopoly, it is, of course, the case that the disclosure of information by ministers, however it is done, is in a quite different category from that of a disclosure by an official. (Peele, 1986, p.151)

The problem of making any hard and fast distinction between authorised and unauthorised leaking, however, is that any leaking at all is usually at the expense of someone in the government. A leak is only authorised in a complete sense if a minister discloses information limited to his or her own arguments or activities. A far more common situation is one where a hostile leak about what minister B has said is 'authorised' by another minister, A. In this case many of the objections made about unauthorised leaking (that it is a breach of confidence, that its cumulative effect will be to undermine the frankness of policy advice used in government, and so on) seem to apply with equal force. The Mayhew letter leak represents a further stage towards non-authorisation, for here information about what minister C has said was leaked by minister A in a way calculatedly hostile to minister B. Two aspects of the leak are additionally problematic. First, the law officers are supposed to stand in an independent professional position *vis-à-vis* the government of which they are members. To involve them without their permission in a media ploy clearly undermines this special status in addition to the normal impacts of hostile leaking. Second, even leaving the character of minister C on one side, it is unclear who within government, even the prime minister, could legitimately authorise such a complex hostile leak. Various aspects of the Mayhew leak, such as the restriction of direct quotation from the letter to just two extremely damaging words ('material inaccuracies'), compound the problems in seeing it as 'authorised'.

The prime minister's explanation about why the leak took place is complex. She admitted that on 3 January she and her aides studied the text of Heseltine's alarmist letter to the Euro-consortium, which had not been cleared with any other minister before being despatched. As a result of this meeting Brittan was asked by Number 10 to contact the solicitor-general and to secure his written criticism of Heseltine's letter. Brittan rang Mayhew the following day, a Saturday, and the law officer agreed that there did seem to be mistakes in Heseltine's phrasing and that he would look at the issue first thing on Monday morning. Next day (Sunday) a Thatcher inner-cabinet met at Chequers to draw up the ultimatum to Heseltine for the next (9 January) cabinet meeting. By this stage both the DTI and Westland itself were already briefing journalists that Heseltine's letter was about to be denounced by the government's law officers, as the meeting at Chequers must have known.

Mayhew arrived at his office on Monday morning, studied the file and sent off his letter, a copy of which reached both the DTI and Number 10 by 1.30 p.m. It was seen in Number 10 by the PM's private secretary and her chief press officer, and both were consulted by DTI officials about how the Mayhew letter was to be used. Thatcher claimed in her Commons replies that is was urgent to bring the gist of Mayhew's verdict into the public domain before 4.00 p.m. when a Westland board meeting was taking place and might make a wrong decision on the basis of inaccuracies in Heseltine's letter. The government, she claimed, had a public duty to release the information quickly. Hence well-intentioned officials, acting under severe time pressures and without consulting her, cleared DTI to leak extracts from Mayhew's letter.

The symbolic politics account views this explanation as almost complete whitewash. The timing of the arrival of Mayhew's letter, and of when the Westland board would meet, were both known at least two days in advance. No effort was apparently made by anyone at Number 10 or DTI to contact Mayhew and secure his agreement to publicising the contents of his private and confidential letter before or after it was sent – unlike the strenuous efforts Brittan claimed to be making to protect a similar letter from Sir Austen Pearce. Brittan was explicit with his officials that Number 10 must clear the leak, and Ingham used forceful language to coerce the

DTI press officer into overcoming her scruples about making the disclosures. If Thatcher was not consulted about the clearance to leak, it seems clear that it was because her officials had strong grounds for believing that they were carrying out her expressed intentions and policies. Finally the Mayhew letter leak had almost no commercial significance – when the Press Association report was brought to the attention of the Westland board at their meeting they saw it as adding nothing new of relevance. Indeed Cuckney had known for three days that Heseltine's letter had not been cleared with other ministers and would be publicly ruled out of court by the law officers. The impacts of the leak were exclusively political at all stages.

Thatcher's unchallenged survival despite the inconsistencies surrounding her and her aides' role in the Mayhew letter leak and the Armstrong leak inquiry is a startling testament to British political leaders' ability to rewrite the rule book of good ministerial behaviour to suit their immediate situation. The leaks issue was potentially dangerous for Thatcher in the period when confidence among Conservative MPs and media elites was diminishing, and her leadership seemed to be wobbling and uncertain. But once party support regrouped, the anti-leaking conventions became the pretext justifying withdrawal of governmental solidarity from Brittan, with his subsequent resignation functioning to purge previous leak violations and to draw a line under the affair.

Government–Legislature Relations

The Westland crisis involved some important incidents in the long-running but effectively ritualised conflicts between the executive (as a whole) and Parliament. The *de facto* political impotence of the Commons has of course long existed in an unstable relationship with ideologically important myths of parliamentary control. Crises in government–legislature relations are infrequent, except in circumstances when ministers are discovered to be subverting the residual corporate competence of the Commons. It is indicative of the extent to which the Westland crisis had degenerated out of control that some of its key episodes demonstrated the contempt in which ministers held the much-vaunted but largely symbolic powers of the legislature.

On 13 January, Leon Brittan had to respond to Commons questions about Westland. He had been told by Number 10 just before his speech that a letter had been received, addressed to the prime minister, from Sir Austen Pearce, the chairman of British Aerospace. It protested at the way in which Brittan had tried to lean on the B.Ae managing director Sir Raymond Lygo at a meeting a week earlier. Brittan's answers quite cynically explored the outermost limitations of parliamentary non-accountability:

> [Heseltine] Has the Government received any letter from British Aerospace giving their views on the matter?
> [Brittan] I have not received any such letter.

> [Second questioner] In reply to Mr Heseltine he said: 'I have received no letter.' Did any other member of the Government received any representations or letter from Sir Raymond Lygo or British Aerospace?
> [Brittan] I can only speak for myself.

> [Third questioner] In answer to Mr Heseltine he said he did not receive any letter and when asked whether he knew if any other members of the Cabinet had, he replied: 'I can only speak for myself.' Would it not be more candid to the House if he was to tell us frankly, if he did not read them, the Prime Minister did?
> [Brittan] I have given an account of the meeting [with B.Ae] and I have nothing further to add to it.

> [Fourth questioner] Mr Brittan has been asked questions regarding his meeting with Sir Raymond Lygo. He was asked by Mr Heseltine whether the Government received a letter from the Chairman. He was later asked the same question. He has dodged it on both occasions by saying meekly he could only speak for himself. It is his job to answer for the whole Government. That is why he is at the despatch box. Now come clean.
> [Brittan] I am not aware of any letter from Sir Raymond Lygo to anyone else either.

In the course of giving his apologies for misleading the House later that night, Brittan explained away his very last response in the following way:

> In answer to further questions whether any member of the government had received a letter from Sir Raymond Lygo, I replied that I was not aware of any letter from Sir Raymond Lygo to anyone else either. There has since been an announcement by Downing Street that the Prime Minister received a letter around noon today not from Sir Raymond Lygo but from Sir Austen Pearce, the Chairman of British Aerospace. . . .

In fact a casual inspection of the record shows that none of the four questioners exclusively named either Lygo or Pearce as originating the letter, and all referred to the company in general terms. Brittan himself introduced the misdirection about Lygo, just as he did in response to Heseltine's original question by saying that *he* had not received a letter from BAe. Brittan's explanation then went on to claim that 'in view of the fact that, as I have said, the letter was marked private and strictly confidential, it was essential that I took great care to protect the confidence placed in the Prime Minister by Sir Austen Pearce, while answering questions accurately'.

Most observers interpreted the British Aerospace letter incident in a traditional way, as reflecting the continuing efficacy of Parliament: 'The House of Commons is never more indignant than when it discovers it has been misled by a minister. The following day, Mrs Thatcher and the author of the letter were forced to agree to publish it' (*The Economist*, 18 January 1986, p.21). That Brittan's statement in apology was almost as misleading as his original evasions seems to have been overlooked in such judgements. In addition the immediate aftermath of Brittan's twin statements were almost entirely beneficial for him: British Aerospace (and GEC) completely abandoned their high public profile as the UK face of the Euro-consortium, and B.Ae and Brittan published a joint statement fudging over the dispute between them about what had transpired at the 8 January meeting with Lygo. Of course, a week and more later Brittan's performance may have helped isolate him as the scapegoat for the Mayhew letter leak, since his disregard for Commons sensibilities made him vulnerable to the withdrawal of Tory backbench support. Yet this influence seems secondary in importance to the Conservatives' instrumental need for a scapegoat to take the blame for the Mayhew letter leak, and allow them to rally behind Thatcher's renewed leadership.

Mass Media Battles

A final symbolic 'game' which ran throughout the later stages of the Westland affair was the struggle to dominate mass media coverage between the opposing sets of political/corporate interests. 'Spin merchants' of various kinds played a key role in the critical deliberations of both sides, with print media coverage especially dominating the rival participants' assessments of where they stood. Communication between the opposed camps occurred chiefly through the media, which also functioned as the key means of updating those ministers, high-level officials and MPs who were not directly involved at either Defence or DTI/Number 10. Probably the high point in the use of indirect communication via the mass media was reached on 24 January 1986, when Leon Brittan learnt from the morning press that Bernard Ingham was effectively briefing journalists against him. Ingham was localising the damage to Thatcher from the Mayhew letter leak by saying that Brittan had not been asked to resign, but to make up his own mind what to do. Brittan took these cues as sufficiently strong to indicate that he had lost Thatcher's support and decided to resign, resisting the prime minister's overt attempts later in the day to persuade him to stay on (Linklater and Leigh, 1986, pp.168–70). Brittan apparently preferred to read media stories responding to Ingham's behaviour as a more accurate indication of his diminished standing with Thatcher than her own face-to-face protestations of support.

In its later stages, the mass media battle over Westland seemed to be a game played more for its own sake than because it influenced the flow of events. The corporate battle for control of the company was undoubtedly affected by the ebbs and flows of media coverage during December, but from early January the key determinants became direct share-purchasing activity. And, in political terms, the issues at stake in the Westland crisis were far too complex to be easily processed by the media, other than as a personality battle between Heseltine and Thatcher (with Brittan cast as her hench-man or stooge). The interpretation of the extensive information forthcoming about decision making within Whitehall also focused on a few simplified issues, such as the veracity of ministers' accounts. This concern was well dramatized by the *Sun*'s headline for the Mayhew letter leak, which screamed 'YOU LIAR!' at Heseltine, while the same paper summed up the controversy about Brittan's meeting with B.Ae as 'WHO TOLD THAT CHOPPER WHOPPER?'

Conclusions

Political science is inherently a multitheoretical discipline in which issues of interpretation are of central intellectual interest. Contrasting theories of the relations between the state and civil society provide the starting-points for identifying radically different medium-range accounts of the Westland affair. These views range much more broadly than the concerns of past core executive studies with the balance of prime ministerial and cabinet power. The search for evidence to support or refute these interpretations enhances the importance of applied research, and generates new empirical insights which would otherwise be neglected. Similarly looking at multiple interpretations sharpens the pursuit of rigorous scholarly standards, and makes clear the importance of multiple criteria of theoretical adequacy over and beyond simple descriptive realism. Nor does an emphasis upon comparing interpretations entail lapsing into relativism, or saying that each interpretation is as good as the next or it all depends what assumptions you start from. Accordingly I briefly review the strengths and weaknesses of the four approaches developed here.

The governmental politics model argues that the dynamics of core executive behaviour on Westland were primarily if not exclusively governmental and political. The development of the crisis was crucially influenced by a diverse range of political actors, over and above those involved on either side of the conflict. Decision making took place under a rapid pressure of events, with key actors often failing to anticipate the results of their ploys. This model captures well the complex and unpredictable quality of political decision making, the sense that decisions might easily have gone the other way. In many circumstances, its insistence upon the compartmentalisation of political issues and actors from other influences may be appropriate. But in offering no developed explanation of the political–economic linkages which dominated the Westland affair, the model seems weak.

The Marxist account, by contrast, places these linkages at the centre of its explanation. Its analysis of business predominance in liberal democracies explains both the integral relations between large corporations and the highest echelons of the Conservative government, and the extent to which politicians seem to act at the behest of business interests. The pluralist objection that there is no 'smoking gun' evidence that politicians acted in the way they did *because of* pressure from business is not very compelling. It is inherently difficult to prove such claims with publicly available evidence. A more fundamental difficulty concerns the rifts between different business/government groupings. The 'class fraction' model of conflicts between monopoly/finance capital and medium-sized firms could explain the rifts but it would have to be applied to a wider range of cases before it provided a plausible alternative to the governmental politics analysis.

The policy entrepreneur model sees public/private linkages in the Westland affair as originating not with corporations or capitalists but rather with political actors seeking alliances to pursue goals of their own. Politicians' behaviour was self-interested. The differences between Heseltine and Thatcher chiefly reflect the divergent pressures acting upon middle-ranking politicians and central political actors. This conflict of interests is deeply rooted in a large government machine, hence the rapid escalation of the crisis. The main problems for the policy entrepreneur model are again to show that their account is a general one. Why, for example, should activist ministers not get themselves noticed by cutback strategies, as Heseltine did at the Department of Environment?

The symbolic politics model draws a sharp appearance/reality distinction between the surface issues and arguments around which the Westland affair seemed to be organised and the deeper-lying and overwhelmingly symbolic issues involved. It is the latter which explain why an interministerial squabble over an objectively minor issue should have developed into a damaging political crisis. Heseltine's dissent was correctly decoded as a leadership challenge. The Thatcher camp's breach of previous leaking conventions was seen as inconsistent. Brittan's behaviour, too, clearly highlighted ministers' disdain for Parliament. And throughout the whole affair the key participants charted their successes or failures in terms of mass media publicity. One main problem for this approach is to establish the relative significance of substantive policy questions and of symbolic issues in shaping political dynamics. Again multiple cases need to be studied if symbolic considerations are to be seen as dominating core executive activity.

It would be feasible to construct a single highly inclusive explanation of the Westland affair from the more plausible or interesting elements of the foregoing accounts. Thus one could envisage a modified Marxist account, with an additional emphasis upon symbolic politics, upon Heseltine's hyperactivism and upon the roles played by multiple political actors outside the two main business/political groupings on either side of the affair. Such an account would be descriptively comprehensive but theoretically incoherent, and incapable of being generalised to apply to different issues and decisions. A better strategy seems to me to recognise that a single case study cannot validate any approach on its own. Thus the Marxist account stands up well given the distinctive (and pluralists might argue, highly untypical) features of the Westland affair. Core executive studies should seek to analyse multiple decisions in a way that allows comparative testing of coherent models of the sort analysed here. The lessons of this study are encouraging for such an enterprise. Using systematic documentation searches, it was possible to construct a detailed narrative account of a complex decision, to identify key actors and events, and to bring to the surface relevant interpretations of the data. The challenge is to extend the application of this method to new material.

Note

The author is heavily indebted to Helena Catt and Kenneth Duncan who were the researchers on the 'Heart of the Machine' project during 1986–9, financed by the LSE's Research Fund: they assembled the sources used in the case study. George Jones, Rod Rhodes, Brendan O'Leary, Christopher Pollitt, Alan Beattie, John Bourn, John Barnes and participants at the PSA Annual Conference April 1987 all commented extensively and very helpfully on different earlier drafts of the chapter.

In common with other short policy formulation case studies (such as Polsby, 1984), the chapter is based on published sources. These were: a systematic documentation analysis of all coverage of the Westland issue in *The Times, Financial Times, The Economist, Daily Telegraph* and *Guardian* for 1985 and 1986; the major book-length account of the affair, Linklater and Leigh (1986); and the major House of Commons report (1986). Specific references to these sources are omitted in the narrative to avoid encumbering the text unnecessarily. A chronology of events in the Westland affair and list of documentary sources are available from the author at the LSE. In addition to published material, one senior administrator closely involved in Westland decision making was interviewed and some historical details were cross-checked with informed academics and journalists.

10

Core Executive Decision Making on High Technology Issues: The Case of the Alvey Report

LEO KELIHER

Academic accounts of core executive decision making in Britain often refer in general terms to the growth of the modern state and to the complex technical character of some of the issues which lay politicians are required to consider. These background caveats have little force when set against the discussion of prime ministerial and cabinet 'power' which forms the vivid foreground of debate and controversy. The mass media and political practitioners explain current events in ways which overstate the capability of premiers and cabinet members to control policy across the board. Journalists, opposition parties and government leaders themselves share strong incentives to simplify and personalise issues by representing the prime minister and cabinet as fully responsible for all decisions.

Focusing more on policy-based research (rather than a general description of institutions) can help to construct a more differentiated and disaggregated picture of core executive activity. This chapter analyses high technology issues, an area where the limits on prime ministerial and cabinet influence are at their most restrictive. Complaints about the 'technical ignorance' of MPs and civil servants are equally applicable to the core executive:

> Nuclear power, biotechnology, telecommunications and medicine are good examples of massively capital-intensive developments which affect investment, employment, education and

economic expectations. Parliament has tended to avoid these subjects. . . . We have preferred to debate unemployment levels, inflation . . . subjects where there is a familiar stereotype and political indignation appropriate to the occasion can be triggered. (Lloyd, 1984, p.96)

The specific case to be discussed concerns government funding for advanced research in the information technology (IT) industry, the Alvey project which was considered by the Thatcher cabinet in 1982. Conservative industrial policy at this time was resolutely opposed to attempting to 'second guess' market forces and critical of the philosophy of 'throwing money at problems' and of 'corporatist' negotiations with industry and the unions – all approaches which Tories associated with the Labour government of the late 1970s. Yet the Alvey project proposed to commit substantial government funding to the IT industry, to gear UK companies up to compete more effectively against Japanese, US and European competitors. In addition the programme was to be run by a special, joint government–industry agency on classic 'corporatist' lines. In the climate which prevailed in 1982, these features would seem to stack the odds heavily against the Alvey project's receiving cabinet approval and funding. Yet, in practice, the whole programme passed relatively unscathed through all stages of core executive scrutiny and approval. The changes which were imposed by the prime minister and her colleagues were either marginal or counterproductive in terms of new right policy objectives, or easily evaded by policy community actors at later implementation stages.

This account has five main sections. The first briefly outlines how the IT policy community originated and developed the Alvey project, and the basic chronology of core executive decision making on the issue. The second describes the general methods which the core executive used in scrutinising and evaluating the Alvey proposals, and the extent to which technical ignorance limited ministers' opposition and inhibited outright rejection of the programme. The third section explores a key modification imposed by the cabinet and prime minister which limited the terms on which government funding was committed. The fourth examines how political resistance to the Alvey project was bypassed by presenting the initiative as 'industry's policy', rather than a governmentally directed programme. The fifth examines a further key policy modification, an attempt by the prime minister to shape the organisational structures and personnel implementing the programme. A brief concluding discussion summarises the chapter's implications for core executive research.

Development of the Alvey Project

In mid-1978, the Conservative leader, Margaret Thatcher, outlined the policies which her party would pursue in government if elected, policies designed radically to reduce the scale of public intervention:

> The State should not be allowed, and should not allow itself, to spill outwards ... as if it were the only institution to be relied upon. ... The State's concern in economic affairs should be to ensure that as few obstacles as possible are placed in the way of our own pursuit of enterprise, not to try and organize how we should do that. ... The essence of a free society is that there are whole areas of life where the State has no business at all, no right to intervene. (Thatcher, 1978, pp.6–8)

Some detailed implications of this stance were spelled out by the Tories' ideological guru, Sir Keith Joseph, in a speech three months later, attacking Labour's industrial policies:

> The [current] industrial strategy depends on the government identifying 'winners' and backing them with the public's money. It is flawed because group pressures force the government to back losers rather than winners. Moreover, the government cannot identify winners in advance. Anyway, winners do not need taxpayers' money – and losers waste it. (Joseph, 1978, p.28)

In May 1979, the Conservative election victory brought Thatcher to Downing Street and Joseph to the Department of Industry (DoI), where he promptly initiated a series of seminars with his senior civil servants on whether the ministry should be dismantled or not. Agonised considerations on these lines continued to pre-occupy the minister for almost two years until Joseph was eventually moved sideways to Education. During this period, the Conservatives effectively renounced the use of three out of four key 'tools of government' (Hood, 1983) – finance, legislation or its own personnel – in industrial policy. The fourth resource, nodality, was successfully exploited on a few occasions (such as a conference in 1980 which set a UK standard for Teletext chips that went on to become the *de facto* international standard, with favourable implications for British industry). Otherwise, especially in information technology, the government simply continued Labour initiatives from the late 1970s while pointedly refusing to sponsor active interventions of its own.

During late 1980, however, as unemployment spiralled upwards and the shake-out of labour in manufacturing worsened, Conservative MPs and sections of the party became increasingly uneasy that this stance might not ensure the successful emergence of new 'sunrise' industries, in which the Tories placed their faith for a future economic upturn. In an article entitled 'Mrs Thatcher's new name for intervention', the *Financial Times* detailed the emergence of 'constructive intervention' policies (17 October 1980). This new mood found a ready response in the well-developed industrial/professional 'policy community' (Rhodes, 1988) which existed in information technology areas, and exerted influence upon the detailed operation of government research and industrial support on IT issues. A strongly developed network linked IT managers and researchers in the major private corporations (GEC, Plessey, Ferranti), public enterprises (British Telecom), quasi-government agencies (such as the defence establishments active in IT) and the relevant central departments (DoI and MoD). However, university academics and researchers worked mainly to the Science and Engineering Research Council (SERC, funded by the Department of Education and Science). Links between DoI and the corporations with the universities were less developed.

The principal background factors which stirred these groups into concerted action, and engaged the support of leading industrialists, concerned Britain's international performance in IT. Between 1978 and 1981, Britain's share of the world sales of computers and microelectronics slipped drastically, with Japanese companies in particular continually enlarging the capacities of their integrated circuits and dramatically reducing their price. By the end of 1980, the chances of a British national presence surviving in key areas of information technology such as chip manufacturing or microcomputing seemed slim. Manufacturing companies with interests in the area formed a new pressure group, the United Kingdom Information Technology Organization, and a joint Commons–Lords body was established at Westminster, the Parliamentary Information Technology Committee. Almost simultaneously the Cabinet Office published a report from its Advisory Council on Applied Research and Development which called upon the government to adopt an integrated approach to the information technology industry.

In response to these pressures the appointment of a junior minister for information technology at DoI was announced in November 1980. After two months the lacklustre first incumbent was replaced by the more charismatic Kenneth Baker – described by Hugo Young as 'a shameless critic of the (neo-liberal) faith' and 'a minister who actually believes in the policy of industrial support' (*The Sunday Times*, 11 January 1981). His earliest successes included the launch of a new programme to get microcomputers into all British schools, and the publicity coup of having 1982 designated as information technology year. The DoI also reorganised its internal structure of 'requirements boards' staffed by leading industrialists during 1981, creating a new electronics and avionics board.

At the same time, efforts by the SERC to curtail funding for university microelectronics research on grounds of fairness to other areas of science were thwarted by a coalition of industrialists and researchers. A leading figure in this battle (Dr Thomas of the Rutherford Appleton Laboratory) declared in early 1981 that: 'A prerequisite for future success in information technology could well be the ability to establish and manage large national and international programmes involving massive numbers of staff engaged in cooperative high technology research' (Thomas, 1986, p.40). These views reflected the launching of collaborative research efforts by governments in other advanced industrial states, especially in the USA, Japan and France. In 1980, the European Community appointed consultants to investigate ways of fostering pan-European collaboration with a view to securing research on a scale comparable to that fostered by the huge US and Japanese computer companies. Their report called for a programme of pre-commercial collaborative research involving 12 leading European companies, three of them British, which was eventually approved as the ESPRIT (European Strategic Programme for Research and Development in Information Technology) programme in May 1982.

The specific trigger for the launching of a British national effort on the lines foreshadowed by Thomas came in September 1981. The Japanese Ministry of International Trade and Industry convened a conference in Tokyo launching a 10-year, £700 million project to construct 'fifth generation' computers. They invited the DoI to nominate a team of observers (comprising three academics and three civil servants – one each from DoI, Defence and the Inter-Bank Research Organisation (IBRO)). The British delegation returned from Tokyo deeply alarmed by the extent of the changes in prospect. Japanese ambitions included voice input and output for computers, and the use of artificial intelligence in the new supercomputers. Also startling were the scale of government and company involvement across a wide range of areas – not just on 'fifth generation' computers but also on optoelectronics, laser research, computer peripherals and a host of supporting programmes. Most depressing of all was the speed and effectiveness with which a coordinated Japanese national effort was being implemented.

British industrialists were naturally not invited by the Japanese to attend the Tokyo conference, so a 'debriefing for industry' was arranged at which the members of the UK delegation at first intended to outline their concerns informally. Pressure from industrialists and the SERC and concern amongst DoI civil servants quickly converted this event into the carefully prepared climax of a whole series of smaller workshops in November and December 1981. These events exerted an immense influence on the development of a much more integrated IT policy community, one organised and confident enough to launch a large-scale policy initiative of its own. A joint seminar was held at Abingdon in early January 1982 attended by the Tokyo observers, senior academics and civil servants from DoI, SERC and defence establishments. A DoI note summarised the agreed conclusions:

> A major UK research initiative in IT should be launched immediately, directed at a single focus, Intelligent Knowledge Based Systems. A preliminary estimate of the cost of the programme is £250 million over 5 years, this being seen as additional expenditure over and above that already committed by government and industry.... Long-range research should certainly be funded 100 per cent by government.... The workshop also fully endorsed the conclusion ... that the UK must integrate the efforts of its own IT organizations before considering collaboration with the EEC, with the Japanese or with others. (DoI, 1982, p.2)

However the Abingdon seminar recognised that 'the industry voice must be added before an authoritative national consensus can emerge'.

The industry debriefing took the form of a large conference in London two weeks later, with the Abingdon proposals as its basic agenda. All the major IT companies were well represented and Baker's opening speech stressed the need for a heavy private-sector input in any decision: 'It is very important that British industry should meet together ... to determine what our policy should be in this area' (transcript). Following the industrialists' enthusiastic endorsement of the Abingdon proposals, the way forward was identified as an industry committee of inquiry. Baker immediately sold this idea to a meeting of the National Economic Development Council chaired by Thatcher, and the DoI secured the services of John Alvey (British Telecom, previously in MoD procurement) to head the inquiry. The Alvey committee, together with its steering group, combined managers from major corporations, researchers and academics, and civil servants from the DoI, SERC and MoD research establishments. The committee consulted very widely with information technology interest groups and small business as well as the large firms and quasi-governmental agencies with a stake in IT, but it was the last two groups who most influenced its work.

The big companies' strength in very large-scale integrated circuits (VLSI) technology (which is vital in many defence contracting applications) produced the main change from the original DoI note on the Abingdon seminar, which had stressed Intelligent Knowledge Based Systems. But in all other respects the final Alvey report in September 1981 bore 'a pretty good resemblance to the input that [the] four-day [Abingdon] meeting prepared' (according to one committee member). There were two other main changes. The overall funding recommended was put at £350 million, partly on VLSI and partly because of a committee strategy of 'jam for everybody' (as one IT journalist summarised its approach). But only around two-thirds of this total (£233) was to come from government, with three levels of subsidy: university research would get 100 per cent funding; industrial research 'requiring wide dissemination' would receive 90 per cent government support; and other industrial research work would receive 50 per cent. These figures were apparently plucked out of the air by a DoI civil servant very late in the committee's work. The 90 per cent figure in particular was seen as more acceptable to ministers than 100 per cent state support.

Almost at the same time as the Alvey report was published, the autumn reshuffle of the cabinet brought in another more pragmatic minister, Patrick Jenkin, as successor to Keith Joseph. Together with Baker's strong support and the civil service input into the committee, the departure of Joseph and the perceived failure of his non-interventionist stance guaranteed a very positive DoI response to Alvey. While the Alvey report was widely circulated to the media and in the IT industry, the DoI, supported by SERC and the MoD (who would share some of the extra funding), put a recommendation for its immediate implementation up to cabinet. Consideration by the core executive straddled the period of publication of the 1983–4 public expenditure plans, which made no mention of Alvey. The IT industry and the Confederation of British Industry then lobbied hard for an announcement in the March 1983 budget, but again to no avail.

Not until late April 1983 was a decision to implement the Alvey committee's recommendations finally announced to the Commons by Jenkin. The DoI set up a special unit, the Alvey directorate, with a staff of eight directors composed equally of civil servants and staff seconded from the major IT corporations (such as GEC, Plessey and Logica). Its head was Brian Oakley, a career civil servant. A small steering committee of industrialists and personnel from central departments and quasi-government agencies, was set up to provide strategic advice on the distribution of funding to the directorate. The interpretation promulgated by the government publicity machine stressed: 'The delay turned out to have been caused entirely by indecision about funding and management rather than the programme's content. . . . Apparently the Government tried and failed to persuade several high-powered figures from within the electronics industry to take the Director's job' (*The Times*, 3 May 1983). The Alvey programme got off the ground in commissioning projects slowly because of difficulties in creating the new organisation, setting up routines and soliciting bids. It was only well after the next general election, in April 1984, that Baker was able to announce the first major contract under the Alvey banner (*Financial Times*, 7 April 1984).

Core Executive Scrutiny: General Characteristics

The general approach taken by core executive actors to the scrutiny and assessment of the Alvey project was conditioned by four main factors: the report's vagueness about objectives, the limited ability of non-expert officials in central departments to assess high technology proposals, politicians' use of networking to acquire independent information, and the pressures to make a decision.

Vague Objectives

The Alvey report was notably vague about the objectives which would be served by committing large amounts of government funding to foster long-term research. 'The aim of the programme is to mobilize our technical strengths in IT. This is essential to improve our competitive position in world IT markets' (DoI, 1982a, p.9). The report offered no clear policy indices by which its overall success or failure might be measured, nor did it include a cost–benefit analysis. In some of the subprogramme areas technical objectives were identified, but even at this level much of the report was very vaguely phrased, as the following example of 'technical objectives' suggests:

- Establish a programme aimed at the quantification of software quality and productivity
- Create arrangements for collaboration and information interchange with Ada/APSE (Advanced Project Support Environment) developments
- Support research in a number of areas, including:
  - very high level languages
  - language theory. (DoI, 1982a, p.27)

Critics of the report within central agencies fastened onto these limitations:

> The Alvey report was slightly amateurish . . . this report by a distinguished and experienced set of people did not sufficiently clearly state the objectives and the benefits of [the programme]. I mean, I think it was very qualitative and somewhat ill-defined. It was actually quite professional in terms of the subject areas but as a pure report to a board of directors who were being asked to spend £500 million or whatever it was . . . I thought it lacked professionalism.

A senior Treasury official opined: 'They would not get away with it these days, not since the FMI [Financial Management Initiative] has been implemented . . . We would be worried [by an Alvey-style submission] about the likelihood of . . . generating subsidy addiction, nice cosy relationships between the funders and the private sector.' However, members of the Alvey committee defended the style of their report strongly. As one remarked:

> You are writing the report for a wide range of people ranging from the Prime Minister and politicians, for the experts themselves who had to see something in there that they felt reasonably comfortable with, and then one was writing it for the civil servants, one was writing it a bit for the interested public, certainly for the press on their behalf, and to all of those people it had to make some kind of credible sense. Therefore, my view was you did have to spell out programmes . . . you wouldn't get away with it, if I can put it that way, unless you spelt out the programmes, because people would say 'What the hell are they talking about? What's all this waffle?' . . . But it must also be flexible.

The report's vagueness on economic benefits and dynamic effects, combined with its specificity in only some technical areas,

had distinct advantages in terms of assembling support. As one
insider commented, its multiple, vaguely defined objectives 'meant
that people were left with a whole lot of different ideas of what the
object of the exercise was'.

Difficulties in Assessing the Alvey Proposals

The report's approach also tended to make it very difficult for
officials in central agencies to scrutinise the DoI/SERC/MOD proposals on behalf of the prime minister, chancellor or cabinet as a
whole. The IT policy unit in the Cabinet Office and the government's chief scientific adviser provided some central capability, but
even they tended to turn to outsiders for detailed advice, in particular the Information Technology Advisory Panel (ITAP) set up
to brief the Cabinet Office in 1981. A closely involved official
described it as follows:

> ITAP consisted of half-a-dozen luminaries from the outside
> world – one academic, one sort of generalist, and about four
> industrialists. . . . We deliberately didn't – and this was contro-
> versial – we deliberately didn't go for the really big boys – GEC,
> STC and Plessey. We went for smaller firms partly because the
> Prime Minister herself was very keen to get entrepreneurs in
> rather than what were in some senses bureaucracies like the civil
> service. . . . We are in touch every day with Plessey and GEC, so
> we didn't want that kind of input – the Ministry of Defence
> knows all there is to know about GEC. . . . So this panel was
> formally established to advise the Prime Minister on IT matters.

Yet although ITAP was 'serviced by the Cabinet Office' it also
'serviced Kenneth Baker' and included among its small membership one of the original observers at the Tokyo conference and a
key member of the Abingdon seminar whose proposals Alvey incorporated. Its other members included people from universities and
software firms which had made submissions to Alvey and stood a
good chance of benefiting from its implementation.

The Alvey committee had additionally taken extraordinary steps
not to fall victim to dissident voices from within the IT sector
surfacing at a late stage and influencing core executive consideration. One prominent IT industrialist commented critically:

> One of the problems with Alvey all the way through has been
> a sort of egalitarian approach. Drag anybody who has ever
> had anything to say about [an IT topic] in so then he's

silenced. . . . Alvey bent over backwards to try and satisfy the
little companies in terms of software and systems. . . . They felt
they had a mission to bring technology to a lot of small
companies.

The Alvey committee's success in consensus building tended to
throw central administrators back onto their own limited resources
in framing an assessment. In the Cabinet Office one source summarised their questions about Alvey as: 'Why information technology rather than biotechnology and why collaborative research
rather than the way we have always done it in the past?', rather than
questioning the technical details. Another commented:

> A point which I was very much concerned with and which the
> Prime Minister was very much concerned with was: 'Is collabor-
> ative research and development at a so-called "pre-competitive"
> stage – (a) is it a sensible thing and (b) can it be fitted into the
> British culture of doing things which is obviously very different
> from the Japanese culture where the invention of pre-competi-
> tive collaborative research really occurred?

Nor was the Treasury apparently much better placed to assess
the DoI's proposals. A senior official involved in negotiations
explained: 'We would be concerned to know who would be
receiving the funds, why they need such funds, is it for a part of
their core programme? *We wouldn't ask much about the technicalities
because we wouldn't be able to judge even if someone told us*' (emphasis
added).
Another Treasury man very critical of the Alvey report enlarged
on their approach:

> We often subject what the DTI submits to us by way of these key
> technology proposals to a 'Red Jelly Test'. If we can substitute
> 'Red Jelly' for, say, optoelectronics without any damage to their
> case, then we don't think DTI has presented a very good case
> because it doesn't discriminate between one technology and
> another. . . . It's a good exercise to go through because you
> come up with statements like 'We should support Red Jelly
> because the Red Jelly producers are risk-averse' or 'There are
> fantastic externalities from Red Jelly'. Bullshit. We want to know
> precisely what it is you are claiming for this technology as op-
> posed to any other technology. . . . I mean don't tell me that
> GEC is risk-averse and needs support. For Christ's sake, it's
> sitting on a cash mountain. Why do we need to support GEC in
> this particular technology?

Networking

Politicians in the core executive had to rely on their own resources in seeking to acquire an independent view of the Alvey programme proposal. None of the new right think-tanks, such as the Institute of Economic Affairs or the Centre for Policy Studies, provided any thoughts on the future of the IT industry. The prime minister was most active in looking for advice informally, as one official close to her recalled:

> The Prime Minister feels very uncomfortable if she's getting advice only from one quarter, particularly if it is only from the civil service. She has a group of advisers over a wide range of issues and she is, contrary to popular supposition, she is actually a very good listener and a lot of her time at Number Ten, Downing Street, at Chequers on weekends, at dinners and so on, she listens hard to what people say. So yes, she listened to Lord Weinstock but he was one of many on this issue. . . . But she certainly believes very strongly that many past governments have failed because they have listened to too few people over too narrow a range, and particularly because they listened to the civil service only.

Another elite official with a private sector background argued that linkages between ministers and industrial contacts and informal consultations were an essential part of the policy clearance process:

> I think it is absolutely inevitable that they [ministers] have advisers on all these things. I mean the Chancellor of the Exchequer doesn't understand the details of economic policy any more than the Minister for Trade and Industry understands the details of information technology. In my view there is no difference between those and they have to rely on outside experts and I think . . . they have all had to move as life has become more specialist to getting specialist advice and I think they are very adept at doing this. It was always one of the things that impressed me about Whitehall, coming in from an industrial background, was how adept ministers became at receiving expert advice and being able to assess it. . . . One of the things I have always said since I've come out is that for most of us, you divide the things that are said to you into facts and opinion – facts are facts and opinions are opinions. Ministers treat everything as opinion and are pretty wise to do so in my opinion.

One of the limitations of ministerial networking, however, was its patchy and episodic character. The integration between the Alvey proposal and the European Community's five-year £900 million ESPRIT programme might have been expected to figure prominently in ministers' consideration, not least because the British government was committed to contributing about £40 million to its initial funding. By early 1982, the ESPRIT pilot programme was already under way, yet Alvey–ESPRIT linkages seemed to have been discussed almost by chance. A key official recalled:

> Speaking from the centre of the government, Alvey as an idea pre-dated ESPRIT. The government had very nearly made a decision on Alvey when the Prime Minister happened to sit next to somebody from the European Commission at a dinner and was told all about the ESPRIT programme. The next morning I was sent for and asked 'Why are we doing the same thing twice?' The answer of course was that we weren't but that shows the perception of ESPRIT following on [from Alvey].

Pressures to Make a Decision

The Alvey report was published nearly a year after the Tokyo conference and in the fast-moving world of information technology every month of core executive appraisal was potentially expensive. A senior industrial manager on the Alvey committee remarked:

> We said many times to government – actually I think the example was Ian Barron's [of Inmos] – that while the government were considering this report, about four months or so, the Japanese put 50 per cent more transistors on a chip. So life goes on. You have to be dynamic and flexible.

Private-sector IT people frequently criticised politicians' delays, but those who did a stint inside government formed a very different impression:

> The steamroller of decision making in government is very poorly understood by industry. Industry is able to be really rather relaxed in many cases about its pace of decision making whereas in government . . . there are a whole lot of decisions to be made today and if you don't make them today, you will have twice as many to make tomorrow. The sheer steamroller of the red boxes

each night . . . the decisions that have to be made . . . the efficiency of the administration that is required to make that even
semi-tolerable, which is all it is, I don't think industry recognizes
that at all.

Funding Issues

The limited capabilities of the core executive to assess the technical
case put up by Alvey, and supported by what one DoI official called
'a remarkably large consensus' in the IT policy community, displaced ministers' attention onto more familiar issues of funding
and management. A key sticking point was predictably the level of
government subsidy for research.

The Alvey report recommended that industrial projects where
very 'wide dissemination of the results is required' should be
funded 90 per cent by government. But because other industrial
projects were to be funded at only 50 per cent, the overall government support for corporations involved 'would be roughly 60 per
cent' (DoI, 1982a, p.47). In the early days of the committee's work
the rationale for a 90 per cent level was, according to one member,
'to keep [the companies] round the table' and tie them down to
agreeing the need for precompetitive research. But as the big
firms' enthusiasm for the initiative strengthened so the rationale
shifted towards securing the cooperation of 'software houses,
which are fairly small operations, low capital business'. Alvey's
'egalitarianism' in this respect attracted strong private criticism
from some industrialists in the large firms, one of whom remarked
in our interview:

> Politically there was a sort of attitude that 'Small is Beautiful' and
> we must encourage the creation of one-man companies. Point-
> ing out to them that the British economy was under threat from
> some bloody large Japanese companies – I didn't know that we
> were being screwed by any small ones – just didn't have any
> influence upon them. . . . The idea of discussing the report with
> every two-bit software house in the country – which is what was
> going on – was a nonsense.

Yet the Alvey committee held to its course, maintaining the 90 per
cent proposals as part of its consensus building. One committee
member recalled: 'We had briefly discussed and dismissed the idea
of a sliding scale [for industrial R&D] based on company size,
turnover, etc.' The idea was dropped because all the large companies, such as GEC, had numerous subsidiary companies, many

with small turnovers, so that implementing the scheme was impracticable.

Although the 90 per cent funding level was originated by a DoI civil servant, the idea ran into trouble from ministers in the department, before encountering additional opposition from the Treasury, in cabinet committee and from the prime minister. Interviewees gave two different accounts of how the proposal was eventually struck out. One stressed that even Jenkin and Baker had doubts:

> All of the key senior ministers involved in this decision didn't like the proposal on principle. They argued that, if a company is only putting in one-tenth of the resources, it doesn't then bring to the project the kind of financial discipline which you would expect from the private sector. . . . 90 per cent I think was over the top and I suspect it was knowingly over the top but I think they . . . to some extent the small companies reaped their rough-justice deserts. I think if [Alvey] had gone in and said 'For small companies, it ought to be up to 75 per cent', I think they would have probably won that. By going in and saying up to 90 for small companies, they just irritated ministers and it went against their deeply held convictions about commercial discipline and they said 'No, 50 per cent only.' And the Prime Minister certainly felt that way.

But a Treasury official involved had no doubt that the decision to refuse the 90 per cent funding level was chiefly Thatcher's, because the Treasury agreed in principle to a revised DoI proposal of 60 per cent funding for widely disseminated research:

> I remember that the DTI started off by asking for 80 or 90 per cent funding. We argued for 60 through the Treasury. And I have a feeling that it was the Prime Minister who said '50 or nothing' and got it . . . I remember how devastating that was because, we're supposed to be the tough people, you know, and I'd argued at official levels with ministers, you know – 'If we can get 60 per cent we'll have done very well. Because after all, this isn't going to be the private property of the company paying the money in'. . . . The Prime Minister said '50 or nothing' and got it. It was very humiliating.

Another interviewee explained Thatcher's strong intervention on this one point as part of her overall style:

> As a Prime Minister she became involved in the details of everything where there was decision making. Her management tech-

nique, like many chairmen of major industries, is to ask – to make an assessment of a particular case by asking quite detailed questions and then judging the strategy which is being proposed, not only on its own merits but also by the quality of the answers given to her detailed questions. It is a well-known management technique and she applies it whether it is Trident submarines or the Alvey programme or detente with the Russians or the ANZUS [Australia, New Zealand and United States] pact or whatever. She will always do it that way.

One immediate implication of reducing the public funding ratio was that the government's stake in the programme fell to £200 million, and industry had to make up the shortfall if the overall scale of the Alvey proposals was to be maintained. The cutback was galling for firms in the VLSI sector of Alvey, who had seen the project displace a tentative proposal from the MoD to set up a superchip programme, which would have been 100 per cent government funded.

But by far the most important implication of the decision was, paradoxically, to damage the innovative small firm/entrepreneurial sector upon which Thatcher and the Conservatives placed such reliance. One senior industrialist explained:

> The original proposal [at the Abingdon workshop] suggested a 100 per cent subsidy – no I don't like the word subsidy – 100 per cent support funding for the research programme. This became 90 per cent. When Maggie saw this she dug her heels in and refused on the grounds that scientists would be receiving funds to do all kinds of research with no relevance to the marketplace. What she didn't consider was that, by refusing this level of funding, she automatically excluded all small firms and most medium-sized firms. So if you hear small companies complaining about the 'Big Firm' bias in Alvey, it's not John Alvey or Brian Oakley or the major companies who are to blame. It's her and her alone.

Table 10.1 shows that the principal industrial beneficiaries of Alvey funding were indeed very large companies. Even more interesting, however, was the concentration of industrial grants on companies with strong defence links rather than experience with the civilian applications which the Alvey project was initially supposed to encourage. A former MoD official summarised their attitude:

> I thought it was very important [following the Tokyo mission] that the Ministry of Defence kept up with the running. . . . I

TABLE 10.1   *Top 10 companies attracting government grants from Alvey*

	Alvey funding (£ million)	Proportion (%) of company sales to MoD in 1984
GEC	18.6	61
Plessey	15.6	43
ICL	11.9	n.a.
British Telecom	10.3	n.a.
Ferranti	8.2	61
Standard Telecommunications Laboratories	4.5	n.a.
Racal	4.2	30
Standard Telephone and Cables	3.9	89
Software Sciences Ltd	3.3	n.a.
Systems Designers Ltd	2.3	n.a.

Notes: n.a. = not available.
Source: Keliher (1987, p. 255). Figures are best estimates to June 1987.

don't believe DoI alone could manage the programme. . . . The broad background as I'm sure you must know was, in and around that time, the government was considering whether to go ahead with Alvey – and there was very much a sort of on–off, on–off, on–off. MoD hung in there very, very strongly. There were criticisms that we were running scared of Japan. But in the end, after all the in and out of Cabinet Office, off we went.

In the end MoD administered funding for the VLSI part of the Alvey programme, as well as receiving £40 million in funds (which one official described as 'chicken feed to the MoD').

The final funding hurdle for the Alvey proposal was a hiccup associated with a DoI attempt to secure approval in time for the budget, aided by an MoD pledge to commit existing funding:

The DTI at that time hoped that they might be able to persuade the Chancellor to put in a few R and D things in the budget. Very often Chancellors will take a little theme like 'Helping the Disabled' or 'Modernizing Britain' or something like that which provides a little chapter in the budget, and sometimes you can appease a number of lobbies and get a lot of kudos and lighten the budget up.

In the event, the effort backfired, prompting renewed direct intervention by Thatcher which delayed approval and produced one of the more threatening 'off' periods in decision making.

Industry's Policy, Not Industrial Policy

As the core executive swayed back and forth between approving and rejecting the Alvey recommendations, the critical factor which decided the issue was the homogeneous support of the information technology industry. The backing of SERC and the university sector, as well as MoD and DoI, were influential with officials. But for Conservative ministers, especially the prime minister, the industrialists' voice was decisive. One manager in a large IT firm observed:

> With the sort of government we have at the moment, it is absolutely vital that the thing [the Alvey programme] be seen to be what the industry wants and avoid accusations that we are carrying out government policy and so on. Because it must be remembered that [the] current ministers have no policy for industry at all. . . . So it would, I think, be right [to say] that it be seen purely as the industry's policy.

A different gloss was put on the government's stance by some people in the core executive, such as a senior official who argued:

> I think the government's market policy is often misinterpreted. People say 'The government does not want there to be an industrial strategy.' Actually that's not true in my view. The government is perfectly happy for the chemical industry of the UK to develop a strategy for the chemical industry of the UK. It just doesn't want to have to do it itself because it believes it will get it wrong and all the past records of government intervention in industry in this country, and indeed in others, indicate that that is correct. . . . The government sees programmes like Alvey as oiling the wheels of an industrial strategy without being involved in determining what it is. . . . The basic form of the Alvey programme was determined by groups of people, largely from the private sector, and government did not change it except for fine details such as the 90 per cent problem.

Hence persuading the government to see the Alvey proposals as the industry's policy was critical for success. There were three main strands in this effort. The most important was the informal consultation with ministers by major IT industrialists. One manager recalled:

> It really needed that high degree of commitment from industry to persuade Mrs Thatcher that the programme would go ahead

in the first instance. I recall one crucial time when it [the report] was in for Cabinet discussion as to whether the Alvey programme was going to go ahead and she phoned Lord Weinstock and said something like 'I want to see evidence that GEC and others – you know, will you second people'. . . . [Now] his natural response would be 'What the bloody hell has it got to do with her? You get on with your work and we'll do ours.' But luckily I had a word with him and he said, 'She's asked me to go around and talk about this.' So I gave him a briefing and said, 'Don't just be nice about this, say yes we will [cooperate] because it is important and we don't want to screw the thing up at this stage by saying *No. We won't.*'

A second strand was more formal lobbying by IT interest groups, pressure from the IT press, and more general representations via the Conservative party and other channels. The National Economic Development Council explicitly backed calls for the implementation of Alvey (*The Times*, 9 and 16 February). And a CBI spokesman recalled:

Although in principle the CBI is against profligate government spending and always has been, we nevertheless have supported additional expenditure other than what the government have been planning to do on the infrastructure and on programmes of urgency and of broad importance. We highlighted Alvey as one such [programme] . . . in a thing we do every year, a technical and a policy document prior to the budget . . . called the CBI Budget Representations. . . . We said in a very brief reference that Alvey was the sort of programme where government expenditure was unarguably justified, it was urgent, and we supported that being approved. Now we know from the inside that the Secretary of State who had to argue the case before the Cabinet referred to the fact that even the CBI who are rather against government spending have selected this programme as one we should push.

The third strand in convincing ministers of industrial support involved small firms. One major industrialist summarised this campaign in jaundiced fashion:

When the [Alvey] report was published, the DTI sent out – well it must have been two or three hundred copies to companies asking for their comments. Of course, they all wrote back and said 'What a good idea' or 'Maybe more emphasis should be given to this or that' but the joke of it was that after all this consultation and asking people what they thought, very bloody few of these firms took part in the programme.

Nonetheless the small firms' support helped maintain pressure on policy makers. As one civil servant recalled: 'It wasn't just us who got the feed-back. People contacted their MPs and so on.'

All these indications of backing from corporations and small firms also provided a public rationale for the government, which ministers fully exploited to disguise the tension between the policy decision and their basic ideological stance. Jenkin's announcement of funding to the Commons illustrates the heavy underplaying of governmental subsidies in favour of industrial backing:

> The Alvey Committee was set up last year at the request of the IT industry . . . and after detailed consultation with industry I am now able to announce the Government's response . . . Its theme is the need for collaboration between industry, academic institutions and other research organisations in order to fully mobilise our potential. . . . The task is beyond the resources of any single enterprise. . . . Industry has realised the need for collaborative research in these areas and has agreed to take part in such a programme. This positive involvement of industry in the funding, management and execution of the programme is crucial to its success. (*The Times*, 29 April 1983)

However there was a cost in selling Alvey to the government as the industry's own policy. Ministers, especially Thatcher, demanded a high level of certainty both that industry backed the project and that it would exercise a predominant role in guiding its implementation. One official summarised the politicians' attitudes (and his own views) thus:

> If you are dealing with industrial matters, who actually knows best about the thing? It is very difficult for civil servants to have a culture which understands what is the competitive position on this particular thing [Alvey]. So just to get the right ethos of whether to support this or that, one tends to need industrial people to do it. I am most unhappy when one has the civil servants dominating an area for fear that they don't really understand the commercial imperatives.

This concern opened up a second front on which the prime minister intervened to try to put a distinctive stamp on policy implementation.

Personnel, Organisation and Implementation

If finance is the most predictable area for lay politicians to seek to control complex policy proposals which they cannot assess technically, then exerting influence by picking the people to run the programme is an almost equally important strategy. Thatcher's attention shifted to personnel and organisational structures as soon as it was clear that the programme would reluctantly have to be approved. As in many other policy areas, her concern was to ensure that a small body with firm corporate management was established to run the programme, headed by someone from the private sector, and able to take a strong, decisive line. What she did not want to see was another unit added to the existing government bureaucracy, nor a programme dominated by outside interests influencing government through representative advisory committees. Three aspects attracted her attention: the person to head the Alvey directorate, the shape of the directorate and the role of the steering group.

Personifying Alvey

Controversy about who should head the unit running the intervention programme surfaced in the Alvey committee itself. An industry member recalled:

> During [our] deliberations there was a strong view . . . a strong view that I did not participate in, I thought they were bloody nuts and I kept on telling them that. The majority of the Alvey committee were saying the only way the Alvey programme could run was to find a brilliant whizz-bang manager or director. He would probably have to be an American. Pay him a lot of money and bring him over here and on the day he arrives, say, 'There's the pot of gold, you've got five years to spend the money. You tell the industry what to do, you monitor the programme and control it.'

However, the final version of the Alvey report made no particular commitment on these lines, recommending instead only the creation of a 'slim and compact' directorate within the DoI, led by a director of 'at least' the civil service rank of under-secretary, appointed on a five-year contract (DoI, 1982a, pp.51–2).

Thatcher took a personal interest in the choice of the overall programme director, adding her weight to a general ministerial preference for someone seconded from the IT industry, preferably fitting the 'whizz-bang' model. But all attempts to recruit on these

lines failed dismally since neither their firms nor the private-sector
individuals approached were willing to take on the role. The person eventually appointed was Brian Oakley, the civil service secretary of the SERC. His background was a completely public-sector
one, first in the MoD's Great Malvern Research Establishment,
then as head of the DoI's Research Requirements Division, and
then at SERC. Temperamentally he was described by people involved in Alvey as 'a buccaneer', 'an entrepreneur' and someone
who 'was not afraid to stick his head above the parapet'. But as
an industrialist noted, these qualities had not made him first
choice to run the programme – in fact 'he was not even the third
choice'.

Oakley himself seems to have been sensitive to the charge of not
being an industrial person. One well-placed source suggested that
he had 'refused to accept' nomination 'until all the large firms'
agreed to support him and pledge cooperation: this was 'a form of
blackmail because thereafter they couldn't very well not try to play
the game'.

Size of the Alvey Directorate

When government approval for the Alvey programme and Oakley's
appointment were publicly announced, ministers took pains to
stress that the new directorate would have 'five strong full-time'
staff (*The Times*, 3 May 1983). Thatcher, in particular, interpreted
this restriction almost literally. One civil servant recalled: 'The
remaining legacy of that [her direct interference] . . . was that Mrs
Thatcher said the programme should be run by one man and a
girl. I mean she really did believe the programme could be run by
two or three people, which was of course absolute nonsense'.
Another official, describing implementation difficulties in the
early days of the programme, recalled:

> It all began when the programme was approved. Brian Oakley
> was appointed and the Prime Minister said she did not want a
> bureaucracy, she wanted the whole thing to be run by 'one man
> and a boy'. Brian Oakley had considerable problems in the few
> days before he was appointed persuading the DoI to put in ten
> people, the SERC to put in ten people and the MOD to put in
> ten people: thirty in all. And the Prime Minister was not to be
> told about it and she still doesn't know about it as far as I know.

An industrial manager seconded into the directorate similarly
lamented its slow start in its own offices in June 1983:

There was not even a paper clip. There had been no preparation at all. It was the fault of someone in the government that they had not had enough confidence that this would go ahead, to begin preparing it. So there were no guidelines of what the grants should be, no guidelines on collaboration or anything. Then everyone had to have a mad scramble to get the administration in place. If we only knew, if they had only appointed the director six months ahead. . . . We really tried to arrange all aspects of the programme starting from nothing and that ended up in bureaucratic chaos. Our biggest delays were caused by a lack of staff and Brian [Oakley] had tremendous problems in the early days getting around that. I'm no expert in these matters but I do know that you can't run a £200 million programme over a five-year period with only three or four people. So the bureaucratic delays that occurred were because we couldn't get the people.

The one respect in which ministers' vision of a different agency structure did survive was in the appointments of seven directors to run the component parts of the Alvey project. Four corporation managers from GEC, Plessey, ICL and Logica took half the directors' posts, all in specific technical areas. Officials from MoD and SERC took responsibility for the other two technical areas, with a DoI civil servant in charge of administration. Thus Alvey's eight directors (including Oakley) were half civil servants and half people from the UK's largest IT companies. To this extent Alvey's image of implementing 'the industry's policy' carried through in a partial way to the implementation stage. One of those involved closely in the unit's work explained:

It was really very important that industry felt that this directorate was their body . . . I believe that this is enormously important in the way of doing things. I would think that for the large firms [we] very largely succeeded in that. The large firms . . . think that the policy of the Alvey directorate is the policy that the large firms wanted because they have a very direct input into it. I think some of the smaller firms almost by contrast get worried because of that. Whether they feel that the large firms have captured the policy and therefore they have not had a fair deal – or whether they just feel their normal feeling that government has failed to notice the small firms, I wouldn't care to say.

In later less senior appointments, the Alvey directorate also added some private-sector managers to their 30 civil servants, despite a reluctance by some firms to second people (*Financial Times*,

21 February 1984). 'For industrial people, we went to the obvious top firms. . . . It was a bit *ad hoc* but we tried to get some sort of a balanced team covering the industry – the manufacturing industry.'

The Role of the Steering Group

The Alvey report initially proposed that the director should report simply to the DoI Electronics Applications Requirements Board, but at an early stage in its consideration by the core executive this idea was replaced by a special purpose Alvey steering committee. Again Thatcher intervened directly to make sure that this group fitted in with her ideas, as one senior official rather bitterly recalled:

> The [Alvey] steering committee was unfortunately set up without a proper balance due to the direct interference of our glorious Prime Minister. . . . She wanted . . . the steering committee to be extremely small. She wanted the steering committee to consist of three or four people – and that was directly written in by the Cabinet Office. The result was that, when they came to form the committee, they did so – the Secretary of State made the appointments and so on – I think she probably did approve the appointments herself. . . . But anyway, it was too small. It was a body which didn't really represent the industry, it was an idiosyncratic body of a few individuals.

The steering committee chairman was Sir Robert Telford of GEC–Marconi who worked closely with Oakley. But the initial restriction on the size of the committee had important implications because of a cleavage within the IT industry between people oriented principally to hardware and components (represented mainly by the VLSI part of Alvey) and others oriented to software and systems (represented by other parts of Alvey such as software engineering, intelligent knowledge-based systems and work on the man–machine interface). One insider explained:

> It was a split disguised within the original Alvey committee [of inquiry] itself – it wasn't disguised, it was covered by simply allowing both sides to have their way. But you couldn't do that within the Alvey programme itself. . . . [So] that was a very important issue for the Alvey steering committee, to get that balance right. And we got a dead-set conflict in the middle of the

steering committee between those people who represent the VLSI industry, the few firms who are in that game, and those who represent the systems and software industry. They disagreed entirely about what the programmes should do.

Officials responded to these limitations imposed by Thatcher in a classic 'Yes, Minister' fashion:

We gradually extended the steering committee by one trick and another so that it became a more representative body. I mean it was done with the connivance of everybody but without getting ministers to realize too clearly what was happening because it's not too embarrassing then if Mrs Thatcher should ever notice what had happened. . . . what we did was to have representatives from the other major committees which look after electronics [join] . . . so we got it up, I suppose to seven people, possibly eight and that was much more balanced. You could then ensure that you didn't just have representatives of VLSI, you also had representatives of software and so on.

In fact so successful were these manoeuvres that, a year after being established, the Alvey steering committee had 15 members, and two years on a total of 17. Its 1985–6 composition included eight industrialists or private-sector managers (from GEC–Marconi, GEC, Plessey, Ferranti, ICL, two software firms and one small company), one academic, four DTI civil servants, one MoD official and three of the Alvey directorate (one of whom was seconded from GEC).

Discussion and Conclusions

This analysis of core executive decision making sheds little light directly on the debate about prime ministerial versus cabinet power which has apparently preoccupied most British political scientists specialising in the area. Even when interviewees were keen to criticise Thatcher's 'interference' (as several were), their testimony also tended to provide plenty of references to other cabinet ministers' influence. For example, one senior official complained:

At the moment we have a quite incredible form of government where the Prime Minister makes decisions and sometimes re-members to tell her colleagues. It is, to an old civil servant, quite incredible. . . . The thing that amazes me is why the men put up with it. You know, I really do not understand. Sometimes I think they must be a lot of bloody sheep, although nobody could call Norman Tebbit a sheep. . . . She required a great deal of convincing that Alvey was the right way to go, but there were a considerable number of ministers, not just Kenneth Baker, who really did believe this was the right way to go. . . . I was very surprised when Norman Tebbit became Secretary of State [for Trade and Industry], finding he knew all about the Alvey programme and had taken a personal interest in the battle in Cabinet. Michael Heseltine had too.

Equally, officials, ministers and industrialists had rather different perceptions of the extent of discussion about the policy. Some spoke knowingly of the 'interminable debates' that went on within the cabinet regarding the Alvey report. But other well-placed sources saw the issue as much more briefly and episodically handled, insisting that over the four years 1982–5 Alvey 'as a subject came to Cabinet or cabinet committees on [only] half a dozen occasions'.

Comparison between media coverage and insiders' perceptions suggests that the quality press fairly consistently overstated the role of the prime minister. For example, in explaining why the 1983 budget made no mention of Alvey, *The Times* (22 March 1983) reported: 'Apparently the Treasury are still not happy with the funding system proposed by John Alvey and his team . . . and the Prime Minister has not yet given the proposals her full personal attention.' Similarly, by announcing that the prime minister had stipulated items such as staffing levels, the Number 10 Press Office managed to maintain an image of Thatcher as supreme policy maker which bore a tenuous relationship to her actual administrative influence.

The chief importance of the policy history reviewed here concerns the limits on the ability of the core executive to assess complex high technology issues such as those raised in the Alvey report. The key locus of influence must be firmly located with the IT policy community itself, especially the team of observers who attended the Tokyo conference, the academics and DoI civil servants who attended the Abingdon seminar, and the personnel from large IT corporations who successfully slanted much of the Alvey programme at the implementation stage towards their own, mainly defence- and VLSI-related concerns. Table 10.2 shows the allocation of funding between technical areas proposed by the original Abingdon seminar and the Alvey report, and compares these figures with actual Alvey directorate funding allocations up

TABLE 10.2   *Breakdown of funding across technical areas, 1982 to June 1987*

	Abingdon seminar	Alvey report	Actual total spending	Actual government funding
VLSI and CAD	110	115	132	74
Software engineering	30	70	54	33
Man/machine interface	5	44	48	32
IKBS	30	26	51	33
Demonstrators	30	58	43	26
Communications	8	19	5	4
Others and general	35	20	—	—
Total	248	352	333	202
Total government	248	233	202	·

Notes: VLSI: very large-scale integrated circuits.
CAD: Computer-assisted design.
IKBS: Intelligent, knowledge-based systems.
Sources: DoI (1982d, p.22); DoI (1982); Alvey directorate (1987). For more detailed figures see Keliher (1987, pp.61, 77, 256).

to the end of June 1987. After allowing for some changes of terminology and classifications over time, the table shows a remarkable continuity in the extent and patterning of government involvement.

The technical complexity of the Alvey committee's proposals, together with their success in carefully nurturing an industrial and academic consensus about their report, effectively disabled core executive organisations and actors from scrutinising or modifying their major proposals. Even on issues such as collaborative research, supposedly one key focus of prime ministerial and Cabinet Office attention, Alvey's vagueness was not cracked nor policy objectives specified. One prominent scientist observed that the Alvey report 'went on about pre-competitive R and D but nobody knew what the hell they meant. Did they mean "blue sky" research or research into areas where no products or markets existed? No one knew.' This lack of precision was in the end only 'negotiated' at an implementation stage within the Alvey directorate itself – with a consequent wide variation in the projects funded between development products already in commercial production, through to basic theoretical research.

The most decisive area of core executive involvement was on funding, especially the scrapping of Alvey's suggested 90 per cent support level. Yet the implication of this decision in terms of curtailing total government commitments was rather modest. And there is plenty of evidence that the core executive's intervention

worked against the Conservatives' avowed concern for smaller busi-
nesses. Instead it fostered exactly the kind of cosy corporatist deal
with the large IT companies which Thatcher and the new right said
they wanted to avoid. Nor was this 'backlash' implication unforeseen. Patrick Jenkin still claimed in his Commons announcement
about Alvey that: 'Collaboration will ensure the results of the
research will be widely disseminated, particularly into smaller firms
which have had such an important contribution to make to the
industry.' But the Labour spokesman, John Garret, in denouncing
the government's move as 'penny-pinching' correctly foresaw:
'[This] means that many small companies will not be able to join
the programme yet much innovation comes from these companies.'

Ministers' and the premier's insistence on being assured that
Alvey was 'industry's policy' might be ascribed rather more influence if it could be seen as distinctively influencing the way that the
programme developed. But no such implication stands up to analysis. The critical importance of industrial involvement was recognised by all those who initiated the Abingdon proposals and was
the common currency of debate in the IT policy community as a
whole. Ministers fastened onto it chiefly as a tool for reconciling
themselves to the almost inevitable concession of extra funding,
and as a means of publicly managing tensions between the
programme's corporatist design and their own avowedly anti-
corporatist ideology. The prime minister, it is true, used the
'industry's policy' angle as a means of inserting some of her own
fixed ideas into the details of the programme's administration. But
all the evidence cited here suggests that her efforts either failed
outright (as with the choice of director) or were quickly bypassed
once the programme was up and running (as with limits on the
directorate's staffing and on the size and character of the Alvey
steering committee).

The interest of the story told here lies in the insights which it
gives into how lay politicians and central departments are forced
back onto crude and limited methods of assessing high technology
proposals. The core executive machinery in this area has changed
significantly in the interim, especially with the creation of a Cabinet Committee on Science and Technology chaired by the prime
minister as a (initially secret) part of the government's response
to criticisms by a Lords select committee in 1987. However, subsequent policy decisions in the 1990s show few signs of any change in
the structural limits on the core executive's power to initiate or
modify high technology proposals selectively, or even consider
them in a very sophisticated fashion.

Note

The author would like to thank Professor Patrick Dunleavy of the London School of Economics for his enormous help in preparing the chapter, and Malcolm Grierson and the Queensland Government Centre for Information Technology and Communications who funded and supported the research. The author is grateful to all those interviewees whose frank and informative contributions made this research feasible.

This chapter forms part of a larger project whose research methods and findings are fully documented in Keliher (1987). The main sources of information are a systematic analysis of published documentation; selective access to policy papers from government departments and quasi-governmental agencies; and non-attributable interviews with 62 policy influentials in the IT policy community – mainly civil servants in relevant departments and agencies, industrialists and industrial managers, researchers and academics, specialist journalists and relevant politicians.

11

Joining the ERM: Analysing a Core Executive Policy Disaster

HELEN THOMPSON*

Throughout the whole of the 1980s, British governments confronted a major economic decision: should they join most of the UK's EEC partners in the European Exchange Rate Mechanism (ERM), or should they stay out? The issue was considered no less than eight times between 1979 and October 1990, when the UK did eventually join. In the event Britain stayed in the ERM for less than two years, before being forced out of the system by foreign exchange market pressures in September 1992, partly because the rate at which the UK entered was always unsustainable. Joining early in the decade could have prevented the overvaluation of sterling in the period 1980–82, thereby saving much of Britain's manufacturing capacity and thousands of jobs (NIESR, 1989). But joining very late in 1990 and at the wrong rate brought no benefits to the UK at all. The story of policy making on ERM is thus one of missed opportunities, chronic misperception by British policy makers and huge welfare losses for the British economy.

What makes the ERM story unequivocally a policy disaster, however, is the deep divisions which it opened up within the Conservative governments of the 1980s, between the prime minister and her chief ministers, the chancellor of the exchequer and the foreign secretary. For more than five years, from 1985 to 1990, these three key figures were at loggerheads. At times they warred publicly with each other, at the expense of British national

* I am grateful to those current and former ministers, civil servants and advisers whose interviews inform the account given here.

248

interests in the foreign exchange markets and within the European Community. The legacy of this turmoil remains important in contemporary British politics, in the bitter feud between Eurosceptics and enthusiasts within the Conservative party, in the continuing cabinet divisions about British attitudes towards European monetary union, and in Britain's firmly entrenched and unenviable reputation with her partners as the 'reluctant' member of the European Union.

The chapter has two parts. The first outlines the basic issues involved in the debate about joining the ERM and gives an account of how ERM decision making evolved. My narrative is based largely on non-attributable interviews carried out with 26 top decision makers involved (the unsourced quotes below), plus the conflicting stories offered by Margaret Thatcher and Nigel Lawson in their memoirs. The issues involved were complex, so my summary here is inevitably compressed and simplified (see Thompson, 1994). The second part of the chapter considers the significance of this story for two important debates about where power lies in British political structures.

A Brief History of ERM Decision Making

Since states first started to trade with each other, they have been forced to confront the question of how to organise payment for that trade. There are basically two ways of doing so. Letting currencies float freely against each other allows finance markets to adjust for the relative economic performance of different countries in controlling inflation, maintaining a balance of payments position, and paying interest on deposits in that currency. However, in the modern era in particular, it also creates the possibility that markets will mark currencies up or down, not in accordance with economic 'fundamentals' but in response to all kinds of market sentiment, some of which may be based on few or no foundations. In adverse markets (especially market panics) a currency X will fall, perhaps causing substantial devaluation and possibly increasing inflation. At other times currency X may rise simply because other currencies are falling, making it harder for country X to export goods. The enormous growth in the scale and speed of finance market movements, produced for example by worldwide deregulation of money flows across borders, means that the scale of costs and extent of changes from floating have also increased.

Fixing currencies' positions against each other means that constant small fluctuations are avoided, and major realignments of currencies are resisted, in both cases by the countries in question buying and selling currencies on the market and raising or lowering interest rates to try and manage the levels at which they exchange. If currency X becomes overvalued then that country's central bank needs to buy other currencies to keep their levels up, and possibly cut interest rates to make currency X less attractive to foreign investors. In an adverse market (especially a panic surge) against currency X all the central banks involved in the exchange rate system may buy X to keep its value up. But country X will also need to raise its interest rates and adjust its economic policies so as to maintain a fixed exchange rate (for example, deflating its economy to correct a balance of payments deficit or to control inflation).

The advantages of fixed rates, and therefore of the ERM, are that firms and individuals can plan ahead when exporting or importing goods or capital, without trying to 'second-guess' foreign exchange market trends or fluctuations. Under these circumstances investment and overall levels of economic activity are usually slightly but significantly higher than they would otherwise be. The main disadvantage of fixed exchange rates is that the finance markets may mount a speculative push aiming to break the arrangements and make fast profits for dealers who gamble right. And when such speculation occurs (let alone succeeds) it is costly for the governments involved, in terms of raising interest rates and losing foreign exchange reserves trying to defend a parity which may ultimately be unsupportable. The more inflexible exchange rate arrangements are, the greater the costs of speculative attacks. Furthermore over time *any* exchange rate system will break down. The Bretton Woods system set up in 1947 provided the framework for much of the postwar growth period by fixing the other main currencies against the dollar, but despite its many advantages and the participation of all the major states, the system eventually broke down in 1971.

Just seven years later the countries of the European Economic Community tried again with a much more limited system, an Exchange Rate Mechanism (ERM) which would fix the EEC countries' rates against each other in terms of a weighted composite basket currency called the Ecu (the European Currency Unit). Each EEC country's currency could move up or down against the Ecu, but only within certain bands, thereby, it was hoped, making the EEC an island of relative monetary stability within the overall international environment of free-floating exchange rates. If any ERM currency became subject to intolerable market pressure beyond these limits the initial system provided for joint intervention by European central banks to protect it, and if the pressure became very severe realignments were also possible –

a half-way house solution designed to be more flexible than Bretton Woods, and known technically as a 'dirty float'.

The system was devised by West German and French officials in 1978, initially with the participation of a senior British civil servant, but he quickly became isolated from his counterparts. The Callaghan Labour government decided not to join the ERM when it began working in March 1979. Speaker after speaker at the October 1978 Labour Conference attacked the ERM, so that the cabinet had no appetite for joining, while most of the senior civil servants involved were deeply sceptical that any fixed currency arrangement could work. A senior official recalled that the Treasury 'had considerable doubt as to whether it [the ERM] would survive', while Bank of England officials were still traumatised by the free-fall in sterling's value that had led to the IMF loan to Britain in 1976, just three years earlier.

The Opposition took a different view. When the European summit setting up ERM was concluded, and Britain had not signed up, Thatcher condemned Callaghan in the House of Commons for standing outside the European mainstream on the issue. She insisted that there was no way out of the world recession by standing alone and that the British people were shocked to find themselves 'relegated to the European second division' having been 'the victors in Europe' in 1945 (*The Times*, 11 July 1978, p.1). And when Callaghan announced at the end of 1978 that Britain definitely would not join, Thatcher declared: 'This is a sad day for Europe.' The prime minister, she declared, was content to have Britain 'classified among the poorest and least influential countries' in the EEC.

Not surprisingly, when the Conservatives came to power in May 1979, the new government initiated an immediate review of whether Britain should join the ERM, the first of eight occasions when the policy was seriously considered. I consider this chequered history in three main periods: the early reviews, 1979–82, the years of turmoil, 1984–8 and the endgame on entry, 1989–90.

The Early Reviews (1979–82)

The 1979 Tory manifesto contained no pledges either way on ERM entry, but the new cabinet was markedly more pro-European than the Callaghan government and, at the urging of the Foreign Office, ERM policy was considered as a European question in a desultory manner. In July the government announced that it would postpone the issue to the autumn, effectively killing it, since the chancellor, Geoffrey Howe, had by then introduced his first budget committing the government to a strict monetarist strategy of tightly controlling the money supply and using high interest rates to choke off inflationary pressures in the UK economy. With these changes in place, and an increase in international oil prices, sterling began to appreciate in value against other European currencies. The pound's rise reflected:

- its new position as a petro-currency (thanks to North Sea oil);
- the financial markets' positive view of the government's monetarist rigour; and
- high interest rates paid on sterling holdings as the principal means of controlling money supply growth and inflation.

The Treasury was at first divided about the Conservatives' strategy and there was no enthusiasm for the extra complications an exchange rate target would have introduced.

The Foreign Office pressure in favour of ERM entry quickly ran into the sands, reflecting its weak institutional position on economic issues, as a senior official recalled:

> Although it [the FCO] has consistently had some very bright people on the economic side, who understand the issue as well as anybody else, the Foreign Office is perceived both in Number 10 and the Treasury and elsewhere in Whitehall, as sort of stepping outside of its own parish if it gets involved in financial and monetary discussions.... It's part of the Whitehall one-upmanship.

The only other place where ERM might have found support was the Bank of England, whose governor Gordon Richardson had publicly expressed cautious support for the ERM's objectives. However senior civil servants recall that even in private Richardson was not prepared 'to put its [the Bank's] head very far above the parapet on the issue'. In September 1979, a rumour of British entry swept finance markets, prompting an immediate government denial of intention to join. In October, after the door had been shut, Thatcher held a cabinet meeting with Howe, Richardson and cabinet members and officials. They quickly agreed that membership was not now appropriate and devised a formula that Britain would join when 'the time was right'.

A few months later the ERM issue resurfaced in the context of Thatcher's efforts to negotiate down Britain's EEC budget contributions. The German chancellor, Helmut Schmidt, publicly warned that Britain's chances of a satisfactory settlement would be improved if the UK was seen as becoming a full EEC member by joining the ERM. An official in the Cabinet Office's economic secretariat recalled many less public signals in a similar vein: 'Had we been a full participant in the ERM our general standing could have made the task on the budget that much easier. . . . It would have reduced the antagonism.'

The issue had more steam behind it in the spring of 1980, not only because of Schmidt's offer, but because Gordon Richardson had become opposed to the strict monetary targets of MTFS and now brought the Bank of England round to favouring entry, despite opposition by some of his key staff. As a senior Bank official commented, 'in a way all that matters is what the Governor says'.

However Thatcher quickly stymied the attempt to link the ERM and EEC budget issues. As an FCO official commented: 'It was a constant difficulty to try and persuade her to see things that way [in terms of trade-offs] . . . She would say that was typical Foreign Office stuff.' In public Thatcher told French television that sterling's appreciation 'gave rise to very considerable difficulty' in joining ERM, and within a short period killed off the issue by deciding that 'domestic monetary policy must remain paramount' (Thatcher, 1993, p.692).

The final occasion when joining ERM resurfaced in the first-term Thatcher government was in the second half of 1981, when the economy was at a low ebb after the deflationary budget in April and the government's political fortunes touched an all-time low. Although the budget was designed to achieve a reduction in interest rates and a depreciation in sterling, by autumn 1981 Howe believed that sterling was falling too fast, threatening to increase British inflation levels again. He ordered the Bank of England to raise interest rates in two jumps, eventually producing a 4 per cent rise in UK lending rates.

This experience prompted many ministers to wonder whether British interest rates could not be lowered while safeguarding a non-inflationary value for sterling, if the UK were in ERM. Indeed Nigel Lawson, then financial secretary at the Treasury, started the ball running for a reconsideration of policy in June 1981, but he then left to go to the Energy Department. His efforts did not completely convince Howe, but the chancellor had second thoughts on opposing ERM, as a key Treasury official close to Howe explained:

It was the overvaluation of the pound in 1980 and 1981 and Geoffrey Howe's experiences outside the ERM, when he had to put interest rates up from 12 per cent, in the autumn just before the party conference, to 16 per cent, in order to protect the pound as the pound had started to decline. (Why they wanted to do that I don't know because the pound was still far too high!) It was that that convinced him that stability of exchange rates was an aim that was worth pursuing in the ERM.

Treasury officials remained opposed to ERM, however, especially the chief economic adviser, Terence Burns, and Sir Kenneth Couzens, with the permanent secretary, Douglas Wass, more ambivalent. Despite the interest rate increase, Treasury officials saw their stance as 'looking at all the dials', not just exchange rates. They believed that ERM membership would be too large a shift in policy. A top FCO official agreed that, in autumn 1981, 'I never saw any sign that the Treasury or the Prime Minister was seriously interested in making a move.' Nevertheless Howe's conversion kept the issue very much alive, and preliminary work on entry proceeded well. One of the ministers involved estimated that by the start of 1982 the government was working to a timetable for ERM entry which it came 'within 10 days' of fulfilling.

Thatcher appears to have put an end to this plan at a key meeting in January 1982. The Bank of England and FCO both put up a strong case for membership. The FCO's case was not influential, however, because, as senior officials admit, by late 1981 Thatcher 'tended to discount Foreign Office advice completely'. Moreover, according to one source, the foreign secretary, Lord Carrington, added a sceptical footnote to his presentation, finishing the FCO's pro-ERM brief by saying: 'And that's what my advisers tell me, but I don't believe a word of it.' Lawson's memoirs (1992, pp.111–12) assert that Howe 'could see the attraction but was worried that the ERM might conflict with domestic monetary policy'. But he was not actually at the meeting. At least one person who was there recalls that Howe argued a case for ERM entry with 'modest enthusiasm'. However Thatcher's summing up was decisive, coming down strongly on keeping Britain's 'freedom of manoeuvre', denying advantages in terms of lower interest rates and arguing for delay till UK inflation and interest rates were closer to those of Germany. One participant recalls, 'She destroyed the Bank's case', while another felt: 'She really slammed the door seven or eight times. The arguments were very much in her mind as to why we should not join. The door was slammed, and that was it.'

The Years of Turmoil (1984–8)

Throughout 1982, the election year 1983 and most of 1984 the January 1982 decision stood as the apparently final word. Gordon

Richardson was replaced as governor of the Bank of England by Robin Leigh-Pemberton, and the MTFS enthusiast Peter Middleton took over as permanent secretary at the Treasury. At the same time, the ERM began to operate as a much more fixed exchange rate system, losing many of its previous 'dirty float' characteristics. The discipline of ERM came to be seen as a potent counterinflationary strategy by the member states, especially in France, where inflation dropped from 12 per cent in mid-1983 to 7 per cent two years later. At home the new chancellor, Nigel Lawson, found it increasingly difficult to run a monetarist policy as different indicators of the money supply (which he was supposedly controlling) continued to behave erratically. There was increasing scepticism in financial markets about the government's counterinflationary policy. Yet during this time officials recall Lawson as being 'rather dispassionate' about ERM membership and not seeing 'real positive merit' in entry, a different story from Lawson's memoirs, where he argues that he was a continuous enthusiast from 1981 onwards but did not see 'the right opportunity' to persuade Thatcher.

The decisive event for Lawson was a sterling crisis at the start of 1985. From mid-1984 the government began practising 'benign neglect' towards the currency, allowing sterling to depreciate to around $1.20 in the autumn, and then below that level. In January 1985, the *Sunday Times* ran a story that the government was willing to see a dollar/pound parity (that is, £1 = $1). The story was based on a briefing from Bernard Ingham, Thatcher's chief press officer. Within a week, as the pound fell further, Lawson abandoned 'benign neglect' and raised interest rates by 1 per cent, only to be undermined a day later by another Ingham press briefing denying that Britain's foreign reserves would be 'thrown' into the markets to protect sterling. The Treasury hauled in government information officers from across Whitehall to offset this briefing with saturation denials, and British interest rates were increased a further 1.5 per cent. Lawson told the Commons:

> I am afraid that there was a feeling in the markets that the government had lost their willingness and ability to control their affairs so as to maintain the downward pressure on inflation. (*Hansard*, 13 January 1985)

In February the dollar continued to climb against all currencies and sterling fell as low as $1.03 despite a further interest rate increase (a 4.5 per cent increase in one month). Eventually concerted market interventions by the USA, Japan, Germany, France and Britain stabilised the dollar.

The 1985 sterling crisis raised questions about ERM entry directly, because sterling suffered far more from the dollar's appreciation than did the ERM countries. A conversation between Thatcher and the Dutch premier prompted her to ask Lawson to re-examine the issue, a move he had decided on anyway. As an anti-ERM Treasury official commented, within weeks of the crisis:

> Nigel Lawson decided he wanted to join for reasons that none of us was terribly clear about. It was almost as though, having pursued a successful policy, he wanted to pursue an unsuccessful one for a spell.

At a meeting in mid-February 1985, Lawson lined the Treasury up behind joining ERM, along with the Bank and the FCO (now headed by Geoffrey Howe), while Thatcher seemed less sceptical than in the past, insisting primarily that the UK's foreign currency reserves (depleted by the sterling crisis) were too low to let Britain join the ERM yet. It was left for the chancellor to build up reserves again and come back with a concrete proposal for an entry date.

In public, however, both Lawson and Thatcher denied that staying out of the ERM had made things worse than they would otherwise have been, partly to stem the rising tide of business criticism. The sterling crisis changed CBI and business attitudes quite quickly, as a top CBI official recalls:

> There was a surprising degree of unanimity that, if we were going to set up Britain on a proper basis, if British industry was to be set up satisfactorily, we'd got to have something better than this.

The new ascendency of the City of London in fuelling economic growth also increased pressure for ERM membership, which financiers increasingly saw as a counterinflationary discipline.

Lawson's conversion to ERM entry soon extended to the whole Treasury policy apparatus. In his account, 'I gradually brought my officials round to my way of thinking on the ERM. Since in the end Civil Servants have to support their Minister, they had no real choice' (Lawson, 1992, p.486). One of his senior officials commented: 'He did not require a tremendous amount of advice on all this.' Another recalled that Lawson 'was not a man who relied on the advice of his officials.' So, 'If he says, I want to join the ERM, you talk about it to him, and all the rest of it. But you're not going to say "No, you don't think so".'

Because Lawson's commitment was in absolute form, one senior adviser recalled that 'He was a permanent problem from then on. He basically lost interest in the way we were running economic policy and proceeded to try and run it in a different way, based primarily on the exchange rate.' Nevertheless, to a greater or lesser extent, Middleton, Burns and other senior Treasury officials eventually came to believe for themselves that ERM Membership was the best way forward. 'As far as I could see their conversion was genuine, if in some cases unenthusiastic' (Lawson, 1992, p.486).

In large part the Treasury's switch also reflected a realisation that the MTFS and previous monetarist policies were a busted toolkit: 'We came to the conclusion that there was no single definition of the money supply which is of any utility to a policy operator.' Another official explained: 'We had to take decisions of some sort. We could not just say, we'll continue to think about. That was becoming increasingly untenable.' Two other civil servants argued: 'We never saw it [ERM membership] as a fundamental shift in policy. It's just a question of how you go about the same thing.' And 'It became very attractive simply as a device consistent with what we wanted to do but a damn sight easier to explain.'

Lawson and the Treasury built up ammunition for an autumn 1985 offensive on their terms. A key aide recalls:

> We put a lot of effort into mobilizing allies, and that actually included demobilizing the Foreign Office. . . . They were such an easy target for her [Thatcher] and poor Geoffrey Howe was an easy personal target for her.

In August, Howe gave Lawson a Foreign Office paper advocating ERM entry in the next few months. Lawson was unimpressed by its assumption that realignments would continue to be feasible inside ERM. In September, Lawson, Treasury officials, Robin Leigh-Pemberton and Bank officials, plus Howe and the head of the prime minister's Policy Unit held a seminar with Thatcher at which she remained unconvinced of the desirability of entry and demanded responses to a series of questions. A joint Treasury–Bank team was set up to write a new paper and answer her queries, prepared in large part by Alan Walters, the prime minister's personal economic adviser.

> When the Number 10 questionnaire arrived, it proved to contain no fewer than twenty-three questions and read rather like a rag-bag of every objection to ERM membership that anybody could come up with. (Lawson, 1992, pp.496–7)

Between September and November, optimism grew in the Treasury about the chances of success in convincing Thatcher. One Treasury official commented:

I think I got personally to the point of believing that there might be a slightly better than evens chance. Because we had done our homework well; the seminar had gone not too badly; and the question of Alan Walters, I was inclined to dismiss, and it is something that I still am . . .

The climax of this process was a full ministerial meeting in November 1985. Lawson, Howe and Leigh-Pemberton united behind a Treasury paper advocating entry, supported by Leon Brittan, the Trade and Industry secretary, and backed on the day by Norman Tebbit (then Tory party chairman) and John Wakeham (the chief whip). Only John Biffen, the leader of the House of the Commons (invited as a notorious anti-European sceptic), opposed the recommendation. William Whitelaw, the nominal deputy prime minister, summed up by saying:

'If the Chancellor, the Governor and the Foreign Secretary are all agreed that we should join the EMS that should be decisive. It has certainly decided me.' I suspect he was as surprised as the rest of us when Margaret instantly replied, 'On the contrary: I disagree. If you join the EMS, you will have to do so without me.' There was an awkward silence, and the meeting broke up. (Lawson, 1992, p.499)

A Thatcher confidante present recalled:

Lawson said: 'How can you stand up against it, when your Chancellor and Foreign Secretary are both agreed that it is most urgent that we enter the ERM?' She replied that it was her constitutional responsibility to choose policy.

'At the end of the meeting [when] Margaret swept out, with Griffiths trotting behind her', Lawson's memoirs record that he considered seriously whether to resign, but was then persuaded by the other ministers present to stay on.

Various explanations of Thatcher's opposition have been offered by those involved. The first was an anxiety about having to raise interest rates to defend sterling in the run-up to a general election (the so-called 'Alan Walters question'). A second concern was to avoid previous British financial crises. 'When we go in [to the ERM]', she told the *Financial Times* (11 June 1986), 'we will go in strong and stay in.' Given her carefully cultivated strong leadership image, this concern was a deep one. And finally there was her concept of British national policy being decided in Westminster and Whitehall. A colleague summed up: 'She stood out on grounds of sovereignty, a concept she had read about somewhere but could never tell you where.'

With Thatcher's blank refusal of collective responsibility, Lawson and Howe could have bid the issue up to full cabinet: they never did. A minister commented:

> The nature of British government invests enormous authority in the Prime Minister and if the Prime Minister is a bad loser – and I promise you the previous Prime Minister was a very bad loser – then I think she could have probably survived.

A Foreign Office civil servant observed:

> I dare say there was a bit of reluctance of Treasury officials to plot with Foreign Office officials. The Treasury's view usually is that what is required is for the Prime Minister and the Chancellor of the day to be absolutely at one . . .

This non-cooperation persisted into 1986, despite Lawson and Howe making speeches on 16 April which delicately brought their disagreement with Thatcher out into the public view. Lawson was put off from joint action with Howe because of his perceived weakness as an easy target for Thatcher's criticisms. In addition Lawson was encouraging a depreciation in sterling to stimulate economic growth, and he temporarily lost interest in exchange rate stability as a policy target. Only when sterling threatened to go into free-fall in autumn 1986 did Lawson raise the ERM issue with Thatcher again, as a means of stabilising sterling around the DM3.00 level. However she made it clear that a policy shift could not be discussed before the next general election. Again Lawson and Howe could have coalesced but refused to do so, as an official close to both of them recalled:

> I tried to 'hot' Nigel Lawson and Geoffrey Howe up to demand a Cabinet session on the subject. Because I thought it would be very difficult for her to refuse a firm demand for a Cabinet discussion on the basis of a firm paper from the Chancellor and the Foreign Secretary. And that she would find herself with not too many supporters. I don't know why the hell they didn't do that. They never did.

Instead, by November 1986, Thatcher's second veto had caused the split between the chancellor, Bank of England and foreign secretary, on the one hand, and Thatcher, on the other, to emerge into the open more than ever before. Howe and Lawson publicly affirmed the advantages of ERM entry, and Leigh-Pemberton told a German conference that Britain's non-entry was 'entirely political' (*Financial Times*, 13 November 1986). Treasury officials were alarmed: 'It is absolutely essential that there should be agreement between the Prime Minister and the Chancellor on really important things. If and when they don't agree, you carry on until they do.' Lawson sought approval from Thatcher for raising interest rates to manage the sterling parity, but got only a grudging and partial agreement.

In February 1987, at the international conference of the G7 group of advanced industrial countries, the UK signed up for an accord pledging in general terms to try and achieve exchange rate stability. On the back of this commitment, Lawson returned to the Treasury and began a policy of tying sterling to the ERM's strongest and hence most central currency, the Deutschmark. He maintained an 'informal' rate of three marks to the pound. In the changed market conditions of 1987, with sterling rising, this now meant cutting interest rates. Thatcher later claimed in her memoirs that 'extraordinarily enough' she had no idea of what was going on until November 1987, more than nine months later. She says she found out only when journalists pointed out to her during an interview that the Bank of England had been intervening to maintain the DM3.00 level. Thatcher recalls:

> The implications of this were, of course, very serious at several levels. First, Nigel had pursued a personal economic policy without reference to the rest of the government. How could I possibly trust him again? Second, our intervention in the exchange markets might well have inflationary consequences. Third, perhaps I had allowed interest rates to be taken too low in order that Nigel's undisclosed policy of keeping the pound below DM3 should continue. (Thatcher, 1993, pp.701–2; see also Ridley, 1991, pp.201–2)

However, Lawson denies concealing anything from Thatcher. His then officials point out that each night the prime minister's economic private secretary receives the Treasury's daily market reports:

> Whether she would actually see them depends on the private secretary. But I am pretty sure that, given the size of the movements that were in there, the private secretary would say: 'Here, you'd better have a look at this'.

Lawson's account seems most plausible since Thatcher herself admitted in interviews long before her memoirs were written that she *had* known about the shadowing of the Deutschmark, and described allowing it to go on as her 'great mistake' (*The Times*, 29 June 1991).

The people who were really kept in the dark by Lawson were the Bank of England. Officials there regarded the policy as a 'total disaster':

> Shadowing was the worst of both worlds because the markets don't really believe it. . . . You have to defend the target without credibility. You have to put more effort into defending it because they [the markets] can't really believe you should be defending it.

Another commented:

> He [Lawson] could not give it the proper airing and debate in the decision-making process that should normally attend these things because he was actually wanting to do something which he knew his neighbour next door would not actually agree to. . . . It was a private enterprise attempt to be a proxy member of ERM.

Thatcher started to complain about shadowing in December 1987. By the start of 1988, the financial markets believed that the DM3.00 rate represented a 'ceiling' for sterling, and pressure grew on Lawson to keep the currency from appreciating past this level with reserve interventions and interest rate cuts. A few days before the tax-cutting 1988 budget, Thatcher told Lawson that the level of reserve intervention was unacceptable, demanding an end to the DM3.00 ceiling. Lawson recorded in his memoirs: 'There was no way in which I could contemplate resigning then: I was determined to introduce the 1988 budget for which I had laboured so long and hard. And Margaret knew this' (Lawson, 1992, p.795). Thatcher's thinking moved on the same lines:

> The question arises whether at some point now or later I should have sacked Nigel. I would have been fully justified in doing so. He had pursued a policy without my knowledge or consent and he continued to adopt a different approach from that which he knew I wanted. On the other hand, he was widely – and rightly – credited with helping us win the 1987 election. He had complete intellectual mastery of his brief. He had the strong support of Conservative back-benchers and much of the Conservative press who had convinced themselves that I was in the wrong and that only pettiness or pig-headedness could explain the different line I took. (Thatcher, 1993, p.703)

In the event, the stand-off between the two continued. Shadowing was ended by letting the pound rise against the mark, Thatcher declaring in the Commons that 'there is no way in which one can buck the market'. However she agreed that interest rate cuts to curb sterling's appreciation could continue. Together with the income tax cuts in the budget, this shift created strong inflationary pressure in the economy, which particularly troubled Bank officials, one of whom recalled:

> It was clear that the Bank of England was at the end of its tether at what Lawson was doing. . . . The Bank felt they were put in an impossibly compromised position by the inflationary boom. It was a disastrous policy. Some of them [Bank decision makers] may have come close to resigning, I think.

With the Bank marginalised and Thatcher, Lawson and Howe feuding in public, Thatcher called a meeting at which a compromise was eventually hammered out, postponing an ERM decision, but everyone present at last agreed on the need for exchange rate stability.

The Endgame on Entry (1989–90)

Even as the shadowing fiasco receded, the debacle over ERM began to take on a wholly new dimension, as monetary union moved to the top of the European Community agenda. At the Hanover summit in June 1988, the EC states, including Britain, agreed to create a committee to investigate the means necessary to achieve monetary union. The committee was chaired by Jacques Delors, with the governor of the Bank of England, Robin Leigh-Pemberton, as Britain's representative. By common consent he made a completely inadequate defence of the UK's opposition to monetary union, on which Lawson and Thatcher actually concurred. An FCO civil servant recalls:

> Robin Leigh Pemberton did not have any instructions of any kind in all that year of the Delors Report. . . . He never saw Mrs Thatcher after he signed it to discuss it. I mean she just went around saying that he was a bloody idiot to go along with it.

Bank of England people argue that 'The Treasury were kept in touch with what was happening but more by way of letting them know what had happened at each meeting.' But Treasury insiders are critical, one commenting that Leigh-Pemberton 'was a bit out of his depth in central banking circles. . . . He saw being Governor as a part-time job in his spare time from being Lord Lieutenant of Kent.' Another remembered: 'I think Nigel Lawson was pretty fed up with the way that Robin Leigh-Pemberton allowed himself to be carried along. . . . He spoke scathingly of the inability of the Governor to stop it.'

The result was that Leigh-Pemberton signed the unanimous Delors committee report setting out a timetable for establishing a single currency and a European central bank. Published in April 1989, the Delors report directly contradicted both Thatcher's anti-Europeanism, famously expressed in the autumn 1988 Bruges speech, and Lawson's public criticisms of the monetary union idea. But Whitehall was uncertain what to offer as an official response, as a senior civil servant noted:

> It was quite difficult after the Delors report was actually published to discover what the government's attitude actually was. And as we were supposed to be working for the government, it was a period of some confusion.

The prospect of complete monetary union strengthened ERM in the exchange markets and convinced the City of London that staying out would weaken their position as Europe's leading financial market.

Lawson now started to argue inside Whitehall that the UK needed to join the ERM so that it could slow down the momentum towards monetary union. In contrast, the Delors report only seemed to strengthen Thatcher's opposition. Lawson comments on a May 1989 meeting:

> It was evident to both of us that the discussion was getting nowhere; but the terms in which she brought it to a close were particularly revealing. 'I do not want you to raise the subject ever again,' she said; 'I must prevail.' It was those last three words that said it all. The economic and political arguments had become an irrelevance. Joining the ERM, as she saw it, had become a battle of wills between her and me. (Lawson, 1992, p.918)

The extra dimension of European monetary union, plus Thatcher's increasingly dogmatic rejection of discussion, finally forced Lawson and Howe together into joint action after all their years of dithering and non-cooperation. In mid-June 1989, as a preparation for the EC's Madrid summit, they began work on a joint memorandum about the conditions under which the UK would enter the ERM. A Treasury official recalls: 'What was extraordinarily unusual was something that comes out in the Lawson memoirs, that he and Geoffrey Howe signed a joint minute. That is very, very rare in Whitehall.' At a first meeting Thatcher rejected their arguments, and a strong counter memo from her foreign policy adviser Charles Powell set out strict terms of entry. Lawson and Howe agreed that they would insist on their conditions or both resign. At a Sunday meeting on 25 June 1988, the three met again, hours before Thatcher and Howe were due to leave for the European summit. In Lawson's account:

> The atmosphere was unbelievably tense. As before, Geoffrey opened, and spoke briefly along the lines of the minute. Margaret was unmoveable. Geoffrey then said that if she had not time for his advice, and was not prepared to make the sort of forward move at Madrid necessary to avoid the disastrous outcome he feared, then he would have no alternative but to resign. I then chipped in, briefly to say, 'You should know, Prime Minister, that if Geoffrey goes, I must go too.' There was an icy silence, and the meeting came to an abrupt end, with nothing resolved. (Lawson, 1992, p.933)

In Thatcher's account:

> I would never, never allow this to happen again. I refused to give them any undertaking that I would set a date [for ERM entry]. Indeed, I told them that I could not believe that a Chancellor and a former Chancellor could seriously argue that I should set a date in advance: it would be a field day for the speculators, as they should have known. I said I would reflect further on what to say at Madrid. They left, Geoffrey looking insufferably smug. (Thatcher, 1993, p.712)

At the Madrid summit Thatcher announced a set of conditions for Britain to join the ERM, including convergence of UK inflation with other EC countries' rates and the removal of all exchange controls and barriers to financial competition inside Europe. Thatcher claimed that these conditions were based on a paper by Alan Walters, rather than on the Lawson–Howe memorandums. But, briefed by Ingham, the media saw Thatcher's announcement as a significant shift *towards* ERM. The media reaction made it impossible for Howe and Lawson to resign together. They met and agreed that 'a resignation in those circumstances would have been bizarre and incomprehensible' (Lawson, 1992, pp.934–5).

In fact a close Thatcher confidante recalled:

I would argue that the conditions for our joining ERM were made more difficult by her statement in Madrid, not brought closer and that was a deliberate act of defiance of them [Lawson and Howe]. In effect they had to climb down when she came home and pretend to be satisfied with what they'd done.... What we did was spell out the conditions which would have to be met if sterling were to join the ERM. And when you actually spelled out the conditions, it became quite clear that the hurdles were a good deal higher than the previous rather vague general formulation that we'll join when the time was right.

A cabinet minister concurred: 'She gave sufficient ground to make everyone believe she had given more ground than she had done.'

To compound the confusion, although Thatcher formally accepted the Delors report at the Madrid summit, she declared at a press conference immediately afterwards that Britain would be putting forward its own alternative proposals to the report. Lawson recalls:

The first I and my senior officials knew of this proposal was a report on the radio from Madrid which stated that the Treasury was already working on alternatives to Delors. Peter Middleton [Treasury Permanent Secretary] subsequently told me that he heard the news when driving his car, and was so astonished that he nearly crashed into a tree. (Lawson, 1992, p.939)

Returning to the Commons after the summit, Thatcher also speculated that the ERM might collapse if France and Italy abolished exchange controls, as her conditions required.

Over the summer the feuding and deadlock at the heart of government continued. Thatcher removed Howe from the Foreign Office, demoting him to the nominal role of deputy prime minister, and bringing in John Major to replace him. His chance to resign before Madrid blown, Howe accepted the demotion quietly, biding his time. In the early autumn, the British balance of payments deficit widened and sterling fell on the foreign exchange markets again. Lawson got Thatcher's permission to follow the Germans in raising interest rates in October. But press stories soon began to circulate that Alan Walters opposed doing so, and that Thatcher had now set her face against further rises to defend sterling. On 18 October, extracts from one of Walters' articles were published in the *Financial Times* in which he described ERM as 'half-baked'. Labour attacked the government for again sending out confusing messages and Lawson concluded that he could not carry on if Walters stayed. He demanded that Thatcher sack Walters and, when she failed to do, Lawson resigned. Sterling plunged on the foreign exchange markets and by evening Walters, too, had resigned.

Thatcher now brought Major over from the FCO to be chancellor and appointed Douglas Hurd as foreign secretary. As the finance markets settled down, with both her Madrid opponents moved from their posts, Thatcher felt freer to express in a TV interview her opposition to the ERM:

> The various countries in that particular exchange rate play by different rules. That is nonsense. When you join any system, you must all play by the same rules. . . . You just simply can't have a system with a currency like sterling, which is a big currency, which has London as the most open market, freest market in the world, playing under that higgledy-piggledy set of rules.

Asked if it was true that 'the UK shall not be going into ERM for quite some time,' Thatcher replied: 'That depends on them [the other EC countries], on the gap between what they say and do' (*Financial Times*, 30 October 1989).

Yet within a few months of apparently redominating her government, Thatcher found her blocking stance unsustainable. Both Major at the Treasury and Hurd at the FCO began to re-exert their departments' pressure for ERM entry, even though the Bank of England began to have some backtracking doubts because of the rise in the UK's inflation rate. The European Community's momentum towards monetary union seemed strong and Britain's voice was increasingly marginalised. In December 1989, at the Strasburg summit, the EC states set the starting dates for two critical conferences on monetary and political union for December 1990 over Thatcher's opposition.

Faced with this immediate problem, Hurd persuaded Major in a series of bilaterals to join the FCO in pressing in a low-key way for entry. As UK inflation worsened in 1990, the government was left with a palpably inadequate set of policy measures for controlling it, except high interest rates which increased the risk of recession. In late March 1990, Thatcher met Major and agreed to let it be publicly known that she had agreed in principle to UK membership of ERM, although still declaring the time not yet ripe. Yet this new stance was largely camouflage, designed to reassure the foreign exchange markets and to secure an appreciation in sterling for counterinflationary purposes. Several insiders felt that Thatcher actually did not change her mind on ERM until September 1992. One commented: 'I think the Prime Minister was only convinced quite late, when it appeared that joining the ERM would allow us to control inflation at lower interest rates at a time when the government's economic policies were under attack.' And a Bank insider remarked: 'I don't think a decision was taken early in the year to do it specifically in the autumn.' At the EC's Dublin summit in July 1990, Thatcher again attacked the 'folly' of fixed exchange rates, nearly upsetting the work being done by Hurd and Major to prepare other EC states for Britain's entry.

When it came, the end of Thatcher's resistance was sudden, and not at all preplanned, as D. Smith (1992) and other commentators have presented it. By October 1990, during the Labour party's successful party conference week, Major assembled some senior Treasury officials and Eddie George, the deputy governor of the Bank of England, to go and see Thatcher to obtain her agreement for final planning preparations for entry before the end of the year. A senior official recalls:

> We went to the Prime Minister for an informal discussion about this – she was going out to dinner somewhere; she had to get into a long dress so the whole thing was punctuated by this changing – with a view to joining later in the year. The [Conservative] party conference was coming up and none of us wanted to join close to the party conference. I'm totally allergic to doing things close to party conference, interest rate changes or anything.
>
> It was a Thursday night when we went to see her. She said: 'All right, do you think it will be all right?' 'It will certainly be all right for the next six to seven months.' The Prime Minister said: 'Could you bring down interest rates at the same time?' We said, 'Yes', because we wanted to bring down interest rates anyway. She then said: 'Well, can you do it [join ERM] tomorrow?' 'Well, that would be extremely difficult.'
>
> So we then adjourned to see when we could assemble the monetary committee [of ERM] and we said: 'No, we can't do it tomorrow. But we can have it done by the weekend.' And she said: 'Goodness knows how we are joining at 2.95' [Deutschmarks, the prevailing sterling exchange rate].

The next day, and with no warning to the other ERM countries, John Major announced to the media outside the door of Number 10 that Britain would join ERM immediately. The suddenness of the decision in this account was confirmed by a Bank of England official who commented:

> Discussions most immediately associated with the decision itself were very closely focused on a short period of time. There had

been quite a lot of fairly general discussion about it in the run-up. But then suddenly when things started to coalesce [and] move very fast, it was really a very short period of discussions about things like [the] appropriate rate and [the] precise moment.

The rushed decision meant that no real review of the rate at which Britain would enter the ERM was possible, while all the other member countries were suddenly asked to accept a *fait accompli* without consultation. A former Bank official remarked:

> Typical. After waiting all these years, they [Thatcher and Major] just told them [the other ERM countries]. If they had actually had a meeting [of ERM's monetary committee], had a whole weekend, and said in any kind of an open sense: 'Look, we are thinking of this kind of rate', I'm sure they would have heard from the others, at least privately, if not in open committee, 'Are you sure about this rate?'. . . . It was an extraordinary thing to do.

Something of the importance of entering at DM2.95 can be gleaned from one of the few business voices critical of the decision at the time, an exporting company executive who declared presciently:

> We would have preferred a rate of DM2.65. The current rate is far too high. The internationally tradeable sector will have a very tough time, there could be two years of sub-optimal growth, investment will be cut and I expect a sharp rise in unemployment. (*Financial Times*, 6 October 1990)

A senior decision maker in another top manufacturing company described the DM2.95 rate decision as 'an unmitigated disaster' (*The Times*, 6 October 1990). Some economic estimates suggest that the pound was overvalued by about 15 per cent on its rushed entry. Thus the decade of wrong decisions closed with a botched entry, ironically at just the time when the ERM itself began to suffer from the severe pressures produced by German unification – pressures which UK entry at the wrong rate compounded.

Analysing the ERM Fiasco

The ERM decision-making saga has considerable significance for two contemporary arguments about where power lies and how decision making operated in Britain: disputes about the salience of the core executive compared with 'policy communities'; and arguments about the importance of 'institutional' influences on policy making versus more individualistic, political leadership influences.

Policy Communities v. Core Executive

An important strand in contemporary political science, which in some respects became the 'conventional wisdom' in the discipline during the 1980s, argued that the central policy-making dynamics in the UK focus on interactions between civil service departments, interest groups, professions, quasi-governmental agencies and local authorities, organised as policy 'networks' (in more loosely coordinated or open issues) or as policy 'communities' (in areas with dominant professions or strongly integrated policy implementation systems). Policy communities are basically separated issue areas characterised by frequent consultation between members, a shared specialist language of debate, consensual bargaining and fairly stable policy outcomes (Jordan and Richardson, 1987; Marsh and Rhodes, 1992b). A key implication of this view is that, if the basic dynamics of policy change operate at the interactions between central government and social actors, at what C. Wright Mills termed the 'middle levels of power', the scope for core executive activity is restricted to the 'icing on the cake' (Dunleavy and Rhodes, 1990, p.20; Mills, 1956; and for an extended example see Keliher, Chapter 10 above).

But to affirm that policy communities *normally* predominate across all policy areas and time periods is too sweeping and generalised an assertion. The third-term Thatcher government affords many examples of issues previously the preserve of policy communities being pulled suddenly into the core executive and radically restructured from the top downwards. The policy community approach was always at its least plausible in relation to strategic economic decisions, but this did not put off Jordan and Richardson from pushing their view to its fullest extent: 'Groups do not have insider access to influence all kinds of policy but even where policy is evolved internally, in the longer term it will only be tenable if it can be sold to an influential constituency' (Jordan and Richardson, 1987, p.179). Thus high politics issues (like ERM) are not excluded from the policy communities approach. Instead over time they will be broken up into smaller chunks which can be handled in a policy community fashion: 'the disaggregation of all policy issues into "low" and "manageable" problems' (Jordan and Richardson, 1991, p.161).

Set this approach against the evolution of ERM policy, and its inadequacies and limitations are starkly apparent. On many economic policy issues – not just monetary policy and exchange rate management, but also taxation and public expenditure – the core executive simply executes its own decisions. Policy making is confined within the core executive itself because decisions cannot be made in the stable national environment and cooperative group/government relations described by the policy community literature. The volatility of foreign exchange markets and the interdependence of national economies means that economic policy makers are forced to operate in an unpredictable (increasingly global) environment facing 'acute' issues where there is often not time for consultation or prolonged sifting of options (Polsby, 1984). If there is a run on sterling or the Bundesbank raises its interest rates, the core executive will not wait to ask the CBI's position before deciding on a response.

Similarly, while the policy community literature stresses that policy makers seek to avoid risks, much economic policy is essentially about risk assessment. Policy makers are forced to make recurring choices about the same policy options, notably the level of interest rates, public expenditure and taxation. In each case they are assessing how firms, consumers and financial markets which they cannot control are likely to respond to policy changes. But they make this assessment by forecasting and modelling statistical probabilities and making judgements about dynamics, not via consultations.

On ERM, shifts in business opinion were significant background influences in 1985, when a procession of business leaders affirmed their conversion to embracing membership, and again in the winter and spring of 1988/9, when the Delors report's timetable for monetary union pushed most of the City of London's finance capital interests and the financial press into insisting that the UK could not be left on the sidelines. But the causal effectiveness of these shifts in influencing policy making was extremely limited. Outside interests responded late to issues which core executive actors had anticipated. Internal government actors had made initiatives to change policy and fully defined the decision agenda and available options on both occasions. Business mobilisations were no more than a Greek chorus for the principal players.

Similarly party political considerations and influences impinged on the fringes of the ERM decisions at several points, sometimes giving a particular 'spin' to arguments inside the core executive, as in Thatcher's reluctance to announce changes in the monetarist MTFS strategy long after insiders recognised it as dead, and her 1985–7 worries about being boxed into ERM in difficult circumstances with a general election looming. But party mobilisations and shifts of opinion only became a seriously constraining influence in the ERM endgame, when Thatcher's isolation in the Conservative parliamentary party, lack of alternative ministerial colleagues and declining political popularity pushed her into accepting ERM entry as inevitable. But again the policy logics and internal core executive pressures were so strong that it is hard to know what weight to attach to these influences.

Institutions v. Leaders

If policy influence on ERM unequivocally lies within the core executive, however, there still remains an important issue about which kind of influences prevail there. An important strand in the 1980s revival of so-called 'state-centred' theory has been 'new institutionalist' accounts, whose central proposition is that institutions shape individual actors' behaviour in extensive ways. Individual policy makers, whether cabinet ministers or officials, essentially follow institutional rules and routines rather than making carefully worked-through choices or rationalistic decisions on a case-by-case basis. When new issues arise, actors primarily process them by classifying the issue in terms of previous organisational experiences and the collective historical memory of institutions. Rules and norms exist and are so influential because they are the best means by which both individual and collective actors can avoid disorder and potential chaos. As a result, the logic of institutional action is one of appropriateness so that actors respond to situations with the most appropriate action given prevailing rules and the consequences for institutional stability (March and Olsen, 1989).

In the see-saw debate over ERM membership, a new institutionalist approach would suggest that the major organisational locations – the Treasury, the Bank of England, the Foreign Office and (possibly) Downing Street and the Cabinet Office – would set the agenda, structure the debates, survey the vast majority of policy options, set the rules for sifting and sorting through choices and, overall, dominate the decision process. Individual ministers and officials would appear in this kind of story primarily as representatives of their institution, bearers of its roles and perceptions and culture, more than as autonomous sources of intentionality. In terms of outcomes, we should expect to see policy changing only gradually, and in response to long-run, carefully considered adaptions in the positions of the relevant institutions. Through much of the general academic literature on UK economic policy, the image of an all-powerful Treasury assisted by the Bank of

England also looms large (see Ingham, 1984; Ham, 1984; Keegan and Pennant-Rea, 1979; Hodgeman, 1983).

However, the ERM case shows that a new institutionalist account of UK macroeconomic policy making oriented on these lines would explain only the pitch on which the game is played and some of the enduring rules. It could not tackle the strategies adopted by the central actors (Thatcher and Lawson) or the eventual policy outcomes which resulted. Organisations' established ways of processing issues were important at some junctures. The inability of Lawson and Howe to cooperate was strongly shaped in 1985 and again in 1989 by the Treasury's inhibitions about letting any other department impinge on their turf, or trying to make macroeconomic decisions bypass the premier. But their entrenched attitudes about chancellor–prime minister agreement could not stop Lawson from shadowing the mark in 1987. Indeed Treasury officials' committed attachment to their own bureaucratic predominance facilitated Lawson's decision to keep the Bank of England formally in the dark about his policy. In a broader contextual way, both the Treasury's and the Bank's institutionalised perceptions of fixed exchange rate systems influenced policy making in severely damaging and limiting ways. In the 1978–83 period they were convinced that no element of flexibility could be incorporated into such a system, so that they failed to anticipate the way in which ERM operated as a 'dirty float' until 1983, giving time for currencies to become adjusted to coexistence. This misperception significantly inhibited Britain's chances of joining early on. Later, in 1988–9, no British policy maker, basically, could take the idea of monetary union seriously, so that Leigh-Pemberton was left unbriefed and bemused to sign up for a Delors committee report which he had no chance of influencing.

Institutional rules and perceptions did not determine the development of ERM policy, the options considered, or the outcomes reached. Instead the central, critical working out of policy reflected primarily the disputes between Thatcher and Lawson and Howe. Lawson embraced ERM early on, in 1981 (for a time) and his efforts to shift policy then combined with Howe's own reassessments to alter the chances of entry significantly, even while Treasury attachment to monetarist orthodoxy was unshaken. Again, in 1985, Lawson determined a shift in Treasury policy, against the weight of most of his senior officials and the Treasury's ingrained hostility to fixed exchange rate systems. Nor did either Howe's or Lawson's conversion reflect Bank influence, for their role *vis-à-vis* ministers was quite minimal.

As for Thatcher's long rearguard action against ERM, its sources could only be traced to strong personal and dispositional characteristics, and its effectiveness to the considerable veto power of the prime minister on macroeconomic policy issues. Progressively coming to stand virtually alone in her cabinets in terms of the depth and vigour of her anti-ERM feeling, Thatcher could none the less manipulate cabinet committees, ministerial meetings and bilaterals to ensure that the issue never reached full cabinet. And she repeatedly used her power to damage her chancellor and foreign secretary by publicly taking a different line, especially via her Lobby mouthpiece, Bernard Ingham, pushing always at the limits of irresponsibility in her willingness to infringe clear national interests in pursuit of personal objectives. But she could only pick her ministers within limits, could not fire them at will, and could not secure policy implementation as she wished. 'I must prevail' was less the demand for omnipotence which Lawson perceived, more the plaintive refrain of a dominant leader finding herself able only to block ERM membership, not prevent it from constantly returning and dominating the economic agenda.

Conclusions

The dominance of personalised, non-institutional, leadership influences in ERM decision making raises in an acute and difficult form questions about whether Britain's fundamental arrangements for making strategic decisions are inadequate, especially for macroeconomic policy. The prime minister and chancellor are closeted in a closed and secret policy-making environment against the enormous backdrop of the foreign exchange markets, where their every public word might have huge consequences. They have to give an unremitting 'performance' to the foreign exchange markets and national and international news media. The pressures involved may create a loss of objectivity, overidentification of actors with their chosen public stance and even self-deception as the performer becomes 'convinced at the moment that the impression of reality which he fosters is the one and only reality' (Goffman, 1959, p.86).

Some partial institutional responses to the 1980s fiascos have already been set in place under Major. External and academic economic policy advice is now formally given by the chancellor's 'seven wise men' in an open and public mode. And a record of the regular monthly meetings between the governor of the Bank of England and the chancellor is now published (a month in arrears), part of an effort by ministers to stave off greater demands for institutional independence for the Bank. Both these shifts recognise that only much greater openness in policy deliberations, and much clearer accounting by core executive actors for their decisions, can cure the recurrent problems of 'groupthink' and presenters' self-deception which plagued ERM disputes. But such modest moves in this direction seem unlikely to be sufficient, as the spiralling deterioration in relations between John Major and his chancellor, Norman Lamont, bears witness. After Britain was forced to leave ERM in 1992, the prime minister and chancellor were again at loggerheads, and the Treasury's standing in Whitehall slipped to what some observers regard as a postwar low point.

Nor has policy since 1992 suggested any stronger mastery of the ERM issues amongst ministers or the key departments involved in monetary policy making. When Britain (along with Italy) was forcibly expelled from the ERM in 1992, the Treasury and Bank assumed that the ERM would quickly disintegrate like all fixed exchange rate systems before it, a view reinforced by the currency turbulence of the next year and the ending of ERM's narrow bands in July 1993. So the UK cheerfully embarked on a large unilateral devaluation, with the pound drifting down to a rate of DM2.40 by 1994. Both the Treasury and the Bank then reacted with delayed amazement as the other ERM countries failed to cut loose in the same manner. Instead the franc/D-mark parity and most of the currency alignments supposedly 'destroyed' by the 1993 crisis were quickly restored. Within a year of British ministers proclaiming the end of ERM and Britain's foresight in baling out early, monetary union was back on the agenda for as early as 1999, provoking a startled protest, breaching party discipline, from Michael Portillo, the then Treasury number two minister. The spectre of a two-tier Europe which so spooked City of London firms in 1989 thus returned to haunt British policy makers under John Major.

12

Leaders, Politics and Institutional Change: The Decline of Prime Ministerial Accountability to the House of Commons, 1868–1990

PATRICK DUNLEAVY AND G.W. JONES
WITH JANE BURNHAM, ROBERT ELGIE AND PETER FYSH*

Analysing Institutional Change

Political institutions are created in complex ways: by formal organisational arrangements, by conventions and agreements which surround and insulate these mechanics, by shared understandings and cognitions, and by emotive attachments and identifications (March and Olsen, 1984, 1989). At their core, however, what gives institutional arrangements peculiar moral force may be their 'natural' quality, their apparent analogy with easily understood or larger processes at work in the physical world or the broader society (Douglas, 1987). The practices of legislatures often embody some longstanding basic principles (such as majority voting and the rules of fair debate) whose apparent 'naturalness' and ancient origins play an important part in assuring legitimacy for legislative outcomes. In maintaining the accountability of govern-

*We would like to thank Alan Beattie, Rod Rhodes and Brendan O'Leary, for help and comments on an earlier draft of the chapter, as well as David Sanders and an anonymous referee.

ments, most liberal democratic legislatures rely on apparently simple 'answerability' mechanisms – making members of the executive
directly and personally explain government policies and decisions.
This approach is fundamental, creating potent interactions where
precise verbal formulations and personal responses function as
clues to underlying attitudes in a way that indirect accountability
inherently could never replicate.

In the US congressional system oversight hearings are
always specific, inquisitorial and focused on officials immediately
in control of policy: they never extend to the direct interrogation
of the president and very rarely encompass even their senior staff
or cabinet members. But in Westminster-model systems the integration of the executive into the legislature is emphasised by wide-
ranging and generalised accounting for government actions by
ministers, especially by the prime minister, in various forms of
parliamentary debate and scrutiny. The heart of this relationship
in Westminster systems, symbolically and practically, is the active
attendance of the premier and ministers in the House of Commons. To be accountable, they must first be present in, and involved in the operations of, the legislature – that is the
fundamental assumption of a parliamentary system.

In fact British prime ministers do not take part in many aspects
of the House of Commons' work. They never attend standing
committee discussions and, so far, have never testified before any
of the departmental select committees. With the exception of voting in the division lobbies, their overt and formal parliamentary
participation is limited to answering questions, making statements,
giving speeches in debates and intervening in debates. All these
occur in 'whole House' settings on the floor of the Commons
chamber itself; and under most parliamentary conventions, the
opportunities for the leader of the opposition to perform in Parliament are largely limited to those occasions when the prime minister is there.

Despite their importance, the four kinds of prime ministerial
activity listed above have never been systematically studied before.
However in this chapter we examine a database showing how prime
ministers have behaved in the House of Commons in every year
from 1868 to the dramatic fall of Margaret Thatcher in November
1990, a period that covers 19 different premiers. We examine
questions, statements, speeches and debating interventions in
turn, before looking at overall measures of prime ministers'
activism.

Answering Questions

Figure 12.1 shows the number of times in each session that the prime minister has answered questions since 1868, adjusted to iron out differences solely caused by variations in session lengths. All the data included in the graphs, and most of those reported in the text, are statistically reweighted for comparability to refer to a session of average duration. At a few points in the text we refer to the 'actual scores' (that is unadjusted numbers of times) that prime ministers undertook activity, but these occasions are always explicitly flagged. The data in Figure 12.1 are also smoothed to remove single-year deviations from the general pattern, allowing us to concentrate on the underlying patterns (for details, see Dunleavy, Jones *et al.*, 1993).

At the start of our period prime ministers were still developing the practice of answering questions. The clerks of the House simply entered questions for them on the daily order paper listing questions to ministers in the sequence they were received. A resolution of 1869 formalised the previous practice of grouping ministers' questions together at a fixed point in the day's business, which over the next decade became the start of the day. But the prime minister still had to sit through all of ministers' question time in order to respond to those addressed to him. In the late 1860s and 1870s, Gladstone answered questions on around 70 days a session, but

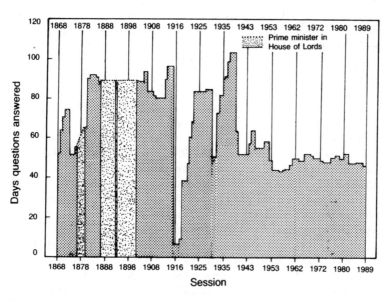

Figure 12.1   *Smoothed adjusted questions per session, 1868–1989*

Disraeli much less, averaging just over 50 days a session before he moved to the House of Lords.

From the 1880s, prime ministers' questions were bunched together and placed last on the order paper for ministers' question time. Simultaneously other methods for backbench MPs to raise grievances were being closed off by revisions to standing orders. Both changes fuelled questions to the prime minister and, during Gladstone's second administration in the early 1880s, he answered questions on 90 days a session on average. This record basically defined the norm for most subsequent premiers up to the Second World War. When the premiership returned to the Commons in 1902, the increased pressure of questions to ministers meant that those for the prime minister were pushed further down the order paper and sometimes were not reached. In 1904, Commons procedures were changed to list the prime minister's questions at a fixed point on the order paper, number 45, on each of the four main parliamentary days of the week. This pattern endured for half a century. The changes meant that Balfour broadly continued Gladstone's pattern and was especially active in the closing years of his premiership. Campbell-Bannerman and then Asquith were both rather more diffident, but Asquith answered questions more frequently with the descent into war in 1914.

Previous norms for question answering were dramatically interrupted in Lloyd George's period as prime minister, beginning in 1916. In his last three wartime sessions as prime minister, Asquith answered questions on 287 days (actual scores), averaging 98 days a session on an adjusted basis. In his three long wartime and peacemaking sessions from 1916 to 1920, Lloyd George answered questions on only 20 days (actual scores), an average score of nine days a session when reweighted. In the same period he made 17 statements, seven major speeches and 34 minor interventions in debates – so that his question-answering slumped far more dramatically than his other forms of parliamentary behaviour.

Constructing a balanced coalition government and replacing the normal cabinet system with a streamlined war cabinet structure allowed Lloyd George to withdraw from routine parliamentary activity altogether. He passed over the role of leader of the House of Commons completely to the Conservative leader, Bonar Law, who also shouldered the main burden of replying for the government to criticism from the Asquithian Liberals (Rowland, 1975, p.379). Even in peacetime Lloyd George never resumed the task of leader of the House. The prime minister explained his absences from the Commons in terms of the pressures of his executive role alone (Riddell, 1933, pp.240–41), but his biographers are in no doubt that his behaviour reflected a strong disposition to avoid routine parliamentary occasions. 'Had he been a genuinely free agent . . . he would probably have dispensed with the House of Commons altogether for the duration of the war' (Rowland, 1975, p.379).

When the Versailles peace conference closed, Lloyd George had to adapt his behaviour to peacetime conditions, and do something to halt the simmering discontent about his remoteness from the mass of Conservative MPs on which the postwar coalition government depended. The prime minister complained that his questions listed at number 45 in the order paper were not being reached, and for two years they were listed higher, at number 25. As a result, Lloyd George's activity increased and he answered questions 121 times (actual scores) in the 1920–22 period, handling many foreign affairs issues (because Foreign Secretary Curzon was in the Lords and later the prime minister was involved in arranging summit conferences) and on Irish matters and industrial relations. Even this increased level of activity still amounted to only 41 days a session, less than half the prewar average. The Commons' resentment of his remoteness continued and helped to fuel the decision by the Carlton Club meeting of Tory MPs to withdraw from the coalition government in October 1922.

After this dramatic interruption of established practices the inter-war period as a whole represented a return to a modified Gladstonian pattern. Bonar Law took back the leader of the House role, an example followed by all other premiers up to Chamberlain, and prime minister's questions were once more scheduled at their traditional point in the order paper (number 45). As a result inter-war prime ministers again basically answered questions on between 80 and 100 days a session, with no overall trend discernible in their frequency of response. Bonar Law in 1922–3 and MacDonald in 1923 had rather lower scores, intermediate between Lloyd George's last sessions and this later pattern. But Baldwin and MacDonald in 1929–31 resumed very much Asquith's peacetime level of activity. The formation of the National Government occasioned an interruption, however. MacDonald's behaviour changed in 1931–3, so that he answered questions on just 50 days a year, around half the normal average. This dip clearly reflected the exceptional conditions of coalition government and MacDonald's general distaste for the Commons, where he was attacked by former Labour colleagues (see below). From the mid-1930s onwards both Baldwin and Chamberlain again answered questions more frequently. Indeed Chamberlain's score was consistently over 100 days a session, largely because his foreign secretary, Lord Halifax, was a peer and the prime minister consequently took most Commons questions on foreign policy.

The formation of another war cabinet with the onset of the Second World War marked the permanent end of the Gladstone pattern. Churchill's wartime attendances to answer questions fluctuated below 50 days a session, partly because he 'found the House uncongenial in the early months of his premiership [and] rarely attended', but also because he effectively assigned the leader of the House of Commons' role to the Labour leader, Attlee, and later formally gave it up altogether (Harris, 1982, pp.180, 192). From 1940 onwards the roles of prime minister and leader of the House were never again combined, so that in the modern era 'Only very rarely are the Prime Minister and the leader of the Opposition directly concerned with parliamentary business' (Wilson, 1976, p.145).

None the less Churchill avoided the trap into which Lloyd George fell, of losing touch with the Commons altogether. Having started by being more active (when he was minister for defence), Attlee also answered questions around 55 days a session, signalling a clear reduction on the prewar level. During the 1950s, even this reduced level of question answering was further eroded. In deference to Churchill's frailty his questions were reduced from four to two days only (Tuesday and Thursday) in 1953; even then his attendance was further reduced by illness. Eden maintained the two-day pattern and answered relatively few questions, especially after Suez. Macmillan's question-answering (again on two days a week only) drifted down to just 37 days in the 1959 session, by which time Labour MPs were understandably critical of the shielding of the prime minister from hostile scrutiny. Although these low years were exceptional single scores, and thus do not show up in the smoothed curves of Figure 12.1, the graph clearly reveals a long-run dip in the late 1950s, with prime ministers answering questions on just 45 days a session on average.

In 1961, a select committee recommended and the Commons accepted a fundamental reform, setting aside two fixed 15-minute slots for prime minister's questions, on Tuesday and Thursday at 3.15 p.m. (the end of question time, just before ministerial statements). MPs' questions for these slots are submitted two weeks ahead and those to be taken selected by lot. This change has endured ever since and had an immediate effect on prime ministerial behaviour, slightly raising the frequency with which they answered questions from the late 1950s level to just over 50 days a session, and then almost completely standardising this pattern across all subsequent premiers. From 1961 onwards virtually every prime minister answered questions on between 47 and 53 days a session.

The institutional evolution of question time did not stop there, however. Although we cannot measure subsequent changes using our data, it is important to review them briefly. At the start of the 1960s, most questions to the prime minister, as to any other minister, focused on specific topics. The new 'prime time' slot encouraged more topical questions than those which could be framed two weeks in advance. When Wilson became prime minister he began 'transferring' many specific questions put down for him to whichever cabinet colleague had immediate policy responsibility for the issue involved, a practice continued by Heath. MPs responded to both developments by shifting over in a large-scale way to 'open' or pro-forma questions, asking about the prime minister's schedule for the day, less commonly when he or she would visit their constituency. After the prime minister has answered this question once, the way is open for MPs lucky in the ballot to ask an oral supplementary on any topical issue, hoping to catch the prime minister out. Although Thatcher announced in 1982 that she would no longer transfer specific questions (Irwin, 1988, p.81), the trend proved irreversible, with between 100 and 200 pro-forma questions listed for each Tuesday and Thursday.

A second change induced by the 'prime time', fixed-length slot has been the increased role of the leader of the opposition. In the early 1960s, various senior members of the shadow cabinet would intervene to ask the prime minister a supplementary question, using the privileges accorded to privy councillors by the speaker. But, in the late 1960s, Heath inaugurated the practice of the leader of the opposition alone regularly intervening. Although Wilson in opposition was more diffident, by the end of the 1970s it became the practice for only the opposing party's leader to question the prime minister. In the 1980s, Michael Foot began *always* intervening, converting prime minister's question time into a 'twice-weekly passage of arms' (Dalyell, 1987, p.xiii), a custom extended by Kinnock who asked multiple supplementaries, pre-empting a large share of the 15 minutes available. The broadcasting and later televising of the Commons have focused extra attention on these interchanges between the prime minister and opposition leader, which are by far the most frequently replayed material in news programmes.

The combined effect of developments since 1961 has been to make prime minister's question time different from that for any other minister: 'In effect the House now allows – for the Prime Minister only – the system of Questions without notice that is standard procedure in the parliaments of Australia and Canada. All that is different is the artificiality of the standard form Question' (Griffith and Ryle, 1989, p.260). Far from its original purpose of 'redressing grievances' and seeking information (Bromhead, 1974, p.141), prime minister's question time in particular has become: 'a kind of stylized minuet . . . For the most part it is a ritual, a primitive expression of the clash of political ideas on the part of those who are playing a game called high politics' (Sedgemore, 1980, pp.190–91).

Summing up on question answering, Figure 12.1 is dominated by just two main periods. The first stretches from 1882 to 1940, during which time virtually all prime ministers answered Commons questions on between 80 and 100 days. A total of 38 sessions conform to this norm, but they are spread across six decades by the interruptions in the late nineteenth century because the premier was in the Lords, and by the dramatic fall in prime ministerial activity under Lloyd George. But all these gaps were clearly seen by ministers, MPs and observers as aberrations from the longer-term 'normal' pattern. The second main period starts during the Second World War, and is marked by a permanent but once-for-all decline in prime ministerial activity to a level around half the previous peaks. Initially oscillating, and with the possibility of secular decline apparent in the 1950s, this new pattern was then frozen into place by the 1961 reforms. Thereafter all prime ministers have spent between 12 and 14 hours a year answering questions spread across 50 separate occasions, and seem likely to continue to do so for the foreseeable future. Inside this mould, further rapid institutional change has occurred, with prime minister's question time becoming more topical, gladiatorial and stylised. We conclude that on question answering the major influences at work in shaping patterns have been institutional shifts. Strong conjunctural and personality effects were apparent only under Lloyd George and otherwise account for fairly minor or short-lived variations in activity.

Making Statements

Since 1868, prime ministers have made statements in the Commons about 10 times less frequently than they have answered questions. But this overall average is misleading, because prime ministers' activity has varied sharply over time. Figure 12.2 shows how many days per session prime ministers made statements, again adjusted to standardise session lengths across the period and smoothed to remove single-year fluctuations. (For unsmoothed data, see Dunleavy, Jones *et al.*, 1993, p.278.)

Three periods are immediately apparent. The first covered essentially the alternation of Gladstone and Disraeli as prime min-

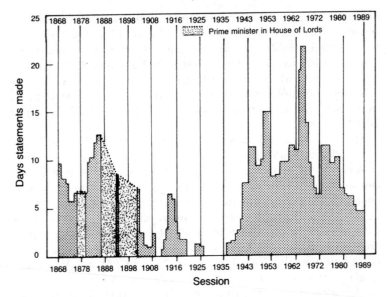

Figure 12.2 *Smoothed adjusted statements per session, 1868–1989*

ister, an era when the practice of ministerial statements was just being formalised. Statements were already linked with question time, and the practice had developed of setting aside a period after questions had finished during which ministers could make statements, which would be followed by a short period of comment or questions from other MPs about what had been said, and responses by the minister. Commons procedures were still cumbersome, however. When Gladstone made a statement in 1884 on the government's proposals for redistributing seats, it was necessary for Sir Stafford Northcote to move the adjournment of the House in order to be able to comment. This situation reflected the fact (unchanged to the present day) that:

> The procedure of Ministers making statements which may be followed by Questions, and indeed, the procedures for questioning Ministers, are not laid down in any formal rule but have evolved in practice, although themselves exceptions to what may be called 'basic procedure' of Parliament. (Griffith and Ryle, 1989, p.177)

Since the prime minister has no specific department, his involvement in statements is potentially minimal, apart from occasional ceremonial orations, on the death of statesmen or monarchs, or marriages in the royal family – all of which we have excluded from our count. However we have included another type of procedure, which Gladstone used in the 1870s and *Hansard* recorded as 'Observations'. Essentially he would set out a problem that seemed troublesome to him, and ask other members of the Commons to comment. This practice died out after 1893. The net effect is that Gladstone regularly made statements on over 10 days a session, far more than Disraeli. In particular years statements were more common, by Disraeli in 1868–9 and by Gladstone in 1872 and 1885.

The second period started in the twentieth century and lasted for four decades. Prime ministers' activity fell sharply to a base level of just one or two statement days per session. Higher levels occasionally occurred, where prime ministers were particularly associated with policy initiatives or with major overseas crises. Peacetime policy statements by the prime minister were made somewhat more often in Balfour's first and last years as premier, and in Lloyd George's last session covering the war in Ireland and recognition of the Irish Free State. The First World War was a larger exception to the early twentieth-century pattern. Asquith made statements on 20 days across two years (three sessions, actual scores) but Lloyd George was much less active in the war years. In the inter-war period prime minister's statements more or less dried up for two decades. Baldwin made statements on only six days across eight sessions as prime minister, MacDonald made statements on only three days across seven sessions, and Chamberlain five statements in four sessions (actual scores).

The third period began in 1940 and marked the renaissance of statements as an important aspect of the prime minister's activity in Parliament. Churchill (who was also minister of defence) made statements on 38 days in six wartime sessions (more than the previous three prime ministers had made between them over 16 years). Attlee carried the change further, making statements on 85 days over six sessions and defining a new peacetime norm for statements. Three presumptions had evidently changed. The first was that prime ministers would account for their attendance at a growing number of international summits or heads of government meetings. Secondly, it came to be expected that prime ministers would commonly make statements about international crises, especially those possibly involving British military forces. Last, prime ministers were expected to comment on negotiations or developments in domestic politics with which they were particularly associated. General rules for ministerial statements were also codified in a postwar set of Cabinet Office guidelines. Parliamentary procedures were also progressively relaxed to make statement-making easier and to allow half-hour sessions where an opposition spokesperson could respond and significant numbers of backbenchers could ask questions.

As a result prime ministers since 1940 have made statements regularly, virtually never slipping below a base level of between six and 10 days per session, with frequent much higher scores of over 15 days' statements in particular sessions. Many of these isolated years' figures (such as Churchill's high score in 1940, or Eden's many statements in 1955–6 covering the Suez invasion) wash out in the smoothed data of Figure 3.

However, three more sustained postwar peaks remain: 1944–6, covering the ending of the war, the general election and the launch of Labour's domestic programme; 1950–52, covering two general elections and the Korean war; and 1964–8, covering the period of two general elections, the devaluation of sterling in 1967 and the declaration of unilateral independence by Rhodesia. In each case an incumbent prime minister (Churchill, Attlee and Douglas-Home respectively) made a high level of statements in the run-up to a general election, a pattern which was carried on for a time by his successor after the election (Attlee, Churchill and Wilson respectively). The peak for this kind of activity came under Harold Wilson, who made statements on no less than 44 days in the 1966–7 session, and on 106 days from 1964 to 1969 (actual scores). Wilson enjoyed his mastery of the Commons at this stage, and used statements to dramatise his personal grip on policy issues. For his first three years in office he put his personal authority behind the effort to sustain sterling's fixed parity within the Bretton Woods agreement, which failed with the 1967 devaluation. Prices and income policy also involved Wilson in making more domestic policy statements. Later industrial crises linked to income policies made necessary extra statements from Heath in 1973–4 and Callaghan in 1978–9. (The latter was coerced by Speaker Thomas to make statements in order to ward off the threat of emergency debates.) The time allocated by Speakers for important statements and the mini-debates which followed them also lengthened, with hour-long slots common by the late 1970s and 1980s (Griffith and Ryle, 1989, pp.334–6; Irwin, 1988, pp.72–87).

Prime ministerial statements twice declined sharply over a run of years. In 1969–70, Wilson first made fewer statements in the run-up to the 1970 election and his successor Heath followed his lead until 1973. A longer and more significant period of gradual decline occurred in the 1980s. Thatcher made statements on only 79 days across 12 years in office (actual scores), reaching the lowest continuous postwar average of under five statements a session in 1985–90. Thatcher confined her statements almost exclusively to foreign affairs issues raised by summit meetings (including European Council meetings which became significant in the 1980s). International issues accounted for 85 per cent of her statement days, compared with only 58 per cent for Callaghan, 42 per cent for Wilson in the 1974–6 period, and 24 per cent for Heath. There is a strong possibility that if Major and future premiers follow Thatcher's example a fourth period of reduced statement making by the prime minister will have been inaugurated by these 1980s changes.

We conclude that the major U-shaped curve apparent in Figure 12.2 reflects primarily long-run institutional features – the early era of general parliamentary activism (including 'observations') under Gladstone, the dying out of significant prime minister's policy statements from 1901 to 1939, and their re-emergence as a key prime ministerial activity from the Second World War onwards. If we shift focus to the changes within the postwar era alone, the culmination of statement-making under Wilson in the late 1960s reflects primarily conjunctural and personality effects, while the marked decline in Thatcher's last years could be similarly attributed. Yet the contrast between the two is also a contrast of institutional patterns, shaped by a perceived failure of the interventionist government style characteristic of Wilson and by British entry into the European Community (EC). Crisis conditions can still force reluctant prime ministers to make statements they would prefer to avoid, as with Heath and Callaghan at the end of their terms, but the forces fostering a lower level of activity and possibly further decline in this form of prime ministerial activity may outlast the Thatcher years.

Giving Speeches

By contrast with both questions and statements, the institutional arrangements governing the prime minister's speeches have remained much more constant. Prime ministers primarily attend and speak in debates on the annual King's/Queen's Speech (setting out the government's programme for a new session) and on very major pieces of legislation – all occasions when they can control their attendance. However, they may also be forced to come to the Commons by the calling of an emergency debate, usually conceded by the Speaker only in extraordinary or crisis circumstances, or by the opposition submitting a motion of no-confidence in the government as a whole. Under normal Commons conventions the prime minister is almost always debating principally with the leader of the opposition.

As with statements, Figure 12.3 shows the days on which prime ministers made speeches per session, with scores adjusted for a standard session length and smoothed to iron out single-year varia- tions. (For unsmoothed data, see Dunleavy, Jones *et al.*, 1993, p.283.) The dominant overall pattern is for prime ministers' speech-making to decline over time. Year-by-year variations and more substantial cycles in speech-making are still apparent. But the underlying base-level of days when prime ministers speak in de- bates has continuously fallen. Four basic periods stand out: the nineteenth century; the early twentieth century from 1906 to 1945; the postwar period; and lastly the 1980s.

In the 1870s and 1880s, Gladstone was an inveterate debater, making speeches on 21 days a year on average across five sessions in the 1870s and seven sessions in the 1880s. The peak of his activity was in 1882–3, when he spoke on 33 days (actual score). Disraeli was markedly less active (averaging 10 days a session), but Balfour approximated Gladstone's pattern (averaging 17 days a session). In 1904–6 he made speeches on 37 days across two sessions (actual scores), reflecting his party's problems over free trade. The import- ance of speech making at this time was captured by one contempo- rary commentator who noted in March 1905:

> Fiscal debate with a most animated speech from Balfour to a very large house. Our party was greatly refreshed and pulled to- gether. The Prime Minister is a wonderful man. He had been

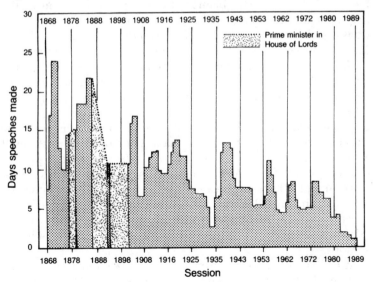

Figure 12.3 *Smoothed adjusted speeches per session, 1868–1989*

suffering from a very bad toothache, slept thirteen hours under opium, had already spoken in the afternoon, now spoke again for a full hour in his very best form. (Quoted in Egremont, 1980, p.189.)

The Liberal landslide of 1906 brought a major change. The new premier, Campbell-Bannerman, was very reluctant to project himself as the voice of the government. Across two sessions, 1906–8, he made only 11 speeches (and only one statement) before becoming ill and absent from Parliament altogether (actual score). His successors from Asquith through to MacDonald's first government followed Disraeli's example rather than Gladstone's. With a couple of exceptions – 1911–12 under Asquith and 1916–18 under Lloyd George – they all made speeches on between nine and 14 days a session.

Under Baldwin after 1926, speeches by the prime minister fell again to just over four days on average in his last three sessions (actual scores), a pattern basically continued by Ramsay MacDonald. In fact, in the last two years of his National Government premiership (1933–5), MacDonald almost gave up making speeches altogether. This pattern closely fitted his reluctance to answer questions during the years 1931–3, his relatively low scores for intervening in debates and almost complete absence of statements. MacDonald became more and more uncomfortable in the Commons because of personal attacks on him from his former Labour colleagues, who blamed him for deserting them at the height of the economic crisis, and in particular for the party's catastrophic 1931 defeat by the coalition. In the late 1920s, MacDonald's diary already recorded his view of the Commons as 'a public institution inhabited by snivelling inmates' (Marquand, 1977, p.402; Wertheimer, 1929, pp.174–5), and he was in many ways a lonely and isolated figure. After his break with Labour, 'More and more he dreaded the prospect of appearing at the dispatch box. The night before making a speech, he would lie awake worrying; after a bad performance, he would torture himself with the memory' (Marquand, 1977, p.698; see also pp.602, 672, 680 and 698–9). With MacDonald's departure, the National Government effectively became a conventional Conservative administration, and Baldwin and later Chamberlain made more speeches (often about the growth of rearmament and overseas crises), a pattern which continued for Churchill's first few wartime sessions.

After 1945, the postwar norm was quickly re-established at 1920s levels, with prime ministers making speeches on only four to eight days a session. There were a number of small peaks in this period, coinciding with crisis periods. Eden made 17 speeches during the long session 1955–6, which included the Suez crisis (actual scores). Wilson made rather more speeches (as well as many statements) in 1964–6 and Heath was unusually active in 1973–4 and Wilson in 1975–6, both crisis periods. But across the postwar period as a whole prime ministers' speech making tended to focus on just four or five days a session.

The fourth period began in 1979. Across 11 sessions, Margaret Thatcher made speeches on only 36 days (actual scores): after 1987, her activity was confined to just one day per session. Unlike Campbell-Bannerman or MacDonald her performance did not reflect personality qualms or coalitional conditions (see below). She assigned her cabinet colleagues to undertake all but the most unavoidable Commons speeches. Leaving aside the debate on the Queen's Speech, Thatcher made only 23 speeches of 15 minutes or more between 1979 and 1990, of which half were on foreign affairs. Her speeches on the economy or social themes totalled 11, less than one a year, whereas her three predecessors as prime minister spoke preponderantly on domestic issues.

The overall pattern for prime ministers' speeches is thus one of a long-run secular decline. This trend has been fairly continuous, although a few premiers have stood out against it for a time. Campbell-Bannerman, MacDonald and Thatcher only represent rather starker changes to prime ministerial reticence than their predecessors or successors. Their personality factors produced sharp downward wobbles, but the trend line itself is much more broadly based. While single-party majority governments persist it is hard to see any process by which prime ministers are likely to begin making more than the odd speech or two per session.

Intervening in Debates

The Commons is founded upon debate, but in what does the essence of debate itself consist? Speeches are important, but they encompass only part of the experience which debate is designed to create. To turn up and make a speech only to leave immediately is barely to participate in 'debate'. The more normal expectation (which Commons procedures embody) is that a speaker will listen to opposing views and very probably respond to them in some small way.

These responses constitute the type of impromptu behaviour we have classed as 'intervening in debates'. Most of the activities involved are fairly minor in themselves – rising to pose a question to an opposing speaker, making points of order and even interjecting remarks, or showing some other sign noted by *Hansard* of active reaction to what has been said. Just as the institutional arrangements governing speeches have remained relatively constant over our period, so the rules about intervening in debates have been little altered. In modern times there has perhaps been a reduced willingness by ministers or the opposition frontbenchers to 'give way' to interjections from the other side of the House, more especially since the broadcasting and televising of the Commons, but this change in leading politicians' behaviour has not been caused by any modifications of the rules of debate.

Before the late 1970s, prime ministers were much *more* likely to intervene in debates in an impromptu way than they were to make a formal speech. Especially in the era when prime ministers were also leaders of the House of Commons, they often sat in on debates to see how colleagues were performing and to gauge the mood of the Commons – and if a point occurred to them they would rise spontaneously to interpose it. Across the period as a whole, therefore, intervening in debates is the second most common prime ministerial activity, after answering questions. Partly as a result intervening is not so subject to the individual-year peaks and troughs found with speeches and statements. For most of the period there is a fairly regular base level of activity, shown in Figure 12.4, which graphs the days on which prime ministers intervened in debates, adjusted for session length and smoothed to remove single-year fluctuations. (For unsmoothed data, see Dunleavy,

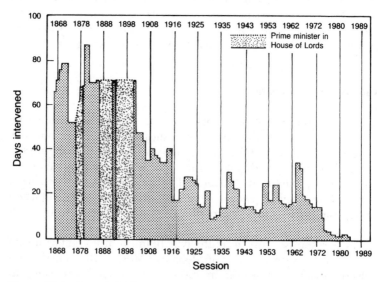

Figure 12.4   *Smoothed adjusted debating interventions per session, 1868–1989*

Jones *et al.*, 1993, p.285.) There are three periods: the late nineteenth century, with a transitional Edwardian era; a long trendless period from Lloyd George through to 1974; and from the mid-1970s onwards.

The view of the late nineteenth century as a high point for Commons debating activity is well supported in our data. Gladstone constantly intervened in debates, averaging 75 days a session during the whole time he was prime minister. In two long sessions, 1882–3 and 1893, he interjected on more than 100 occasions (actual scores). As with other things, Disraeli was markedly less active. A transition began in 1902. Although Balfour was often activist in other ways, he intervened in debates much less than his predecessors, around 45 days a session. Asquith followed Campbell-Bannerman's lead in intervening rather less before the First World War, rising slightly with the onset of war.

The second and longest period was inaugurated by Lloyd George. During the war years and 1919 his interventions dropped to around 15 days a session, barely more than his not very frequent speeches. In the closing years of his government he became somewhat more active, setting a base level for the rest of the 1920s of about 25 days. From 1927 onwards, Baldwin intervened less, and when MacDonald became prime minister in the National Government he was conspicuously reluctant to utilise debating opportunities – intervening only 40 times across four sessions (actual scores). From this low point the base level for intervening rose again slightly after the Second World War, averaging around 15 days a session through to 1974. There were periodic but smaller peaks in prime ministers' Commons activity, notably during 1938–41, 1951–2, 1955–8 and 1964–7. Some Tory prime ministers, such as Churchill and Eden, believed in the importance of impromptu debating, while others such as Macmillan and Heath were active only in those particular sessions when they made more formal speeches, notably Heath in the 1973–4 session.

The final period started in 1974 and marked the almost complete disappearance of prime ministers' intervening in debates. After narrowly winning the October 1974 general election Harold Wilson became something of a recluse from Parliament in the 1974–5 session. Although he was more active in the 1975–6 session leading up to his resignation, he intervened on only 20 days across three sessions (actual scores). Callaghan intervened only 15 times in four sessions, and his lead was imitated by Thatcher, who intervened only 16 times in her first five sessions (both actual scores). From 1985 onwards, Thatcher made no recorded interventions at all until a solitary instance in her last days as Conservative leader in

1990. Following Callaghan's lead, she gave up completely any impromptu or unscripted interventions.

The overall pattern for debating interventions is again one of decline, but not the long and gradual decline evident in speech making. Interventions in debate fell from a peak in the late nineteenth century, through a period of transition in the early 1900s, to a long plateau of fairly modest activity which lasted from the 1920s to the 1970s. From there, in the space of a decade and a half, the tradition of prime ministers actively participating in debates beyond making their own speeches has completely withered and died. It seems unlikely that it will be revived spontaneously.

Prime Ministers' Overall Activism

How can these differing trends be summarised from our data? If we simply looked at the days when prime ministers undertook any one or more of the four kinds of parliamentary activity we would obtain a misleading picture, because question-answering would dominate the resulting index. In addition we would miss an important change since the late nineteenth century. At that time a parliamentarian like Gladstone would commonly undertake several activities on any given day – answering questions, giving a speech or making a statement, and certainly intervening in debate. By contrast a modern prime minister rarely if ever undertakes multiple activities on the same day.

To meet this difficulty we first standardise prime ministers' scores for each activity, using the following calculation for each session's data:

$$\text{standard score} = \frac{\text{actual score} - \text{mean score}}{\text{standard deviation}}$$

This procedure produces a set of scores for each activity with a mean of zero and a standard deviation of one, irrespective of the original level and spread of the data. Secondly, we sum the scores for the four kinds of activities to derive an overall index showing how active or inactive each prime minister was in each session, compared with the data set as a whole. This index is not then dominated by any one activity, but rather reflects how exceptional or routine each session's scores were for all four activities. However we should note a limitation of the index, namely that each activity has the same weight as any other. No greater importance is assigned to answering questions than to intervening in debates, for example.

Graphing this smoothed index for the whole period shows an interesting pattern which fits closely the analyses in the previous four sections (Figure 12.5). Prime ministers' activism is above the 1868–1990 average throughout the period before 1916. (The only slight exception is Campbell-Bannerman's last two sessions in office, for much of which he was ill.) By contrast prime ministers' activism since Lloyd George has only ever reached the long-run average in three brief periods: Chamberlain's premiership and the run-up to the Second World War; the 1944–6 sessions under Churchill and Attlee; and 1964–7 under Wilson. Since 1916, the general run of prime ministerial scores has been below the mean for the period as a whole, albeit with frequent wobbles towards that average. But there have been three very marked periods of prime ministerial inactivity: Lloyd George's wartime sessions; MacDonald's time as prime minister in the National Government; and the whole of Margaret Thatcher's time as prime minister. Thatcher's record is the longest and most consistently below-average set of scores for any prime minister.

As with any calculation of this kind, Figure 12.5 depends crucially on which figures are used to compute the standardised scores. We have repeatedly noted the importance of 1940 as a break point, especially for prime ministers making statements. There are therefore good reasons for looking in more detail at the

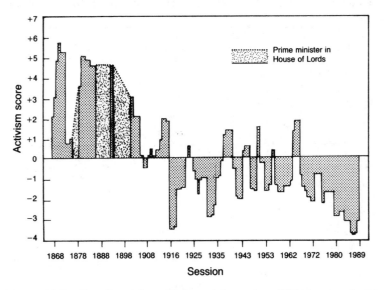

Figure 12.5 *Overall activism of prime ministers since 1868 (compared with mean, 1868–1989)*

1940–90 period, and seeing how prime ministers' activism scores compare if they are standardised against the means and standard deviations for this part of the data alone. Figure 12.6 shows that, compared with postwar averages, there was an abrupt change. Until the mid-1970s, most prime ministers' scores were above or very close to the 1940–90 average: from 1976, the scores for first Callaghan and then Thatcher are consistently negative, becoming sharply worse in the late 1980s.

The decline under Thatcher is so marked because both her speech making and her interventions in debates dwindled away to virtually nothing during her long tenure of office, while her statements also declined after 1985. A number of explanations have been suggested. First, like Lloyd George, Thatcher prioritised her role as an executive prime minister, involving herself in successive efforts to reorganise the whole public sector by the time of her third term. She undoubtedly developed a strong preference for running the core executive, and in particular operating with her own powerful staffs, rather than performing in Parliament – in the process repeating Lloyd George's costly mistake of distancing herself from her backbenchers. Although she began her period as Conservative leader resolved not to repeat Heath's 'remoteness', many Tory MPs elected after 1987 claimed almost never to have met her or visited Downing Street. Even during the critical leadership contest of 1990, Thatcher absented herself at an

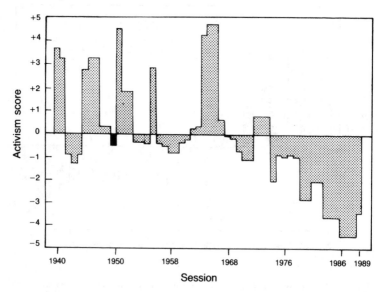

Figure 12.6   *Overall parliamentary activism of prime ministers since 1940 (compared with mean, 1940–1989)*

overseas summit in the days leading up to the parliamentary party's vote.

A second explanation is that Thatcher's political style was built upon being carefully prepared. Far more than previous premiers, she relied on a whole squad of advisers, speechwriters, her political office and assorted media-fixers and spin-merchants. By 1983, she had completely abandoned conventional electioneering in which she might encounter ordinary voters (Dunleavy and Husbands, 1985, p.86). Her preparations for question time, the one unavoidable parliamentary chore, were reputedly exhaustive – usually a minimum of three hours for each 15-minute slot. Thatcher seems to have wanted to be shielded from or highly prepared for potentially discomforting experiences, a trait which her normally bellicose and confident parliamentary manner would otherwise belie. Her concern to have cabinet colleagues undertake speeches fits this pattern; for example, her refusal to speak in the debate following Britain's 1990 entry into the EC's Exchange Rate Mechanism, which she had almost single-handedly opposed for four years within government. Facing huge Tory majorities in the 1980s, the Labour opposition was also reluctant to use no-confidence motions to force the prime minister to attend, further compounding her record.

A final explanation of Thatcher's reclusiveness in the Commons is that she was the first woman at 10 Downing Street, operating in an overwhelmingly male parliamentary context. At times she seemed to view the Commons in very different terms from the friendly male debating club which some previous premiers enjoyed dominating: 'One tends, particularly with the kind of atmosphere in the House of Commons at Question Time, when you are always attacked, to defend yourself. Most women defend themselves. It is the female of the species. It is the tigress and the lioness in you which tends to defend when attacked' (Margaret Thatcher, quoted in *Daily Mail*, 4 May 1989). This perception of the Commons as a hostile environment could help explain Thatcher's distinctive efforts to reduce her exposure there.

Conclusion

The traditional assumption has been that for the parliamentary accountability of the prime minister to have any value or meaning he or she must be physically present in the Commons and undertaking some specific task (Birch, 1964, pp.131–70). Our data suggest that this condition is no longer being met in the way that it was. Prime ministerial activity in the Commons has decreased overall and narrowed down to a few forms of participation, especially the now highly formalised and very brief prime minister's question time. We have shown that speech-making and intervening in debates have both declined markedly in the postwar period; that question-answering remains more regular but is much less frequent than before 1940 and is far more constrained than in earlier eras; but that prime ministers have made many more statements – albeit with another decline and narrowing of the subjects of prime ministerial statements evident in the 1980s. These results establish unequivocally that the *direct* parliamentary accountability of the prime minister has fallen sharply over the whole period since 1868, and that this change has accelerated in the last decade and a half.

We have also documented a number of partly countervailing trends: for question-answering to stabilise at 50 days a session since 1961; the growth of open questions to the prime minister since the 1970s; and the generally more frequent postwar use of statements by prime ministers. It is also possible that this decline in direct accountability will be reversed under Major or future prime ministers. However the probabilities involved here seem small. After being socialised into leadership within the parliamentary expectations of the last decade, new leaders are highly unlikely to return to the status quo ante. There seems no plausible mechanism by which the House of Commons could gradually re-engage the participation of national political leaders and hence little prospect of achieving a homeostatic rebalancing of direct accountability.

We have argued elsewhere that the decline of *direct* prime ministerial accountability charted here also applies to more *indirect* or *mediated* forms of accountability, those which operate via the parliamentary party, the whips system, cabinet colleagues or the mass media (see Dunleavy, Jones *et al.*, 1993, pp.290–96). No convincing evidence exists to suggest that there are strong countervailing trends in any of these areas which make prime ministers more continuously answerable to or responsive to MPs. Even if some mysterious process has partly offset the decline in direct accountability to the Commons which we have demonstrated, any substitute mechanism must occur outside the ambit of constitutionally regulated institutions, and it cannot be primarily focused on the Commons.

An important final question to consider is how we should explain the diverse patterns of change in prime ministerial activity analysed above. General explanations in terms of across-the-board influences will not work, because they should have produced parallel changes across all forms of activity. For example, the patterns we have charted cannot be easily attributed to strengthened party discipline or changes in the Commons' standing orders, all of which were firmly in place by 1902, when Balfour broadly continued the Gladstonian tradition. Most changes have occurred in the twentieth century, well within the period of established strong party discipline.

As an alternative, pluralist writers might be tempted to explain the prime minister's reduced presence in the Commons as a product of increased 'complexity' and 'growth' in British government. How this 'complexity' is measured seems unclear, since at the start of our period Britain ran a vast overseas empire, and by the end ranked as a minor regional power with a rather run-down welfare state. But even if we accept the thesis as plausible for a moment, why should increased 'complexity' on its own elicit more prime ministerial statements, a standardised level of answers to questions and yet a drastically reduced number of speeches and debating interventions? A more promising possible explanation is that some of the prime minister's parliamentary role has been displaced to cabinet colleagues or a wider range of ministers. Their increased activity may compensate in part or in whole for the prime minister's reduced role, but we have no hard data at present on that. Premiers could also have become less active in Parliament simply because MPs have allowed the Commons to become less important in policy-making terms. Hence prime ministers' behaviour could have lagged behind rather than caused declining accountability. This explanation also might explain the diverse patterns set out in our figures: as parliamentary roles have become specialised, so premiers have adjusted to accord emphasis to those of their activities which matter most to MPs. Systematic evaluation of these and other possible explanations could provide important research avenues for future core executive and legislative studies.

13

Estimating the Distribution of Positional Influence in Cabinet Committees under Major

PATRICK DUNLEAVY

For all the rhetorical importance of 'cabinet government' as an ideal, no one informed about British politics believes that a great deal of business is or can be effectively transacted at weekly meetings of 23 ministers lasting for around an hour and a half. Ministers, officials, journalists and academics agree that the 'real' business of government is transacted elsewhere – in the cabinet committee system, bilateral or trilateral meetings between ministers and inside the Whitehall departments. Cabinet committees (known in officialese as 'ministerial standing committees') form perhaps the most central and least documented part of the modern core executive. Their task is to pre-process issues, and relieve the burden on full cabinet meetings. Each committee consists of only a selection of the cabinet members, those with relevant departmental interests plus others assigned by the prime minister. Some include a few junior ministers as well. Subcommittees below standing committees exist in areas where there are numerous issues. And in addition to the permanent standing committees a wide range of temporary committees have been set up at different times to handle specific policy decisions or especially pressing issues. Finally cabinet committees are paralleled by 'official committees' of civil servants which meet in advance of ministerial meetings: they seek to establish areas of agreement, clarify the remaining problems and help each department to best work out its options and position.

The network and membership of the cabinet committees is determined largely by the prime minister and the cabinet secretary, the official who is head of the Cabinet Office (and now also head of the civil service as a whole). The cabinet secretary chairs the Joint Intelligence Committee, an official committee which has responsibility for coordinating the security and intelligence services. The Cabinet Office staff manage the entire cabinet committee network, recording discussions, collating papers and ensuring that government decisions are reliably implemented by departments.

This chapter has four main parts. The first briefly reviews the origins and growth of cabinet committees, and explains why they have so far been buried in obscurity because of official secrecy rules. The second part uses information first released only in 1992 to rank ministers in terms of their committee influence and to measure their linkages with cabinet colleagues. I show that committee influence is considerably segmented between domestic policy ministers, cabinet members involved in overseas and defence policy committees, and non-departmental ministers chairing committees. Each of these groups acquires influence in different ways, with the prime minister as an additional special case. The third section analyses the extent to which committee influence can be seen as concentrated or fragmented, and how easy or difficult it is for different 'coalitions' of cabinet ministers to control the overall committee system. Finally the conclusions explore some implications of these findings for public discussion and understanding of core executive operations, and for future core executive studies.

The Cabinet Committee System: Origins, Growth and Reasons for its Obscurity

In many key respects the shape of British government in the 1990s still reflects the period when the Whitehall system was decisively modernised nearly a century ago, between the 1860s and the 1920s, largely to cope with the demands of managing the enormous British imperial state (see also Beattie, Chapter 8 above). This was certainly true of the cabinet committee system which began life as a long overdue effort to coordinate the policies for the defence of the Empire. A Colonial Defence Committee was first established in the 1880s, the prototype of the later Chiefs of Staff Committee and a stimulus to an informal 'defence committee' of the cabinet set up in 1895, which met only episodically. In 1902, this committee was remodelled as the Committee of Imperial

Defence (CID), including the prime minister and the secretaries of state from the India Office, War Office and Admiralty, with a secretariat provided by the director of naval intelligence and the director of military intelligence. After 1904, an independent secretarial staff was created (from the Foreign Office), the CID's powers were expanded and its membership increased to include the foreign secretary and colonial secretary. The troubled Conservative premier, Arthur Balfour, stayed in office primarily to get this powerful committee established before the Liberals gained power. For a long time the CID was taken as unique in showing:

> how far the Cabinet system has progressed in the direction of committee government. Its peculiarity in this direction is due to the division of defence functions among three separate [military] departments and services and the further dispersion of administration that arises from the need to defend the several territories governed by or related with the Dominions Office, the Colonial Office, and the India Office. (Jennings, 1936, p.247)

Others noted:

> shortly after the outbreak of the recent [1914] war, the Committee of Imperial Defence was strengthened, and became a body having almost executive power to advance its own decisions; but it remained, in theory, a committee of the Cabinet (which was then a larger body) supplemented by expert assistance. Its relations to the Cabinet, however, were obscure and not very satisfactory, until the drastic rearrangements which took place in December 1916 once more left it the great expert War Council of the Empire. (Jenks, 1923, p.206)

The cabinet reorganisation for peacetime after 1919 reaffirmed the CID as the leading edge of core executive change, with no parallels in domestic politics, where committees were episodic and less formalised. In particular the Cabinet Office was developed in peacetime as the secretariat for the cabinet on exactly the lines which had governed the CID's secretariat, absorbing its ethos and procedures and generalising them across the whole gamut of business. The Cabinet Office also took over the top control of intelligence in a new official coordination device, the Joint Intelligence Committee.

In the 1930s, the cabinet committee system for domestic policy was still poorly developed, with no developed hierarchy of committees or regular and systematic system for processing issues. Contemporary observers noted:

The extension of the Committee [of Imperial Defence]'s methods to the economic field has often been suggested. But the problem is far more difficult. Economic changes defy the forecasts of experts. A 'Crisis Book' for the next 'economic blizzard' [analogous to the 'War Book' contingency plans prepared by CID] is impossible. If, however, the planning of trade and industry were adopted as a policy, the method would no doubt be a system not essentially different from that of the Committee of Imperial Defence. (Jennings, 1936, p.247)

This prescient forecast was borne out within a very few years, as the Second World War inaugurated the vast expansion of formalised committee government, with powers delegated extensively away from cabinet. The postwar Labour government converted CID into a regular ministerial standing committee, in theory normalising its status and bringing it fully within the ambit of cabinet control. Its modern name later became the Overseas Policy and Defence (OPD) Committee. But the twin decisions to commit Britain to building an independent nuclear deterrent and to wage the Korean war rapidly pushed the new committee into the same tradition of semi-autonomous and secret action which had characterised its predecessor. Successive nuclear decisions were made in complete secrecy quite outside the formal reporting or decision conventions of cabinet by an OPD subcommittee (Hennessy, 1986, ch. 4).

The wartime expansion of government intervention altered domestic policy-making irreversibly. The postwar Attlee government employed an 'engine room' of over 300 different cabinet committees to help accomplish its lasting changes in British society and the economy (Hennessy and Arends, 1983). The committees began to divide formally between ministerial 'standing groups' and *ad hoc* groups. Of the 244 *ad hoc* groups which were set up in the 1945–51 period, only 11 met more than 10 times. Over time the Cabinet committee system progressively became less anarchic. The welter of *ad hoc* and temporary committees became more coordinated, especially on the domestic policy side, with a powerful economic affairs committee and home affairs committee emerging. Generally the domestic cabinet committee system became progressively more formalised, compartmentalised and fragmented into permanent 'partial governments'.

During his premiership (1964–70) Harold Wilson added a powerful impetus to this development by decreeing that no issue could go to cabinet without first having been processed by ministerial committee, and that only in unusual circumstances could ministers dissatisfied with a cabinet committee decision raise the issue involved in full cabinet. The rules governing this situation (set out in the Cabinet Office document, 'Questions of Procedure for Ministers', see James, Chapter 3 above) came to be increasingly important for ministers. In the Westland affair, for example, the specific trigger for Michael Heseltine's resignation was dissatisfaction with the committee consideration of his plans (see Dunleavy, Chapter 9 above).

It is difficult to be more precise about the modern development of committee structures after the 1950s and before 1992 because throughout the twentieth century British governments followed the extraordinary policy of refusing to divulge which committees existed. The names of committees were official secrets, as were details of which ministers sat on them, or who acted as the committee chair. As late as February 1978 the Labour prime minister, James Callaghan, signed a solemn memo explaining why he proposed to continue the long-standing practice of refusing to disclose any details at all of the cabinet committee system. After dismissively noting 'some Press allegations about Whitehall obscurantism', he argued:

> The method adopted by Ministers for discussing policy questions is however *essentially a domestic matter*; and a decision by a Cabinet Committee, unless referred to the Cabinet, engages the collective responsibility of all Ministers and has exactly the same authority as a decision by Cabinet itself. Disclosure that a particular Committee had dealt with a matter might lead to argument about the status of the decision or demands that it should be endorsed by the whole Cabinet. (Hennessy, 1986, p.89: emphasis added)

By 'a domestic matter' Callaghan meant that how ministers came to take a decision was not a matter of legitimate public interest, but rather a purely private internal decision of the government members themselves, fundamentally a housekeeping issue.

His defence of total secrecy went on to cite the usual repertoire of Whitehall memos down the ages. He claimed that committees existed solely to ease the decision-making burden on cabinet itself; that any disclosure of committee details (even the existence of committees) would be misleading, since some of them could not be revealed on security grounds and others were ephemeral; and that disclosing anything at all would lead to parliamentary select committees asking committee chairs to give the reasons for decisions, instead of (or as well as) the departmentally responsible ministers (who might have been outvoted). His conclusion was that the existing policy of saying nothing at all about committees, not even to confirm the names of the main committees, was the only defensible position. Anything else would open up a crack through which would slip progressively more numerous details of the government's operations.

As a testimony to the self-serving (almost paranoid) suspicion which prevailed for well over half a century in core executive 'reasoning' about these issues, Callaghan's memo could hardly be bettered. As Hennessy (1986, p.88) notes, he was 'an arch traditionalist' in his constitutional attitudes, as was Margaret Thatcher throughout the 1980s. In the whole farrago of nonsense justifying blanket official secrecy, by far the most bizarre claim was that cabinet committee arrangements were 'essentially domestic' in character. The logic of committee decision is a push towards creating more 'partial' governments, in the twin sense of vesting the power to decide issues in more restricted sets of people, who are also (potentially) more biased – more selective in what they take into account, and less broadly representative of the government as a whole in their values or experiences. Probably in no other governing system in the Western world would senior elected officials so blandly attempt to deny that the forums used to make decisions can affect the quality of consideration accorded them or the nature of the outcomes reached. Notice too that British official doctrine says nothing about cabinet committees *improving* the quality of decisions, for example, by bringing to bear more concentrated expertise in more specialised settings. Implicitly the justification of committees as a simple load-shedding device to relieve full cabinet seems to admit that committee decisions are inherently less collegial and hence less legitimate than full cabinet consideration.

In May 1992, John Major consigned the more farcical Whitehall defences of secrecy to the junkheap of history by publishing a full listing of the names and membership of the cabinet's standing ministerial committees and subcommittees. No details were given of the already established network of temporary committees (those labelled as GEN committees under one prime minister, and as MISC committees under the next). But Major did begin announcing details of any *new* temporary committees set up from 1992 onwards. No information was released either about the official committee network which parallels the ministerial committees and pre-processes issues which they consider. However details of ministerial committee memberships and chairs were provided, together with brief terms of reference and a few lines on the way subcommittees report to the full committees. This official disclosure for the first time makes feasible an attempt to assess the distribution of influence within the permanent structures of the cabinet committee system, and the extent to which different ministers share in committee decision making.

Measuring the Distribution of Positional Influence in the Cabinet Committee System

Table 13.1 gives the salient details of committees and subcommittees as at May 1992, including names and abbreviations, the committee's chair, its size, number of non-cabinet ministers and a weighting score (explained below). The prime minister chairs all of the full committees in the OPD fields, which generally have a smaller membership. In addition the prime minister chairs two committees in very cognate fields, dealing with the intelligence services and with Northern Ireland. Five of these committees have either four or five members only. In addition the prime minister chairs two larger domestic policy committees, EDP, the premier committee dealing with strategic economic policy-making, and the ministerial committee on science and technology (EDS), handling technology issues. These additions bring the average size of all nine of the prime minister's committees up slightly, to seven members. Only one minister from outside the cabinet sits on any of the committees chaired by the prime minister.

All but one of the remaining domestic full committees have over 12 members, and in July 1992 were chaired either by the Lord Privy Seal (then Lord Wakeham) or the Lord President of the Council (Tony Newton). The five committees prefixed ED generally include two or three area ministers (for Scotland, Wales and Northern Ireland) plus one or two non-departmental ministers, the chancellor and one or more heads of economic departments (such as the Board of Trade, or Employment, or the chief secretary) and the heads of major spending departments in domestic policy. One of the full committees deals with civil service pay (civil servants are defined as public-sector employees directly controlled by ministers). Two domestic committees deal with legislation and future legislation: they have more of a technical character and include several junior ministers from outside the cabinet dealing with legal matters and parliamentary timetabling and discipline.

There seem to be three kinds of ministerial subcommittee. The three OPD subcommittees form a distinct group with significant responsibilities and memberships composed of cabinet ministers. The subcommittee on European questions is larger because its European Community role involves domestic departments, whereas the other two (covering terrorism and Eastern Europe) are closer to the OPD norm with eight members each. A second

TABLE 13.1   *The cabinet committee structure in May 1992*

Committee name & abbreviation	Chair	Size	A	B
Overseas policy and cognate committees				
Overseas Policy and Defence OPD	PM	6	0	100
Nuclear Defence Policy OPDN	PM	4	0	100
MC on the Gulf OPDG	PM	4	0	100
European Security OPDSE	PM	4	0	100
Hong Kong OPDK	PM	8	1	88
Intelligence Services IS	PM	5	0	100
Northern Ireland NI	PM	7	0	100
Domestic policy committees				
Economic and Domestic Policy EDP	PM	13	0	100
Science and Technology EDS	PM	12	0	100
Home and Social Affairs EDH	LPS	18	1	94
Industrial, Commercial and Consumer Affairs EDI	LPS	13	0	100
Environment EDE	LPS	13	0	100
Local Government EDL	LPS	15	1	93
Civil Service Pay EDC	LPC	12	1	92
The Queen's Speech and Future Legislation FLG	LPC	9	4	56
Legislation LG	LPC	12	6	50
Overseas policy subcommittees				
Eastern Europe OPD(AE)	FS	9	1	44
European Questions OPD(E)	FS	15	1	47
Terrorism OPD(T)	HS	8	0	50
Domestic subcommittees				
Public Sector Pay EDI(P)	LPS	12	0	50
Health Strategy EDH(H)	LPC	13	3	35
Drug Misuse EDH(D)	LPC	10	9	5
Alcohol Misuse EDH(A)	CDL	12	11	4
Women's Issues EDH(W)	EMP	13	12	4
Coordination of Urban Policy EDH(U)	ENV	14	13	4
London EDL(L)	ENV	12	11	4

Notes: A = non-cabinet members; B = weighted Influence score.
   The first three letters of the abbreviation for a subcommittee indicate the full committee to which it reports.
   The *Chair* column uses the following abbreviations: PM (prime minister), LPS (lord privy seal), LPC (lord president of the council), FS (foreign secretary), HS (home secretary), CDL (chancellor of the Duchy of Lancaster), EMP (secretary of state for employment), ENV (secretary of state for the environment).

group includes two domestic subcommittees with multiple cabinet members. One covers public sector pay, paralleling the full committee on civil service pay. Its lower status seems to stem chiefly from the fact that it meets only episodically, before the annual pay round starts; but its membership is virtually the same as that of a full cabinet committee. The other covers the government's health strategy and includes nine cabinet members and four junior ministers. By contrast with these important OPD and domestic subcommittees, the remaining six domestic subcommittees (covering alcohol abuse, drug abuse, women's issues, coordination of the government's urban policy and London issues) have a different character. Their membership is almost entirely composed of junior ministers, with only a single cabinet member acting as chair in each case. These subcommittees have very low salience in political terms. They are often set up more for 'window-dressing' or symbolic purposes, to serve as a visible governmental response to social problems, or as a reaction to the need to accommodate relatively minor issues, rather than to transact key quantities of government business.

In summary, the official two-level distinction between committees and subcommittees masks an underlying structure of four different levels of committee. In the first rank are the small full committees with the OPD prefix and the IS committee. The second rank includes the domestic policy full committees. The third rank includes the OPD subcommittees and the two domestic subcommittees with multiple cabinet members. And the fourth rank consists of the remaining 'symbolic' domestic subcommittees.

To make full use of this new information we need to develop some generally accepted indices of the extent to which ministers are advantaged or disadvantaged by their placings within the cabinet committee system. A first step is to measure the relative importance of committees described above. I suggest the following formula:

$$\text{Committee weighting} = 100 * S * (C/N)$$

Here S means the official status of the committee, and can be scored by counting a full ministerial committee as one, and a subcommittee as 0.5. (For a discussion of alternative weightings, see Dunleavy, 1994, Appendix.) C means the number of cabinet members who sit on the committee and N denotes the total number of ministers who are members. Thus a committee's weighting depends on its formal status and its salience (as measured by the proportion of its members who are cabinet ministers). Table 13.1 above gives these weightings for all 26 committees. Full committees with cabinet members exclusively score 100, while those with one junior minister drift downwards into the 90s. The two legislation committees are unusual as full domestic committees because they are fairly small and have several non-cabinet ministers as members: their scores accordingly dip down to around

50. Ministerial subcommittees with cabinet members exclusively score 50, while those with one or two junior ministers score in the 40s. The 'symbolic' domestic subcommittees score just four or five on this index. In the cabinet committee system as a whole there are a total of 1719 score points. So a committee with 100 points absorbs 5.8 per cent of the total, a subcommittee with 50 points counts for 2.9 per cent and a 'symbolic' subcommittee for 0.3 per cent.

The next step is to partition out the weighting of each committee among its members. Since we have no information about ministers' behaviour on committees, the simplest rule would be to divide the weighting score for each committee by the number of members, regarding each as equal to all others in influence. But an obvious difficulty here has been raised by earlier authors who suggested that committee chairs enjoy considerable influence, by virtue of their central role in agenda-setting and controlling discussion:

> The job of chairing Cabinet committees is of very high political status. In effect, the chairman is over other ministers. The chairman's task is to resolve differences between ministers in ways acceptable to the disputants, while also promoting the general interest of the government, that is, the Prime Minister's interest. (Rose, 1987, p.88)

To cope with this widely recognised importance, we can simply consider the chair as an additional role to be assigned influence. So in attributing shares of the committee's weighting score we divide the total by $N + 1$ and assign a double share to the chair (one share in virtue of their membership and another for chairing). Thus, for a normal committee member, their personal weighted score is:

$$[100 * S * (C/N)]/(N + 1)$$

The score for committee chairs will be twice this amount.

Table 13.2 shows the results of this calculation for all members of the cabinet and some of the most important junior ministers involved in cabinet committees in 1992, together with counts of their committee and subcommittee memberships and chairs. This analysis assumes that the weighted scores for positional influence will produce an overall increment or decrement to the other sources of influence accorded to cabinet members, such as departmental ministers' control of large-scale resources, and the prime minister's influence as party leader and 'team manager' of the cabinet. Aggregate patterns of committee influence will show up

TABLE 13.2   *Committee influence scores for senior ministers, 1992*

Minister	Committee influence		Committee places	Chairs
	Weighted score	% of total		
Prime minister	256	14.9	9 + 0	9 + 0
Foreign secretary	155	9.0	10 + 3	0 + 2
SS for defence	138	8.0	9 + 2	0 + 0
Chanc. exchequer	110	6.4	9 + 3	0 + 0
Home secretary	82	4.8	7 + 3	0 + 1
Ld pres of council	76	4.4	8 + 3	3 + 2
Chanc. Duchy Lanc	76	4.4	9 + 3	0 + 1
Pres Bd of Trade	75	4.4	7 + 4	0 + 0
Lord privy seal	74	4.3	7 + 1	4 + 1
SS for Scotland	66	3.8	8 + 4	0 + 0
Attorney-general	65	3.8	5 + 2	0 + 0
SS for environment	62	3.6	7 + 6	0 + 2
SS for Nthn Ireland	57	3.3	6 + 3	0 + 0
Chief secty, Treasury	56	3.3	7 + 1	0 + 0
SS for transport	45	2.6	5 + 3	0 + 0
SS for Wales	41	2.4	6 + 2	0 + 0
SS employment	38	2.2	4 + 4	0 + 1
Min. agriculture	32	1.9	3 + 3	0 + 0
SS health	25	1.4	3 + 2	0 + 0
SS for education	22	1.3	3 + 1	0 + 0
FCO min of state*	21	1.2	2 + 2	0 + 0
SS social security	20	1.2	3 + 1	0 + 0
SS natl heritage	18	1.0	3 + 0	0 + 0
Chief whip*	17	1.0	2 + 1	0 + 0
Finan sec, Treasury*	16	1.0	3 + 0	0 + 0
Lord chancellor	14	0.8	3 + 0	0 + 0
Lord advocate*	9	0.5	2 + 0	0 + 0
Govt whip, Lords*	9	0.5	2 + 0	0 + 0
Environment min. state*	6	0.3	1 + 1	0 + 0
Home off min. state*	4	0.2	1 + 3	0 + 0
All others	17	1.0	0 + 58	0 + 0
Total	1719	100	154 + 119	16 + 10

Notes: In the third column, the first figure shows committee memberships and the second figure subcommittee memberships. The fourth column follows a similar format for chairs of committees or subcommittees.

In the list of ministerial titles SS means 'secretary of state' (the basic cabinet rank). The titles lord president of the council, lord privy seal and chancellor of the Duchy of Lancaster are traditional titles for equivalently ranked non-departmental posts. The chancellor of the exchequer, president of the Board of Trade and the minister for agriculture, fisheries and food are departmental heads of the Treasury, the DTI and MAFF, respectively. The attorney-general and lord chancellor are law officers. The chief secretary to the Treasury is the second-in-command at the Treasury, but a cabinet member.

Non-cabinet ministers are indicated by an asterisk. The ministers of state at the Foreign Office and Home Office are the deputies to the foreign secretary and home secretary, and the financial secretary is third-in-line at the Treasury. The lord advocate is a law officer for Scotland. The chief whip's formal title is parliamentary secretary to the Treasury, and that of the government whip in the Lords is the captain of the gentlemen at arms.

---

across a range of issues and a long period of time, but need not be discernible in the outcomes of any particular round of a single issue.

One striking feature of Table 13.2 is the prominence of the prime minister's score, more than 100 points above a group of three major rivals, the foreign secretary, defence secretary and chancellor of the exchequer. Together these four roles clearly constitute a 'first division' in the ranking. The defence secretary's relatively high ranking compared with the chancellor is surprising. It may reflect a greater tendency for overseas and defence issues to be formally handled by the cabinet committee system (dating back to the long history of earlier committee organisation on defence issues than on domestic policy). By contrast a great deal of Treasury influence may be exercised in department–Treasury bilaterals without formally running through the committee system. In addition, unlike any other department, the Treasury's committee places are split between the chancellor and the chief secretary. Their combined score (166) surpasses that for any other department's cabinet representative.

A second-ranked group of ministers includes two prominent departmental ministers, the home secretary and president of the Board of Trade. Since the home secretary's role is conventionally described as one of the 'four great offices of state', its lower position here is noteworthy. Also in this second division are three non-departmental ministers (sometimes deprecatingly called 'floaters' by departmental colleagues) two of whom are the Lord President and Lord Privy Seal: between them they chair all the domestic committees and non-symbolic subcommittees which the prime minister does not attend. Traditionally one or both these people are the fixers and business managers of the system, lubricants, swing-voters in finely balanced committees and guardians of electoral and party interests. The third minister without portfolio is the chancellor of the Duchy of Lancaster, who in 1992 was William Waldegrave, head of the relatively small Office for Public Service and Science in the Cabinet Office (OPSS), with responsibility for science policy and Major's Citizen's Charter initiative.

In the somewhat larger third-ranked group there are several types of ministers. The heads of the three area ministries

(Scotland, Wales and Northern Ireland) sit on considerably more committees because of the multifunctional interests of their departments (see Parry, 1989; Thomas, 1989; Bell, 1989). The attorney-general (the government's chief law officer) and the chief secretary (the Treasury's second cabinet member, with responsibility for controlling public spending) have specialised roles which bring them assignments to influential committees. The environment secretary and the transport secretary are the most prominent of the departmental spending ministers, the Environment brief including responsibility for local government. And two lower-ranked 'economic' departments, Employment and the Ministry for Agriculture, sit on relatively fewer committees.

The 'fourth division' of ministers in Table 13.2 is composed of five cabinet members and three others from outside its ranks. The low-ranked secretaries of state include the heads of the three biggest spending welfare state departments, Social Security (whose budget alone accounts for over a third of public spending), Health (with responsibility for the NHS) and Education. Also in this group is the newest and smallest Whitehall spending department, National Heritage (set up only in 1992 to provide a role for a Major ally, David Mellor, and supervising broadcasting and conservation). The lowest ranked of all cabinet members in committee influence is the lord chancellor, whose highly untypical and rather separate department administers the operations of the courts and selects the judiciary. One interpretation of these results is that single-track ministries sit more on the fringes of the committee system, because their work is more self-contained, while less important but conglomerate departments (such as the three area ministries) play a more prominent role. Another view sees significance in the marginalisation of 'welfare state' departments (Social Security, Health and Education) from the committee process, despite their huge budgetary size and social importance, while relatively low-spending 'economic' ministries (DTI, Employment and MAFF) play more central roles.

Three non-cabinet ministers have comparable committee influence rankings with the bottom rungs of the cabinet: the Foreign Office minister of state (the deputy for the foreign secretary, in 1992 the influential Tristan Garel-Jones); the chief whip, in charge of all parliamentary discipline; and the financial secretary, the third Treasury minister in the rankings.

Finally, for comparative purposes, Table 13.2 includes individual scores for a number of other junior ministers who serve not on the 'symbolic' subcommittees but on one of the more salient committees with a preponderance of cabinet members. Junior ministers serving only on the symbolic subcommittees are classed as 'others', and account for less than 1 per cent of the overall weighting score in the cabinet committee system.

The approach in Table 13.2 focuses on aggregating ministers' positional influence across all their committees to reach an estimate of their influence across the cabinet committee system as a whole. It might be objected that what matters to ministers is instead only their degree of influence within the committees on which they actually sit. If we ignore the fact that some ministers sit on very few committees, and instead focus on how likely they are to get their way on the decisions they are involved in, will different conclusions follow? Figure 13.1 shows each cabinet minister's share of influence on the committees where they do sit along the vertical axis, plotted against their percentage of the total amount of influence in the cabinet committee system (taken from Table 13.2) on the horizontal axis.

The prime minister scores top on both measures, but with a higher mean influence score on the vertical axis (28 per cent, rather than 15 per cent in Table 13.2), because the premier chairs all the committees he or she sits on. The foreign secretary and

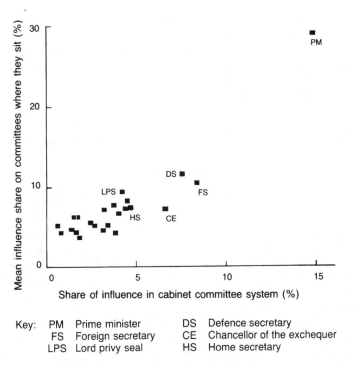

Figure 13.1   *Two measures of cabinet ministers' positional influence*

defence secretary stand out as the 'first division' group of cabinet members because they sit mainly on small and powerful committees, but the chancellor of the exchequer does not have the same advantage. The remaining cabinet members are more equal in their influence in terms of their mean influence on committees where they sit, than on the measures in Table 13.2. Thus Figure 13.1 shows a second group of minister scoring 7–9 per cent on the vertical axis, including the three non-departmental ministers, the chief secretary, attorney-general, home secretary, president of Board of Trade and Northern Ireland secretary. The remaining cabinet ministers are the third group. They sit solely on larger committees, almost entirely handling domestic policy, and their mean influence scores are virtually identical, between 5 and 6 per cent, with only minor variations across committees. (The lord chancellor is the only slight exception, with a mean score below 3.)

The spread of ministers along the vertical axis of Figure 13.1 suggests a less differentiated (perhaps more 'equal') cabinet, where the median minister has a mean score of 6.3 per cent across the committees where they sit. Ministers' influence is fairly standardised: 15 out of 23 cabinet members have mean scores within plus or minus 1.5 points of this median. The prime minister has a mean score four and a half times greater than the average minister, and the foreign and defence secretaries' mean scores are both roughly twice as great. Yet we should not exaggerate the differences between ministers' two scores shown in Figure 13.1. The correlation between ministers' positions on the horizontal and vertical axes is 0.93, so that they are very closely related. (Correlation scores can range from zero, which denotes a complete lack of association between the two measures, to 1.0, which means they are completely identical.)

There is a third way in which to assess the information on cabinet ministers' allocations, this time looking simply at who comes into contact with whom in the committee system, rather than trying to uncover measures of relative influence. This exercise covers all full committees and all the subcommittees which include two or more cabinet members (thereby excluding only the 'symbolic' domestic subcommittees). For each minister an interaction table was computed, showing the number of colleagues with whom their committee work brings them into contact. (For details, see Dunleavy, 1994, Appendix Table B.) With 23 ministers this table is too complex to be easily analysed. And a simple numerical comparison of contacts (as in a network analysis) would anyway be distorted, since some ministers sit on larger committees than others. Table 13.3 abstracts the most salient details.

TABLE 13.3   *The linkages between cabinet members created by joint membership of committees and subcommittees*

Minister	Average linkages	Number of colleagues with links	
		4 or over	1 or 0
SS Scotland	5.7	17	0
SS environment	5.4	17	2
Chanc. Duchy Lancaster	5.0	17	1
Chancellor of exchequer	5.0	16	1
President Bd of Trade	4.9	16	2
Lord president of council	4.5	12	0
SS Northern Ireland	4.3	13	2
SS transport	4.2	16	2
Home secretary	4.0	14	2
SS Wales	4.0	13	2
Foreign secretary	3.9	11	7
Lord privy seal	3.8	12	3
SS employment	3.5	11	4
Chief secretary	2.9	7	4
SS defence	2.8	6	8
Minister agriculture	2.7	9	7
SS health	2.6	5	5
Prime minister	2.3	5	11
SS education	2.3	5	7
SS social security	2.1	4	7
Attorney general	1.9	2	9
SS national heritage	1.9	0	7
Lord chancellor	1.1	0	17
Average cabinet members	3.5	9.7	3.7

Notes: Coverage includes the 16 ministerial committees and the five subcommittees which include multiple members of the cabinet.

The second and third columns show the number of colleagues with whom each minister has more than the average of 3.5 committee linkages or, on the other hand, has colleagues with whom their committee places produce little overlap. At the top of the table, the Scottish secretary will see over four-fifths of his or her cabinet colleagues in four or more committees, whereas the prime minister overlaps to this extent with only a fifth of the cabinet (primarily those who sit on the OPD network of committees). The last column shows that the lord chancellor and the prime minister have the largest number of cabinet colleagues with whom they barely overlap in committees, the lord chancellor because he or she sits on so few committees, and the prime minister because he or she is primarily involved in the OPD network.

Whereas Table 13.2 and Figure 13.1 suggested basically consistent rankings of ministers, the ordering in Table 13.3 is quite different. Heading the list of ministers with committee links to colleagues are the Scottish secretary (who is almost omnipresent in the committee system) and the environment secretary (who sits on all the large domestic committees). The chancellor of the exchequer, chancellor of the Duchy of Lancaster and president of the Board of Trade are also prominent. Some of the top-ranked ministers in Table 13.2, such as the prime minister, defence secretary and the attorney-general, come well down the list on Table 13.3, reflecting their role on the smaller OPD committees. Other ministers at the bottom of Table 13.3 are the same as on Table 13.2, however, such as the education, social security, health and national heritage secretaries, and the lord chancellor. Their low influence scores derive from their restricted committee places, which also reduce the extent of their contacts with colleagues.

An interesting problem is to estimate how these various dimensions of cabinet members' committee roles feed through into the overall index of their positional influence. An appropriate method for trying to partition the various factors involved is multiple regression, with each minister's weighted committee influence score acting as the dependent variable, and denoted by I. After considerable investigation, three explanatory variables were entered:

- the minister's average number of committee links to Cabinet colleagues, denoted by L;
- the number of chairs of cabinet committees or subcommittees held by the minister, denoted by C; and
- a dummy variable denoted by D indicating whether the minister is involved in two or more OPD committees (scored 1) or not (scored 0): the ministers scored 1 are the prime minister, chancellor of the exchequer, foreign secretary, defence secretary and attorney-general.

A final dummy variable (denoted P) was included to estimate the extra influence attaching to the prime minister's role (score 1 for the prime minister and 0 for everyone else): this is equivalent to running the equation on the data set excluding the prime minister. The final equation is then:

$$I = 11.0\,L + 12.6\,C + 8.6\,D + 103.8\,P - 3.4$$

In other words, the basic expected influence score of most cabinet members is simply 11 times their average number of committee links, minus a constant of 3.4. If they are also a committee chair then 12.6 times their number of chairs is added to their expected score. If they are a core member of the smaller OPD committees an increment of 80.6 is added to their basic score. And if they are the prime minister, a further increment of 103.8 is added. This model has an R^2 of 92 per cent, outperforming all the other models tested.

Yet the result needs to be interpreted cautiously, since the number of chairs a cabinet member has is directly built into the calculation of the overall influence score. In addition the number of committee linkages is related to the number of committee placements a minister has, and placements are also built into the calculation of overall influence scores. So the purpose of the regression is not to *explain* the influence scores, whose construction is completely artefactual. But the model does allow us to estimate numerically the relative importance of the various components of the scores as constructed. In particular it clearly demonstrates that most cabinet ministers' committee influence depends primarily on cumulating committee positions on the larger domestic committees. By contrast, those ministers on the mainly separate OPD network gain influence from its exclusivity, while the non-departmental ministers accumulate influence by chairing committees. Finally the prime minister has a substantial increment of influence simply in virtue of her or his office, accounting for around two-fifths of their overall committee influence score. These results can be regarded as a first ranging shot at estimating the importance of the different factors underlying committee influence.

Coalitions and the Fragmentation of Positional Influence in the Cabinet Committee System

Despite the prominence of the prime minister's large lead over other ministers, his or her committee influence is by no means dominant. The prime minister absorbs almost 15 per cent of the total scores available, equivalent to the influence of more than three high-salience cabinet committees. On the other hand, any two of the other 'first division' ministers can wield rather more committee influence, in addition to controlling their own important departments. If we can assume that senior and junior ministers in departments take the same positions then the combined Treasury score in Table 13.2 (for the chancellor, chief secretary and financial secretary) rises to 182 points (or 10.6 per cent), while that for the foreign secretary and FCO minister of state rises to 176 (10.2 per cent). A coalition of both departments would then push past the prime minister in committee influence, as would a coalition of either with the defence secretary. However, by the same logic, a careful prime minister would ensure that the non-departmental ministers in the 'second division' group (the lord president, lord privy seal and chancellor of the Duchy of

Lancaster) were particularly loyal colleagues. If these three ministers always acted cohesively with the prime minister, the bloc would control 28 per cent of committee influence, including chairing all full cabinet committees.

There are a number of different ways of assessing the degree of fragmentation of influence in the cabinet committee system. One measure (the Hirschman–Hirfindahl index) derives from work on industrial concentration ratios, and has been applied to assessing the number of effective parties contesting elections (Taagepera and Shugart, 1989, pp.77–91). It entails dividing one by the sum of the squares of each ministers' share of the overall committee influence (expressed as a fraction rather than a percentage). On this basis the fragmentation of the cabinet committee system is very high, with the number of effective actors in the system being 18. However, if we could assume that the non-departmental ministers act with the prime minister in one bloc, and that the Treasury, Foreign Office and Home Office ministers act cohesively in departmental mini-blocs, the number of effective actors would be rated much lower, at just over nine (out of a cabinet of 23).

A second approach is to ask how many ministers would be required to act together so as to control the overall operations of the cabinet committee system. We have no definite information about what would be needed here, but it is feasible to proceed on the assumption that a winning coalition of ministers would need to assemble just over half the overall total of influence scores in the cabinet committee system (that is more than 860 out of the 1719 points). In practice the threshold involved is likely to be considerably lower, since many cabinet ministers will choose not to become involved in issues which do not affect their departments. However, if we assume a 50.1 per cent threshold, the lessons drawn will apply to lower thresholds pro rata.

To assess the viability of different coalitions we assume that a set of central actors who have concerted their stance must seek the support of extra actors. If they are being rational, the central actors will seek additional support by working down the list of other ministers in the order of their influence scores ranking. In this way they will be able to construct a 'minimum winning coalition' (one commanding 50.1 per cent influence) which has the fewest number of actors in it: the smaller the number of actors in a coalition the easier it will be to construct and to maintain its cohesion.

A basic finding of considerable significance from Table 13.2 is that almost any winning coalition constructed in this manner (and hence including the prime minister and other first division ministers in it) will have seven actors. Another important criterion for assessing an individual minister's influence is how easy it is for other ministers to organise a winning coalition excluding her or him; that is, to construct a *hostile* coalition. Forming a hostile coalition excluding the prime minister or another of the first division ministers involves recruiting a larger number of members. For example, keeping out the prime minister (influence score 256 points) may entail recruiting four ministers with influence scores of 70–80 points, a net increase of three people in the minimum coalition size. Similarly, excluding the defence secretary (influence score 138 points) may entail recruiting two ministers with influence scores of 70 points, increasing the minimum coalition size by one member. By contrast, excluding ministers lower down the rankings will rarely trigger an increase in the size of the minimum winning coalition. The difference between the sizes of a coalition involving the actor and that of a hostile coalition can be taken as indicating that minister's *advantage* in coalition forming.

Table 13.4 presents the salient data for coalitions where the central actors are either individual ministers or groups of ministers. The first row shows the data for the home secretary, the top-scoring 'second division' minister in Table 13.2, with 4.8 per cent of total influence scores. If he or she recruits other ministers in the sequence in Table 13.2 (that is including the prime minister and first division ministers) then he or she will need six extra actors to succeed, making seven members in all. But a hostile coalition excluding the home secretary could also be constructed with seven

TABLE 13.4   *The coalitional prospects for cabinet ministers*

Central actors	% of total scores	Extra actors needed	Size of hostile coalition	Advantage
HS or other minister	4–5	6	7	0
FS/CE/DS	6–9	6	8	1
PM	15	6	10	3
PM + 1[FS/DS/CE]	24	5	11	4
PM + NDMs	28	3	10	3
PM + NDMs + 1[FS/DS/CE]	37	2	12	5
PM + 2[FS/DS/CE]	33	4	13	6
PM + NDMs + 2[FS/DS/CE]	45	1	–	max

Notes: The following abbreviations are used: PM (prime minister), FS (foreign secretary), DS (defence secretary), CE (chancellor of the exchequer), NDMs (the three non-departmental ministers, lord president, lord privy seal and chancellor of the Duchy of Lancaster).

The sign/means 'or'; + 1[. . .] means 'and one of'. Hence PM + 1[FS/DS/CE] means the prime minister and one of the foreign secretary or the defence secretary or the chancellor of the exchequer; +2 [. . .] means 'and two of'.

actors, so his or her advantage is zero. If the central actor is the foreign secretary (or the chancellor or defence secretary), because they control more of the total influence score a hostile coalition would have to be slightly larger than a friendly coalition, giving an advantage of one. And for the prime minister alone the advantage rises to three. Combinations of the prime minister and one or two other first division ministers will enjoy proportionately larger advantages.

The prime minister may select the three leading non-departmental ministers carefully so that they act as a cohesive bloc with her or him. But although this bloc would need to recruit only three more actors to succeed, hostile coalitions could form more easily against it than against a coalition involving the prime minister and one of the first division ministers – because the non-departmental ministers carry less influence than the foreign secretary or defence secretary or chancellor of the exchequer. If the prime minister plus bloc can also involve at least one first division minister then opponents must recruit more than half of the cabinet to outvote them. Similarly the prime minister plus two first division ministers requires a hostile coalition to recruit 13 cabinet members to outweigh them. If the prime minister plus the non-departmental ministers can recruit any two of the foreign secretary or the defence secretary or the chancellor of the exchequer then no hostile coalition is feasible. The six central actors here would need to recruit only one additional voice to control the committee system, and they would already be a 'blocking coalition' in their own right, since there is insufficient weighted influence among the remaining cabinet members to reach over 50 per cent of the total. We could strengthen these results somewhat if we assume that all the Treasury ministers (inside and outside the cabinet) act cohesively together, as do the Foreign Office ministers.

These results throw a new light upon the experience of the 1980s, when the prime minister, Margaret Thatcher, had two rather different coalitional experiences. In the early 1980s, in coalition with her chancellor of the exchequer and defence secretary plus the non-departmental ministers, she easily pushed through her monetarist economic policies against probably a majority of her cabinet, including two sceptical foreign secretaries. But from the mid-1980s until 1990, she failed to secure her own way against a coalition in favour of entering the European Exchange Rate Mechanism which included two successive foreign secretaries and two chancellors of the exchequer. As a detailed decisional study by Thompson (1994) makes clear, Thatcher could manage only a blocking rearguard action against ERM entry, and eventually conceded defeat in October 1990 (see Chapter 11). There seems to be a close fit between the empirical evidence here and the conclusions suggested by Table 13.4.

That the prime minister is in a powerful coalitional position despite commanding only 15 per cent of the total influence scores in the committee system might suggest that he or she is in a position akin to that of a shareholder who manages to control a publicly quoted company despite holding much less than 51 per cent of the shares. A minority shareholder can have a controlling stake because many of the other shareholders are inactive, often because they are so fragmented that the costs of organising prevent them exercising their formally assigned influence over the company. Something analogous often goes on in the cabinet committee system, where ministers tend to stay out of other people's battles and look after their own department's interests first, perhaps extending a lower level of support to colleagues pushing issues which are important to that minister's particular faction within the governing party.

Many features of core executive operations in Britain reinforce this basic separatism – including the importance of departmentalism in Whitehall's 'federal' structure, the fragmentation of the committee system and the predominance of bilateral deals between the Treasury and individual spending ministers in the budget process (see Dunleavy and Rhodes, 1990, and Chapter 1 above). In addition cabinet government conventions frown on any overt 'log-rolling' between spending ministers and stress large majority or 'consensus' decisions (which are virtually impossible to achieve without the consent of the prime minister and the other first division ministers). The only ministers who have the freedom to roam more broadly over the issues that cabinet committees consider are the prime minister, the non-departmental ministers and the chancellor of the exchequer/chief secretary – who are highly likely to operate as a coalition on issues such as determining overall public expenditure levels or holding spending ministers to compliance with budget targets.

Conclusions: Committee Influence and Research on the Core Executive

Given that information on cabinet committees has only recently become available, this study has necessarily been exploratory; we must be cautious in interpreting the numerical estimates given above. These scores should not be fetishised, nor should any fine or precise significance be attached to them. Their value is primarily heuristic, in providing pegs which help us to think further about the ways that cabinet committees and ministerial influence over decision making may be patterned. If in future some alternative construct can better perform this role – for example, if we can develop improved data about ministers' actual committee behaviour – then the indices used here will be obsolete.

However, for the moment even the modest advances made here open up some substantial research opportunities. An obvious question is whether the 1992 pattern of committees is different from that of other governments or not. In recent years some good quality work on comparing across cabinet systems has begun to be carried out (Burch, 1993). There is obvious scope for this trend to be developed further, especially since most of this work seems to lack the necessary analytic concept of the 'core executive' to guide it and hence largely neglects to discuss committees (Blondel and Müller-Rommel, 1993; but see Andeweg, 1993, p.34).

In Britain earlier work on cabinet committee structures has established only a basic listing of which committees existed, even in the period for which full Public Record Office files are available. Hennessy and Arends (1983) provide a full listing of 'Mr Attlee's Engine Room', the committee structure of the postwar Labour government. Even the 'standing groups' here are virtually unrecognisable in 1992 terms, with only the Defence Committee, Future Legislation, and King's Speech and Legislation Committees having any close contemporary counterparts. Even here, however, no systematic information is available about the Attlee committees' memberships, or even most of the chairs, although the number of meetings is recorded. A full listing is also given of 244 *ad hoc* groups, only 11 of which met more than 10 times.

The next available comparison point seems to be December 1985, where again Hennessy (1986) provides an unofficial but broadly reliable listing of 27 Cabinet standing committees and subcommittees (excluding the 'symbolic' subcommittees which barely involve cabinet members). Comparing 1984 and 1992 shows some

TABLE 13.5   *Committee/main subcommittee chairs*

Minister	1984	1992
Prime minister	10	9
Lord president	7	4
Chanc. exchequer	6	0
Lord privy seal	1	5
Foreign secretary	1	2
Home secretary	1	1
Total	26	21

commonalities, notably in the prime minister's committees and those of the foreign secretary (apart from an extra OPD subcommittee coping with the post-1989 changes in Eastern Europe) and the home secretary. But it also shows some differences: see Table 13.5. In 1984, the lord president chaired far more of the domestic committees than the lord privy seal, whereas in 1992 they split the roles more evenly. In 1984, the chancellor of the exchequer chaired six forums, but by 1992 none – an apparently substantial change.

However Major's change in policy towards openness about cabinet committees was a permanent one, and in 1993 a new listing was produced. In preparation for the winter 1993 budget a new cabinet standing committee (EDX) was set up to decide on public expenditure cutbacks, given the prospect of a £50 billion public sector borrowing requirement: and this key committee was chaired by the chancellor of the exchequer. Later in 1993, a new cabinet committee (EDR) was set up to coordinate the economic regeneration of the regions, further illustrating the fairly constant change in the committee structure.

The next agenda for research should be to establish comparable data about cabinet committee memberships for the whole of the postwar period not covered by the thirty-year rule. However the Callaghan/Whitehall doctrine that committee structures were 'domestic' matters continues to exert a baneful influence. It apparently means that no revelations about committee structures inside the thirty-year rule period can take place without the permission of the premier involved – which is unlikely to be forthcoming, certainly for the Thatcher and Wilson years. But as the 'open government' period stretches into the future, and as the thirty-year rule progressively unrolls, so the closed gap will reduce in significance, and comparable data for the period before 1965 and after 1992 will increasingly dominate our thinking about committee government.

By maintaining complete secrecy about cabinet committees, previous British governments in the twentieth century continued the Bagehot tradition of urging citizens 'to venerate what they cannot presently comprehend'. Now that the official stance has cracked a little, the onus is on political science research to widen the gap further.

Guide to Further Reading

R.A.W. RHODES

This guide is selective, personal and gives full details for each item, even if it is also included in the Bibliography. As explained in the introduction, this collection focuses on the UK and does not include any comparative material.

Prime minister and cabinet are among the cast of characters in many academic books about British government and politics but they are rarely the lead. The best single introduction covering both prime minister and cabinet is Simon James, *British Cabinet Government* (London: Routledge, 1992) but he would be the first to admit that he has written a textbook, not an authoritative study.

On the prime minister there is no single-author, contemporary book of note. John Mackintosh, *British Cabinet Government* (London: Stevens, 1st edn, 1962) was the definitive text but it is out of date, better on the period before 1945 than after, and few would now accept his interpretation. The 'classic' debate about the power of the prime minister is most conveniently covered in Anthony King (ed.), *The British Prime Minister: a reader* (London: Macmillan, 1969) and the revised and updated second edition of this collection (London: Macmillan, 1985) also contains some good articles, including King's oft-cited essay, 'Margaret Thatcher: The Style of a Prime Minister' (pp.96–140). Michael Foley, *The Rise of the British Presidency* (Manchester: Manchester University Press, 1993) provides a distinctive twist to the prime ministerial power thesis. Thereafter, the best material is in academic journals and chapters in books. George Jones is always worth reading; see 'Development of the Cabinet', in W. Thornhill (ed.), *The Modernisation of British Government* (London: Pitman, 1975) pp.31–62; 'The Prime Minister's Power', in A. King (ed.), *The British Prime Minister*, 2nd edn (London: Macmillan, 1985) pp.195–220; and 'Mrs Thatcher and the Power of the Prime Minister', *Contemporary Record*, vol. 3, no. 4, pp.2–6. Especially noteworthy is Richard Rose, 'The Job at the Top', in R. Rose and E. Suleiman (eds), *Presidents and Prime Ministers* (Washington DC: American Enterprise Institute, 1980) pp.1–49.

On advising prime ministers, Bernard Donoughue, *Prime Minister: The Conduct of Policy under Harold Wilson and James Callaghan* (London: Cape, 1987); and Tessa Blackstone and William Plowden, *Inside the Think Tank: Advising the Cabinet, 1971–1983* (London: Heinemann, 1988) are illuminating but do not cover the bulk of the Thatcher era.

On the cabinet, see the relevant chapters in Simon James, *British Cabinet Government* and Peter Hennessy, *Cabinet* (Oxford: Blackwell, 1986). The latter is engagingly written, with excellent sections (on, for example, the cabinet machine), but episodic. Val Herman and J.E. Alt (eds), *Cabinet Studies: A Reader* (London: Macmillan, 1975) is out of date but contains some excellent articles (for example, Roy Jenkins, 'On Being A Minister', pp.210–20).

On ministers there is still only Bruce Headey, *British Cabinet Ministers* (London: Allen & Unwin, 1974). On junior ministers, there is Kevin Theakston, *Junior Ministers in British Government* (Oxford: Blackwell, 1987). On government departments, there is an excellent survey of the literature by Martin Smith, David Marsh and David Richards, 'Central Government Departments and the Policy Process', *Public Administration* vol. 71, 1993, pp.567–94 (Chapter 2 above is an extract).

On the civil service and its relationship to the executive, the best introduction is Gavin Drewry and Tony Butcher, *The Civil Service Today*, 2nd edn (Oxford: Blackwell, 1991). The *tour de force*, however, is Peter Hennessy, *Whitehall* (London: Secker & Warburg, 1988; new edn, London: Fontana, 1990). On recent changes see: William Plowden, *Ministers and Mandarins* (London: Institute for Public Policy Research, 1994).

There are several books on specific aspects of cabinet government. On life in the Whitehall village, there is still nothing to surpass Hugh Heclo and Aaron Wildavsky, *The Private Government of Public Money: Community and Policy Inside British Politics*, 2nd edn (London: Macmillan, 1981), although the successor volume by Colin Thain and Maurice Wright, *The Treasury and Whitehall: the planning and control of public expenditure 1976–1993* (Oxford: Oxford University Press) is due by spring 1995 at the latest. On the constitutional conventions of cabinet government, the collection edited by Geoffrey Marshall, *Ministerial Responsibility* (Oxford: Oxford University Press, 1989) is useful, although his *Constitutional Conventions: the rules and forms of political acountability* (Oxford: Clarendon Press, 1984) may well be definitive. Diana Woodhouse, *Ministers and Parliament: Accountability in Theory and Practice* (Oxford: Clarendon Press, 1994) is relentlessly thorough on trends in accountability in the 1980s and 1990s, covering resignations, non-resignations, departmental select committees and agencies.

There is little on the impact of the European Community on the British executive but Simon Bulmer, Stephen George and Andrew Scott (eds), *The United Kingdom and EC Membership Evaluated* (London: Pinter, 1992) and Stephen George (ed.), *Britain and the European Community: the politics of semi-detachment* (Oxford: Clarendon Press, 1992) are both helpful.

I have left until last accounts by and of politicians. Diaries, memoirs, biographies and autobiographies are a major political and publishing industry. All I do is note some personal favourites for the 1970s and 1980s. Anthony King, *British Prime Minister*, 2nd edn, pp.261–5 provides a useful listing for all postwar prime ministers; Peter Hennessy and Anthony Seldon (eds), *Ruling Performance: British Governments from Attlee to Thatcher* (Oxford: Blackwell, 1987) provides both brief portraits of all postwar prime ministers and extensive bibliographies.

Since these two books were published there have been some important additions, especially Alistair Horne, *Macmillan 1894–1956* (London: Macmillan, 1988); Alistair Horne, *Macmillan 1957–1986* (London: Macmillan, 1989); John Campbell, *Edward Heath* (London: Cape, 1993). The former is the official biography and Volume 1 is particularly fine. The latter is informative but strangely inconclusive about its subject.

For the Labour governments of the 1960s and 1970s the diaries of Tony Benn, Barbara Castle and Richard Crossman are essential reading. Although no student will read them from cover to cover, they should be dipped into as source material. See Tony Benn, *Out of the Wilderness: Diaries 1963–67* (London: Hutchinson, 1987); *Office Without Power: Diaries 1968–72* (London: Hutchinson, 1988); and *Against the Tide: Diaries 1973–76* (London: Hutchinson, 1989); Barbara Castle, *The Castle Diaries 1974–76* (London: Weidenfeld & Nicolson, 1980); and *The Castle Diaries 1964–70* (London: Weidenfeld & Nicolson, 1984); R.H.S. Crossman, *The Diaries of a Cabinet Minister, Volume 1, Minister of Housing 1964–66* (London: Hamilton & Cape, 1975); *The Diaries of a Cabinet, Minister, Volume 2, Lord President of the Council and Leader of the House of Commons 1966–68* (London: Weidenfeld & Nicolson, 1976); and *The Diaries of a Cabinet Minister, Volume 3, Secretary of State for Social Services 1968–70* (London: Weidenfeld & Nicolson, 1977).

Of the memoirs, Denis Healey, *The Time of My Life* (London: Michael Joseph, 1989) and Roy Jenkins, *A Life at the Centre* (London: Macmillan, 1991) are most informative. Of the biographies, Ben Pimlott, *Harold Wilson* (London: HarperCollins, 1992) is essential reading. Finally on Labour governments, to demonstrate that politics can be fun, I recommend Gerald Kaufman, *How To Be a Minister* (London: Sidgwick & Jackson, 1980); and Joel

Barnett, *Inside the Treasury* (London: André Deutsch, 1982), especially his Peter Shore stories.

The outpourings of Conservative ministers of the 1980s are invariably self-serving and rarely enlivened by wit or insight. Encyclopaedic, unreadable from cover to cover but an essential source is Nigel Lawson, *The View From No. 11: Memoirs of a Tory Radical* (London: Bantam Press, 1992). Less informative but no more readable is Margaret Thatcher, *The Downing Street Years* (London: HarperCollins, 1993). Thereafter 'you pays your money and takes your choice'. I enjoyed Alan Clarke, *Diaries* (London: Weidenfeld & Nicolson, 1993), but for all the wrong reasons! There are useful sections on policy making in Kenneth Baker, *The Turbulent Years: My Life in Politics* (London: Faber & Faber, 1993); Norman Fowler, *Ministers Decide: A Personal Memoir of the Thatcher Years* (London: Chapman, 1991); Lord Young, *The Enterprise Years: A Businessman in the Cabinet* (London: Headline, 1990). As Simon James comments, with true English understatement, these volumes are 'unexciting'. Finally there is an excellent biography of Margaret Thatcher: Hugo Young, *One of Us: A Biography of Margaret Thatcher* (London: Macmillan, 1st edn, 1989). The final edition (London: Pan Books, 1993) covers her last two years in office.

Little of value has yet been published on John Major, apart from Philip Norton, 'The Conservative Party from Thatcher to Major', in Anthony King *et al.* (eds), *Britain at the Polls 1992* (Chatham, NJ: Chatham House, 1993) pp.29–69; and Dennis Kavanagh and Anthony Seldon (eds), *The Major Effect* (London: Macmillan, 1994).

Bibliography

Alderman, R.K. (1976) 'The Prime Minister and the Appointment of Ministers: An Exercise in Political Bargaining', *Parliamentary Affairs*, vol. 29, no. 2, pp.101–34.

Alderman, R.K. and Carter, N. (1991) 'A Very Tory Coup: The Ousting of Mrs Thatcher', *Parliamentary Affairs*, vol. 44, no. 2, pp.125–39.

Alderman, R.K. and Carter, N. (1992) 'Logistics of Ministerial Reshuffles', *Public Administration*, vol. 70, no. 4, pp.519–34.

Alderman, R.K. and Cross, J.A. (1985) 'The Reluctant Knife; Reflections on the Prime Minister's Powers of Dismissal', *Parliamentary Affairs*, vol. 38, no. 4, pp.387–407.

Alderman, R.K. and Cross, J.A. (1986) 'Rejuvenating the Cabinet: The Record of Post-War British Prime Ministers Compared', *Political Studies*, vol. 34, no. 4, pp.639–49.

Alderman, R.K. and Smith, M.J. (1990) 'Can British Prime Ministers be given the push by their Parties?', *Parliamentary Affairs*, vol. 43, no. 3, pp.260–76.

Alford, R. and Friedland, R. (1985) *Powers of Theory: Capitalism, the State and Democracy* (Cambridge: Cambridge University Press).

Allison, G. (1969) 'Conceptual Models and the Cuban Missile Crisis', *American Political Science Review*, vol. 63, no. 3, pp.689–718.

Allison, G. (1971) *The Essence of Decision: Explaining the Cuban Missile Crisis* (Boston: Little, Brown).

Allison, G. and Halperin, M. (1972) 'Bureaucratic Politics: A Paradigm and some Implications', in R. Tanter and R. Ullman (eds), *Theory and Policy in International Relations* (Princeton: Princeton University Press), pp.40–79.

Allison, G. and Szanton, P. (1976) *Remaking Foreign Policy* (New York: Basic Books).

Almond, G. (1988) 'The Return to the State', *American Political Science Review*, vol. 82, no. 3, pp.853–74.

Alt, J. and Chrystal, K.A. (1983) *Political Economics* (Brighton: Wheatsheaf).

Alvey Directorate (1987) *Alvey Programme: Annual Report* (London: Department of Industry).

Amery, L.S. (1947) *Thoughts on the Constitution* (London: Oxford University Press).

Anderson, B. (1991) *John Major: The Making of the Prime Minister* (London: Fourth Estate).

Andeweg, R. (1993) 'A Model of the Cabinet System', in J. Blondel and F. Muller-Rommel (eds), *Governing Together: The Extent and Limits of Joint Decision-Making in West European Cabinets* (London: Macmillan), pp.23–42.

Anton, T. (1967) 'Roles and Symbols in the Determination of State Expenditures', *Mid-West Journal of Political Science*, vol. 11, February, pp.27–43.

Ashworth, J. (1982) 'On the Giving and Receiving of Advice (in Whitehall and Salford)', *Transactions of the Manchester Statistical Society.*

Earl of Oxford and Asquith (1928) *Thirty Years of Parliament* (London: Cassell).

Attiyah, P.S. (1979) *The Rise and Fall of Freedom of Contract* (Oxford: Clarendon Press).

Attiyah, P.S. and Summers, R.S. (1987) *Form and Substance in Anglo-American Law* (Oxford: Clarendon Press).

Bagehot, W. (1867) 'The English Constitution', in N. St John Stevas (ed.), *The Collected Works of Walter Bagehot*, Vol. V, 1974 (London: The Economist).

Baker, K. (1993) *The Turbulent Years: My Life in Politics* (London: Faber & Faber).

Baldwin, N.D. (1991) 'The Demise of a Prime Minister', *British Politics Group, Newsletter*, no. 64, spring.

Baldwin, R. (1988) 'The Next Steps: Ministerial Responsibility and Government by Agency', *Modern Law Review*, vol. 51, no. 3, pp.273–95.

Barber, J. (1991) *The Prime Minister Since 1945* (Oxford: Blackwell).

Barber, J. (1984) 'The Power of the Prime Minster', in R.L. Borthwick and J.E. Spence (eds), *British Politics in Perspective* (Leicester: Leicester University Press), pp.73–101.

Barber, J.S. (1972) *The Presidential Character* (Englewood Cliffs, New Jersey: Prentice-Hall).

Barnes, J. (1989) Contribution to a roundtable symposium on 'The British Cabinet in the 1980s', Annual Conference of the Political Studies Association, University of Warwick, 5 April.

Barnett, J. (1982) *Inside the Treasury* (London: André Deutsch).

Barnett, M.J. (1969) *The Politics of Legislation: The Rent Act 1957* (London: Weidenfeld & Nicolson).

Bassett, R. (1964) *The Essentials of Parliamentary Democracy* (London: Frank Cass).

Beattie, A. (ed.) (1970) *English Party Politics 1660–1970*, Vol. 1 (London: Weidenfeld & Nicolson).

Beattie, A. (1975) 'The Two Party System: Room for Scepticism?', in S.E. Finer (ed.), *Adversary Politics and Electoral Reform* (London: Anthony Wigram), pp.293–316.

Beattie, A. (1989) 'Conservatives, Consensus and the Constitution', *LSE Quarterly*, vol. 3, no. 2.

Beer, S.H. (1956) *Treasury Control* (Oxford: Clarendon).

Beer, S.H. (1965) *Modern British Politics* (London: Faber).

Beer, S.H. (1982) *Britain Against Itself* (London: Faber).

Bell, P.N. (1989) 'Direct Role in Northern Ireland', in R. Rose (ed.), *Ministers and Ministries: A Functional Analysis* (Oxford: Clarendon Press), pp.189–226.

Benn, T. (1980) 'The Case for a Constitutional Premiership', *Parliamentary Affairs*, vol. 3, no. 1, pp.7–22.

Benn, T. (1981) *Arguments for Democracy* (London: Cape).

Benn, T. (1988) *Office Without Power: Diaries 1968–72* (London: Hutchinson).

Benyon, J. (1991) 'The Fall of a Prime Minister', *Social Studies Review*, vol. 6, no. 3, January, pp.102–7.

Berger, P. and Luckman, T. (1967) *The Social Construction of Reality* (Harmondsworth: Penguin).

Berrill, K. (1985) 'Strength at the Centre – The Case for a Prime Minister's Department', in A. King (ed.), *The British Prime Minister*, 2nd edn (London: Macmillan), pp.242–57.

Berrington, H. (1974) 'Review Article – The Fiery Chariot: British Prime Ministers and the Search for Love', *British Journal of Political Science*, vol. 4, no. 3, pp.345–69.

Birch, A.H. (1964) *Representative and Responsible Government* (London: Allen & Unwin).

Birkinshaw, P. (1988) *Freedom of Information* (London: Weidenfeld & Nicolson).

Birkinshaw, P., Harden, I. and Lewis, N. (1990) *Government by Moonlight* (London: Unwin–Hyman).

Blackstone, T. and Plowden, W. (1988) *Inside the Think Tank: Advising the Cabinet, 1971–1983* (London: Heinemann).

Blondel, J. and Müller-Rommel, F. (eds) (1993) *Governing Together: The Extent and Limits of Joint Decision-Making in West European Cabinets* (London: Macmillan).

Bogdanor, V. (1981) *The People and the Party System* (Cambridge: Cambridge University Press).

Bogdanor, V. (1983) *Multi-Party Politics and the Constitution* (Cambridge: Cambridge University Press).

Brazier, R. (1988) *Constitutional Practice* (Oxford: Clarendon Press).

Bridges, Lord (1964) *The Treasury* (London: George Allen & Unwin).

Brittan, S. (1964) *The Treasury under the Tories* (London: Penguin).

Brittan, S. (1971) *Steering the Economy* (Harmondsworth: Penguin).

Bromhead, P. (1974) *Britain's Developing Constitution* (London: Allen & Unwin).

Brown, A.H. (1968a) 'Prime Ministerial Power (Part I)', *Public Law*, spring, pp.28–51.

Brown, A.H. (1968b) 'Prime Ministerial Power (Part II)' *Public Law*, summer, pp.106–18.

Bruce-Gardyne, J. and Lawson, N. (1976) *The Power Game* (London: Macmillan).

Bunyan, T. (1976) *The History and Practice of the Political Police in Britain* (London: Quartet).

Burch, M. (1983) 'Mrs Thatcher's Approach to Leadership in Government, 1979–83', *Parliamentary Affairs*, vol. 36, no. 4, pp.399–416.

Burch, M. (1985) 'The Demise of Cabinet Government?', *Teaching Politics*, vol. 14, no. 3, pp.345–62.

Burch, M. (1988) 'The British Cabinet: A Residual Executive', *Parliamentary Affairs*, vol. 41, no. 1, pp.34–48.

Burch, M. (1989) Contribution to a roundtable symposium on 'The British Cabinet in the 1980s', Annual Conference of the Political Studies Association, University of Warwick, 5 April.

Burch, M. (1990) 'Cabinet Government', *Contemporary Record*, September.

Burch, M. (1993) 'Organizing the Flow of Business in West European Cabinets', in J. Blondel and F. Muller-Rommel (eds), *Governing Together:*

The Extent and Limits of Joint Decision-Making in West European Cabinets (London: Macmillan), pp.99–130.

Butler, Lord (1975) 'Reflections on Cabinet Government', in V. Herman and J. Alt (eds), *Cabinet Studies* (Basingstoke: Macmillan), pp.193–209.

Butler, R. (1989) 'Louder than Words', Radio 4, BBC, 10 September.

Butler, Sir Robin (1992) 'The New Public Management: The Contribution of Whitehall and Academia', *The PAC Annual Conference*, University of York, 7 September.

Butler, Sir Robin (1993) 'The Changing Civil Service: A Progress Report', *The PSA Annual Conference*, University of Leicester, 20–22 April.

Butt, R. (1967) *The Power of Parliament* (London: Constable).

Byrd, P. (ed.) (1988) *British Foreign Policy Under Thatcher* (Oxford: Philip Allan).

Cabinet Office (1992a) *Questions of Procedure for Ministers* (London: Cabinet Office).

Cabinet Office (1992b) *Ministerial Committees of the Cabinet: Membership and Terms of Reference* (London: Cabinet Office).

Callaghan, J. (1987) *Time and Chance* (London: Collins).

Campbell, C. (1983) *Governments Under Stress: Political Executives and Key Bureaucrats in Washington, London and Ottawa* (Toronto: University of Toronto Press).

Carpenter, W.S. (1952) *The Unfinished Business of Civil Service Reform* (Princeton: Princeton University Press).

Carter, N. (1988) 'Measuring Government Performance', *Political Quarterly*, vol. 59, no. 3, pp.369–75.

Carter, N. (1991) 'Learning to Measure Performance: the use of indicators in organizations', *Public Administration*, vol. 69, no. 1, pp.85–101.

Carter, N., Day, P. and Klein, R. (1992) *How Organizations Measure Success* (London: Routledge).

Castle, B. (1973) Mandarin Power, *The Sunday Times*, 10 June.

Castle, B. (1980) *The Castle Diaries 1974–1976* (London: Weidenfeld & Nicolson).

Castle, B. (1984) *The Castle Diaries 1964–70* (London: Weidenfeld & Nicolson).

Central Statistical Office (1987–91) *Financial Statistics* (London: HMSO).

Chester, D.N. and Willson, F.M.G. (1968) *The Organisation of British Central Government 1914–1964*, 2nd edn (London: Allen & Unwin).

Clark, A. (1993) *Diaries* (London: Weidenfeld & Nicolson).

Clarke, D. (1947) *The Conservative Faith in the Modern Age* (London: Conservative Political Centre).

Clarke, M. (1988) in M. Smith, S. Smith and B. White (eds), *British Foreign Policy Tradition, Change and Transformation* (London: Unwin–Hyman).

Clarke, R. (1971) *New Trends in British Government* (London: HMSO).

Clarke, R. (1975) 'The Machinery of Government', in W. Thornhill (ed.), *The Modernization of British Government* (London: Pitman), pp.63–95.

Clegg, S. (1989) *Frameworks of Power* (London: Sage).

Cockburn, C. (1977) *The Local State* (London: Pluto Press).

Cockerell, M. (1988) *Live From Number 10* (London: Faber).

Cockerell, M., Hennessy, P. and Walker, D. (1985) *Sources Close to the Prime Minister: Inside the Hidden World of the News Manipulators* (London: Macmillan).

Cornford, J. (1974) 'Review Article – The Illusion of Decision', *British Journal of Political Science*, vol. 4, no. 2, pp.231–43.

Cox, A., Furlong, P. and Page E. (1985) *Power in Capitalist Society* (Brighton: Wheatsheaf).

Craig, P.P. (1990) *Public Law and Democracy in the United Kingdom and the United States of America* (Oxford: Clarendon Press).

Cranston, R. (1985) *Legal Foundations of the Welfare State* (London: Weidenfeld & Nicolson).

Crewe, I. (1974) *British Political Sociology Yearbook, Vol 1: Elites in Western Democracy* (London: Croom Helm).

Crewe, I. (1990) 'The State of the Parties', *Social Studies Review*, vol. 6, no. 1, pp.21–31.

Crick, B.R. (1964) *The Reform of Parliament* (London: Weidenfeld & Nicolson).

Crick, B.R. (1968) *The Reform of Parliament*, 2nd edn (London: Weidenfeld & Nicolson).

Crick, M. and van Klaveren, A. (1991) 'Mrs Thatcher's Greatest Blunder', *Contemporary Record*, vol. 5, no. 3, pp.397–416.

Crosland, S. (1982) *Tony Crosland* (London: Cape).

Cross, J.A. (1970) *British Public Administration* (London: University Tutorial Press).

Crossman, R.H.S. (ed.) (1963) 'Introduction', in W. Bagehot (ed.), *The English Constitution* (London: Fontana).

Crossman, R.H.S. (1972) *Inside View* (London: Jonathan Cape).

Crossman, R.H.S. (1975) *The Diaries of a Cabinet Minister, Volume 1, Minister of Housing* (London: Hamilton and Cape).

Crowther Hunt, Lord, and Kellner, P. (1980) *The Civil Servants: An Inquiry into Britain's Ruling Class* (London: Macdonald).

Cunningham, C. (1992) 'Sea Defences: A Professionalized Network', in D. Marsh and R.A.W. Rhodes (eds), *Policy Networks in British Government* (Oxford: Oxford University Press).

Curtis, L.P. (1963) *Coercion and Conciliation in Ireland 1880–1892* (Princeton: Princeton University Press).

Dalyell, T. (1987) *Misrule: How Mrs Thatcher Has Misled Parliament from the Sinking of the Belgrano to the Wright Affair* (London: Hamilton).

Davies, A. and Willman, J. (1991) *What Next? Agencies, Departments and the Civil Service* (London: Institute of Public Policy Research).

De Smith, S.A. (1977) *Constitutional and Administrative Law* (Harmondsworth: Penguin).

Delafons, J. (1982) 'Working in Whitehall: Changes in Public Administration 1952–1982', *Public Administration*, vol. 60, no. 3, pp.253–72.

Department of Industry (1982a) *A Programme for Advanced Information Technology: The Report of the Alvey Committee of Inquiry* (London: DoI).

Department of Industry (1982b) 'Proposal for Project IT87: Management Report', confidential memorandum, DoI, 19 January.

Department of Industry (1982c) 'Proposal for Project IT87: Summary Report', confidential memorandum, DoI, 19 January.

Department of Industry (1982d) 'Proposal for Project IT87: Technical Report', confidential memorandum, DoI, 19 January.

Dicey, A.V. (1915) *Introduction to the Study of the Law of the Constitution*, 8th edn (London: Macmillan).

Doherty, M. (1988) 'Prime Ministerial Power and Ministerial Responsibility in the Thatcher Era', *Parliamentary Affairs*, vol. 41, no. 1, pp.49–67.

Doig, J.W. and Hargrove, E.C. (eds) (1987) *Leadership and Innovation: A Biographical Perspective on Entrepreneurs in Government* (Baltimore: Johns Hopkins University Press).

Donoughue, B. (1985) 'The Conduct of Economic Policy 1974–1979', in A. King (ed.), *The British Prime Minister* (Basingstoke: Macmillan), pp.47–71.

Donoughue, B. (1987) *Prime Minister: The Conduct of Policy under Harold Wilson and James Callaghan* (London: Cape).

Donoughue, B. (1988) 'The Prime Minister's Day', *Contemporary Record*, vol. 2, no. 2, p.17.

Douglas, M. (1987) *How Institutions Think* (London: Routledge & Kegan Paul).

Dowding, K. (1991) *Political Power and Rational Choice* (Aldershot: E. Elgar).

Drewry, G. (ed.) (1989) *The New Select Committees* (Oxford: Clarendon).

Drewry, G. and Butcher, T. (1988) *The Civil Service Today* (Oxford: Blackwell).

Drucker, H., Dunleavy, P., Gamble, A. and Peele, G. (eds) (1986) *Developments in British Politics 2* (London: Macmillan).

Dunleavy, P. (1987a) 'Analysing the Heart of the Machine: Theories of the State and Core Executive Decision-Making', paper to the Annual Conference of the Political Studies Association, University of Aberdeen, 6 April.

Dunleavy, P. (1987b) 'Political Science', in V. Bogdanor (ed.), *The Blackwell Encyclopedia of Political Institutions* (Oxford: Blackwell), pp.468–72.

Dunleavy, P. (1989a) 'The Architecture of the British Central State, Part I: Framework for Analysis', *Public Administration*, vol. 67, no. 3, pp.249–75.

Dunleavy, P. (1989b) 'The Architecture of the British Central State, Part II: Empirical Findings', *Public Administration*, vol. 67, no. 3, pp.391–417.

Dunleavy, P. (1991) *Democracy, Bureaucracy and Public Choice* (Hemel Hempstead: Harvester Wheatsheaf).

Dunleavy, P. (1992) 'Understanding the Structure of Public Sector Agencies', paper to the *Institutional Design Conference*, Research School of the Social Sciences, Australian National University, Canberra, 16 July.

Dunleavy, P. (1994) 'Estimating the Distribution of Influence in Cabinet Committees Under Major', paper to the PSA Annual Conference, University of Swansea, 29 March–30 April.

Dunleavy, P. and Husbands, C.T. (1985) *British Democracy at the Crossroads: Voting and Party Competition in the 1980s* (London: Allen & Unwin).

Dunleavy, P. and Jones, G.W. (1993) 'Leaders, Politics and Institutional Change: The Decline of Prime Ministeral Accountability to the House of Commons, 1968–1990', *British Journal of Political Science*, vol. 23, pp.267–98.

Dunleavy, P. and O'Leary, B. (1987) *Theories of the State: The Politics of Liberal Democracy* (London: Macmillan).

Dunleavy, P. and Rhodes, R.A.W. (1990) 'Core Executive Studies in Britain', *Public Administration*, vol. 68, no. 1, pp.3–28.

Dunleavy, P., Jones, G.W. and O'Leary, B. (1990) 'Prime Ministers and the

Commons: Patterns of Behaviour, 1868 to 1987', *Public Administration*, vol. 68, no. 1, pp.123–40.

Dunsire, A. and Hood, C. (1989) *Cutback Management in Public Bureaucracies: Popular Theories and Observed Outcomes in Whitehall* (Cambridge: Cambridge University Press).

Dyson, K. (1980) *The State Tradition in Western Europe* (Oxford: Robertson).

Eatwell, J. (1981) *Whatever Happened to Britain?* (London: Duckworth).

Eckstein, H. (1975) 'Case Study and Theory in Political Science', in F.I. Greenstein and N. Polsby (eds), *Handbook of Political Science. Volume 7: Strategies of Inquiry* (Reading, Mass: Addison-Wesley), pp.79–137.

Edelman, M. (1964) *The Symbolic Uses of Politics* (Urbana, Illinois: University of Illinois Press).

Edwards, G. (1992) 'Central Government', in S. George (ed.), *Britain and the European Community: The Politics of Semi-Detachment* (Oxford: Oxford University Press).

Efficiency Unit (1988) *Improving Management in Government: The Next Steps (Ibbs Report)* (London: HMSO).

Efficiency Unit (1991) *Making the Most of the Next Steps: The Management of Ministers' Departments and their Executive Agencies* (London: HMSO).

Egremont, M. (1980) *Balfour: A Life of Arthur James Balfour* (London: Collins).

Elder, C.D. and Cobb, R.W. (1983) *The Political Uses of Symbols* (New York: Longman).

Ellis, N.W. (1991) *John Major: The Authorised Biography* (London: Faber & Faber).

Emmerson, H. (1956) *The Ministry of Works* (London: Allen & Unwin).

Erickson, B.H. and Nozanchuk, T.A. (1977) *Understanding Data* (Milton Keynes: Open University Press).

Ewing, K.D. and Gearty, C.A. (1990) *Freedom Under Thatcher* (Oxford: Oxford University Press).

Fabbrini, S. (1988) 'The Return to the State: Critique', *American Political Science Review*, vol. 82, no. 3, pp.891–901.

Fine, B. and Millar, R. (1985) *Policing the Miners' Strike* (London: Lawrence & Wishart).

Finer, H. (1937) *The British Civil Service* (London: The Fabian Society).

Finer, S.E. (1980) *The Changing British Party System 1945–1979* (Washington, DC: American Enterprise Institute).

Finer, S.E. (1987) 'Thatcherism and British Political History', in K. Minogue and M. Biddiss (eds), *Thatcherism: Personality and Politics* (London: Macmillan), pp.127–40.

Finer, S.E. (1989) 'The Individual Responsibility of Ministers', in G. Marshall (ed.), *Ministerial Responsibility* (Oxford: Oxford University Press), pp.115–26.

Finer, S.E., Berrington, H. and Bartholomew, J.B.' (1961) *Backbench Opinion in the House of Commons, 1955–9* (London: Oxford University Press).

Flynn, A., Gray, A. and Jenkins, W.I. (1990) 'Taking the Next Steps: The Changing Management of Government', *Parliamentary Affairs*, vol. 43, no. 2, pp.159–78.

Foley, M. (1993) *The Rise of the British Presidency* (Manchester: Manchester University Press).

Foucault, M. (1980) *Power/Knowledge* (Brighton: Harvester).

Fowler, N. (1991) *Ministers Decide: A Personal Memoir of the Thatcher Years* (London: Chapman).

Freedman, L. (1976) 'Logic, Politics and Foreign Policy Processes', *International Affairs*, vol. 52, pp.434–49.

Freedman, L. (1980) *Britain and Nuclear Weapons* (London: Macmillan).

Frohlick, N., Oppenheimer, J. and Young, O. (1971) *Political Leadership and Collective Goods* (Princeton: Princeton University Press).

Gamble, A. (1988) *The Free Economy and the Strong State: The Politics of Thatcherism* (London: Macmillan).

Gamble, A. (1990) *Britain in Decline* (London: Macmillan).

Gamble, A. (1991) 'The End of Thatcherism?', *Social Studies Review*, vol. 6, no. 3, pp.86–91.

Gamble, A. and Walkland, S. (1984) *The British Party System and Economic Policy* (Oxford: Clarendon Press).

Geelhoed, E.B. (1991) *Margaret Thatcher in Victory and Defeat, 1987 and 1990* (New York: Praeger).

Giddens, A. (1986) *The Constitution of Society* (Oxford: Policy Press).

Giddings, P. and Drewry, G. (1991) 'Parliament and the Next Steps', *RIPA* (London: RIPA).

Gilbert, M. (1988) *Never Despair* (The Official Biography of Winston Churchill) (London: Heinemann).

Gilmour, I. (1969) *The Body Politic* (London: Hutchinson).

Gilmour, I. (1992) *Dancing with Dogma: Britain Under Thatcherism* (London: Simon & Schuster).

Goffman, E. (1959) *The Presentation of Self in Everyday Life* (Harmondsworth: Penguin).

Goldsworthy, D. (1991) *Setting up Next Steps* (London: HMSO).

Gordon-Walker, P. (1972) *The Cabinet* (London: Fontana).

Gorman, R. (1970) 'On the Inadequacies of a Non-Philosophical Political Science: A Critical Analysis of Decision-Making Theory', *International Studies Quarterly*, vol. 14, no. 4, pp.395–411.

Grant, W. (1982) *The Political Economy of Industrial Policy* (London: Butterworths).

Grant, W. (1987) *Business and Politics in Britain* (London: Macmillan).

Grant, W. and Marsh, D. (1977) *The CBI* (London: Hodder & Stoughton).

Grant, W. and Wilks, S. (1983) 'British Industrial Policy: Structural Change, Policy Inertia', *Journal of Public Policy*, vol. 3, no. 1, pp.13–28.

Gray, A. and Jenkins, W.I. (1985) *Administrative Politics in British Government* (Brighton: Wheatsheaf).

Gray, A. and Jenkins, W.I. (1991) 'Government and Public Administration 1990–1991', *Parliamentary Affairs*, vol. 44, no. 4, pp.572–92.

Gray, A., Jenkins, W.I., Flynn, A. and Rutherford, B. (1991) 'The Management of Change in Whitehall: The Experience of FMI', *Public Administration*, vol. 69, no. 1, pp.41–59.

Greaves, H.R.G. (1947) *The Civil Service in the Changing State: A Survey of Civil Service Reform and the Implications of a Planned Economy on Public Administration in England* (London: Harrap).

Greenaway, J. (1985) 'Historical Perspectives Upon the Thatcher Government's Whitehall Reforms', *Public Administration Bulletin*, vol. 47, pp.5–17.

Greenaway, J. (1991) 'All Change at the Top?', *Social Studies Review*, vol. 6, pp.136–40.

Greenberg, E.S. (1979) *Understanding Modern Government: The Rise and Decline of the American Political Economy* (New York: Wiley).

Greenleaf, W.H. (1983) *The British Political Tradition: Volume 1: The Rise of Collectivism* (London: Methuen).

Greenleaf, W.H. (1987) *The British Political Tradition: Volume 2, Part I: A Much-Governed Nation* (London: Methuen).

Griffith, J.A.G. (1974) *Parliamentary Scrutiny of Government Bills* (London: Allen & Unwin).

Griffith, J.A.G. (1979) 'The Political Constitution', *Modern Law Review*, vol. 42, no. 1, pp.1–21.

Griffith, J.A.G. and Ryle, M. (1989) *Parliament* (London: Sweet & Maxwell).

Haines, J. (1977) *The Politics of Power* (London: Cape).

Haldane, R.B. (1918) *Report of the Machinery of Government Committee*, Ministry of Reconstruction, Cd 9230 (London: HMSO).

Hall, P. (1986) *Governing the Economy* (Oxford: Polity Press).

Hall, S. and Jacques, M. (eds) (1983) *The Politics of Thatcherism* (London: Lawrence & Wishart).

Halperin, M. (1974) *Bureaucratic Politics and Foreign Policy* (Washington, DC: Brookings Institution).

Ham, A. (1984) *Treasury Rules: Recurrent Themes in British Economic Policy* (London: Quartet).

Hanson, A.H. (1961) *Parliament and Public Ownership* (London: Cassell).

Harden, I. and Lewis, N. (1986) *The Noble Lie* (London: Hutchinson).

Harlow, C. and Rawlings, R. (1984) *Law and Administration* (London: Weidenfeld & Nicolson).

Harris, K. (1982) *Attlee* (London: Weidenfeld & Nicolson).

Harris, R. (1990) *Good and Faithful Servant: The Unauthorised Biography of Bernard Ingham* (London: Faber & Faber).

Hawkins, A. (1989) '"Parliamentary Government" and Victorian Political Parties 1830–1880', *English Historical Review*, CIV, 412.

Hayek, F.A. (1963) *The Constitution of Liberty* (London: Routledge).

Headey, B. (1974) *British Cabinet Ministers* (London: Allen & Unwin).

Healey, D. (1989) *The Time of My Life* (London: Michael Joseph).

Heclo, H. and Wildasky, A. (1974) *The Private Government of Public Money: Community and Policy Inside British Politics*, 1st edn (London: Macmillan).

Heclo, H. and Wildavsky, A. (1977) *The Private Government of Public Money: Community and Policy Inside British Politics* (London: Macmillan).

Heclo, H. and Wildavsky, A. (1981) *The Private Government of Public Money: Community and Policy Inside British Politics*, 2nd edn (London: Macmillan).

Hennessy, P. (1985) 'Whitehall Contingency Planning for Industrial Disputes', in P.J. Rowe and C.J. Whelan (eds), *Military Intervention in Democratic Societies* (Beckenham: Croom Helm), pp.94–109.

Hennessy, P. (1986) *Cabinet* (Oxford: Blackwell).

Hennessy, P. (1987a) 'Sir Robert Armstrong', *Contemporary Record*, vol. 1, no. 4, pp.28–31.

Hennessy, P. (1987b) 'The Attlee Governments 1945–51', in P. Hennessy and A. Seldon (eds), *Ruling Performance* (Oxford: Blackwell), pp.28–62.

Hennessy, P. (1988) *Whitehall* (London: Secker & Warburg).

Hennessy, P. (1989) 'The Westland Affair', in G. Marshall (ed.), *Ministerial Responsibility* (Oxford: Oxford University Press), pp.80–91.

Hennessy, P. (1990) *Whitehall* (London: Fontana).

Hennessy, P. and Anstey, C. (1991) 'Diminished Responsibility', *Strathclyde Papers on Government and Politics, no. 2* (Glasgow: University of Strathclyde).

Hennessy, P. and Arends, A. (1983) 'Mr Attlee's Engine Room: Cabinet Committee Structure and the Labour Governments, 1945–51', *Strathclyde Papers on Government and Politics, no. 26* (Glasgow: University of Strathclyde).

Herman, V. and Alt, J.E. (eds) (1978) *Cabinet Studies: A Reader* (London: Macmillan).

Hermann, M.G. (1986) 'Ingredients of Leadership', in M.G. Hermann (ed.), *Political Psychology: Contemporary Problems and Issues* (San Francisco: Jossey-Bass), pp.167–92.

Heseltine, M. (1987) *Where There's a Will* (London: Hutchinson).

Heseltine, M. (1989) *The Challenge of Europe* (London: Weidenfeld & Nicolson).

HMSO (1987) *Civil Research and Development. Government Response to the First Report of the House of Lords Select Committee on Science and Technology, 1986–1987 Session.* Cmnd 328 (London: HMSO).

HMSO (1988) *Supply Estimates 1988–9 for the year ending. 31 March 1989: Summary and Quide.* Cmnd 185 (London: HMSO).

HMSO (1994) *The Civil Service: Continuity and Change*, Cm 2627 (London: HMSO).

Hodgeman, D. (1983) 'The Political Economy of Monetary Policy', Proceedings of a Conference held at Perugia, Italy, July.

Hogwood, B. (1984) 'The Rise and Fall and Rise of the Department of Trade and Industry', paper presented to the Conference on the Structure and Organisation of Government Group of the International Political Science Association, Manchester, 15–18 November.

Hogwood, B. (1990) 'Development in Regulatory Agencies in Britain', *International Review of Administrative Science*, vol. 56, pp.595–612.

Hogwood, B. (1992a) 'Government Departments', mimeo, University of Strathclyde.

Hogwood, B. (1992b) *Trends in British Public Policy* (Milton Keynes: Open University Press).

Hogwood, B. (1993) 'The Uneven Staircase: Measuring up to Next Steps', *Strathclyde Papers on Government and Politics, no. 92* (Glasgow: University of Strathclyde).

Holm, R. and Elliott, M. (1988) *Time for a New Constitution* (London: Macmillan).

Hood, C. (1983) *The Tools of Government* (London: Macmillan).

Hood, C. (1991) 'A Public Management for all Seasons', *Public Administration*, vol. 69, no. 1, pp.3–19.

Hood, C. and Dunsire, A. (1981) *Bureaumetrics* (Farnborough, Hants: Gower).

Hood, C., Dunsire, A. and Thompson, S. (1978) 'So you think you know what Government Departments are?', *Public Administration Bulletin*, vol. 27, pp.20–32.

House of Commons (1986) *Fourth Report of the Defence Committee. Westland Plc: The Government's Decision Making*, Session 1985–86, HC 519 (London: HMSO).

Howard, M. (1993) 'The World This Weekend', interview, BBC Radio 4, 30 May.

Hudson, J. (1984) 'Prime Ministerial Popularity in the UK, 1960–81', *Political Studies*, vol. 32, no. 2, pp.86–97.

Hurd, D. (1993) 'Chairing from the Front', *The Spectator*, 6 November 1993.

Ingham, B. (1991) *Kill the Messenger* (London: HarperCollins).

Ingham, G. (1984) *Capitalism Divided: The City and Industry in British Social Development* (London: Macmillan).

Iremonger, L. (1970) *The Fiery Chariot: British Prime Ministers and the Search for Love* (London: Secker & Warburg).

Irwin, H. (1988) 'Opportunities for Backbenchers', in M. Ryle and P.G. Richards (eds), *The Commons Under Scrutiny* (London: Routledge), pp.76–98.

James, S. (1992) *British Cabinet Government* (London: Routledge).

Janis, I. (1972) *Victims of Groupthink* (Boston, Mass.: Houghton Mifflin).

Jeffery, K. and Hennessy, P. (1983) *States of Emergency: British Governments and Strikebreaking Since 1919* (London: Routledge).

Jenkins, G. (1959) *The Ministry of Transport and Civil Aviation* (London: Allen & Unwin).

Jenkins, K., Caines, K. and Jackson, A. (1988) *Improving Management in Government: The Next Steps: Report to the Prime Minister (Ibbs Report)* (London: HMSO).

Jenkins, R. (1971) 'A Study in Whitehall Style', *Sunday Times*, 17 January.

Jenks, E. (1923) *The Government of the British Empire*, 3rd edn (London: John Murray).

Jennings, I. (1936) *Cabinet Government* (London: Cambridge University Press).

Jennings, I. (1963) *Party Politics: Vol. 2. The Growth of Parties* (Cambridge: Cambridge University Press).

Jennings, R.F. (1977) *Education and Politics: Policy Making in Local Education Authorities* (London: Batsford).

Jessop, R. (1982) *The Capitalist State* (Oxford: Martin Robertson).

Johnson, N. (1980) *In Search of the Constitution* (London: Methuen).

Johnson, N. (1988) 'Departmental Select Committees', in M. Ryle and P.G. Richards (eds), *The Commons under Scrutiny* (London: Routledge), pp.157–85.

Jones, G.W. (1975) 'Development of the Cabinet', in W. Thornhill (ed.), *The Modernisation of British Government* (London: Pitman), pp.31–65.

Jones, G.W. (1980) 'The Prime Minister's Aides', *Hull Papers in Politics, No. 6* (Hull: Hull University Department of Politics).

Jones, G.W. (1983) 'Prime Ministers' Departments Really Create Problems: A Rejoinder to Patrick Weller', *Public Administration*, vol. 61, no. 1, pp.79–84.

Jones, G.W. (1985a) 'The Prime Minister's Aides', in A. King (ed.), *The British Prime Minister*, 2nd edn (London: Macmillan), pp.72–95.

Jones, G.W. (1985b) 'The Prime Minister's Power', in A. King (ed.), *The British Prime Minister*, 2nd edn (London: Macmillan), pp.195–220.

Jones, G.W. (1987a) 'The United Kingdom', in W. Plowden (ed.), *Advising the Rulers* (Oxford: Blackwell), pp.36–66.

Jones, G.W. (1987b) 'Cabinet Government and Mrs Thatcher', *Contemporary Record*, vol. 1, no. 3, pp.8–12.

Jones, G.W. (1987c) 'Stand up for Ministerial Responsibility', in A. Robinson, R. Shepherd, F.F. Ridley and G.W. Jones (eds), 'Symposium on Ministerial Responsibility', *Public Administration*, vol. 65, no. 1, pp.87–91.

Jones, G.W. (1989) 'A Revolution in Whitehall? Changes in British Central Government Since 1979', *West European Politics*, vol. 12, no. 3, pp.238–61.

Jones, G.W. (1990) 'Mrs Thatcher and the Power of the Prime Minister', *Contemporary Record*, vol. 3, no. 4, pp.2–6.

Jordan, A.G. (1976) 'Hiving off and Departmental Agencies', *Public Administration Bulletin 21*.

Jordan, A.G. (1981) 'Iron Triangles, Woolly Corporatism and Elastic Nets: Images of the Policy Process', *Journal of Public Policy*, vol. 1, no. 1, pp.95–123.

Jordan, A.G. (1990) 'Sub-Governments, Policy Communities and Networks: Refilling the Old Bottles', *Journal of Theoretical Politics*, vol. 2, pp.319–38.

Jordan, A.G. and Richardson, J. (1985) *Governing Under Pressure: Politics in a Post-Parliamentary Democracy* (Oxford: Basil Blackwell).

Jordan, A.G. and Richardson, J. (1987) *British Politics and the Policy Process: An Arena Approach* (London: Unwin–Hyman).

Jordan, A.G. and Richardson, J. (1991) *Government and Pressure Groups in Britain* (Oxford: Clarendon Press).

Joseph, K. (1978) *Conditions for Fuller Employment: A Speech to the Bow Group*, 24 August (London: Bow Group).

Kavanagh, D. (1987) *Thatcherism and British Politics* (Oxford: Oxford University Press).

Kavanagh, D. (1990) *Thatcherism and British Politics* (Oxford: Oxford University Press).

Kavanagh, D. (1991) 'Prime Minister Power Revisited', *Social Studies Review*, vol. 6, pp.131–5.

Keegan, W. (1989) *The Battle for Downing Street* (London: Hodder & Stoughton).

Keegan, W. and Pennant-Rea, R. (1979) *Who Runs the Economy: Control and Influence in British Economic Policy* (London: Maurice Temple Smith).

Keeton, G.W. (1970) *Government in Action* (London: Ernest Benn Ltd).

Keliher, L. (1987) 'Policy Making in Information Technology: A Decisional Analysis of the Alvey Programme', PhD thesis, London School of Economics and Political Science.

Kellner, P. and Lord Crowther Hunt (1980) *The Civil Servants* (London: Macdonald).

King, A. (1985a) 'Introduction: The Textbook Prime Ministership', in A. King (ed.), *The British Prime Minister: A Reader*, 2nd edn (London: Macmillan), pp.1–11.

King, A. (1985b) 'Margaret Thatcher: The Style of a Prime Minister', in A. King (ed.), *The British Prime Minister: A Reader*, 2nd edn (London: Macmillan), pp.96–140.

King, A. (1991) 'The British Prime Ministership in the Age of the Career Politician', in G.W. Jones (ed.), *West European Prime Ministers* (London: Frank Cass), pp.25–47.

Kingdom, J. (1991) *Government and Politics in Britain* (Cambridge: Polity Press).

Klein, R. (1989) *The Politics of the NHS* (London: Longman).

Kogan, M. (1971) *The Politics of Education* (Harmondsworth: Penguin).

Kogan, M. (1975) *Educational Policy Making* (London: Allen & Unwin).

Kogan, M. (1978) *The Politics of Educational Change* (London: Fontana).

Krasner, S.D. (1972) 'Are Bureaucracies Important? (or Allison in Wonderland)', *Foreign Policy*, no. 7, pp.159–79.

Laumann, E.O. and Knoke, D. (1987) *The Organizational State* (Wisconsin: University of Wisconsin Press).

Lawson, N. (1992) *The View from No. 11: Memoirs of a Tory Radical* (London: Bantam Press).

Lawton, A. and Rose, A. (1991) *Organisation and Management in the Public Sector* (London: Pitman).

Lee, J.M. (1974) ' "Central Capacity" and Established Practice: The Changing Character of the "Centre of the Machine" in British Cabinet Government', in B. Chapman and A. Potter (eds), *WJMM: Political Questions – Essays in Honour of W.J.M. McKenzie* (Manchester: Manchester University Press), pp.162–89.

Lee, J.M. (1980) 'The Machinery of Government: The Prospect of Redefining the Issues under Mrs Thatcher's Administration', *Parliamentary Affairs*, vol. 33, pp.434–47.

Lee, J.M. (1990) 'The Ethos of the Cabinet Office: A Comment on the Testimony of Officials', *Public Administration*, vol. 68, no. 3, 235–42.

Lewis, N. (1990) 'Corporatism and Accountability: The Democratic Dilemma', in C. Crouch and R. Dore (eds), *Corporatism and Accountability* (Oxford: Oxford University Press), pp.63–101.

Lewis, N. (1991) 'Next Steps and Accountability: The Concern of the Constitutional Lawyer', in *RIPA*, 1991.

Linklater, M. and Leigh, D. (1986) *Not with Honour: The Inside Story of the Westland Scandal* (London: The Observer).

Lloyd, I. (1984) 'The Work of PITCOM and Parliament's Role in New Technology', *Information Technology and Public Policy*, vol. 2, no. 2, pp.96–100.

Lowe, P. and Goyder, J. (1983) *Environmental Groups in Politics* (London: George Allen & Unwin).

Lowell, A.L. (1920) *The Government of England*, vol. I (New York: Macmillan).

Lowi, T. (1988) 'The Return to the State: Critique', *American Political Science Review*, vol. 82, no. 3, pp.885–91.

Luhmann, N. (1982) *The Differentiation of Society* (New York: Columbia University Press).

Lynn, J. and Jay, A. (eds) (1984) *The Complete Yes Minister* (London: BBC Books).

McAuslan, P. and McEldowney, J.F. (eds) (1985) 'Legitimacy and the Constitution: The Dissonance Between Theory and Practice', in P. McAuslan and J.F. McEldowney (eds), *Law, Legitimacy and the Constitution* (London: Sweet & Maxwell), pp.1–38.

McCall, M.W. (1977) 'Leaders and Leadership: Of Substance and Shadow', in J.R. Hackman, E. Lewler and L.W. Porter (eds), *Perspectives on Behaviour in Organisations* (New York: McGraw-Hill), pp.375–86.

McInnes, D. (1990) 'Policy Networks within the Department of Energy and Energy Policy', *Essex Papers in Politics and Government* (Colchester: University of Essex).

McKenzie, R.T. (1964) *British Political Parties* (London: Mercury Books).

Mackie, T. and Hogwood, B.W. (1985) *Unlocking the Cabinet: Cabinet Structures in Comparative Perspective* (London: Sage).

Mackintosh, J. (1962) *The British Cabinet*, 1st edn (London: Stevens).

Mackintosh, J. (1968) *The British Cabinet*, 2nd edn (London: Stevens).

Mackintosh, J. (1977) *The British Cabinet*, 3rd edn (London: Stevens).

McLean, S. (1986) *How Nuclear Weapons Decisions are Made* (London: Macmillan/Oxford Research Group).

Macmillan, H. (1972) *Pointing the Way* (London: Macmillan).

Madgwick, P. (1986) 'Prime Ministerial Power Revisited', *Social Studies Review*, vol. 1, no. 5, pp.28–35.

Madgwick, P. (1991) *British Government: The Central Executive Territory* (London: Philip Allan).

March, J. and Olsen, J. (1984) 'The New Institutionalism', *American Political Science Review*, vol. 78, pp.734–49.

March, J. and Olsen, J. (1989) *Rediscovering Institutions* (New York: Free Press).

Margach, J. (1978) *The Abuse of Power: The War Between Downing Street and the Media from Lloyd George to James Callaghan* (London: W.H. Allan).

Marquand, D. (1977) *Ramsay MacDonald* (London: Cape).

Marsh, C. (1988) *Data Analysis for Social Scientists* (Cambridge: Polity Press).

Marsh, D. (1992) *The New Politics of British Trade Unionism: Trade Unions and the Thatcher Legacy* (London: Macmillan).

Marsh, D. and Rhodes, R.A.W. (1992a) *Implementing Thatcherism: An Audit of an Era* (Milton Keynes: Open University Press).

Marsh, D. and Rhodes, R.A.W. (eds) (1992b) *Policy Networks in British Government* (Oxford: Clarendon Press).

Marsh, P. (1978) *The Discipline of Popular Government: Lord Salisbury's Domestic Statecraft 1881–1902* (Brighton: Harvester).

Marshall, G. (1980) *Constitutional Theory* (Oxford: Clarendon Press).

Marshall, G. (1984) *Constitutional Conventions: The Rules and Forms of Political Accountability* (Oxford: Clarendon Press).

Marshall, G. and Moodie, G.C. (1967) *Some Problems of the Constitution*, 4th edn (London: Hutchinson).

Marshall, G. and Moodie, G.C. (1971) *Some Problems of the Constitution*, 5th edn (London: Hutchinson).

Maude, J. and Szeremey, J. (1982) *Why Electoral Change?* (London: Conservative Political Centre).

May, A. and Rowan, K. (1982) *Inside Information: British Government and the Media* (London: Constable).

Merton, R.K. (1968) *Social Theory and Social Structure* (New York: Free Press).

Metcalfe, L. (1991) 'Next Steps: The Need for a Comparative Perspective', in *RIPA*, 1991.

Middlemas, K. (1991) *Power, Competition and the State* (London: Macmillan).

Miliband, R. (1969) *The State in Capitalist Society* (London: Weidenfeld & Nicolson).

Miliband, R. (1982) *Capitalist Democracy in Britain* (Oxford: Oxford University Press).

Miliband, R. (1983) *Class Power and State Power: Political Essays* (London: Verso).

Miller, C. (1990) *Lobbying the Government* (Oxford: Blackwell).

Mills, C.W. (1956) *The Power Elite* (New York: Oxford University Press).

Minogue, K. (1963) *The Liberal Mind* (London: Stenval Press).

Minogue, K. (1978) 'On Hyper-Activism in Modern British Politics', in M. Cowling (ed.), *Conservative Essays* (London: Cassell), pp.117–30.

Minogue, K. (1988) 'Introduction: The Context of Thatcherism', in K. Minogue and M. Biddiss (eds) (1988) *Thatcherism: Personality and Politics* (London: Macmillan), pp.x–xvii.

Minogue, K. and Biddiss, M. (eds) (1988) *Thatcherism: Personality and Politics* (London: Macmillan).

Moran, M. (1984) *The Politics of Banking* (London: Macmillan).

Morrison, H.S. (1954) *Government and Parliament* (Oxford: Oxford University Press).

Morrison, H.S. (1964) *Government and Parliament*, 3rd edn (Oxford: Oxford University Press).

Mosley, R.K. (1969) *The Story of the Cabinet Office* (London: Routledge & Kegan Paul).

NIESR (1989) 'The Consequences of Full ERS Membership', *National Institute Economic Review*, 8 August.

Niskanen, W. (1971) *Bureaucracy and Representative Government* (New York: Aldine-Atherton).

Nordlinger, E. (1981) *On the Autonomy of the Democratic State* (Cambridge, Mass.: Harvard University Press).

Nordlinger, E. (1988) 'The Return to the State: Critique', *American Political Science Review*, vol. 82, no. 3, pp.875–85.

Norton, P. (1975) *Dissension in the House of Commons: Intra-Party Dissent in the House of Commons Divisions Lobbies, 1945–74* (London: Macmillan).

Norton, P. (1980) *Dissension in the House of Commons, 1974–79* (Oxford: Clarendon Press).

Norton, P. (1981) *Parliament in Perspective* (London: Martin Robertson).

Norton, P. (1984) *The British Polity* (New York: Longman).

Norton, P. (1987) 'Prime Ministerial Power. A Framework for Analysis', *Teaching Politics*, vol. 16, no. 3, pp.325–45.

Norton, P. (1988) 'Prime Ministerial Power', *Social Studies Review*, vol. 3, no. 2, pp.108–15.

Norton, P. (1990) 'Choosing a Leader: Margaret Thatcher and the Parliamentary Conservative Party', *Parliamentary Affairs*, vol. 43, no. 3, pp.249–59.

Norton, P. (1991) 'Did Mrs Thatcher Fall Or Was She Pushed?', *British Politics Group*, no. 63, winter.

Norton, P. (1992) 'The Conservative Party from Thatcher to Major', in A. King (ed.), *Britain at the Polls 1992* (New Jersey: Chatham House), pp.29–69.

Nossal, K.R. (1979) 'Allison through the (Ottawa) Looking Glass: Bureaucratic Politics and Foreign Policy in a Parliamentary System', *Canadian Journal of Political Science*, vol. 22, pp.610–26.

Oakeshott, M. (1962) 'On Being Conservative', in *Rationalism in Politics* (London: Methuen), pp.168–96.

O'Leary, B. (1987a) 'The Anglo-Irish Agreement: Statecraft or Folly?', *West European Politics*, vol. 10, no. 1, pp.5–32.

O'Leary, B. (1987b) 'Why was the GLC Abolished?', *International Journal of Urban and Regional Research*, vol. 11, no. 2, pp.193–217.

Oliver, D. (1989) 'The Parties in Parliament', in J. Jowell and D. Oliver (eds), *The Changing Constitution* (Oxford: Clarendon), pp.441–61.

Oliver, D. and Austin, R. (1987) 'Political and Constitutional Aspects of the Westland Affair', *Parliamentary Affairs*, vol. 40, no. 1, pp.20–40.

Osborne, D. and Gaebler, T. (1992) *Reinventing Government* (Reading, Mass.: Addison-Wesley).

Parkinson, C. (1992) *Right at the Centre: An Autobiography* (London: Weidenfeld & Nicolson).

Parkinson, M. and Duffy, J. (1984) 'Government's Response to Inner City Riots: The Minister for Merseyside and the Task Force', *Parliamentary Affairs*, vol. 37, pp.76–96.

Parris, H. (1969) *Constitutional Bureaucracy* (London: Allen & Unwin).

Parry, R. (1989) 'The Centralization of the Scottish Office', in R. Rose (ed.), *Ministers and Ministries: A Functional Analysis* (Oxford: Clarendon Press), pp.97–141.

Pearce, E. (1991) *The Quiet Rise of John Major* (London: Weidenfeld & Nicolson).

Peele, G. (1986) 'The State and Civil Liberties', in H. Drucker, P. Dunleavy, A. Gamble and G. Peele (eds), *Developments in British Politics 2* (London: Macmillan), pp.144–74.

Pennock, J.R. (1952) 'Responsiveness, Responsibility and Majority Rule', *American Political Science Review*, vol. XLVI, no. 3.

Phillips, R. (1977) 'The British Inner Cabinet', *London Review of Public Administration*, vol. 10, pp.5–27.

Pickthorn, K. (1925) *Some Historical Principles of the Constitution* (London: Philip Allan).

Pile, W. (1979) *The Department of Education and Science* (London: Allen & Unwin).

Pitt, D.C. and Smith, B.C. (1981) *Government Departments* (London: Routledge).

Piven, F.F. and Cloward, R. (1982) *The New Class War* (New York: Pantheon).

Pliatsky, L. (1982) *Getting and Spending* (Oxford: Blackwell).

Pliatsky, L. (1984) *Getting and Spending* (Oxford: Blackwell).

Pliatsky, L. (1989) *The Treasury under Mrs Thatcher* (Oxford: Blackwell).

Pollard, S. (1982) *The Wasting of the British Economy* (London: Croom Helm).

Pollitt, C. (1984) *Manipulating the Machine: Changing the Pattern of Government Departments* (London: Allen & Unwin).

Polsby, N.W. (1984) *Political Innovation in America: The Politics of Policy Initiation* (New Haven: Yale University Press).

Ponting, C. (1986) *Whitehall: Tragedy and Farce* (London: Hamish Hamilton).

Poulantzas, N. (1978) *State, Power, Socialism* (London: New Left Books).

Price Waterhouse (1990) *Executive Agencies: Facts and Trends* (London: Price Waterhouse), annual series.

Prosser, T. (1986) *Nationalised Industries and Public Control: Legal, Constitutional and Political Issues* (Oxford: Blackwell).

Pym, F. (1984) *The Politics of Consent* (London: Hamish Hamilton).

Radcliffe, J. (1991) *The Reorganization of British Central Government* (Aldershot: Dartmouth).

Ranelagh, J. (1991) *Thatcher's People* (London: HarperCollins).

Raz, J. (1983) 'The Rule of Law and its Virtues', in *The Authority of Law: Essays on Law and Morality* (Oxford: Clarendon Press), pp.3–27.

Rees, J.R. (1977) 'Interpreting the Constitution', in P. King (ed.), *Study of Politics* (London: Cass), pp.97–117.

Regan, C. (1986) 'Anonymity in the British Civil Service: Facelessness Diminished', *Parliamentary Affairs*, vol. 39, no. 4, pp.421–36.

Rhodes, R.A.W. (1981) *Control and Power in Central–Local Government Relations* (Farnborough: Gower).

Rhodes, R.A.W. (1988) *Beyond Westminster and Whitehall: Sub-Central Governments in Britain* (London: Allen & Unwin).

Rhodes, R.A.W. (ed.) (1991) *The New Public Management*, special issue of *Public Administration*, vol. 69.

Rhodes, R.A.W. (1993) 'The Changing Nature of the British Executive: A Research Proposal', Report to the ESRC, May.

Rhodes, R.A.W. (1994) 'The Hollowing Out of the State', *The Political Quarterly*, vol. 15, no. 2, pp.138–51.

Richelson, J.T. and Ball, D. (1985) *The Ties that Bind: Intelligence Co-operation between the UKUSA Countries* (Boston: Allen & Unwin).

Riddell, Lord (1933) *Lord Riddell's Intimate Diaries of the Peace Conference and After* (London: Gollancz).

Riddell, P. (1990) *The Thatcher Government*, 2nd edn (Oxford: Blackwell).

Riddell, P. (1991) 'Review of A. Watkins: A Conservative Coup', *The Times Literary Supplement*, 29 November.

Ridley, F. (1988) 'There is no British Constitution', *Parliamentary Affairs*, vol. 41, no. 3, pp.340–61.

Ridley, N. (1991) *My Style of Government: The Thatcher Years* (London: Hutchinson).

Robinson, A. (1987) 'Accountability', in A. Robinson, R. Shepherd, F.F. Ridley and G.W. Jones (eds), 'Symposium on Ministerial Responsibility', *Public Administration*, vol. 65, no. 1, pp.62–8.

Roll, E. (1966) 'The Machinery for Economic Planning: 1. The Department of Economic Affairs', *Public Administration*, vol. 44, no. 1, pp.1–11.

Rose, R. (1974) *The Problem of Party Government* (London: Macmillan).

Rose, R. (1980a) 'British Government: The Job at the Top', in R. Rose and E.N. Suleiman (eds), *Presidents and Prime Ministers* (Washington, DC: American Enterprise Institute), pp.1–49.

Rose, R. (1980b) *Do Parties Make a Difference?* (London: Macmillan).

Rose, R. (1984) *Understanding Big Government* (London: Sage).

Rose, R. (1987) *Ministers and Ministries: A Functional Analysis* (Oxford: Clarendon Press).

Rose, R. (1990) 'Inheritance Before Choice in Public Policy', *Journal of Theoretical Politics*, vol. 2, no. 3, pp.263–91.

Roseveare, H. (1969) *The Treasury: The Evolution of a British Institution* (London: Allen Lane).

Rowland, P. (1975) *Lloyd George* (London: Barrie & Jenkins).

Royal Institute of Public Administration (RIPA) (1987) *Top Jobs in Whitehall* (London: Royal Institute of Public Administration).

Royal Institution of Public Administration (RIPA) (1991) *The Civil Service Reformed: The Next Steps Initiative*, Proceedings of a RIPA Research Seminar 28 June (London: RIPA).

Rush, M. (1984) *The Cabinet and Policy Formation* (London: Longman).

Russell, S. (1989) 'Power Politics: Explaining the Introduction – Or Absence – Of Energy Technology', *Science and Technology Analysis Research programme Working Paper*, University of Wollongong, NSW, no. 2.

Salter, B. and Tapper, T. (1981) *Education, Politics and the State* (London: Grant McIntyre).

Sanders, D. (1991) 'Government Popularity and the Next General Election', *Political Quarterly*, vol. 62, no. 2, pp.235–61.

Saran, R. (1973) *Policy Making in Secondary Education* (Oxford: Clarendon).

Scruton, R. (1980) *The Meaning of Conservatism* (London: Penguin).

Sedgemore, B. (1980) *The Secret Constitution* (London: Hodder & Stoughton).

Seldon, A. (1990) 'The Cabinet Office and Coordination', *Public Administration*, vol. 68, no. 1, pp.103–21.

Seldon, A. and Pappworth, J. (1983) *By Word of Mouth* (London: Methuen).

Self, P. (1985) *Political Theories of Modern Government* (Sydney: Allen & Unwin).

Seymour-Ure, C. (1984) 'British "War Cabinets" in Limited Wars: Korea, Suez and the Falklands', *Public Administration*, vol. 62, no. 3, pp.181–200.

Sharp, E. (1969) *The Ministry of Housing and Local Government* (London: Allen & Unwin).

Shaw, E. (1988) *Discipline and Discord in the Labour Party 1951–1987* (Manchester: Manchester University Press).

Shell, D. (1991) 'The British Constitution in 1990', *Parliamentary Affairs*, vol. 44, no. 3, pp.265–82.

Shepherd, R. (1991) *The Power Brokers* (London: Hutchinson).

Simmonds, N.E. (1984) *The Decline of Judicial Reason* (Manchester: Manchester University Press).

Simonton, D.K. (1987) *Why Presidents Succeed* (New York: Wiley).

Sisson, C.H. (1959) *The Spirit of British Administration* (London: Faber).

Sisson, C.H. (1976) 'The Civil Service After Fulton', in W.J. Stankiewicz (ed.), *British Government in an Era of Reform* (London: Collier Macmillan), pp.252–62.

Skocpol, T. (1985) 'Bringing the State Back in: Strategies of Analysis in Current Research', in P.B. Evans, D. Rieschemeyer and T. Skocpol (eds), *Bringing the State Back in* (Cambridge: Cambridge University Press), pp.3–37.

Smith, B. and Stanyer, J. (1976) *Administering Britain* (London: Fontana).

Smith, D. (1992) *From Boom to Bust: Trial and Error in British Economic Policy* (Harmondsworth: Penguin).

Smith, M. (1990) *The Politics of Agricultural Support in Britain* (Aldershot: Dartmouth).

Smith, M. (1991) 'From Issue Network to Policy Community: Salmonella in Eggs and the New Politics of Food', *Public Administration*, vol. 69, no. 2, pp.235–55.

Smith, M. (1992) 'The Institutional Organization of Group/Government Relations', paper presented to joint sessions of ECPR Workshops, Limerick, 30 March–6 April.

Smith, M., Marsh, D. and Richards, D. (1993) 'Central Government Departments and the Policy Process', *Public Administration*, vol. 71, no. 4, pp.567–94.

Spender, J.A. (1923) *The Life of Sir Henry Campbell-Bannerman: Volume II*

(London: Hodder & Stoughton).

Stack, F. (1983) 'Imperatives of Participation', in F. Gregory (ed.), *Dilemmas of Government: Britain and the EEC* (London: Robertson), pp.124–52.

Steed, M. (1983) 'The Formation of Governments in the United Kingdom', *Political Quarterly*, vol. 54, no. 1, pp.54–65.

Street, J. (1988) 'British Government Policy on Aids', *Parliamentary Affairs*, vol. 41, pp.490–507.

Taagepera, R. and Shugart, M. (1989) *Seats and Votes* (New Haven: Yale University Press).

Tant, A.P. (1990) 'The Campaign for Freedom of Information: A Participatory Challenge to Elitist British Government', *Public Administration*, vol. 68, no. 4, pp.477–91.

Thain, C. and Wright, M. (1990a) 'Coping with Difficulty: The Treasury and Public Expenditure, 1976–89', *Policy and Politics*, vol. 18, no. 1, pp.1–15.

Thain, C. and Wright, M. (1990b) 'Running Costs Control in UK Central Government', *Financial Accounting and Management*, vol. 6, no. 2, pp.115–31.

Thain, C. and Wright, M. (1992) 'Planning and Controlling Public Expenditure in the UK, Part I: The Treasury's Public Expenditure Survey; Part II: The Effects and Effectiveness of the Survey', *Public Administration*, vol. 70, no. 1, pp.3–24 and 193–224.

Thane, P. (1990) 'Government and Society in England and Wales 1750–1914', in F.M.L. Thompson (ed.), *The Cambridge Social History of Britain 1750–1914: Vol. 3 Social Agencies and Institutions* (Cambridge: Cambridge University Press), pp.1–61.

Thatcher, M. (1978) *The Ideals of an Open Society: A Speech to the Bow Group*, 6 May (London: Bow Group).

Thatcher, M. (1993) *The Downing Street Years* (London: HarperCollins).

Theakston, K. (1987) *Junior Ministers in British Government* (Oxford: Blackwell).

Theakston, K. and Fry, G. (1989) 'Britain's Administrative Elite', *Public Administration*, vol. 67, no. 2, pp.129–47.

Thomas, D. (1986) *At Alvey and Afterwards: A Seminar for the Press* (Saint-Paul-de-Vence, France: Sperry Limited).

Thomas, I.C. (1989) 'Giving Direction to the Welsh Office', in R. Rose (ed.), *Ministers and Ministries: A Functional Analysis* (Oxford: Clarendon Press), pp.142–88.

Thompson, H. (1994) 'Joining the Exchange Rate Mechanism: Core Executive Decision-Making and Macro-Economic Policy, 1979–90', unpublished PhD Thesis, London School of Economics and Political Science.

Treasury and Civil Service Committee (1990) *The Next Steps Initiative: Report Together with the Proceedings of the Committee and the Minutes of the Evidence*, HC 531 (London: HMSO).

Tukey, J. (1977) *Exploratory Data Analysis* (Reading, Mass.: Addison-Wesley).

Turpin, C. (1989) 'Ministerial Responsibility: Myth or Reality?', in J. Jowell and D. Oliver (eds), *The Changing Constitution*, 2nd edn (Oxford: Clarendon Press), pp.53–86.

Veljanovski, C. (1987) *Selling the State: Privatisation in Britain* (London: Weidenfeld & Nicolson).

Vile, M.J.C. (1967) *Constitutionalism and the Separation of Powers* (Oxford: Clarendon Press).

Wakeham, Lord (1993) 'Cabinet Government', lecture at Brunel University, 10 October.

Walker, P. (1991) *Staying Power* (London: Bloomsbury).

Walker, P.G. (1970) *The Cabinet* (London: Cape).

Wallace, W. (1986) 'What Price Independence? Sovereignty and Interdependence in British Politics', *International Affairs*, vol. 62, pp.367–89.

Wapshott, N. and Brock, G. (1983) *Thatcher* (London: Fontana).

Ward, H. (1990) 'Environmental Politics and Policy', in P. Dunleavy, A. Gamble and G. Peele (eds), *Developments in British Politics 3* (London: Macmillan), pp.221–45.

Wass, D. (1984) *Government and the Governed* (London: Routledge & Kegan Paul).

Watkins, A. (1991) *A Conservative Coup* (London: Duckworth).

Weller, P. (1983) 'Do Prime Ministers' Departments Really Create Problems?', *Public Administration*, vol. 61, no. 1, pp.59–78.

Weller, P. *et al.* (1995) *The Hollow Centre: Executive Government in the Modern State* (Buckingham: Open University Press).

Wertheimer, E. (1929) *Portrait of the Labour Party* (London: Putnam).

White, R.W. (ed.) (1964) *The Conservative Tradition* (London: Kaye).

Whitehead, P. (1985) *The Writing on the Wall* (London: Michael Joseph).

Whitelaw, W. (1989) *The Whitelaw Memoirs* (London: Aurum Press).

Whiteley, R. (1974) 'The City and Industry', in P. Stanworth and A. Giddens (eds), *Elites and Power in British Society* (Cambridge: Cambridge University Press), pp.65–80.

Wilks, S. (1987) 'Administrative Culture and Policy Making in the Department of the Environment', *Public Policy and Administration*, vol. 2, no. 1, pp.25–41.

Williams, S. (1980) 'The Decision-Makers', *RIPA* (London: RIPA), pp.79–102.

Williamson, P.J. (1989) *Corporatism in Perspective* (London: Sage).

Willson, F.M.G. (1955) 'Ministries and Boards: Some Aspects of Administrative Development Since 1832', *Public Administration*, vol. 33, no. 1, pp.43–58.

Wilson, E. (1992) *A Very British Miracle: the Failure of Thatcherism* (London: Pluto Press).

Wilson, H. (1974) *The Labour Government 1964–70* (Harmondsworth: Penguin).

Wilson, H. (1976) *The Governance of Britain* (London: Weidenfeld & Nicolson).

Wilson, H. (1979) *Final Term: The Labour Government 1974–76* (London: Weidenfeld & Nicolson).

Wilson, J.Q. (1973) *Political Organizations* (New York: Basic Books).

Wilson, S. (1975) *The Story of the Cabinet Office to 1945* (London: HMSO).

Winnifrith, J. (1962) *The Ministry of Agriculture, Food and Fisheries* (London Allen & Unwin).

Yin, R.K. (1984) *Case Study Research: Design and Methods* (London: Sage).

Young, H. (1989) *One of Us* (London: Macmillan).

Young, H. (1991) *One of Us*, 2nd edn (London: Macmillan).

Young, H. and Sloman, A. (1982) *No Minister* (London: BBC).

Young, H. and Sloman, A. (1983) *But Chancellor: An Inquiry into the Treasury* (London: BBC).

Young, H. and Sloman, A. (1984) *But Chancellor: An Inquiry into the Treasury* (London: BBC).

Young, H. and Sloman, A. (1986) *The Thatcher Phenomenon* (London: BBC).

Zysman, J. (1983) *Governments, Markets and Growth* (Ithaca: Cornell University Press).

Author/Name Index

Subject Index